PHP Object-Oriented Solutions

David Powers

PHP Object-Oriented Solutions

ISBN-13 (pbk): 978-1-4302-1011-5

ISBN-13 (electronic): 978-1-4302-1012-2

Printed and bound in the United States of America (POD)

Distributed to the book trade worldwide by Springer-Verlag New York, Inc., 233 Spring Street, 6th Floor, New York, NY 10013. Phone 1-800-SPRINGER, fax 201-348-4505, e-mail orders-ny@springer-sbm.com, or visit www.springeronline.com.

For information on translations, please e-mail info@apress.com, or visit www.apress.com.

Apress and friends of ED books may be purchased in bulk for academic, corporate, or promotional use. eBook versions and licenses are also available for most titles. For more information, reference our Special Bulk Sales—eBook Licensing web page at http://www.apress.com/info/bulksales.

The source code for this book is freely available to readers at www.friendsofed.com in the Downloads section.

Credits

CONTENTS AT A GLANCE

CONTENTS

Chapter 8: Generating XML from a Database 289

Chapter 9: Case Study: Creating Your Own RSS Feed 321

Index 355

ABOUT THE AUTHOR

 **David Powers** is the author of a series of highly successful books on PHP, including *PHP Solutions: Dynamic Web Design Made Easy* (friends of ED, ISBN: 978-1-59059-731-6) and *The Essential Guide to Dreamweaver CS3 with CSS, Ajax, and PHP* (friends of ED, ISBN: 978-1-59059-859-7). As a professional writer, he has been involved in electronic media for more than 30 years, first with BBC radio and television, both in front of the microphone (he was a BBC correspondent in Tokyo from 1987 to 1992) and in senior editorial positions. His clear writing style is valued not only in the English-speaking world—several of his books have been translated into Spanish and Polish.

Since leaving the BBC to work independently, David has devoted most of his time to web development, writing books, and teaching. He is active in several online forums, giving advice and troubleshooting PHP problems. David's expertise was recognized by his designation as an Adobe Community Expert in 2006.

When not pounding the keyboard writing books or dreaming of new ways of using PHP and other programming languages, David enjoys nothing better than visiting his favorite sushi restaurant. He has also translated several plays from Japanese.

ABOUT THE TECHNICAL REVIEWER

Seungyeob Choi is the lead developer and technology manager at Abraham Lincoln University in Los Angeles, where he has been developing various systems for online education. He built the university's learning platform and has been working on a development project for Student Lifecycle Management. Seungyeob has a PhD in computer science from the University of Birmingham, England.

ACKNOWLEDGMENTS

The book you're holding in your hand (or reading on the screen) owes its genesis to a tongue-in-cheek exchange with Steve Fleischer of Flying Tiger Web Design (www.flyingtigerwebdesign.com), who suggested I should write *Powers Object-Oriented PHP*. Actually, he phrased it rather differently. If you take the initial letters of the suggested title, you'll get the drift . . . But Steve had an important point: he felt that books on object-oriented programming (OOP) frequently assumed too much prior knowledge or weren't easily adaptable to PHP in a practical way. If you like what you find in this book, thank Steve for planting the idea in my brain. If you don't like it, blame me, because I'm the one responsible for writing it the way it is.

Thanks must also go to everyone at Apress/friends of ED for helping bring "my baby" into the world. Books are uncannily like real babies. This one took exactly nine months from conception to birth with the expert help of editor Ben Renow-Clarke, project manager Beth Christmas, and many other "midwives." I owe a particular debt of gratitude to Seungyeob Choi for his perceptive technical review. Seungyeob's eagle eye and deep knowledge of PHP and OOP saved me from several embarrassing mistakes. Any remaining errors are my responsibility alone.

I would also like to thank everyone who has supported me by buying this or any of my previous books. I realize not everyone can afford to buy books, but the royalties from new—not second-hand—books ensure that authors get some reward for all the hard effort that goes into writing. Even the most successful computer books can never aspire to the stratospheric heights of Harry Potter, so every little bit helps—and is much appreciated.

The biggest thanks of all must undoubtedly go to the developers of PHP, who have given the rest of the world a superb programming language that continues to go from strength to strength.

INTRODUCTION

My first experiments with object-oriented programming in PHP took place about six years ago. Unfortunately, the book that introduced me to the subject concentrated on the mechanics of writing classes and paid little heed to principles underlying OOP. As a result, I wrote classes that were closely intertwined with a specific project ("tightly coupled," to use the OOP terminology). Everything worked exactly the way I wanted, but the design had a fundamental flaw: the classes couldn't be used for any other project. Worse still, it was a large project—a bilingual, searchable database with more than 15,000 records—so any changes I wanted to make to it involved revising the whole code base.

The purpose of this book is to help you avoid the same mistake. Although most chapters revolve around mini-projects, the classes they use are project-neutral. Rather than being a "how to" cookbook, the aim is to help developers with a solid knowledge of PHP basics add OOP to their skill set.

So, what is OOP? To oversimplify, OOP groups together functions (known in OOP-speak as "methods") in classes. In effect, a class can be regarded as a function library. What makes OOP more powerful is the fact that classes can be extended to add new functionality. Since many of the new features added to PHP 5 are object-oriented, this means you can easily extend core PHP classes to add new functionality or simply make them work the way you want them to. In fact, Chapter 3 does precisely that: it extends the PHP DateTime class to make it easier to use. The project in Chapter 4 takes the PHP filter functions and hides them behind a much more user-friendly interface.

Chapter 5 shows how to create a class that retrieves a text file from a remote server by automatically detecting the most efficient available method. Chapters 6 and 7 cover two of the most important OOP features added to core PHP in version 5: SimpleXML and the Standard PHP Library (SPL). The XML theme continues in the final two chapters, which use the PHP XMLWriter class to generate XML on the fly from a database and show you how to create a news feed from your site.

The need for OOP has come about because PHP is being used increasingly for large-scale web applications. Object-oriented practices break down complex operations into simple units, each responsible for a defined task. This makes code much easier to test and maintain. However, ease of maintenance is just as important in small-scale projects, so OOP can play a role in projects of any size. This is an introductory book, so the object-oriented solutions it contains are designed for use in small projects, but the principles they demonstrate apply equally to large-scale projects.

By the time you have finished this book, you should understand what OOP is and how to write PHP classes that conform to current best practices, making your code easier to maintain and deploy across multiple projects. The information contained in this book will also provide a solid foundation for anyone planning to use an object-oriented framework, such as the Zend Framework (www.zend.com/en/community/framework).

Although everything in this book is devoted to OOP, it's important to emphasize that OOP is only *part* of PHP. OOP helps you create portable, reusable code. Use it where appropriate, but there's no need to throw out all of your existing PHP skills or code.

Another important thing to emphasize is that all the code in this book requires a minimum of PHP 5, and preferably PHP 5.2 or 5.3. It has also been designed to work in PHP 6. *The code will not work in PHP 4*, nor will any support be provided for converting it to PHP 4. Even though at the time of publication, it's estimated that more than half of all PHP-driven websites still run on PHP 4, all support for PHP 4 officially ended on August 8, 2008. PHP 4 is dead. Long live PHP 5 (and PHP 6 when it's released). If you haven't yet made the switch from PHP 4, now is the time to do it.

Who should read this book

If you develop in PHP, but haven't yet got your feet wet with OOP, this is the book for you. No previous knowledge of OOP is necessary: Chapter 1 covers the basic theory and explains how OOP fits into PHP; Chapter 2 then goes into the mechanics of writing object-oriented code in PHP. The remaining seven chapters put all the theory into practice, showing you how to create and use your own classes and objects, as well as covering object-oriented features that have been built into core PHP since version 5.

You don't need to be a PHP expert to follow this book, but you do need to know the basics of writing your own PHP scripts. So, if you're comfortable with concepts such as variables, loops, and arrays, and have ever created a function, you should be fine. Throughout the book, I make extensive use of core PHP functions. In some cases, such as with the filter functions in Chapter 4, I go into considerable detail about how they work, because that knowledge is essential to understanding the chapter. Most of the time, though, I explain what the function is for and why I'm using it. If you want a more in-depth explanation, I expect you to look it up for yourself in the PHP online documentation at http://docs.php.net/manual/en/.

The book aims to be a gentle introduction to OOP in PHP, but it moves at a fairly fast pace. The code involved isn't particularly difficult, but it might take a little more time for some of the concepts to sink in. The best way to achieve this is to roll up your sleeves and start coding. Exercises at strategic points demonstrate what a particular section of code does and help reinforce understanding.

Using the download code

All the files necessary to work with this book can be downloaded from the friends of ED website by going to www.friendsofed.com/downloads.html and scrolling down to the link for *PHP Object-Oriented Solutions*. Download the ZIP file, and unzip its contents into a new folder inside your web server document root. I named the folder OopSolutions, but you can call it whatever you want. In addition to a series of folders named ch2_exercises through ch9_exercises, the folder should contain the following:

- Ch2: This contains example class definitions for use with ch2_exercises.
- class_docs: This contains full documentation in HTML format for all the classes developed in the book. Double-click index.html to view them in your browser.
- finished_classes: This contains a full set of completed class definitions.
- Pos: *This folder is empty.* It is where you should create your own versions of the class definitions as you work through each chapter. If you don't want to type out everything yourself, you need to copy each class definition from finished_classes to this folder for the files in the exercise folders for each chapter to work.

Understanding the file numbering system

Most download files have a filename ending in an underscore and a number before the .php filename extension (e.g., Book_01.php, Book_02.php). This is because the files represent a class definition or exercise at a particular stage of development.

If you are typing out the exercises and class definitions yourself, leave out the underscore and number (e.g., use Book.php instead of Book_01.php). Throughout the text, I indicate the number of the current version so you can compare the appropriate supplied version with your own, or simply use it directly if you don't want to type everything yourself.

To get the best out of this book, I strongly urge you to type out all the exercises and class definitions yourself. It's a lot of work, but hands-on practice really does reinforce the learning process.

What to do if things go wrong

Every effort has been made to ensure accuracy, but mistakes do slip through. If something doesn't work the way you expect, your first port of call should be www.friendsofed.com/book.html?isbn=9781430210115. A link to any known corrections since publication will be posted there. If you think you have found a mistake that's not listed, please submit an error report to www.friendsofed.com/errataSubmission.html. When friends of ED has finished with the thumbscrews and forced me to admit I'm wrong, we'll post the details for everyone's benefit on the friends of ED site.

If the answer isn't on the corrections page, scan the chapter subheadings in the table of contents, and try looking up a few related expressions in the index. Also try a quick search through Google or one of the other large search engines. My apologies if all this sounds obvious, but an amazing number of people spend more time waiting for an answer in an online forum than it would take to go through these simple steps.

If you're still stuck, visit `www.friendsofed.com/forums/`. Use the following guidelines to help others help you:

- Always check the book's corrections page first. The answer may already be there.
- Search the forum to see if your question has already been answered.
- Give your message a meaningful subject line. It's likely to get a swifter response and may help others with a similar problem.
- Give the name of the book and a page reference to the point that's giving you difficulty.
- "It doesn't work" gives no clue as to the cause. "When I do so and so, x happens" is a lot more informative.
- If you get an error message, say what it contains.
- Be brief and to the point. Don't ask half a dozen questions at once.
- It's often helpful to know your operating system and which version of PHP you're using.
- Don't post the same question simultaneously in several forums. If you find the answer elsewhere, have the courtesy to close the forum thread and post a link to the answer.

Please be realistic in your expectations when asking for help in a free online forum. I'm delighted if you have bought one of my books and will try to help you if you run into problems; but I'm not always available and can't offer unlimited help. If you post hundreds of lines of code, and expect someone else to scour it for mistakes, don't be surprised if you get a rather curt answer or none at all. And if you do get the help that you need, keep the community spirit alive by answering questions that you know the answer to.

Layout conventions

To keep this book as clear and easy to follow as possible, the following text conventions are used throughout.

Important words or concepts are normally highlighted on the first appearance in **bold type**.

Code is presented in `fixed-width` font.

New or changed code is normally presented in **`bold fixed-width font`**.

Pseudocode and variable input are written in *`italic fixed-width font`*.

Menu commands are written in the form Menu ➤ Submenu ➤ Submenu.

Where I want to draw your attention to something, I've highlighted it like this:

> *Ahem, don't say I didn't warn you.*

Sometimes code won't fit on a single line in a book. Where this happens, I use an arrow like this: ➥.

```
This is a very, very long section of code that should be written all ➥
on the same line without a break.
```

1 WHY OBJECT-ORIENTED PHP?

élite	£9.99
�lite	�9.99
Ã©lite	Â£9.99

Correct encoding

iso-8859-1 served as utf-8

utf-8 served as iso-8859-1

```
78        $this->errors = array();
79        $this->booleans = array()
80    ↑
81    } ↑
82      parse error
83      Unexpected '}'
```

Let's get things straight right from the start: PHP (PHP Hypertext Preprocessor) is not an object-oriented language, but it does have extensive object-oriented features. These underwent comprehensive revision and enhancement when PHP 5 was released in July 2004, and the PHP 5 object-oriented programming (OOP) model remains essentially unchanged in PHP 6. The purpose of this book is to help you leverage those features to make your code easier to reuse in a variety of situations. I assume you're familiar with basic PHP concepts, such as variables, arrays, and functions. If you're not, this isn't the book for you—at least not yet. I suggest you start with a more basic one, such as my *PHP Solutions: Dynamic Web Design Made Easy* (friends of ED, ISBN13: 978-1-59059-731-6).

> *The techniques and code used in this book require PHP 5 or PHP 6. They will not work with PHP 4.*

In this introductory chapter, you'll learn about the following topics:

- How OOP evolved and the thinking behind it
- What an object is and how it differs from a class
- What terms such as encapsulation, inheritance, and polymorphism really mean
- How the object-oriented model has developed in PHP
- Which tools make it easier to work with classes in PHP

I don't intend to bombard you with dense theory. The emphasis will be on gaining practical results with a minimum of effort. If you're lazy or in a hurry, you can just use the PHP classes in the download files (available from `www.friendsofed.com/downloads.html`) and incorporate them into your own scripts. However, you'll get far more out of this book if you type out the code yourself, and follow the description of how each section works and fits into the overall picture.

The techniques taught in this book are intended to improve the way you work with PHP, not replace everything you've learned so far. However, should you decide to delve deeper into OOP, they lay a solid foundation for further study. You'll find the knowledge in this book indispensible if you intend to use a PHP framework, such as the Zend Framework (`www.zend.com/en/community/framework`). Although frameworks take a lot of the hard work out of writing code, without a working knowledge of OOP, you'll be completely lost.

So what is OOP, and how does it fit into PHP?

Understanding basic OOP concepts

Object-oriented programming (OOP) is one of those great buzzwords that tend to mystify or intimidate the uninitiated. Part of the mystique stems from the fact that OOP was originally the preserve of graduates in computer science—a mystique deepened by concepts with obscure sounding names, such as encapsulation, polymorphism, and loose coupling. But OOP is finding its way increasingly into web development. ActionScript 3, the language behind Adobe Flash and Flex, is a fully fledged OOP language, and the many JavaScript frameworks, like jQuery (http://jquery.com/) and script.aculo.us (http://script.aculo.us), that have recently become so popular—although not 100 percent OOP—make extensive use of objects.

In spite of all the high sounding words, the underlying principles of OOP are very simple. To begin with, let's take a look at why OOP developed.

How OOP evolved

Object-oriented programming traces its roots back to the 1960s, when computer programmers realized that increasingly complex programs were becoming harder to maintain. Programs sent a series of instructions to the computer to be processed sequentially, in much the same way as PHP is usually written. This approach—known as **procedural programming**—works fine for short, simple scripts, but once you get beyond more than a few hundred lines of code, it becomes increasingly difficult to spot mistakes. If you make a change to part of the program's logic, you need to ensure that the same change is reflected throughout.

The answer was to break up long, procedural code into discrete units of programming logic. In many ways, this is similar to creating custom functions. However, OOP takes things a step further by removing all functions from the main script, and grouping them in specialized units called classes. The code inside the class does all the dirty work—the actual manipulation of data—leaving the main script like a set of high-level instructions. To take a common example that will be familiar to PHP developers, before using input from an online form, you need to make sure it doesn't contain anything that could be used to sabotage your database or relay spam. The procedural approach looks at the specific project, and writes tailor-made code, usually a series of conditional statements designed to check each input field in turn. For instance, this sort of code is commonly used to make sure a username is the right length:

```
if (strlen($username) < 6 || strlen($username) > 12) {
    $error['username'] = 'Username must be between 6 and 12 characters';
}
```

OOP looks at programming in a more generic way. Instead of asking "How do I validate *this* form?" the object-oriented approach is to ask "How do I validate *any* form?" It does so by identifying common tasks and creating generic functions (or methods, as they're called in OOP) to handle them. Checking the length of text is one such task, so it makes sense to have a method that checks the length of any input field and automatically generates the error message. The method definition is tucked away inside the class file, leaving something like this in the main script:

```
$val->checkTextLength('username', 6, 12);
```

At this stage, don't worry about what the code looks like or how it works (this object-oriented approach to input validation is explained fully in Chapter 4). Don't worry about the terms, class, and method, either; they will be described shortly.

The approach taken by OOP has two distinct advantages, namely:

- **Code reusability**: Breaking down complex tasks into generic modules makes it much easier to reuse code. Class files are normally separate from the main script, so they can be quickly deployed in different projects.

- **Easier maintenance and reliability**: Concentrating on generic tasks means each method defined in a class normally handles a single task. This makes it easier to identify and eliminate errors. The modular nature of code stored outside the main script means that, if a problem does arise, you fix it in just one place. Once a class has been thoroughly tried and tested, you can treat it like a black box, and rely on it to produce consistent results.

This makes developing complex projects in teams a lot easier. Individual developers don't need to concern themselves with what happens inside a particular unit; all that matters is that it produces the expected result.

So, how's it done? First, let's take a look at the basic building blocks of OOP: classes and objects.

> *See* http://en.wikipedia.org/wiki/Object-oriented_programming *for a more detailed background to OOP.*

Using classes and objects

Many computer books begin explaining OOP by using a car as an example of an **object**, describing the number of wheels or color of the bodywork as typical properties, and accelerate or brake as methods. Although this is a conceptually appealing way of illustrating some basic OOP terminology, it has nothing to do with building a web site, which involves practical things such as processing forms, validating input, and so on.

So, forget all about cars—and even objects—for the moment. Let's think in terms of code. The fundamental building block of all object-oriented code is called a **class**. This is simply a collection of related variables and functions, all wrapped up in a pair of curly braces and labeled with the name of the class. In OOP-speak, a variable associated with a class is referred to as a **property**, and a function is called a **method**—nothing scary or mysterious at all. If you have built up a library of your own custom PHP functions for reuse in different projects, creating a class will seem very familiar. We'll look at the actual syntax in the next chapter, but the main difference is that a class groups everything together.

> *Not all variables in a class are properties. A property is a special type of variable that can be used anywhere inside a class and sometimes outside as well. The distinction between ordinary variables and properties will become clearer later.*

So, if you want to validate user input, you could create a class called Validator (by convention, class names always begin with an initial capital) to group together a series of methods (in other words, functions) to perform such tests as these:

- Is this a number?
- Is it within a specified range?
- Is this a valid email address?
- Does this text have potentially malicious content?

In fact, you'll build just such a class in Chapter 4. Since other developers are likely to create classes for similar purposes, it's recommended that you prefix class names with a three- or four-letter prefix followed by an underscore. All classes in this book will be prefixed with Pos_ (for **P**HP **O**bject-Oriented **S**olutions), so the class in Chapter 4 will be called Pos_Validator.

When you want to use any of the class's properties or methods, you need to create an **instance** of the class by using the new keyword like this:

```
$val = new Pos_Validator();
```

This creates an **object** called $val. As you can see, it looks just like an ordinary PHP variable, so what is an object? In this particular case, it's principally a device that gives you access to all the methods defined in the Pos_Validator class. Without $val, you have no way of using them. In addition to methods, a class can have properties. In the case of Pos_Validator, one of them stores an array of required fields that the user has failed to fill in; another property stores an array of error messages. Because of the way the class has been designed, these arrays are populated automatically, holding the information until you're ready to use it. In programming terms, you might think of an object as a supercharged multidimensional array that controls functions as well as variables. However, in conceptual terms, the $val object is the tool that validates the user input. It uses its methods to run specific validation tests, and stores all the results. In other applications, objects can be envisaged in a similar way to real life objects. An e-commerce application might use a Product class to represent items of stock, or an online forum might have a Member class to represent individual contributors.

Let's take a quick look at an example of the Pos_Validator class in action. As I said earlier, you need to create an instance of the class to be able to use it. This is known as **instantiating an object**. As you probably noticed, when instantiating the $val object earlier, I placed a pair of empty parentheses after the name of the class. In the same way as you pass arguments to functions, you can also pass arguments to an object at the time of instantiation. The Pos_Validator class accepts two arguments, both of them optional. The first optional argument is an array of required form fields. So, the script to instantiate a Pos_Validator object to validate a simple form might look like this:

```
// create an array of required form fields
$required = array('age', 'name', 'comments');

// instantiate a validator object, and pass it the $required array
$val = new Pos_Validator($required);
```

The way you access an object's properties and methods is with the -> operator (a dash followed by a greater-than sign, with no space in between). Even if you don't know anything about OOP, it shouldn't take long to work out what the following code does (try to guess, and then read the next paragraph to see if you were right):

```php
// use class methods to validate individual fields
$val->isInt('age');
$val->removeTags('name', 0, 0, 1);
$val->checkTextLength('comments', 5, 500);
$val->removeTags('comments', 0, 0, 1);
$val->isEmail('email');

// validate the input and get any error messages
$filtered = $val->validateInput();
$missing = $val->getMissing();
$errors = $val->getErrors();
```

> *To save space, opening and closing PHP tags have been omitted throughout this book, except where required for clarity.*

The $val object begins by checking if age is an integer. It then removes HTML tags from the name field, checks that the comments field contains between 5 and 500 characters, and strips all tags from it before checking that the email field contains a properly formed email address. The final three lines validate the input, and get the names of missing fields and details of errors. It might look mysterious at the moment, but it's a lot easier to read than dozens of lines of conditional statements.

Another advantage is that objects are independent of each other, even if they're instances of the same class. You can create two separate instances of the Pos_Validator class to validate user input from both the $_POST and $_GET arrays. Because the objects are separate, you can identify where an error message has come from and take appropriate action.

Each object acts like a black box, keeping the data passed to each one completely separate from the other. The black box analogy also applies to one of the main concepts behind OOP: encapsulation.

Protecting data integrity with encapsulation

The idea of **encapsulation** is to ensure that each part of an application is self-contained and doesn't interfere with any others, except in a clearly defined manner. OOP breaks down complex tasks into their component parts, so it's necessary to ensure that changing the value of a property doesn't trigger an unintended chain effect through other parts of the application. When defining a property in a class, you must specify whether it's public, private, or protected. Public properties are accessible to all parts of a PHP script, both inside and outside the class definition, and their values can be changed in the same way as any variable. Protected and private properties, on the other hand, are hidden from external scripts, so they cannot be changed arbitrarily.

1

Methods can also be public, protected, or private. Since methods allow objects to do things, such as validate input, you frequently need them to be public. However, protected and private methods are useful for hiding the inner workings of a class from the end user.

You'll see how this works in the next two chapters when you start working with actual code, but one of the properties of the Pos_Validator class is $_inputType, which determines whether the input being validated comes from the $_POST or $_GET array. To prevent the value of $_inputType from being changed, the class definition declares it protected like this:

```
protected $_inputType;
```

The value of $_inputType is set internally by the class at the time of instantiating the object. If you attempt to change it directly, PHP generates a fatal error, bringing everything to a grinding halt. Inconvenient though this might sound, this preserves the integrity of your code by preventing an attacker from tricking a validation routine to handle variables from the wrong type of source. As long as a class is well designed, encapsulation prevents the values of important properties from being changed except by following the rules laid down by the class.

> *It's a common convention to begin the names of protected and private properties with an underscore as a reminder that the property's value should be changed only in strictly controlled circumstances. You'll learn more about public, protected, and private properties and methods in the next chapter.*

Encapsulation also makes the final code much simpler and easier to understand, and this is where the example of a car as an object begins to make sense. Unless you're a motor mechanic or enthusiast, you don't need to know the details of the internal combustion engine to get in a car and drive. It doesn't matter whether it's an old-fashioned gas guzzler or one that runs on biofuel; all you need to do is turn on the ignition and put your foot down on the accelerator. What this means in terms of OOP is that you can create a class with a method called accelerate(), and the user doesn't need to worry about the internal code. As long as the accelerate() method performs the expected task, the user is happy.

This leaves the developer free to make improvements to the method's internal code without forcing users to make similar changes throughout their own scripts. If you're working on your own, this might not seem all that important, as you're both the developer and end user. However, if you're working in a team, or decide to use a third-party class or framework, knowing what goes on inside the black box of the object is irrelevant. All you want to know is that it works and provides consistent results.

Encapsulation is a great advantage for the end user, but it places an important responsibility on the developer to ensure that changes to the internal code don't produce unexpected changes in output. If a method is expected to return a string, it shouldn't suddenly return an array. The black box must work consistently. Otherwise, all dependent code will be affected, defeating the whole purpose of OOP.

Closely related to this is another key feature of OOP: polymorphism.

Polymorphism is the name of the game

In spite of its obscure-sounding name, **polymorphism** is a relatively simple concept. It applies to both methods and properties and means using the same name in different contexts. If that doesn't make it any clearer, an example from the real world should help. The word "polymorphism" comes from two Greek words meaning "many shapes." A human head is a very different shape from a horse's head, but its function is basically the same (eating, breathing, seeing, and so on), so we use the same word without confusion. OOP applies this to programming by allowing you to give the same name to methods and properties that play similar roles in different classes.

Each class and object is independent, so method and property names are intrinsically associated with the class and any objects created from it. There's no danger of conflicts, so when a method or property is used similarly in different classes, it makes sense to use the same name each time. Continuing the example from the previous section, accelerate() makes a car go faster, but the way this is achieved depends on its type. In a regular car, you put your foot down on the accelerator pedal; but in a car specially adapted for a wheelchair user, the accelerator is usually on the steering wheel; and in a child's pedal car, you need to move your legs backward and forward quickly. There's no confusion, because each type of car is different, and they all achieve the same effect in different ways. It doesn't matter how many new classes are created to cover different types of cars, you can use accelerate() for all of them, leaving the implementation of how they go faster encapsulated inside the class. This is far more convenient than having to use footDown(), squeezeHandle(), or pedalFaster() depending on the type of car. Polymorphism and encapsulation go hand in hand, with polymorphism providing a common interface and encapsulation taking care of the inner details.

In a web site context, you might create different classes to interact with MySQL and SQLite databases. Although the code needed to connect to each database and run queries is different, the concepts of connecting and running queries are common to both, so it makes sense to give both classes connect() and query() methods, and a $_result property. A MySQL object will automatically use the code encapsulated in its black box, and a SQLite object will do likewise. But thanks to polymorphism, both classes use methods and properties with common names.

Contrast this to the need in procedural programming to use different functions, such as mysql_connect() and sqlite_open(). If you want to change the database your web site uses, you need to change every single line of database code. With the object-oriented approach, the only changes you need to make are the connection details and instantiating a MySQL object instead of a SQLite object, or vice versa. As long as your SQL is database-neutral, the rest of the code should work seamlessly.

This brings us to the final basic concept in OOP: inheritance.

Extending classes through inheritance

Since a class is simply a collection of related functions and variables, one way of adding new functionality is to amend the code. In the early stages of development, this is usually the correct approach, but a fundamental aim of OOP is reusability and reliability. Once a class has been developed and tested, it should be a stable component that users can rely on. Once the wheel has been invented, there's no need to reinvent it—but you can improve it or adapt it for specialized uses. However, there's no need to code everything from scratch; you can base a new class on an existing one. OOP classes are extensible through **inheritance**.

Just as you have inherited certain characteristics from your parents, and developed new ones of your own, a **child class** or **subclass** in OOP can inherit all the features of its **parent** (or **superclass**), adapt some of them, and add new ones of its own. Whereas humans have two parents, in PHP, a child class can have only one parent. (Some object-oriented languages, such as Python and C++, permit inheritance from more than one parent class, but PHP supports only single inheritance.)

The subclass automatically inherits all the properties and methods of its superclass, which can be a great timesaver if the superclass contains a lot of complex code. Not only can you add new methods and properties of your own, but you can also **override** existing methods and properties (this is polymorphism at play), adapting them to the needs of the new class. You see this in action in Chapter 3, when you extend the built-in PHP DateTime class. The extended class inherits all the basic characteristics of the DateTime class and creates an object to store a date, time, and time zone. Some of the original class's methods, such as for setting and getting the time zone, are fine as they are, so they are inherited directly. However, the original DateTime class doesn't check a date for validity, so you'll override some methods to improve their reliability, as well as adding new methods to format and perform calculations with dates.

Generally speaking, you can extend any class: one you have built yourself, a third-party one, or any of those built into PHP. However, you cannot extend a class or method that has been declared final. I explain the significance of final classes and methods in the next chapter, and in Chapter 3, you'll learn how to inspect a class to find out which properties and methods can be inherited and/or overridden.

Deciding on a class hierarchy

The ability to create subclasses through inheritance is undoubtedly one of the main benefits of OOP, but it also poses a dilemma for the developer: how to decide what each class should do. The object-oriented solutions in this book take a relatively simple approach, either extending an existing PHP class or creating a class that stands on its own. However, if you plan to go more deeply into OOP, you will need to give considerable thought to the structure of your inheritance hierarchy.

Say, for example, that you have an e-commerce site that sells books. If you create a Book class, you run into problems as soon as you decide to sell DVDs as well. Although they share a lot in common, such as price, weight, and available stock, DVDs don't need a property that stores the number of pages, and books don't have a playing time. Add T-shirts to your *product* range, and the inheritance problems become even worse. Hopefully, you picked up the clue in the previous sentence: start with a generic concept, such as product, and use inheritance to add the specific details.

Inheritance is extremely powerful, but there is a danger of overusing it. So, to round out this brief overview of OOP principles, I want to take a quick look at two principles of best practice: loose coupling and design patterns.

Using best practice

Once you appreciate the advantages of OOP, there's a temptation to go overboard and use it for everything, particularly creating lots of child classes. Well designed classes are said to be **loosely coupled**. This means that changes to one part of the code don't have a domino effect forcing changes elsewhere. Loose coupling is achieved by giving classes and objects clearly defined tasks, so that one class is not dependent on the way another works. For example, you might have two classes: one to query a database, and the other to display the results. If the second expects a `mysql_result` resource, it's tightly coupled to the class performing the query. You can't switch to using a different database without changing both classes. If the first class returned an array instead, the second class would continue working regardless of where the data came from.

The general advice about loose coupling is to avoid coding for a particular project. However, this is easier said than done. At some stage, you need to get down to the specifics of the project in hand, and it's often necessary to create classes that you won't be able to reuse elsewhere. Don't worry about this too much. When creating a new class, just ask yourself whether the same technique could be useful in other projects. If it could be, then you know it should be loosely coupled—made more generic.

Many of the problems you try to solve, while new to you, are likely to be the same issues that countless other developers have come across before. If you can find a tried and tested way of doing something, it's often best to adopt that solution, and spend your time tackling issues specific to your own project. Over the years, the accumulated wisdom of OOP developers has been crystallized into what are known as design patterns. A **design pattern** isn't a block of code that you can pick off the shelf and plug into your project; it describes an approach to a problem and a suggested solution. The Pos_Validator class in Chapter 4 is an example of the Facade design pattern, the purpose of which is to define "a higher-level interface that makes the subsystem easier to use." PHP 5.2 introduced a set of filter functions designed to validate user input. Unfortunately, it relies on a large number of predefined constants, such as `FILTER_FLAG_ALLOW_THOUSAND`, that are difficult to remember and tedious to type out. The Pos_Validator class encapsulates this complexity and hides it behind a set of user-friendly methods.

In the course of this book, I make use of some design patterns and describe them briefly at the appropriate point. However, this isn't a book about PHP design patterns. The emphasis is on learning how to write PHP classes and put them to practical use in the context of website development. If you want to study design patterns in detail, I suggest *PHP Objects, Patterns, and Practice, Second Edition* by Matt Zandstra (Apress, ISBN13: 978-1-59059-909-9). Another good book is *Head First Design Patterns* by Eric Freeman and Elizabeth Freeman (O'Reilly, ISBN13: 978-0-596-00712-6). Even though all the examples in the second book are written in Java, they are easy to understand, and the unconventional approach brings the subject to life.

> *The names and descriptions of most design patterns come from* Design Patterns: Elements of Reusable Object-Oriented Software *by Gamma, Helm, Johnson, and Vlissides (Addison-Wesley, ISBN13: 978-0201633610), affectionately known as the "Gang of Four (GoF) book."*

How OOP has evolved in PHP

As I said before, PHP is not an object-oriented language. In fact, support for OOP wasn't added until PHP 3. Unfortunately, the way OOP was originally incorporated into PHP lacked many essential features. The biggest problem was the way variables were handled internally, resulting in unexpected behavior. These shortcomings weren't addressed in PHP 4 because the main emphasis was on preserving backwards compatibility.

The addition of support for OOP was unexpectedly popular, but it was impossible to rectify the shortcomings without breaking existing scripts. So, when PHP 5 was released in July 2004, the way classes and objects work in PHP was changed radically. PHP 4 objects are incompatible with those designed for PHP 5. The good news is that, apart from a few advanced features beyond the scope of this book, the way PHP 6 handles objects is identical to PHP 5.

> All the code in this book is designed to work in both PHP 5 and PHP 6. To ensure full compatibility, you should be using a minimum of PHP 5.2.

OOP since PHP 5

PHP's handling of objects was completely rewritten in PHP 5 to improve performance and conform to standards common to other object-oriented languages. Aside from a long list of new features, the biggest change from PHP 3 and 4 is the way objects and their properties are handled. Take the following line of code:

```
$objectB = $objectA;
```

In PHP 3 and 4, this makes a *copy* of $objectA and stores it as $objectB. Both objects then act independently of each other; changes made to $objectA don't affect $objectB, and vice versa. This is known as **copying by value** and is the way PHP handles variables. In short, PHP 3 and 4 treated objects like any other variable.

Since PHP 5, objects are treated differently from other variables. Instead of making a copy of $objectA, the previous line of code stores a *reference* to $objectA in $objectB. Both variables refer to *the same object*; changes made to one affect the other. This is known as **copying by reference**. If you find this difficult to grasp, it's like adopting a nickname in an online forum. In public, you might call yourself Haven'tAClue, but you remain the same person. To make a copy of an object since PHP 5, you need to use the clone keyword like this:

```
$objectB = clone $objectA;
```

> The clone *keyword is used only with objects. All other variables act the same way as in PHP 4. To learn more about references in PHP, see* http://docs.php.net/manual/en/language.references.php.

Other important differences include the addition of the following features:

- Modifiers to control access to properties and methods (essential for encapsulation)
- A unified constructor name, __construct()
- Support for explicitly cleaning up resources through a destructor function
- Support for interfaces and abstract classes
- Final classes
- Static classes, properties, and methods
- Automatic class loading

All these features are covered in the remaining chapters. If you have worked with objects and classes in PHP 4, you'll find some things familiar, but I advise you to forget most of what you already know. The new OOP model is very different.

Preparing for PHP 6

PHP 6 has been a long time in the making. It was originally expected to come out in early 2007. The timetable then slipped to the end of 2007, but even as 2008 dawned, the months rolled by with still no sign of PHP 6. One factor behind the delay was the need to continue supporting PHP 4, which still represented nearly three-fourths of all PHP installations at the end of 2007. Since PHP 5 was released in 2004, this meant the development team was maintaining two major releases at the same time as trying to develop the next one. The pressure was too great, so a decision was made to terminate support for PHP 4. All support came to an end on August 8, 2008 after the release of the final security update (PHP 4.4.9). By the time you read this, PHP 4 should have been consigned to the dustbin of history. It served the web community well, but it's time to move on. If you're still using PHP 4, you're living on borrowed time.

With PHP 4 out of the way, the development team could finally concentrate on the future of PHP, rather than patching up the past, but the task is enormous. The main goal of PHP 6 is to make it Unicode-compliant. Computers store letters and characters by assigning a number to each one. The problem is that different encoding systems have evolved to cope with the different writing systems used around the world. To make things worse, different computer operating systems don't always use the same numbers to indicate a specific character. Unicode changes all that by providing a unique number for every character, no matter what the platform, no matter what the program, no matter what the language (www.unicode.org/standard/WhatIsUnicode.html).

If you work exclusively in English, and never use accented characters, the switch to Unicode is nothing to worry about, as the 26 letters of the alphabet and basic punctuation use the same encoding in both Latin 1 (iso-8859-1) and the most common Unicode standard (utf-8). However, as Figure 1-1 shows, accented characters cause major problems if you mix encodings. Even English-speaking Britain isn't safe, as the encoding for the pound sterling symbol (£) is different.

Figure 1-1. Mixing character encoding results in garbled output onscreen.

Since PHP manipulates character data, making PHP 6 Unicode-compliant means updating thousands of functions. It has also generated a vigorous debate about whether to make Unicode the default. As of mid-2008, a final decision had still not been made. The problems posed by the transition to Unicode resulted in a decision to bring forward many of the features originally planned for PHP 6. The most important of these, support for namespaces in OOP, was introduced in PHP 5.3.

One of the core developers, Andi Gutmans, is on record as saying "the migration path may be extremely hard moving from PHP 5 to PHP 6" (http://marc.info/?l=php-internals&m= 120096128032660&w=2), and there is a widespread expectation that PHP 5 will remain the common standard for a long time to come. Even if you decide to postpone the move to PHP 6, it's important to make sure you don't use code that will break when you finally make the transition. In addition to becoming Unicode-compliant, PHP 6 is dropping support for many deprecated features that could be lurking in existing scripts. The following guidelines should help you future-proof your PHP applications:

- Unify the way you gather and store data, making sure that the same encoding, preferably utf-8, is used throughout.
- Be aware that versions of MySQL prior to 4.1 do not support utf-8. Any data imported from older versions needs to be converted.
- Eliminate $HTTP_*_VARS from existing scripts, and replace them with the shorter equivalents, such as $_POST and $_GET.
- PHP 6 does not support register_globals. Make sure you don't have any scripts that rely on register_globals.
- Magic quotes have been removed from PHP 6.
- Replace all ereg_ functions with their preg_ equivalents, and use Perl-compatible regular expressions (PCRE). Support for ereg_ and Portable Operating System Interface (POSIX) regular expressions is turned off by default.

Those are the main issues you need to address to prepare for PHP 6, as code that relies on deprecated features just won't work. However, since they already represent best practice, there's nothing arduous about implementing these guidelines. Other best practice that you should adopt includes the following:

- Always use the full opening PHP tag, <?php. It's the only one guaranteed to work on all servers.
- Although function and class names are not case-sensitive, always treat them as such, because there are moves to make them case-sensitive in the same way as variables.

The code in this book was developed before the final release of PHP 6. Any changes that affect its operation in PHP 6 will be listed on the friends of ED web site (www.friendsofed.com) and my web site at http://foundationphp.com/pos/.

Choosing the right tools to work with PHP classes

PHP code is written and stored on the web server in plain text. The web server compiles PHP scripts into byte code at runtime, so there's no need for any special tools or a compiler. All you need is a text editor to write the scripts and a PHP-enabled server to run them on. Since you need to be familiar with PHP basics before embarking on this book, I assume that you already have access to a web server. Although you can test the code on a remote web server, you'll find a local testing environment is much more efficient. Detailed instructions for setting up a local testing environment are in my earlier books, *PHP Solutions: Dynamic Web Design Made Easy, Foundation PHP for Dreamweaver 8*, and *The Essential Guide to Dreamweaver CS3 with CSS, Ajax, and PHP* (all friends of ED), so I won't go over the same ground here.

If you don't want to configure a testing environment yourself, I suggest you try XAMPP for Linux or Windows (www.apachefriends.org/en/xampp.html) or MAMP for Mac OS X (www.mamp.info/en/mamp.html). Both are easy to set up and have a good reputation. Alternatively, you might want to invest in a specialized PHP integrated development environment (IDE), such as Zend Studio for Eclipse (www.zend.com/en/products/studio/) or PhpED (www.nusphere.com/products/phped.htm). Both have built-in PHP servers for testing.

Let's take a quick look at choosing a suitable program to write PHP classes.

Using a specialized script editor

Although you can write PHP classes in Notepad or TextEdit, you can make your life a lot easier by choosing a specialized editor with built-in support for PHP. A good script editor should offer at least the following features:

- **Line numbering**: Being able to find a specific line quickly makes troubleshooting a lot easier, because PHP error messages always identify the line where a problem was encountered.
- **A "balance braces" feature**: Parentheses, square brackets, and curly braces must always be in matching pairs, but the opening and closing ones can be dozens or even hundreds of lines apart. Some editors automatically insert the closing one as soon as you type the opening one of the pair; others simply provide a way of identifying the matching pairs. Either way, this is a huge time-saver.
- **Syntax coloring**: Most specialized script editors highlight different parts of code in distinctive colors. If your code is in an unexpected color, it's a sure sign that you have made a typing mistake.

- **Code collapse or folding**: When working with long scripts, it's useful to be able to hide sections of the code that you're not currently working on. Some editors automatically identify related code blocks making them easy to collapse; others rely on you selecting the code you want to hide manually.

- **Code hints and code completion**: Unless you have a phenomenal memory, you'll probably be grateful for a reminder of the spelling of PHP functions and the arguments they take. Most dedicated PHP editors have hints for several thousand functions and automatically complete the name when you select it from a pop-up window.

In *PHP Solutions: Dynamic Web Design Made Easy*, I said my personal choice for writing PHP scripts was Dreamweaver (www.adobe.com/products/dreamweaver/). Dreamweaver offers all the features just listed, so I still think it's a good choice for PHP, particularly if you're involved in designing the front end of PHP web sites. However, for serious work with OOP, Dreamweaver lacks the more advanced features offered by a dedicated PHP IDE, such as Zend Studio for Eclipse or PhpED.

I won't go through all the extra features, but those I have found most useful are as follows:

- **Instant error analysis:** If you have ever hunted for a missing semicolon (and who hasn't?), this is one of the most useful features of a dedicated editor. The editor constantly scans your code looking for syntax errors. If it spots one, PhpED underlines the error with a wavy red line and displays an appropriate message as a tooltip when you hover your mouse pointer over it, as shown in Figure 1-2.

```
78          $this->errors = array();
79          $this->booleans = array()
80       }
81       }
82          parse error
83          Unexpected '}'
```

Figure 1-2. PhpED picks up syntax errors as you type and displays them as tooltips.

Zend Studio for Eclipse also draws a wavy red line under syntax errors but draws your attention to them by displaying a white × in a red circle next to the number of the affected line (see Figure 1-3). In case you miss it, the error is also listed in the Problems view (panel).

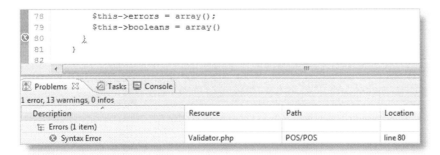

Figure 1-3. Zend Studio for Eclipse highlights syntax errors alongside the line number and in the Problems view.

As you can see, both programs highlight the closing brace on line 80, rather than the missing semicolon at the end of line 79. But this is the way PHP reports syntax errors, and it's a lot quicker than testing the script in a browser and then hunting for the rogue semicolon.

- **Code introspection**: This is really important when working with OOP. The IDE keeps track of user-defined classes, variables, and functions in the current project and enables code completion for them, too. Figure 1-4 shows the code hints generated by PhpED for the Pos_Validator class in Chapter 4.

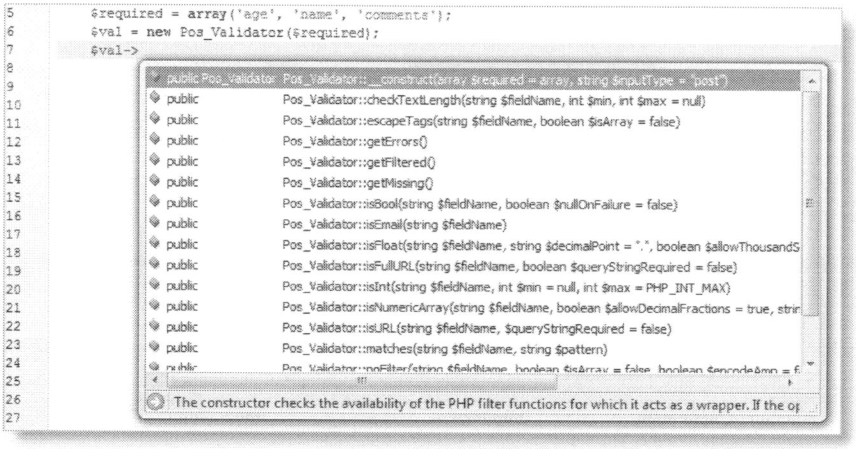

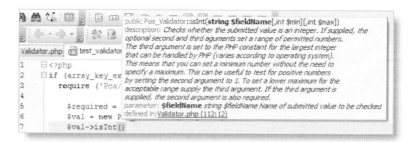

Figure 1-4. Code hints for the Pos_Validator class as displayed in PhpED

- **Automatic documentation**: If you comment your code using the PHPDoc format, as described in Chapter 2, both PhpED and Zend Studio generate automatic documentation that is displayed as part of the code hints, although they display them in slightly different ways. Figure 1-5 shows how PhpED handles automatic documentation, displaying the full description in a pop-up window when the cursor is between the parentheses of a function or method. If you use a heavily documented framework, such as the Zend Framework, this can look rather overwhelming onscreen.

Figure 1-5. PhpED displays the full documentation for each method of a custom-built class as a code hint.

Zend Studio for Eclipse takes what I think is a more practical approach. Instead of displaying the full description, it displays just a summary at the same time as the code hints pop-up menu, as shown in Figure 1-6. This is easier to read and helps you choose the appropriate method. Once you make your choice, code hints showing only brief details of the arguments are displayed (see Figure 1-7).

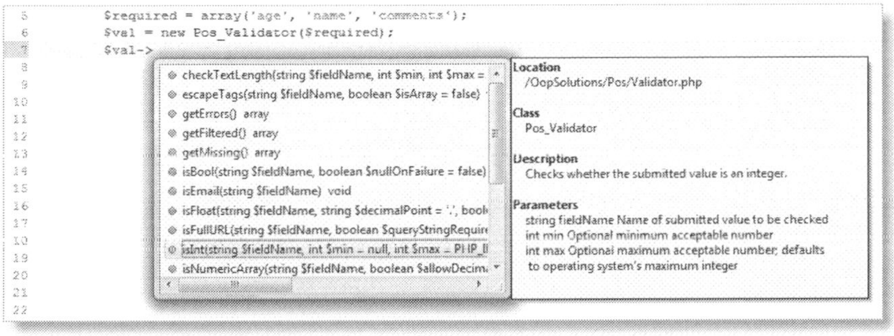

Figure 1-6. Zend Studio for Eclipse displays abbreviated documentation alongside the code hints pop-up menu.

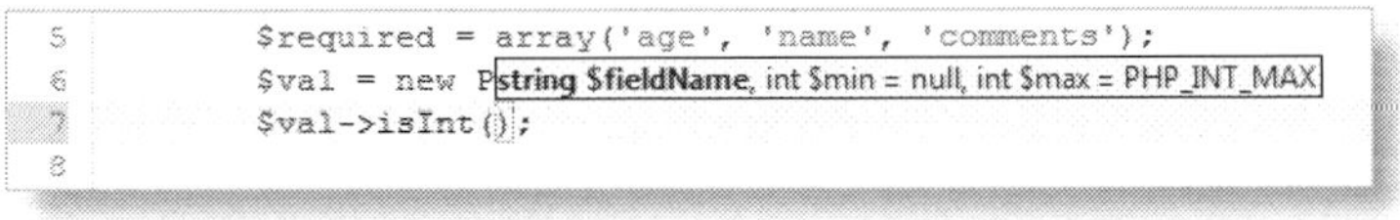

Figure 1-7. Code hints are less obtrusive in Zend Studio for Eclipse.

Both Zend Studio for Eclipse and PhpED are commercial products, costing several hundred dollars, so it's worth downloading the trial versions and giving them a thorough test before deciding which one is right for you—or, indeed, if either of them is. PhpED is Windows only, but Zend Studio is available for Linux, Windows, and Mac OS X 10.4 or higher. At the time of this writing, a license for Zend Studio includes both the Eclipse version, which was released at the beginning of 2008, and the original stand-alone version. However, this might change as Zend plans to focus future development on the Eclipse version. Zend Studio for Eclipse automatically installs everything on your computer; there is no need to install Eclipse separately beforehand.

If your budget is restricted, you might want to try PHP Development Tools (PDT), a free plug-in for Eclipse. You can find more details at `www.eclipse.org/pdt/`.

It doesn't matter which editor you use for writing your PHP classes. This book is completely software-neutral.

Chapter review

Object-oriented programming evolved in response to the problems of maintaining complex code by breaking it down into discrete units of programming logic. The aims were reusability of code and ease of maintenance through a modular, generic approach to common programming tasks. Purists might argue that if you're going to adopt OOP, every-thing should be object-oriented, but with PHP, that's neither necessary nor—in many cases—desirable. Building classes takes time and effort, so OOP isn't necessarily the best approach for simple, one-off tasks. Unless you know the code is going to be reused in other projects, it can feel like building a steam hammer to crack open a hazelnut. However, an advantage of OOP is that you create the basic code once, test it, and then for-get about it—well, almost.

The fundamental building block of object-oriented code is a collection of related variables and functions gathered together as a class. To use the variables and functions defined by a class, you create an instance of the class, which is referred to as an object. The variables associated with an object are called its properties, and the functions are referred to as methods. A major difference from procedural programming is that the properties and methods of an object can be declared protected or private. This ability to hide from view the inner workings of a class is one of the three most important characteristics of OOP, namely:

- **Encapsulation**: This hides the details from the end user and prevents direct access to key values.

- **Polymorphism**: This means giving the same name to methods and properties that play similar roles in different classes. Polymorphism extends encapsulation by hid-ing the details of how individual methods work by using a common name.

- **Inheritance**: New classes can be derived from existing ones, automatically inherit-ing all the methods and properties of the parent or superclass. The new class can not only add new properties and methods of its own, it can override those of its parent.

Another key concept is loose coupling—designing code so that changes in one part don't cascade down through the rest of the code. All these concepts are interrelated and can be difficult to grasp at the outset. However, don't get hung up on the terminology. Once you start using classes and objects, you're likely to see quite quickly the important benefits of reusable code that's easy to maintain. And as you become more familiar with OOP, the abstract concepts that underpin the object-oriented approach should become much clearer.

In the next chapter, we'll start fleshing out some of this theory by studying the nuts and bolts of PHP OOP syntax.

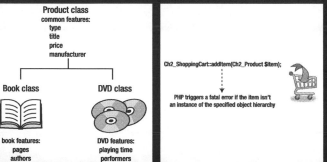

Creating your own PHP classes is remarkably simple. As I explained in the previous chapter, a class is basically a collection of related variables and functions surrounded by a pair of curly braces and labeled with the class name. Of course, there is more to it than that, so this chapter explains the finer details.

By the end of this chapter, you should have a good understanding of the following:

- Creating a class and instantiating objects from it
- Controlling access to class properties and methods with visibility modifiers
- Creating a subclass and overriding its parent's properties and methods
- Preventing a class, its properties, or methods from being overridden
- Loading classes automatically
- Throwing and catching exceptions
- Writing comments in the PHPDoc format to generate automatic documentation

I'll also cover some more advanced subjects, such as using interfaces, and abstract classes and methods. To illustrate how to write the code, I'll use an example from the section on inheritance in the previous chapter and show how to create a Product class and related subclasses. The examples are deliberately simple to illustrate the principles behind writing OOP and are not intended for use in a real-world situation. At times, the exercises will backtrack, undoing things that you have just created. Again, this is deliberate. When developing code in real life, it's frequently necessary to **refactor** (redesign or improve the code structure). It's also easier to assimilate new concepts one step at a time, rather than having everything thrown at you at once. You'll get down to writing real live code in Chapter 3.

If you're completely new to OOP, you might find some of this chapter heavy going. However, it's important to have an understanding of the basic syntax and concepts before diving into real code. The chapter is divided into two halves, with advanced material in the second half. Read through the first half of this chapter and do the exercises, but don't attempt to memorize all the details. This chapter is designed to act as a reference that you can come back to later when you need to refresh your memory about a particular aspect

> *If you skipped the introduction and first chapter, be warned that the code in this book does not work with PHP 4. This book concentrates exclusively on the OOP syntax used in PHP 5 and PHP 6, although I occasionally point out major changes for the benefit of readers who have worked with the old object-oriented model.*

First of all, since classes are often reused by other people, I think it makes sense to follow an accepted standard for formatting code.

Formatting code for readability

One of the joys of PHP is that it's very flexible, and that flexibility extends to how you lay out your code. As long as you observe the basic rules, such as terminating each command with a semicolon and wrapping code blocks in curly braces, you can format your code however you like, because PHP ignores whitespace inside code blocks. As a result, many different styles of coding have sprung up. There's nothing inherently right or wrong with any of them. As long as the code is readable—and works—that's all that really matters.

However, if you exchange code with others or work on a team project, it makes sense for everybody to adhere to an agreed standard. The standard I have chosen for this book is the Zend Framework PHP Coding Standard. There's no obligation for you to follow the same conventions, because that's all they are—conventions. If you prefer to use your own style, ignore the next section.

Using the Zend Framework PHP Coding Standard

I have chosen this particular set of coding conventions because it comes from the source. Zend is the company founded by the creators of the core PHP scripting engine, Zeev Suraski and Andi Gutmans, who remain key contributors to PHP. The standard was developed for the Zend Framework, a vast library of advanced PHP classes that you should explore after finishing this book. The emphasis throughout is on making your code easy to read and understand. The full details are at http://framework.zend.com/manual/en/coding-standard.html, so I'll go through only the main points.

- Naming conventions:
  - Use class names that map to the directory structure in which the class is stored by prefixing the class name by the name of each directory followed by an underscore. All classes in this book are in the Pos directory, so the class in Validator.php is called Pos_Validator.
  - Capitalize only the first letter of each word in file and directory names.
  - Use descriptive names for methods and properties. They should be as verbose as practical to increase understandability. Names should begin with a lowercase character, but where they consist of more than one word, each subsequent word should begin with an uppercase letter (camel case).
  - Begin the names of private and protected properties with an underscore (private and protected properties are explained later in this chapter).
  - Use uppercase characters only for constants, and separate each word with an underscore.
- Coding style:
  - Always use the full opening PHP tag (<?php).
  - Omit the closing PHP tag (?>) in files that contain only PHP code. The closing PHP tag is optional, provided nothing else (e.g., HTML) comes after the PHP code. Leaving out the closing tag has the advantage of preventing unwanted

whitespace triggering the "headers already sent" error when using includes (http://docs.php.net/manual/en/language.basic-syntax.instruction-separation.php).

- Indent code four spaces (I have followed this convention in the download files, but I have used only two spaces in the book because of restrictions of the printed page).
- Where practicable, restrict lines to a maximum of 80 characters. The printed page allows me only 72, so I have used an arrow like this ➡ to indicate code written on the same line.
- Always use single quotes for strings, unless they contain variables to be processed or other quotation marks.
- Use a combination of single and double quotes in preference to escaping quotes.
- Put a space either side of the concatenation operator (.) for readability.
- Insert a trailing space after commas for readability.
- Break associative arrays into multiple lines, and use whitespace padding to align both keys and values.
- Put the opening and closing braces of classes and functions on separate lines.
- Put the opening brace of a conditional statement on the same line as the condition, but the closing brace on a line of its own.
- Use PHPDoc formatted comments.

Choosing descriptive names for clarity

Even if you don't follow the Zend Framework guidelines to the letter, it's a good policy to use verbose, descriptive names for methods and properties. Descriptive names act as a reminder of the role played by a particular property or method and help make much of your code self-documenting. There can be little doubt, for example, what the checkTextLength() method in the Pos_Validator class does. Yes, it means more typing, but this isn't a problem if you use a dedicated PHP IDE, such as Zend Studio for Eclipse or PhpED, that automatically generates code hints. Since PHP code remains on the server, there's no advantage in obfuscating code to prevent others from stealing your brilliant ideas. The only people likely to be confused are yourself when, in six months' time, you come to review your code or your colleagues if you're working in a team.

Creating classes and objects

PHP has many built-in classes, some of which you will use later in the book, such as DateTime, XMLWriter, and XMLReader. However, the focus in this chapter is on building your own classes. Once a class has been defined, you use it in exactly the same way as any of the built-in ones.

Defining a class

A class normally contains both properties and methods. There are no rules about the order in which they should appear inside the class, but the normal convention is to declare all the properties first, followed by the methods. Throughout this chapter, I'm going to use examples based on an imaginary e-commerce application that sells a small range of products. So, this is how you define a class called Product:

```
class Product
{
  // properties defined here
  // methods defined here
}
```

That's actually a valid class. It doesn't do anything because it contains only comments, but it's perfectly valid.

There are no rules about where you should define classes, but it's considered best practice to define each class in a file of its own, as it makes it easier to redeploy classes in different projects. Unlike some languages, such as ActionScript, there's no restriction on what you call the file, but it makes life easier if you use the same name as the class. So, the Product class would be defined in Product.php. Since Product is likely to be a common class name, it's recommended to give it a three- or four-character prefix to avoid name clashes. I'm following the Zend Framework PHP Coding Standard, so I'll give it a name that maps to the Ch2 directory where all the examples for this chapter are stored: Ch2_Product. Figure 2-1 shows the structure of my site and the basic skeleton for the class in Zend Studio.

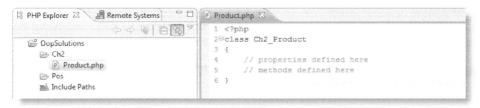

Figure 2-1. To prevent clashes, it's common practice to prefix a class name with the name of the directory it is stored in.

The class is no use without any properties or methods. These are the same as variables and functions, but before adding them, you need to understand visibility modifiers.

Controlling access to properties and methods

As I explained in Chapter 1, encapsulation is a key concept in OOP, so you need to control the **visibility** of a class's properties and methods. Visibility determines whether a property or method can be accessed directly by any part of a script that uses a class, or whether it remains internal to the class. This is the principle of the black box. To maintain the reliability of a finely tuned car engine, a mechanic doesn't want any Tom, Dick, or Harriet to tinker with the timing of the plugs. Equally, if a class is to produce reliable results, certain parts of its inner workings need to be hidden from sight. You do this by preceding the property or method definition with one of the following keywords: public, protected, or private. Table 2-1 explains the meaning of each keyword.

Table 2-1. PHP visibility (access control) modifiers

Modifier	Meaning
public	This means the property or method can be accessed by any part of a script both inside and outside the class definition. All methods are regarded as public unless preceded by a different modifier.
protected	This prevents external access to a property or method, but permits access internally and to parent and child classes.
private	Private properties and methods can be accessed only within the class where they are defined.

Although you can omit the visibility modifier for a method, in which case it will default to public, it's not considered good practice.

Properties must *always* be preceded by a visibility modifier. It's a common convention (and one followed by this book) to use an underscore as the first character of protected or private properties. This serves as a reminder to the developer that access is restricted.

So, which should you choose? At the risk of oversimplification, methods often serve as the interface to a class's functionality, so they need to be public. Properties, on the other hand, should almost always be hidden away as protected or private to prevent them from being changed accidentally. When you need to expose or change the value of a property, the normal way to do so is through a getter or setter method.

However, there are no hard and fast rules. It's often useful to create methods that solely perform a task inside the class. For example, in Chapter 4 you'll build a class to validate user input. You don't want anyone to be able to change the source of the input arbitrarily, so the method that retrieves the values from the $_POST or $_GET array needs to be hidden away inside the class as either protected or private.

> If in doubt as to which visibility modifier to use, select protected, as it lets you extend the class. Use private only if you definitely don't want a method or property to be accessed outside the class.

If this sounds confusing, all should become clear through the following exercise.

The code for all the exercises in this chapter is in the Ch2 and ch2_exercises folders of the download files. Each file has a basic name, such as Product.php or product_test.php.

To show the code at different stages of development, the download files are numbered in sequence (e.g., Product_01.php, Product_02.php, and so on). When doing the exercises yourself, I suggest that you use the basic name for each file, just updating the code in each step. If you need to check your code—or simply want to test the download versions— refer to the numbered versions listed at the appropriate point of each exercise.

Experimenting with visibility

This exercise shows what happens when you attempt to access a protected property outside the class definition and demonstrates how to create getter and setter methods.

1. Create a PHP site within your server root. The name is unimportant, but I have called mine OopSolutions.

2. Create a folder called Ch2, and create a file called Product.php within the Ch2 folder.

3. Insert the following code in Product.php:

```php
<?php
class Ch2_Product
{
    // properties defined here
    protected $_type = 'Book';

    // methods defined here
}
```

This defines the Ch2_Product class with a single protected property called $_type. For convenience, I have given the $_type property a default value of Book, but setting a default value isn't necessary. The value of a property can be set in a number of different ways.

> *As noted earlier, the Zend Framework PHP Coding Standard omits the closing PHP tag to avoid problems with unwanted whitespace. In subsequent code listings, I'll also omit the opening tag to save space, but you should always use it, as only the closing tag is optional.*

4. In the site root, create a folder called ch2_exercises. Inside the new folder, create a file called product_test.php, and insert the following code:

```php
// include the class file
require_once '../Ch2/Product.php';
```

To use a class, it must be included in your script. Later in the chapter, I'll explain how to load classes automatically, but for the moment I have used require_once. When you include a class file like this, the PHP engine defines the class ready for use. Like functions, classes can be defined only once in a script, so it's a good idea to use require_once, rather than just require, to prevent triggering a fatal error.

5. Next, you need to create an instance of a class. Add the following code to product_test.php:

```
// create an instance of the Ch2_Product class
$product = new Ch2_Product();
```

The syntax is very simple. You use the new keyword in front of the class name and place an empty pair of parentheses after the class name. The parentheses aren't strictly necessary in this case, but it's good practice to use them. As you'll see later in the chapter, you can pass arguments to a class in the same way as with a function.

The instance of the class is stored in an ordinary variable, in this case $product. $product is now an object.

6. Let's try to display the value of the object's $_type property. To access an object's properties or methods, you use the -> operator (a dash followed by a greater-than symbol with no space in between).

Add the following code to product_test.php:

```
// display the $_type property
echo $product->_type;
```

When accessing properties with the -> operator, you drop the dollar sign ($) from the beginning of the property name, so $product->_type refers to the $_type property of the $product object.

7. Save both files, and launch product_test.php in a browser. You should see a result similar to Figure 2-2. (If you just want to look at the code in the download files, use product_test_01.php and Product_01.php.)

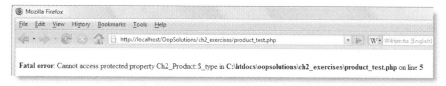

Figure 2-2. Attempting to access a protected property results in a fatal error.

This is visibility and encapsulation at work. The $_type property is so well protected that attempting to access it triggers a fatal error.

> *If you see only a blank screen, it means the* display_errors *directive is turned off. For development and testing, it's essential to be able to see error messages. Either turn on* display_errors *in* php.ini, *or add the following command at the top of each script:* set_ini('display_errors', '1');. *Throughout this book, I assume that* display_errors *is on.*

8. Go back to product_test.php, and try changing the value of $_type like this (the code is in product_test_02.php):

```
$product->_type = 'DVD';
```

If you test the page again, the result should be the same: a fatal error. You can neither display $_type with echo nor change its value. The property is protected inside the class and cannot be accessed by an external script.

9. To access a protected or private property, you need to create getter and setter methods inside the class file. Both are very simple, and use a special variable called $this, which refers to the current object. Add the following code to the Ch2_Product class (the code is in Product_02.php):

```
// methods defined here
  public function getProductType()
  {
    return $this->_type;
  }

  public function setProductType($type)
  {
    $this->_type = $type;
  }
```

Both methods need to be accessed from outside the class, so their visibility is set to public. Although OOP refers to them as methods, they are, in fact, functions, and you use the function keyword in exactly the same way as in procedural code.

Note that I have used verbose, descriptive names. This not only makes it easier to understand what they do, I needed to avoid using getType(), which is the name of a built-in PHP function.

The getter function, getProductType(), returns $this->_type, in other words, the $_type property of the current object.

The setter function, setProductType(), takes a single argument, $type, and assigns its value to $this->_type. Note the use of $type (without an underscore). It's common practice to give an argument the same name—minus the underscore—as the property to which you assign its value. This makes the code easy to understand, but be careful not to mix up the two.

10. To display the value of $_type, change the code in step 6 like this (the code is in product_test_03.php):

```
echo $product->getProductType();
```

If you run product_test.php now, you should see Book displayed onscreen.

11. To change the value of $_type, alter the code in the previous step like this (the code is in product_test_04.php):

```
$product->setProductType('DVD');
echo $product->getProductType();
```

Run the script again, and you should see DVD onscreen. So, although the $_type property is protected, you can change its default value from Book by using setProductType().

12. Try changing the visibility of the setProductType() and getProductType() methods to protected or private. When you do, it should come as no surprise that the script in step 11 triggers a fatal error. The visibility modifiers control methods in the same way as properties.

31

As you can see, protecting properties comes at the expense of longer code. Newcomers to OOP (and some old hands, too) often find this tedious, but the ability to restrict access to properties and methods gives you much greater control over the integrity of your data.

At this stage, you're probably wondering, "What's the point? Why go to all the bother of protecting a property if it can be changed with a setter method?" In the preceding exercise, there is very little point, indeed, apart from demonstrating the basic syntax. However, once you start working with real classes, you'll see that most protected and private properties don't have getter and setter methods. They remain encapsulated within the class.

Some properties have only getter methods. This allows an external script to access the property's value, but the lack of a setter method means you cannot change it. For example, the class in Chapter 4 validates and filters user input and stores it in a property called $_filtered. By declaring $_filtered protected and creating only a getter method, the class gives access to the filtered values but prevents anyone from tampering with them. Setter methods tend to be used mainly for initializing the value of a property. Once the value has been set, the protected or private status of the property prevents the value from being changed accidentally.

> *Give yourself a bonus point if you spotted that* setProductType() *exercises no control over what sort of value is assigned to the $_type property. In a real-world situation, you need to check the data passed to the method as an argument. I kept the script deliberately simple to illustrate the basic principle.*

Quick review

Although that was quite a trivial example, it contained a lot of information, which is probably worth reviewing. Here are the main points to remember:

- All properties must be declared and be preceded by one of the visibility keywords: public, protected, or private. (As with every rule, there is one exception when the visibility keyword is optional. This is explained in "Creating static properties and methods" later in the chapter.)
- Using a visibility keyword is optional when defining a method, but is recommended. If no visibility keyword is used, the method is automatically treated as public.
- "Method" is simply OOP terminology for a function inside a class. Use the function keyword when defining a method.
- You must include the class file in your script for the class to be available. Use require_once to avoid accidentally redefining the class, as this triggers a fatal error.
- Use the new keyword to create an instance of a class (an object).
- The $this variable inside a class refers to the current object.
- Use the -> operator to access an object's methods or properties.
- When accessing a property with the -> operator, omit the $ sign.

- Attempting to access a protected or private property or method from an external script triggers a fatal error.
- Use getter and setter methods to access protected and private properties and methods from an external script.

> *In PHP 3 and PHP 4, you could reassign the value of $this to another object. Doing so now causes a fatal error. Since PHP 5, $this refers only to the current object.*

Setting default values with a constructor method

In the preceding exercise, you gave the $_type property a default value. Although that's sometimes what you want, you gain more flexibility by specifying properties at the time of instantiating the object. You do this in exactly the same way as passing an argument to a function. When you create an instance of a class, PHP automatically looks for the class's **constructor** method (or constructor). As the name suggests, a constructor builds the object, applying default values and assigning to properties values passed to the class when an object is instantiated.

In many languages, the constructor is a method that shares the same name as the class. This is how PHP objects were built in PHP 3 and 4. However, since PHP 5, the constructor for all classes is called __construct() (with two leading underscores). As you saw from the previous exercise, using a constructor is optional, but most classes do use one.

> *For backward compatibility, PHP looks for a method with the same name as the class if it can't find __construct(), but this might not always be the case, so you should always use __construct().*

The constructor works like a setter method, so any values passed to it as arguments can be assigned to properties by using $this to refer to the current object like this:

```
public function __construct($value)
{
  $this->_property = $value;
}
```

> *The constructor method is used exclusively for creating a new object, so it should not use return.*

Let's update the Ch2_Product class to use a constructor.

Passing values to a constructor

This exercise builds on the previous one by adding a constructor that takes two arguments: one to set the product type and the other to set its title. Continue working with the same files as before.

1. Since the product type will be set by passing an argument to the constructor, you need to remove the default value of $_type (Book). Also create a new protected property called $_title. The properties at the top of the Ch2_Product class should now look like this:

```
// properties defined here
protected $_type;
protected $_title;
```

2. The constructor needs to take two arguments, one for each of the properties, and assign them to the object's protected properties. Add the following code immediately after the properties (and remember that there are two underscores before "construct"):

```
// constructor
public function __construct($type, $title)
{
  $this->_type = $type;
  $this->_title = $title;
}
```

3. Because the value of $_type is being set by the constructor, you no longer need the setter method. So delete it, and add a getter method to retrieve the value of the $_title property. The amended class (which is in Product_03.php) should look like this:

```
class Ch2_Product
{
  // properties defined here
  protected $_type;
  protected $_title;

  // constructor
  public function __construct($type, $title)
  {
    $this->_type = $type;
    $this->_title = $title;
  }

  // methods defined here
  public function getProductType()
  {
    return $this->_type;
  }
```

```
  public function getTitle()
  {
    return $this->_title;
  }
}
```

4. You instantiate the object in exactly the same way as before, using the new keyword. However, the class constructor now expects two arguments. To keep the
   code simple, I haven't added any code to check the type of data passed as arguments, but let's assume that both are meant to be strings. Test the revised class by
   amending the code in product_test.php as follows (it's in product_test_05.php
   in the download files):

```
$product1 = new Ch2_Product('Book', 'PHP Object-Oriented Solutions');
$product2 = new Ch2_Product('DVD', 'Atonement');
echo '<p>$product1 is a ' . $product1->getProductType();
echo ' called "' . $product1->getTitle() . '"</p>';
echo '<p>$product2 is a ' . $product2->getProductType();
echo ' called "' . $product2->getTitle() . '"</p>';
```

When you run product_test.php, you should see something similar to Figure 2-3.

Figure 2-3.
The objects now have different
product types and titles assigned
by the constructor.

Admittedly, this isn't the most exciting result in the world, but the purpose at this stage is
to understand basic PHP OOP syntax without introducing any distractions.

The code in the final step of the exercise created two independent objects: one a Book, the
other a DVD. On the face of it, this might not seem any different from creating two associative arrays like this:

```
$product1 = array('type'  => 'Book',
                   'title' => 'PHP Object-Oriented Solutions');
$product2 = array('type'  => 'DVD',
                   'title' => 'Atonement');
```

However, the differences are enormous, namely:

- The values of an array element can be changed at any time. Protected and private
  properties of an object cannot be changed unless the class provides a method to
  do so.

- You have no control over the type of data stored in an array, so a string could be
  changed arbitrarily to a number or a database resource. Code inside a class constructor or setter method can reject any data that doesn't conform to its specifications

35

(e.g., you could use is_string() to ensure that the value is a string before assigning it to the property).

- Unlike array elements, objects can have methods capable of processing data. Up to now, the only methods you have seen are very simple, but you'll see increasingly complex ones as you work through the book.

The previous exercise used the constructor to assign values passed in from outside to the object's properties, but you can use the constructor to do any initial setup for all objects of the same class. So, for example, if all products are made by the same manufacturer, you could use the constructor to assign the default value to a protected property called $_manufacturer. If you want all objects to share the same value, there's no need to pass it to the constructor as an argument.

Using a constructor has made the Ch2_Product class more flexible, but it also introduces a problem. Although you can create objects to represent different types of products, books and DVDs have different features. Books have pages, but DVDs don't. DVDs have a duration or playing time, but books don't. You could get around this by creating a property called $_length and using conditional statements to determine whether this refers to the number of pages or the playing time, depending on the type of product. You *could*, but it's messy. A much better solution is to use inheritance and create specialized subclasses.

Using inheritance to extend a class

The Ch2_Product class started out handling only books. Then you added DVDs. Even if you add a whole range of new products, all will have some features in common, such as price, available stock, and so on. Even though the values are different, the properties are common to all of them, so they can be handled by a common class. An appropriate subclass should handle features particular to a specific type of product. Figure 2-4 illustrates the inheritance hierarchy that you might adopt for books and DVDs.

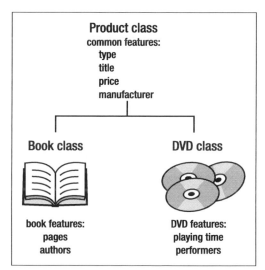

Figure 2-4. The parent class contains the common features, which are inherited by the child classes.

Defining a child class

To define a child class, simply use the extends keyword together with the name of the parent class like this:

```
class ChildClassName extends ParentClassName
{
  // class definition goes here
}
```

The child class needs access to the file where the parent class is defined, so you need to include the parent file before defining the child class. Since the child class depends on it, you should normally use require_once to include the parent file.

So let's create two child classes that inherit from Ch2_Product.

Creating the Book and DVD child classes

This exercise creates two child classes from Ch2_Product and shows what happens when you add a new property to a child class. Continue working with Product.php and product_test.php from the preceding exercise. You can see the finished code in Book_02.php and DVD_01.php in the Ch2 folder and product_test_07.php in ch2_exercises.

1. Create a new file called Book.php in the Ch2 folder, and insert the following code (it's in Book_01.php in the download files):

```
require_once 'Product.php';

class Ch2_Book extends Ch2_Product
{
  // class definition goes here
}
```

This includes the parent class with require_once and uses the extends keyword to indicate that the Ch2_Book class is a child of Ch2_Product. There is no need to add anything between the curly braces. As it stands, this is a complete definition of the new class, which inherits all the properties and methods of its parent.

2. Create a new file called DVD.php in the Ch2 folder, and insert the following code (see DVD_01.php in the download files):

```
require_once 'Product.php';

class Ch2_DVD extends Ch2_Product
{
  // class definition goes here
}
```

Apart from the name of the child class, this is identical to the code in the previous step.

3. Amend the code in product_test.php like this (the code is in product_test_06.php):

```php
require_once '../Ch2/Book.php';
require_once '../Ch2/DVD.php';

$product1 = new Ch2_Book('Book', 'PHP Object-Oriented Solutions');
$product2 = new Ch2_DVD('DVD', 'Atonement');
echo '<p>$product1 is a ' . $product1->getProductType();
echo ' called "' . $product1->getTitle() . '"</p>';
echo '<p>$product2 is a ' . $product2->getProductType();
echo ' called "' . $product2->getTitle() . '"</p>';
```

Instead of including Ch2_Product, this includes the two child class files and creates one instance each of the Ch2_Book and Ch2_DVD classes.

4. Run product_test.php. The output should be exactly the same as before (see Figure 2-3).

5. At the moment, the child classes are identical to their parent class. So let's add a new property called $_pageCount to the Ch2_Book class and set its value by passing a third argument to the constructor. Make the new property protected, and add a getter method to retrieve its value. Amend the code in Book.php like this (it's in Book_02.php):

```php
class Ch2_Book extends Ch2_Product
{
  protected $_pageCount;

  public function __construct($type, $title, $pageCount)
  {
    $this->_pageCount = $pageCount;
  }

  public function getPageCount()
  {
    return $this->_pageCount;
  }
}
```

6. To check that everything is working as expected, amend product_test.php like this (the code is in product_test_07.php):

```php
require_once '../Ch2/Book.php';

$book = new Ch2_Book('Book', 'PHP Object-Oriented Solutions', 300);
echo '<p>"' . $book->getTitle() . '" has ' . $book->getPageCount() . ➥
' pages</p>';
```

When you run the script, you should see the output shown in Figure 2-5.

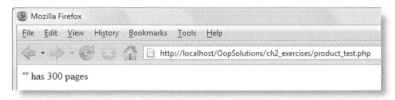

Figure 2-5. The title is missing from the output.

2

The script doesn't generate any warnings, so there are no syntax errors. The getTitle() method of the parent class has been inherited by the child class, so it's legitimate to use it. However, it has produced no output. I expect that most readers will already be yelling, "Of course it hasn't, because you haven't assigned the value of $title to the object's $_title property."

That's true, but I also said that a child class inherits all its parent's properties and methods. So you would also be justified in wondering why it didn't use the Ch2_Product constructor. After all, it did so when you tested the child classes in step 4. The answer is that this is polymorphism in action: a child class inherits its parent's methods and properties, but you can also redefine (or override) them. You're no longer creating a Ch2_Product object, but a Ch2_Book object.

By defining a constructor in the child class, you have overridden the parent constructor. The child class does only what its own constructor tells it to do. It accepts three arguments but does nothing with the first two ($type and $title). To assign the value of these arguments to the $_type and $_title properties, you either need to do so explicitly in the child class's constructor or find some way of invoking the parent constructor.

First, let's take a look at this second option.

Accessing a parent class's methods and properties

The ability to override a parent class's methods or properties is very convenient, but there are times when you want to access them in a child class. To do this, you need to use the scope resolution operator.

Using the scope resolution operator

The **scope resolution operator** is a pair of colons (::). The name of the class goes on the left side of the operator, and the name of the method or property goes on the right like this:

    ClassName::methodOrPropertyName

PHP doesn't object if you put whitespace on either side of the scope resolution operator, but the normal convention is to write everything as a single entity.

The scope resolution operator has the following uses:

- It gives access to overridden properties or methods of a parent class.

- It is used to call the static methods and properties of a class (this is covered in "Creating static properties and methods" later in this chapter).

- It gives access to class constants (see "Using class constants for properties" later in the chapter).

- It is the conventional way of referring to a class method or property in documentation. For example, instead of referring to "the getPageCount() method of the Ch2_Book class," this is shortened to Ch2_Book::getPageCount().

Because Ch2_Book overrides the Ch2_Product constructor, you need to call the parent constructor inside the child constructor. Using the syntax outlined earlier, you could call the Ch2_Product constructor like this:

```
Ch2_Product::__construct($type, $title);
```

However, PHP provides two handy keywords that work with the scope resolution operator, namely:

- **parent**: This refers to the parent or any ancestor of the current class.

- **self**: This refers to the current class. Although this sounds the same as $this, which you met earlier, self refers to the class in general, whereas $this refers to the current *instance* of the class (in other words, an object created from the class).

So, to call the parent constructor of the Ch2_Book class, you can amend the previous code like this:

```
parent::__construct($type, $title);
```

The advantage of the parent and self keywords is that you don't need to change them if you rename any of the classes to which they refer. The next exercise shows how to call the parent constructor in an overridden method.

> *The scope resolution operator has the unusual name,* paamayim nekudotayim, *the Hebrew for "double colon." It was chosen by the creators of the original Zend engine that powered PHP 3 (Zeev Suraski and Andi Gutmans) and for some reason has stuck. As well as being a fascinating piece of trivia that might come in handy during a pub quiz for geeks, it's useful to be able to recognize this name, as it occasionally pops up in error messages. If you see it, you know to look for the double colon.*

Calling the parent constructor

This brief exercise amends the code in the preceding exercise to call the parent constructor when overriding it in a child class. Continue working with the same files.

1. Amend the constructor in Book.php to look like this (the full code is in Book_03.php):

```
public function __construct($type, $title, $pageCount)
{
  parent::__construct($type, $title);
  $this->_pageCount = $pageCount;
}
```

This calls the constructor from the parent class (Ch2_Product) and passes it $type and $title as arguments. The parent constructor method assigns these values to the $_type and $_title properties, respectively. Since both properties are inherited, they become properties of the child class. The value of the $_pageCount property is assigned in the same way as before.

2. Run product_test.php. This time you should see the result shown in Figure 2-6. (If you're using the download files, the code is in product_test_08.php. The only difference is that it calls the updated version of the Ch2_Book class.)

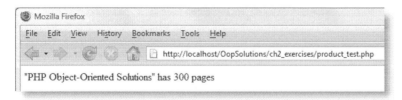

Figure 2-6. The title of the book is now displayed correctly.

I won't bother making the same changes to the Ch2_DVD class, because you have probably realized there's no point setting the $_type property in the constructor when you have separate classes for different types of products. However, this was a handy way of demonstrating the use of parent with the scope resolution operator.

Setting the $_type property in the constructor is not only redundant but it breaks the principle of encapsulation by allowing an arbitrary value to be assigned to a property that should be fixed. A book is a book is a book . . . Instead of calling the parent constructor to set its value, I'm going to hard-code the $_type property in the child constructor. As you'll see later in the chapter, the parent constructor is no longer needed. For those of you who already know the basics of OOP, I plan to turn the Ch2_Product class into an abstract class. If you don't know what that means, don't worry; by the end of the chapter, you will.

Creating separate constructors for books and DVDs

When you originally added the $_pageCount property to Ch2_Book, the child constructor overrode the parent one without setting the $_type and $_title properties. Let's now put that right. Continue working with the same files.

1. The $_type property of a Ch2_Book object will always be book, so you can hard-code that value in the constructor, but the $_title property needs to be set by passing an argument to the constructor. This means you need to pass only two arguments to the Ch2_Book constructor (for the title and page count). Amend the class like this (the code is in Book_04.php):

```php
class Ch2_Book extends Ch2_Product
{
  protected $_pageCount;

  public function __construct($title, $pageCount)
  {
    $this->_title = $title;
    $this->_pageCount = $pageCount;
    $this->_type = 'book';
  }

  public function getPageCount()
  {
    return $this->_pageCount;
  }
}
```

Notice that the $_title and $_type properties are not declared at the top of the child class, yet they are referred to in the constructor as $this->_title and $this->_type. This is because the child class inherits the properties of the parent class, and *treats them as its own*.

> *Although the properties come from the parent, they have not been overridden, so you don't refer to them with the parent keyword. You're creating a Ch2_Book object, which is an enhanced form of Ch2_Product. It's important to realize that inheritance is a one-way process. A Ch2_Product object has no access to the $_pageCount property or getPageCount() method. These are exclusive to Ch2_Book objects.*

2. When creating a Ch2_Book object, you now pass it only two arguments: the title and page count. Amend the code in product_test.php like this (it's in product_test_09.php):

```php
$book = new Ch2_Book('PHP Object-Oriented Solutions', 300);
echo '<p>The ' . $book->getProductType() . ' "' . $book->getTitle() . 
'" has ' . $book->getPageCount() . ' pages</p>';
```

The extra code in the echo statement uses $book->getProductType() to display the value of $_type.

3. Run product_test.php. You should see the result shown in Figure 2-7.

Figure 2-7. The product type has been added to the display.

4. Instead of a page count, the Ch2_DVD class needs a property to store the playing time and a getter method to retrieve its value. The code is very similar to the revised version of Ch2_Book, so it doesn't require any explanation. The full listing is here (and in DVD_02.php):

```php
class Ch2_DVD extends Ch2_Product
{
  protected $_duration;

  public function __construct($title, $duration)
  {
    $this->_title = $title;
    $this->_duration = $duration;
    $this->_type = 'DVD';
  }

  public function getDuration()
  {
    return $this->_duration;
  }
}
```

The constructor method in each of these rewritten child classes does everything you need, so it no longer uses the parent keyword to call the parent constructor. Deciding whether to call the parent constructor depends entirely on the design of the child class. Let's say you have a class with two properties, $_a and $_b, which are set by passing two arguments to the constructor like this:

```php
class ParentClass
{
  protected $_a;
  protected $_b;

  public function __construct($a, $b)
```

43

```
  {
    $this->_a = $a;
    $this->_b = $b;
  }
}
```

You want to create a child class that has another property $_c in addition to $_a and $_b. The best way to extend it is like this:

```
class ChildClass extends ParentClass
{
  protected $_c;

  public function __construct($a, $b, $c)
  {
    parent::__construct($a, $b);
    $this->_c = $c;
  }
}
```

In this deliberately simple example, calling the parent constructor saves only one line of code, but a real class might have a constructor that is much longer. However, the important consideration is not how much typing you save, but the principle of inheritance. Any changes you make to the parent constructor will automatically apply to the child class. If you override the parent constructor completely, as I have done in Ch2_Book and Ch2_DVD, the parent-child relationship becomes much more tenuous. However, as the chapter progresses, you will see that I have done this deliberately as a prelude to converting Ch2_Product into an abstract class. Abstract classes are an advanced OOP concept covered in the second half of this chapter.

Overriding is very useful, but there are times when you don't want it to happen. The main reason you might want to prevent something from being overridden is because doing so would violate the logic of your application or perhaps some business principle. For example, you might create a method that uses a fixed formula to calculate the commission earned by a sales person. If you allow the method to be overridden, someone could create a child class and double the commission. Nice for the sales people; not so nice for the integrity of your class.

Controlling changes to methods and properties

You can prevent a whole class from being overridden or apply restrictions to individual methods and properties. The way you handle individual properties is different, so I'll describe that after dealing with whole classes and individual methods.

Preventing a class or method from being overridden

To prevent a class or method from being overridden, precede the class name or the method's visibility modifier (see Table 2-1) with the keyword final.

So, to prevent the Ch2_Book class from being overridden, just change the first line like this:

```
final Ch2_Book extends Ch2_Product
{
  // class definition omitted
}
```

This covers the whole class, including all its methods and properties. Any attempt to create a child class from Ch2_Book would now result in a fatal error.

However, if you want to allow the class to be subclassed but prevent a particular method from being overridden, the final keyword goes in front of the method definition like this:

```
class Ch2_Book extends Ch2_Product
{
  protected $_pageCount;

  public function __construct($title, $pageCount)
  {
    $this->_title = $title;
    $this->_pageCount = $pageCount;
    $this->_type = 'book';
  }

  final public function getPageCount()
  {
    return $this->_pageCount;
  }
}
```

This lets you create as many subclasses of Ch2_Book as you want, but none of them will be able to override the getPageCount() method. This particular example has little practical value, but declaring a method as final can be extremely useful if you want to ensure that certain aspects of subclasses work in exactly the way you designed.

In practice, you are unlikely to need to use the final keyword very often, but it's important to understand the following subtle differences in its use:

- Declaring a *class* as final prevents it from being subclassed—period; it's the end of the line.

- Declaring every method in a class as final allows the creation of subclasses, which have access to the parent class's methods, but cannot override them. The subclasses can define additional methods of their own.

- The final keyword controls only the ability to override and should not be confused with the private visibility modifier (see Table 2-1). A private method cannot be accessed by any other class; a final one can.

Using class constants for properties

You can't use the final keyword with properties. The closest equivalent to final is to use a class constant. You should be familiar with constants from core PHP syntax. A **constant** is a value that never changes like π (pi) or the conversion ratio from pounds to kilograms. Unlike variables, constants don't begin with a dollar sign, and they are normally written entirely in uppercase. The normal way to define a constant in PHP is with define() like this:

```
define('MILES_TO_KILOMETERS', 1.609344);
```

When you use define(), PHP creates a global constant. In other words, it's available to every part of your script. In OOP, this isn't always what you want, so PHP provides a way of defining class constants. You declare a class constant in a similar way to assigning a value to a variable (except without the dollar sign) and precede the declaration with the const keyword. So, to create a POUNDS_TO_KILOGRAMS constant for the Ch2_Product class, you would add it to the list of properties in the class definition like this:

```
class Ch2_Product
{
  // properties defined here
  protected $_type;
  protected $_title;
  const POUNDS_TO_KILOGRAMS = 0.45359237;

  // rest of class omitted
}
```

Defined inside the class like this, the POUNDS_TO_KILOGRAMS constant becomes available to the Ch2_Product class and all classes derived from it. However, to use it anywhere inside the class hierarchy, you need to prefix it with the self keyword and the scope resolution operator like this:

```
self::POUNDS_TO_KILOGRAMS
```

With class constants, the self keyword refers to a constant defined not only in the current class but in any ancestor class further up the hierarchy.

Because constants don't change, it can sometimes be useful to use them outside a class. There's no need to instantiate an object to do so. As long as your script has access to the class, just use the class name and the scope resolution operator like this:

```
Ch2_Product::POUNDS_TO_KILOGRAMS
```

Although the value of a class constant cannot be changed inside its own class, you can override it in a child class, as the following example shows (the code is in override_constant.php in ch2_exercises):

```
class classA
{
    const FIXED_NUMBER = 4;
}
```

```
class classB extends classA
{
    const FIXED_NUMBER = 20;
}

echo classA::FIXED_NUMBER . '<br />';
echo classB::FIXED_NUMBER;
```

If you run the preceding script, it displays 4 and 20. Preventing changes to the value of a property by declaring it as a class constant is limited to the class itself. If you need to guarantee that a value can never be changed, you need to create a global constant with define(). However, global constants are slower than class constants, so you need to weigh the balance of speed against the need for an immutable value.

The value assigned to a constant cannot be the result of a calculation, a variable, or something like a database resource. However, you can use a different type of construct to handle more complex elements that you want to have fixed values by making them static.

Creating static properties and methods

A **static** property or method is sometimes referred to as a class property or class method in the sense that it belongs to the whole class and not to an individual instance of the class (or object).

To make a property or method static, insert the keyword static after the visibility modifier. In some respects, a static property acts very much like a class constant, but unlike a constant, you can restrict its scope by using the protected or private keywords. For example, instead of creating a class constant POUNDS_TO_KILOGRAMS as in the previous section, you could restrict its use to the Ch2_Product family of classes by making it protected like this:

```
protected static $_lbToKg = 0.45359237;
```

The first thing to notice is that a static property looks like any other variable in that it must start with a dollar sign. However, the similarity ends there. To use a static property inside its own class or any of its descendents, use self with the scope resolution operator like this:

```
self::$_lbToKg
```

Since $_lbToKg has been defined as protected, you cannot access it outside the Ch2_Product hierarchy. However, if you use the public keyword when defining a static property, or omit the visibility modifier altogether, you can access it anywhere. The following definitions are the equivalent of each other:

```
public static $lbToKg = 0.45359237;
static $lbToKg = 0.45359237;
```

The $lbToKg static property can now be accessed in any part of a script using the class name and the scope resolution operator like this:

```
Ch2_Product::$lbToKg
```

47

Note that I removed the leading underscore from the property's name to indicate that it's publicly accessible. The underscore doesn't have any magic properties; it's simply a convention. What controls where you can use a property is the visibility modifier.

> *Defining a property as static is the only time you can omit the visibility modifier when declaring a property. Leaving out the modifier automatically makes a static property public. This is for backward compatibility with PHP 4. However, best practice is always to specify the visibility explicitly, as it leaves no room for doubt about the way you intend the property to be used.*

The preceding example assigns a fixed value to the static property, but unlike constants, static properties can represent dynamically generated values. Static properties are commonly used to store a database connection, as you normally don't want multiple connections to be created by a script.

In fact, the value of a static property can change as the result of internal calculations inside the class, as demonstrated by the following example, which can be found in static_counter.php in ch2_exercises:

```php
class classC
{
  protected static $_counter = 0;
  public $num;

  public function __construct()
  {
    self::$_counter++;
    $this->num = self::$_counter;
  }
}

$object1 = new classC();
echo $object1->num . '<br />';
$object2 = new classC();
echo $object2->num;
```

In this example, $_counter is declared both protected and static, so its value can't be changed outside the class definition. However, each time you create an instance of classC, the value of $_counter is increased by 1, and the result is assigned to the public property $num. If you run the script in static_counter.php, you should see the numbers 1 and 2 displayed onscreen. So in this case, static doesn't indicate an unchanging value; it means that the class as a whole, as opposed to individual objects, is keeping track of the value.

You create a static method the same way by prefixing the method's definition with the static keyword. Since the conversion ratio of pounds to kilograms is little use on its own, you could replace it with a static method like this:

```
public static function convertLbToKg($pounds)
{
    return $pounds * 0.4535923;
}
```

To use this static function inside the class where it is defined or any of its descendent classes, use self like this:

```
$weight = self::convertLbToKg(5); // $weight is 2.2679615
```

To use it elsewhere, use the class name instead of self like this:

```
$weight = Ch2_Product::convertLbToKg(5); // $weight is 2.2679615
```

Of course, you can use a static method outside its class hierarchy only if it is declared public. The class where it is defined also needs to be accessible to the script.

Quick review

The last few pages have covered a lot of ground, so let me try to summarize the main features:

- To define a child class (or subclass), use the extends keyword followed by the name of the parent class.
- The child class must have access to the parent class, either by being included or being loaded automatically (see the following section).
- A child class can have only one parent but can have many children of its own.
- A child class inherits and has access to all the properties and methods of its parent, as well as to any other classes higher up the hierarchy. The only exception is if the property or method is declared as private.
- Inherited methods and properties can be overridden by redefining them in the child class.
- To access a parent's overridden method or property, use the parent keyword followed by the scope resolution operator (::).
- Use the final keyword to prevent a class or individual methods from being overridden.
- If the class itself has been declared final, no further child classes can be created from it.
- If a method has been declared final, it can be inherited, but not overridden, by a child class.
- Define class constants with the const keyword.
- Use the static keyword in combination with one of the visibility modifiers to create static methods and properties.
- Access class constants and static methods and properties through parent, self, or the class name, followed by the scope resolution operator.

Loading classes automatically

Before you can use a class, you need to include it in your script, usually with require_once. The more classes you use, the more include commands you need. On a big project, this becomes time consuming, so PHP provides a way of automating the process with __autoload(). Like __construct(), the name begins with two underscores.

Using __autoload() depends on two things, namely:

- Each class must be defined in a separate file.
- You must adopt a consistent naming convention for both classes, and the file structure they are stored in.

If you give each class the same name as the file where it is defined, __autoload() is very simple. Just add the following code at the beginning of the main file of your application:

```
function __autoload($class)
{
  require_once $class . '.php';
}
```

This concatenates the .php file name extension onto the class name and calls require_once. So, if you have a class called MyClass and store it in MyClass.php, PHP will automatically search your include_path for MyClass.php the first time that you create an instance of MyClass.

The naming convention that I have adopted in this book combines the folder name with the file name. So Ch2_Product is in Ch2/Product.php. This involves just a little extra coding inside __autoload() to create the correct file path like this:

```
function __autoload($class)
{
  $parts = explode('_', $class);
  $path = implode(DIRECTORY_SEPARATOR, $parts);
  require_once $path . '.php';
}
```

This breaks the class name at each underscore into an array and rebuilds it into the path name using the PHP DIRECTORY_SEPARATOR constant. Finally, it concatenates the .php file name extension onto the class name and includes the class file.

Attempting to redefine a function causes a fatal error, so it's a good idea to put the __autoload() definition in an external file and include it using require_once. Needless to say, it must be included before your script attempts to instantiate any objects.

Both examples of __autoload() assume that your classes are in your PHP include_path. If they are outside the include_path, you need to define the full path in the __autoload()

function. For example, on my Windows testing machine, the OopSolutions site is located in C:\htdocs\OopSolutions. So, I need to amend the second example like this:

```
function __autoload($class)
{
  $parts = explode('_', $class);
  $path = 'C:\htdocs\OopSolutions\\' . implode(DIRECTORY_SEPARATOR, ➡
$parts);
  require_once $path . '.php';
}
```

The double backslash is needed at the end of the path to prevent PHP from interpreting the closing quote as an escaped character. On a Mac or Linux, the path is written with forward slashes, so the final slash should not be doubled. Note that you need to use a physical path to the folder containing the classes, not a URL.

With __autoload() there's no need to use require_once to include a class file before using it. PHP loads the class definition on the fly. It does this only once for each class, so the impact on performance is normally minimal.

Throughout the rest of this book, I use require_once instead of __autoload(), because the projects and examples use only a small number of files, and the relative paths should work on any test installation. If you set up your own __autoload() script, you can omit all the include commands in subsequent chapters.

> *The chapter so far has covered all the basic syntax of writing OOP in PHP. Most of the rest of the chapter is devoted to more advanced topics, which you might want to skip on a first read through, although you should take a quick look at "Handling errors with exceptions." Come back to the other parts of the chapter later when you encounter a new concept.*

Exploring advanced OOP features

All the examples of inheritance in the first half of this chapter extend a class that can be instantiated in its own right, but PHP also lets you define classes that cannot be instantiated— abstract classes and interfaces. An **abstract class** defines the basic structure of its child classes but cannot be instantiated on its own. An **interface** dictates which methods a class should have but leaves the actual implementation up to the individual classes.

At first glance, this might sound rather pointless; but these are common features in OOP languages, and once you understand how they work, you'll find them very useful. Seeing actual examples should make things clearer. Other advanced features covered in this section are type hinting, magic methods, and destructors. First, though, let's take a look at abstract classes.

Creating abstract classes and methods

If you worked through the exercises from the beginning of this chapter, you might be wondering if the Ch2_Product class is really necessary. As a result of inheritance, you have specialized classes for books and DVDs. If further products are added to the range, you can create new child classes and would probably never create a Ch2_Product object on its own. In fact, to maintain control, it's a good idea to prevent generic products from being created. However, without the parent class, it would be necessary to declare the common properties and methods in each child class. By making the parent class abstract, you get all the benefits of inheritance but prevent the parent class from being instantiated.

To make a class abstract, add the keyword abstract in front of class and the class name in the class definition. So, the revised Ch2_Product class looks like this (the code is in Product_04.php):

```
abstract class Ch2_Product
{
  // properties defined here
  protected $_type;
  protected $_title;

  // methods defined here
  public function getProductType()
  {
    return $this->_type;
  }

  public function getTitle()
  {
    return $this->_title;
  }
}
```

The only differences are the addition of the abstract keyword in the first line and the removal of the constructor. I could have left the constructor if all child classes used the same one, but they don't. All that's left are the common properties and methods.

However, let's say you want all child classes to implement a particular method but know that the details of the method will be different for each class. Instead of defining a method in the abstract class and overriding it in each child class, you can define an **abstract method**. An abstract method simply names the method and sets its visibility but leaves the details to the child class. In our theoretical online store, you might want to create a method to display the details of each product. Because the details of each type of product are different, the implementation will differ. The following listing shows the Ch2_Product class with the addition of an abstract method called display() (the code is in Product_05.php):

```php
abstract class Ch2_Product
{
  // properties defined here
  protected $_type;
  protected $_title;

  // methods defined here
  public function getProductType()
  {
    return $this->_type;
  }

  public function getTitle()
  {
    return $this->_title;
  }

  abstract public function display();
}
```

Declaring an abstract method like this forces all child classes to define the details of the method. Failure to do so triggers a fatal error. So, in essence, this says all classes in the Ch2_Product hierarchy must have a display() method, but acknowledges that the implementation will be different for each class. For the Ch2_Book class, it might look like this (the code is in Book_05.php):

```php
public function display()
{
  echo "<p>Book: $this->_title ($this->_pageCount pages)</p>";
}
```

For Ch2_DVD, it might look like this (the code is in DVD_03.php):

```php
public function display()
{
  echo "<p>DVD: $this->_title ($this->_duration)</p>";
}
```

You can then create instances of both classes and use the display() method to output the appropriate data for each type of object. The following code (in product_test_10.php) outputs the display shown in Figure 2-8:

```php
$book = new Ch2_Book('PHP Object-Oriented Solutions', 300);
$movie = new Ch2_DVD('Atonement', '2 hr 10 min');
$book->display();
$movie->display();
```

Figure 2-8. By declaring an abstract method, each child class is forced to implement its own version.

> *An abstract class does not need to contain any abstract methods, but as soon as you declare an abstract method within a class, the whole class must be declared abstract.*

Simulating multiple inheritance with interfaces

An interface is very similar to an abstract class, but it has no properties and cannot define how methods are to be implemented. Instead, it is simply a list of methods that must be implemented. Moreover, all methods must be public. While this sounds bizarre, it has two main purposes, namely:

- An interface ensures that all classes that implement it have a common set of functionality.

- Although a child class can have only one parent, it can implement multiple interfaces.

This second characteristic is what makes interfaces very powerful. Let's say that the hypothetical e-commerce application in the examples throughout this chapter sells both downloadable products and ones that need to be delivered. It makes sense for all downloadable products to have a common set of features that won't be applicable to the deliverable goods. An interface offers a way of inheriting from a single parent while sharing an extra set of common features that don't necessarily apply to all child classes.

To create an interface, use the `interface` keyword followed by the name of the interface and a pair or curly braces. Inside the braces, declare the methods without defining their contents. A common convention is to prefix the name of an interface with an uppercase I, but the Zend Framework PHP coding standard that I'm following in this book ends the name with _Interface instead. Because the coding standard maps class and interface names to the directory structure, an interface called Ch2_Downloads_Interface would be stored as Interface.php in a folder called Ch2/Downloads. This can result in a large directory structure, but it has the advantage of consistency and clarity. However, you can choose whichever convention you like. An interface for downloadable items might look something like this:

```
interface Ch2_Downloads_Interface
{
  public function getFileLocation();
  public function createDownloadLink();
}
```

To use an interface, include it automatically with __autoload() or manually with require_once and follow the class name with the keyword implements and the name of the interface in the class definition like this (since I haven't implemented the methods, there are no download files for this example):

```
require_once 'Downloads/Interface.php';
class Ch2_Ebook extends Ch2_Product implements Ch2_Downloads_Interface
{
  // properties and other methods

  public function getFileLocation()
  {
    // details of method
  }

  public function createDownloadLink()
  {
    // details of method
  }
}
```

A class can implement multiple interfaces. Just list them as a comma-delimited list after the implements keyword. The big question is, "Why bother?" To understand that, we need to take another look at class hierarchy.

Understanding which class an object is an instance of

The obvious value of inheritance from a common class is that it avoids the need to repeat code in the child classes. But if that were the only advantage, inheritance and overriding would be little more than a glorified way of selectively including code from a common file. A fundamental aspect of OOP is exercising greater control over the way code works. Inheritance ensures that all related objects share common features and work in a similar way—just like all dogs bark and wag their tails when happy.

In the same way that a dachshund and a spaniel are instances of their own breeds (in object-oriented terms, classes), they are also both dogs. In turn, they are also animals, but they belong to a specialized branch of animals known as mammals. So, a dachshund can be classified as an instance of any of these particular types.

The same applies to objects in PHP. If you created an object from the Ch2_Ebook example in the preceding section, it would not only be an instance of the Ch2_Ebook class but also of Ch2_Downloads_Interface and Ch2_Product.

To find out which class an object belongs to, use the get_class() function like this:

```
$book = new Ch2_Book('PHP Object-Oriented Solutions', 300);
echo get_class($book);  // displays Ch2_Book
```

To find out its parent class, use get_parent_class() like this:

```
echo get_parent_class($book);  // displays Ch2_Product
```

There are two ways to find out whether a class is a subclass of another. The first is to use the is_subclass_of() function. This takes two arguments: the object you want to check and a string containing the name of the class that you want to know whether it's one of the object's parents, for example:

```
if (is_subclass_of($book, 'Ch2_Product'))   // equates to true
```

The other way is to use the instanceof operator like this (note that the name of the class is not in quotes):

```
if ($book instanceof Ch2_Product)   // equates to true
```

The important thing to note about instanceof is that it can also be used to determine whether an object implements a particular interface. The functions, get_class(), get_parent_class(), and is_subclass_of(), test only for direct inheritance.

> *The* instanceof *operator replaces the PHP 4 function* is_a()*, which has now been deprecated.*

Knowing whether an object is an instance of a particular class or interface is important in being able to control program flow. To go back to the animal analogy from earlier, you might be happy to let such animals as cats and dogs into your home, but few people are likely to welcome a crocodile. In object-oriented terms, checking whether an animal implements the Pet interface could save you from a nasty shock.

Restricting acceptable data with type hinting

Let's say that you have developed the simple examples in this chapter ready for deployment in an e-commerce application. Such an application is likely to have a class for the shopping cart and a method called addItem() to add the user's purchases to the cart. To avoid errors, you need to check that the item being added belongs to an acceptable data type. One way of doing so would be to use the instanceof operator like this:

```
public function addItem($item)
{
  if ($item instanceof Ch2_Product) {
    // It's OK, add it to the cart
  } else {
    // Reject it
  }
}
```

PHP also offers a limited version of **type hinting**, a common feature in OOP languages that restricts the type of acceptable data. PHP supports type hinting for objects and (since PHP 5.1) arrays when passed as arguments to methods or functions. You create type hints at the time of defining a function or method by preceding the argument with the type of data you require. If you want a particular type of object, use the class name; for an array, use the word array. The basic syntax looks like this:

```
function functionOrMethodName(TypeRequired $argumentName)
```

If an argument passed to the function or method is of the wrong type, it generates a fatal error.

The data type of a Ch2_Book object is not only Ch2_Book but also Ch2_Product. Figure 2-9 summarizes how to restrict the type of data accepted by the addItem() method of a shopping cart; and the following exercise shows the basic code involved.

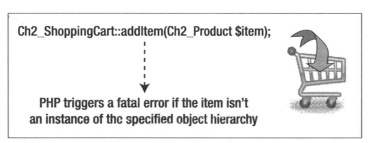

Ch2_ShoppingCart::addItem(Ch2_Product $item);

PHP triggers a fatal error if the item isn't an instance of the specified object hierarchy

Figure 2-9. Type hinting ensures that only the right data type is accepted.

Experimenting with type hinting

This exercise creates the world's least fully featured shopping cart to demonstrate how type hinting restricts the type of data that can be passed as an argument.

1. Create a file called ShoppingCart.php in the Ch2 folder, and define the Ch2_ShoppingCart class like this (the code is in ShoppingCart_01.php in the download files):

```
class Ch2_ShoppingCart
{
  public function addItem(Ch2_Book $item)
  {
    echo '<p>' . $item->getTitle() . ' added</p>';
  }
}
```

The class has a single method, addItem(), which displays the title of the item together with the word "added." To start off with, the method will accept only Ch2_Book objects, so the Ch2_Book class name is added as a type hint in front of the $item parameter. That's all there is to it. (I told you it was the world's least featured shopping cart).

2. Create a file called cart_test.php in the ch2_exercises folder, and insert the following code (it's in cart_test_01.php):

```
require_once '../Ch2/Book.php';
require_once '../Ch2/ShoppingCart.php';

$book = new Ch2_Book('PHP Object-Oriented Solutions', 300);
$cart = new Ch2_ShoppingCart();
$cart->addItem($book);
```

This includes the class files for the Ch2_Book and Ch2_ShoppingCart classes, creates an instance of each class, and adds the $book object to the cart.

> *As explained earlier, the exercises refer to individual files by a basic name. If you have been doing the exercises yourself,* Book.php *should contain the correct code. However, the class definition has changed several times throughout the chapter, so the download files use numbers at the end of each filename to ensure the correct one is loaded.*

3. Test the page, and you should see the result shown in Figure 2-10. No surprises: $book is a Ch2_Book object, and that's what the type hint in Ch2_ShoppingCart::addItem() specifies.

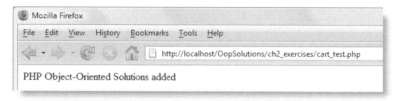

Figure 2-10. The book has been added to the cart.

4. Now let's try adding a DVD to the cart. You need to include the Ch2_DVD class file and create an instance of the class. Amend the code in cart_test.php like this (it's in cart_test_02.php):

```
require_once '../Ch2/Book.php';
require_once '../Ch2/ShoppingCart.php';
require_once '../Ch2/DVD.php';

$book = new Ch2_Book('PHP Object-Oriented Solutions', 300);
$cart = new Ch2_ShoppingCart();
$cart->addItem($book);
$movie = new Ch2_DVD('Atonement', '2 hr 10 min');
$cart->addItem($movie);
```

5. Test the page again. This time you should see the error of your ways (well, mine since I told you to do it), as shown in Figure 2-11.

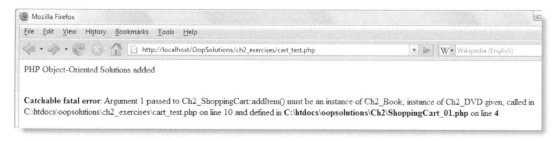

Figure 2-11. The DVD is of the wrong data type and generates a fatal error.

6. To fix the problem, change the type hint in Ch2_ShoppingCart::addItem() like this (the code is in ShoppingCart_02.php):

```
public function addItem(Ch2_Product $item)
```

7. Test the page again (the download file is cart_test_03.php because it needs to include the amended Ch2_ShoppingCart class). This time, both items are accepted, as shown in Figure 2-12, because the addItem() method expects an object of their parent class, Ch2_Product.

Figure 2-12. Using the parent class for the type hint results in both the book and DVD objects being accepted.

When using type hints, you can specify only one type, so you need to be careful how you structure your class hierarchy. This is where interfaces can be handy. If you have a method that applies only to downloadable items, all of which implement an interface called Downloads_Interface, you can use Downloads_Interface as the type hint to prevent the wrong type of object being passed to it.

Type hinting is optional, so even if you provide a type hint for one argument, it's not necessary to provide one for every argument in the same method or function. In fact, you very often can't. Unlike other languages, there is no type hinting support for other data types, such as integers or strings; nor can you specify the type of data to be returned by the method or function. In spite of these limitations, the support for object type hinting means that you can easily test that the right type of object is being passed as an argument.

If you look closely at Figure 2-11, you'll see that the fatal error is described as "catchable." This refers to the error handling model known as exceptions introduced in PHP 5. Exceptions and how to catch them are explained In "Handling errors with exceptions" later in this chapter.

Using magic methods

PHP reserves all function names beginning with a double underscore (like __construct() and __autoload()) as "magical" in the sense that they are automatically invoked in specific circumstances. For example, __construct() is run automatically when you instantiate an object with the new keyword. You can find details of the magic methods in the PHP online documentation at http://docs.php.net/manual/en/language.oop5.magic.php. The following sections cover the most important ones.

Converting an object to a string

One of the first things you learn about working with arrays in PHP is that you can't use echo or print to display the contents of an array. All you see onscreen is the word Array. If you attempt to use echo or print with an object, the result is even less user friendly. Using an object in any situation where a string is expected results in a fatal error.

However, it's often useful to be able to display an object as a string, so the magic method __toString() lets you specify what to display in such a context. The method simply needs to return a string; what it contains is entirely up to you. For example, if you want the Ch2_Book class to display the title of the book when used with echo, define the __toString() method inside the class like this (you can see the full class definition in Book_06.php):

```
class Ch2_Book extends Ch2_Product
{
  // existing properties and methods

  public function __toString()
  {
    return $this->_title;
  }
}
```

You can test this by running product_test_11.php in Ch2_exercises. It simply displays the title of this book, but you could expand the definition of __toString() to display a much more detailed description of the object.

> *Don't use* echo *or* print *inside* __toString(). *The method must* return *a string, not try to display it.*

Cloning an object

Since PHP 5, when you assign an object to another variable, you don't make a copy of it; instead, PHP creates a reference to the same object. Take this simple example:

```
$x = new MyObject();
$y = $x;
```

If you do this, $x and $y both point to the same object. Any changes you make to the properties of object $y will automatically be made to object $x. They are indivisible.

To make a copy of an object, you need to clone it with the clone keyword like this:

```
$y = clone $x;
```

2

This creates what is known as a **shallow copy** of the original object's properties. This means a copy is made of each property that contains a value, which can then be changed independently. However, any property that contains a reference to another object or resource *remains a reference*.

An example should make this clearer. I'm going to create a Ch2_Manufacturer class to store the details of a product's manufacturer. To keep things simple, the class has only one property, but in the real world, it would store many more: contact details, bank account, credit rating, and so on. The class looks like this (the code is in Manufacturer.php in the Ch2 folder of the download files):

```
class Ch2_Manufacturer
{
  protected $_name;

  public function setManufacturerName($name)
  {
    $this->_name = $name;
  }

  public function getManufacturerName()
  {
    return $this->_name;
  }
}
```

To associate the manufacturer with a particular product, you use a technique known as **aggregation**. This simply means that one object acts as a container for one or more other objects. To add a manufacturer to the Ch2_Book and Ch2_DVD classes, you need to amend the abstract Ch2_Product class like this (the code is in Product_06.php in the Ch2 folder):

```
require_once 'Manufacturer.php';

abstract class Ch2_Product
{
  protected $_type;
  protected $_title;
  protected $_manufacturer;

  public function __construct()
  {
    $this->_manufacturer = new Ch2_Manufacturer();
  }

  public function getProductType()
  {
    return $this->_type;
  }
}
```

```
public function getTitle()
{
  return $this->_title;
}

abstract public function display();

public function setManufacturerName($name)
{
  $this->_manufacturer->setManufacturerName($name);
}

public function getManufacturerName()
{
  return $this->_manufacturer->getManufacturerName();
}
}
```

The changes to the Ch2_Product class are highlighted in bold. The constructor creates a new instance of the Ch2_Manufacturer class and assigns it to the $_manufacturer property. This property is an object, but it doesn't exist in its own right; it's wrapped inside a Ch2_Product. So, to set or get its name, getter and setter methods inside the Ch2_Product class use the $_manufacturer object (referred to as $this->_manufacturer) to call the equivalent Ch2_Manufacturer methods.

Because the Ch2_Product class now has a constructor, the child classes need to call the parent constructor like this (for simplicity, I'm showing just the Ch2_Book constructor; the full code is in Book_07.php):

```
public function __construct($title, $pageCount)
{
  parent::__construct();
  $this->_title = $title;
  $this->_pageCount = $pageCount;
  $this->_type = 'book';
}
```

With these changes to the classes, you can create a Ch2_Book object and assign the name of the manufacturer like this:

```
$book = new Ch2_Book('PHP Object-Oriented Solutions', 300);
$book->setManufacturerName('friends of ED');
```

The problem arises if you decide to clone the $book object. To demonstrate the different way clone treats properties depending on whether they refer to an object or resource, the revised version of Ch2_Book in Book_07.php contains a method that lets you change the title of the book. The three lines of code highlighted in bold in the following script in product_test_12.php clone $book and give the cloned version a new title and manufacturer:

```
require_once '../Ch2/Book_07.php';

$book = new Ch2_Book('PHP Object-Oriented Solutions', 300);
$book->setManufacturerName('friends of ED');
echo '<p>' . $book->getTitle() . ' is manufactured by '. ⮕
  $book->getManufacturerName() . '</p>';
$book2 = clone $book;
$book2->setTitle('Website Disasters');
$book2->setManufacturerName('enemies of ED');
echo '<p>' . $book2->getTitle() . ' is manufactured by '. ⮕
  $book2->getManufacturerName() . '</p>';
echo '<p>' . $book->getTitle() . ' is manufactured by '. ⮕
  $book->getManufacturerName() . '</p>';
```

Figure 2-13 shows what happens when you run this script. The $_title property is a string, so changing the title of the cloned object doesn't affect the original. However, even though the manufacturer's name is also a string, it belongs to a Ch2_Manufacturer object inside $book. The shallow copy performed by the clone keyword results in the cloned object still pointing to the original Ch2_Manufacturer object. Changing the manufacturer's name for $book2 changes it for both books.

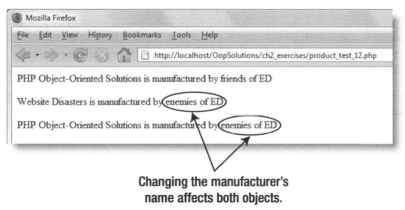

**Changing the manufacturer's
name affects both objects.**

Figure 2-13. Cloning an object can have unexpected consequences when other objects are aggregated.

The __clone() magic method gets around this problem. Whenever you copy an object using the clone keyword, PHP checks if you have defined a __clone() method and calls it automatically. This magic method lets you specify any changes you want made to the object being cloned. If a property contains a reference to another object, you need to clone the property itself. Doing so breaks the reference by producing a copy of the object, which can then be changed without affecting the original. You define __clone() just like any other method. So, to break the reference to the original Ch2_Manufacturer object in the $_manufacturer property, you need to add the following to the Ch2_Product class definition (the full code is in Product_07.php):

```
public function __clone()
{
  $this->_manufacturer = clone $this->_manufacturer;
}
```

If you run the same script as before, the manufacturers' names are now independent of each other, as shown in Figure 2-14. You can test this in product_test_13.php in the download files. (product_test_13.php includes a different version of Ch2_Book, because Ch2_Book needs to inherit the revised version of Ch2_Product. The only difference in the code is the addition of the __clone() method in the Ch2_Product class.)

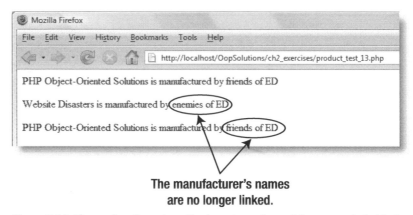

The manufacturer's names
are no longer linked.

Figure 2-14. The __clone() magic method creates a clone of the aggregated object, making it independent of the original.

You can also use the __clone() magic method to change any other values when cloning an object. For instance, you might want to reset an ID property to zero, so the clone doesn't end up with the same ID as the original object.

> *For a more detailed discussion of aggregation, see PHP 5 Objects, Patterns, and Practice, Second Edition by Matt Zandstra or Head First Design Patterns by Eric Freeman and Elizabeth Freeman.*

Accessing properties automatically

Some developers find writing getter and setter methods for private and protected properties tedious, so PHP provides two magic methods, __get() and __set(), that handle everything automatically for you. Before you get too excited by this prospect, I should warn you that if you create both __get() and __set(), the value of any property handled this way is treated as public and can be changed arbitrarily by outside code. Although creating individual getter and setter methods is more time consuming, it gives you much greater control over how protected and private properties can be changed or inspected.

A common way of using __get() and __set() is to create a protected or private property to store the values of undeclared properties as an associative array. The __get() method checks whether the array element exists; if it does, it returns the value. The __set() method simply adds the value to the array. This behavior is not enabled by default, so you need to define the __get() and __set() methods explicitly in your class like this:

```php
class Lazy
{
  // property to hold undeclared properties
  protected $_props;

  // magic methods
  public function __get($name)
  {
    if (isset($this->_props[$name])) {
      return $this->_props[$name];
    } else {
      return false;
    }
  }

  public function __set($name, $value)
  {
    $this->_props[$name] = $value;
  }
}
```

Using __get() isn't always bad. As you'll see in the next chapter, it's useful for creating read-only properties.

Accessing methods automatically

The __call() magic method is used to call methods that don't exist in the current class. While this might sound illogical, it's useful when using aggregation. In the section titled "Cloning an object" earlier in the chapter, I wrapped the getter and setter methods for the Ch2_Manufacturer class in methods of the same name in Ch2_Product. Doing this for just one or two methods is fine, but it becomes a burden in terms of code manageability when there are a lot of them.

Even though a Ch2_Product object can store a reference to a manufacturer object, it can't invoke any of the other class's methods. If you define the __call() magic method, though, PHP calls the other class's method as if it belonged to the Ch2_Product class.

The __call() magic method takes two arguments: the method name and an array of arguments to be passed to the method. You pass these in turn to call_user_func_array() and return the result. However, you need to tell call_user_func_array() which class the

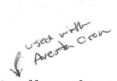

method belongs to. So, the first argument to call_user_func_array() must be an array that contains the aggregated object and the local variable containing the method name.

The code for the __call() magic method is always the same. The only thing that you need to change is the name of the property (highlighted in bold in the following script) that contains the object whose methods you want to call automatically. Taking the example of an object stored by aggregation in a protected property called $_manufacturer, this is how you would define the __call() magic method:

```php
public function __call($method, $arguments)
{
  // check that the other object has the specified method
  if (method_exists($this->_manufacturer, $method)) {
    // invoke the method and return any result
    return call_user_func_array(array($this->_manufacturer, $method), ➡
$arguments);
  }
}
```

The download files contain a revised version of Ch2_Product in Product_08.php. The setManufacturerName() and getManufacturerName() methods have been deleted, and the __call() magic method has been defined.

If you run the script in product_test_14.php, you should see the same result as in Figure 2-14. Instead of using its own getter and setter methods for the manufacturer's name, the Ch2_Product class now directly accesses those defined in the Ch2_Manufacturer class.

Cleaning up with a destructor method

Normally, PHP handles memory management through **garbage collection**—the automatic removal of variables and objects when they're no longer needed by a script. However, there are occasions when you might want to delete a resource, such as a database connection, when an object is no longer needed. Just as PHP calls the __construct() method whenever you create a new object, it looks for the __destruct() magic method immediately before removing an object from memory and runs the destructor automatically if it has been defined.

You define a destructor just like any other method:

```php
public function __destruct()
{
  // code to clear up resources before object is deleted
}
```

A destructor cannot take any arguments. It's also advisable to avoid calls to other objects in a destructor, as there is no way to dictate the order in which objects are deleted, and the other object might already have been deleted by the time the destructor attempts to access it.

Handling errors with exceptions

PHP 5 introduced a new way of handling errors known as exceptions, a concept that is common in many other languages. An **exception** is when something goes wrong in a block of code. Instead of handling the error at that particular point, you **throw** the exception and **catch** it in a special block. This has the advantage of keeping all your error handling in a single place, rather than being scattered throughout your script. PHP has a built-in Exception class, which you can either use as is, or extend to create your own custom exceptions. If you're new to exceptions, it might sound esoteric, but it's quite simple in practice. First, let's look at how to throw an exception.

Throwing an exception

When writing scripts, it's normal practice to test the type of data passed to a function. This often results in complex conditional statements that determine what should happen if the data is of the wrong type. The advantage of using exceptions is that it reduces complexity by handling what should be done in a separate part of the script. This is particularly important with OOP, because classes should be designed to be as project neutral as possible. So, when a problem arises with data passed to a method, keep things simple by throwing an exception inside the method, and leave it to the main application script to determine how to handle it.

The way you throw an exception is with the throw keyword like this:

```
if (the sky falls in) {
    throw new Exception('Oops, the sky has fallen in!');
}
```

Following the throw keyword, you instantiate a new Exception object, which takes one argument: a string that identifies the nature of the problem. Technically speaking, this argument is optional; if you omit it, PHP uses the default value, "Unknown exception." You can also pass a number as an optional second argument. The number has no significance other than to identify the exception. This allows you to set up your own system of error codes.

Once an exception has been thrown, it needs to be caught.

Catching an exception

Whenever you use code that might throw exceptions, wrap the code in a try block and catch any exceptions in a catch block. This structure is similar to an if . . . else conditional statement, except that it uses try and catch instead of if and else. The basic structure looks like this:

```
try {
    // code that might throw exceptions
} catch (Exception $e) {
    // handle the exception here
}
```

67

The try block could be dozens, even hundreds of lines long. If the code throws an exception, the script jumps immediately to the catch block, where the code decides how to handle the problem. In a development environment, you normally want to display a descriptive error message; but in a production environment, you could redirect the user to a custom error page, while sending an email with details of the problem to the server administrator.

The parentheses after the catch keyword should contain a variable to capture the details of the exception. It's also a good idea to use type hinting (see "Restricting acceptable data with type hinting" earlier in the chapter) to indicate what type of exception you want to deal with. In addition to the basic Exception class, the Standard PHP Library (SPL) defines a number of specialized exception classes that you can use in your class definitions (see Chapters 8 and 9). You can also create your own custom exceptions. Using different types of exceptions enables you to have multiple catch blocks that handle problems in different ways. For example, you might create custom exceptions called InvalidDataException and DatabaseErrorException. You could then handle them like this:

```
try {
  // script to be processed
} catch (InvalidDataException $e) {
  // redirect user to input page with appropriate error message
} catch (DatabaseErrorException $e) {
  // redirect user to database error page
} catch (Exception $e) {
  // handle any generic exceptions
}
```

The catch block for generic exceptions must come last. Otherwise the type hinting won't work, as custom exceptions need to extend the built-in Exception class, and therefore belong to the same data type.

Extracting information from an exception

Once you have caught an exception in a catch block, you can extract information about the error and where it occurred by using the Exception class's built-in methods. Table 2-2 lists the methods and the type of information they provide.

Table 2-2. Methods provided by the Exception class

Method	Type/visibility	Description
getMessage()	final	The text of the message passed as the first argument to the exception.
getCode()	final	The error code passed as the optional second argument to the exception. The default is 0.

Method	Type/visibility	Description
getFile()	final	Not the current script, but the file containing the class definition.
getLine()	final	The number of the line on which the exception was thrown—again, not the current script, but the class definition.
getTrace()	final	An associative array containing details of the script that resulted in the exception being thrown, including filename, line, function (method), and arguments.
getTraceAsString()	final	The same information as provided by getTrace() formatted as a string.
__toString()	public	Combines the output of getMessage() and getTraceAsString(). This magic method can be overridden in a custom exception class. All other methods are final, so cannot be overridden.

Because the Exception class has a built-in __toString() method, the simplest way to find out the details of the error is to use echo followed by the variable used to catch the exception like this:

    echo $e;

It can't get much simpler than that.

As you can see from Table 2-2, all the built-in methods, except __toString(), are final. This means __toString() is the only one that can be overridden.

The other methods provide a finer level of detail, so you can display or log the information in a more user-friendly way. Note that the getLine() method refers to the class definition. This reflects the fact that it's the *class* that throws the exception, not the script that utilizes the class. However, what you're usually interested in is locating whatever it was in your script that caused the class to throw an exception. To find that information, you need to extract it from the line element of the array returned by getTrace(). An actual example should clarify how exceptions work.

Throwing and catching an exception

This exercise expands the Ch2_Book class from the examples earlier in the chapter to demonstrate how to throw an exception when invalid data is passed to a Ch2_Book object. It also shows what happens when you fail to catch the exception, and the type of information that can be extracted from an exception that has been caught. Continue working with Book.php from earlier in the chapter. If you no longer have the file, save Book_09.php in the Ch2 folder as Book.php.

1. The Ch2_Book class as defined earlier in the chapter performs no checks on the data passed to the constructor, so it doesn't generate an error if completely meaningless data is passed to it. This is a good case for throwing an exception. For the sake of this exercise, we'll check only that the page count is a number. Amend the constructor method like this:

```php
public function __construct($title, $pageCount)
  {
    if (!is_numeric($pageCount) || $pageCount < 1) {
      throw new Exception('Page count must be a positive number');
    }
    parent::__construct();
    $this->_title = $title;
    $this->_pageCount = (int) $pageCount;
    $this->_type = 'book';
  }
```

The conditional statement (in bold type) uses is_numeric() with the negative operator to check if $pageCount isn't a number, and since there's no point in allowing a negative number, also whether the value is less than 1. If either condition evaluates to true, the code inside the braces throws a new exception with an appropriate message. There's no need for an else clause, because throwing an exception terminates whatever PHP was doing and jumps straight to the first available catch block, assuming there is one.

Just for the sake of tidiness, I have added (int) in front of $pageCount in the line that assigns its value to the $_pageCount property. This casts the value to an integer, if anyone decides to add a decimal fraction to the number. For details of type casting, see the PHP online manual at http://docs.php.net/manual/en/language.types.type-juggling.php#language.types.typecasting.

2. Let's see what happens if you now try to pass invalid data as the second argument to the Ch2_Book constructor. Create a new file called exception_test.php in ch2_exercises, and insert the following code (it's in exception_test_01.php):

```php
require_once '../Ch2/Book.php';

$book = new Ch2_Book('PHP Object-Oriented Solutions', 'Wednesday');
$book->display();
```

This passes the string "Wednesday" instead of a number as the second argument to the Ch2_Book object.

3. Since the Ch2_Book class can now throw exceptions, you should wrap the code in exception_test.php in a try . . . catch block. But let's first see what happens if you don't. Test the page. You should see a result similar to Figure 2-15.

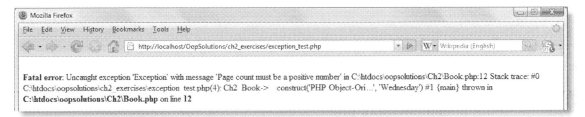

Figure 2-15. Even if you don't catch an exception, PHP generates an error message with all the details.

As you can see, PHP displays a lengthy error message, giving all the details of the exception. If you're being lazy in a development environment, this is all you really need. However, failing to catch exceptions in a production environment is very bad practice, so get into good habits by catching them in your development environment as well.

4. Let's see what information is provided by each of the Exception class methods listed in Table 2-2. Wrap the last two lines of the code in step 2 in a try block, and display the output of each method in the catch block. The code should look like this (if you don't want to go to the trouble of typing out everything yourself, use exception_test_02.php in the download files):

```
try {
  $book = new Ch2_Book('PHP Object-Oriented Solutions', 'Wednesday');
  $book->display();
} catch (Exception $e) {
  echo '<p><strong>Message:</strong> ' . $e->getMessage() . '</p>';
  echo '<p><strong>Code:</strong> ' . $e->getCode() . '</p>';
  echo '<p><strong>File:</strong> ' . $e->getFile() . '</p>';
  echo '<p><strong>Line:</strong> ' . $e->getLine() . '</p>';
  echo '<p><strong>Trace:</strong> ';
  print_r($e->getTrace());
  echo '</p>';
  echo '<p><strong>Trace as string:</strong> ' . ➥
$e->getTraceAsString() . '</p>';
  echo '<p><strong>Using echo:</strong> ' . $e . '</p>';
}
```

5. Test the page now, and you should see the output shown in Figure 2-16.

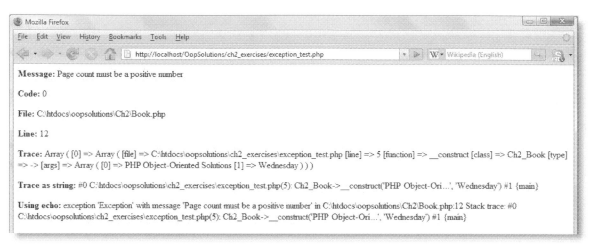

Figure 2-16. Examining the output of the Exception class methods

As you can see, the output of getFile() and getLine() doesn't refer to the current script, but to the location of the conditional statement that throws the exception in the Ch2_Book class. The reference to the part of the script that triggered the exception (line 5 in exception_test.php) is contained in the output of getTrace(), getTraceAsString(), and __toString().

This exercise shows only the information that you can extract from the Exception class methods. What you put in a catch block is entirely up to you. Since an exception brings a script to a halt, the catch block in a production environment should find some way of handling the error gracefully without exposing sensitive details about your server or online application.

Extending the Exception class

In addition to the methods listed in Table 2-2, the Exception class has the four properties described in Table 2-3.

Table 2-3. Default properties of the Exception class

Property	Visibility	Default value	Description
$message	protected	Unknown exception	Message describing error
$code	protected	0	User-defined exception code

Property	Visibility	Default value	Description
$file	protected		Name of the file containing the class that triggered the exception
$line	protected		Line in the class file where the exception was triggered

Because these properties are protected, they are available in any custom class that extends the Exception class.

I won't go into detail about extending the Exception class, because you extend it in exactly the same way as any other class. You can define your own properties and methods. If you override the constructor in your custom class, it is recommended that you call the parent constructor explicitly to ensure that all available data has been properly assigned. The following example taken from the PHP manual shows how you should do it:

```php
// Redefine the exception so message isn't optional
public function __construct($message, $code = 0)
{
  // your own custom code
  // make sure everything is assigned properly
  parent::__construct($message, $code);
}
```

Using comments to generate code hints

Commenting scripts is a chore but a necessary one. It doesn't matter whether you're working on your own or in a team, you need to comment your scripts. Even if no one else ever uses your scripts, you still need to remind yourself of how you intended everything to work, as it's a lot quicker to read comments than to try to fathom things out by reading the code several weeks or months later.

One practice that makes a lot of code virtually self-documenting is to use descriptive names for properties and methods, as recommended in the Zend Framework PHP Coding Standard, which I'm following in this book. Another valuable technique is to use the PHPDoc format. If you're using an IDE such as Zend Studio for Eclipse or PhpED that offers code introspection, PHPDoc comments are automatically converted into code hints (see Figures 1-4 through 1-7 in the previous chapter).

The download files for the remaining chapters contain comments in PHPDoc format. The next section gives just a brief overview to enable you to understand how they're written. You can find full details of PHPDoc at www.phpdoc.org, and a tutorial at www.phpdoc.org/tutorial.php.

73

Writing PHPDoc comments

The normal practice with PHPDoc is to place a comment block before each function (or method) describing its purpose, the arguments it expects, and what it returns (if anything). You can also use comment blocks to describe properties and other variables.

The following example comes from the Pos_Date class in the next chapter and describes the setDate() method.

```
/**
 * Changes the date represented by the object.
 *
 * Overrides the default DateTime setDate() method, and checks
 * that the arguments supplied constitute a valid date.
 *
 * @param  int    $year    The year as a four-digit number.
 * @param  int    $month   The month as a number between 1 and 12.
 * @param  int    $day     The day as a number between 1 and 31.
 */
```

The comment block begins with a forward slash followed by two asterisks (/**). This is a signal to the PHPDoc parser that a PHPDoc comment block is starting. Each subsequent line should also begin with an asterisk. The comment block ends like a normal multiline comment with an asterisk followed by a forward slash (*/).

The first line of the comment block should contain a brief description of what's being commented. The second section contains a more detailed description. The final section contains PHPDoc tags. Each tag must be on a new line and begin with an @ mark. Nothing should precede the tag except whitespace and the asterisk at the start of the line. The preceding example contains three instances of the @param tag.

The @param tag describes an argument accepted by the method. Each argument is listed in the order expected by the method. Following @param is a keyword indicating the required data type. In this case, all three arguments are expected to be integers (int). Then follow the name of the argument, and a brief description.

Table 2-4 lists the most commonly used PHPDoc tags, what should follow the tag, and a description of its use. Where more than one type of data is expected after a tag, separate them with whitespace, not commas.

The following PHPDoc tags should not be used: @abstract, @final, and @static. They were created for PHP 4, which didn't support the abstract, final, or static keywords. Using the keywords in the class definition is now sufficient.

> *The code listings in this book don't include PHPDoc comments, because the purpose of each method and how it works is described in the text. However, the download class files are fully commented.*

Table 2-4. Commonly used PHPDoc tags

Tag	Expected data	Description
@author	Author's name	The author's name can be followed by an email address, which should be enclosed in angle brackets, for example, @author David Powers <david@example.com>.
@copyright	Copyright information	The information is displayed unaltered.
@deprecated	Version information	Notifies users that an element should no longer be used. The version information is displayed unaltered, so can contain anything (or be left blank).
@param	Data type, variable name, description	Describes a parameter (argument) expected by a function or method. The data type should be a valid PHP type. If more than one data type is acceptable, use mixed or separate them with a vertical pipe, for example, int|string.
@return	Data type, description	Describes the return value of a function or method.
@var	Data type, description	Describes a property or variable.
@version	Version details	The information is displayed unaltered, so it can be in any format.

Chapter review

This chapter has covered just about everything you need to know about OOP syntax in PHP. None of it is particularly difficult if you are already familiar with creating your own functions, but absorbing it all at one sitting is likely to be a challenge. I have deliberately put all the theory in this chapter so you can come back to it to refresh your memory whenever necessary.

In the next chapter, you'll start to put this theory into practice by creating a class that extends the built-in DateTime class, giving you hands-on experience of class definition, inheritance, and overriding.

3 TAKING THE PAIN OUT OF
WORKING WITH DATES

It's a well-known fact that most of the formatting characters used by date() and strftime() seem to bear no logical relationship with the values they represent. Even the formatting characters, m (month) and d (date), used with date() aren't completely straightforward. Do they output a leading zero or not? (They do.) But if you don't want the leading zero, can you remember the right characters to use? OK, I'll put you out of your misery; it's n for month and j for date.

Wouldn't it be great if you could format dates in PHP without the need to look up the formatting characters in a book or the online manual every time? Well, that's what this chapter is about. A little-known fact is that a new DateTime class was added in PHP 5.2 (an experimental version can be enabled in PHP 5.1—see http://docs.php.net/manual/en/datetime.installation.php). For some unexplained reason, this class has a rather limited set of methods; and the DateTime::format() method uses exactly the same formatting characters as date(). However, one of the great principles of OOP is encapsulation—hiding the details from the end user—so you can create your own class to handle and format dates in a more user-friendly way.

In this chapter, you will

- Use the PHP Reflection API to inspect class methods and properties
- Use inheritance to extend the built-in PHP DateTime class
- Override the DateTime parent constructor to check the validity of the date
- Use encapsulation to hide the standard date formatting characters
- Create a static method to calculate the number of days between two dates
- Build a series of methods to perform date-related calculations

If this is your first experience of working with OOP in PHP, you'll see very quickly that much of the code inside each method of a custom class is exactly the same as you would use in procedural coding. The only real difference is that, instead of typing little snippets of code to do a specific job in a single project, you're building a generic set of functions that will come in useful across a wide range of projects. Although each section of code is quite short, the finished class definition is several hundred lines long.

Before getting down to the actual code, it's always a good idea to set out the objectives of the new class.

Designing the class

OOP is all about code reuse, so the first step in designing a class should be to consider what's already available within core PHP and how it might be recycled or improved. A quick check of the Date and Time Functions page in the PHP Manual (http://docs.php.net/manual/en/function.date-format.php) shows that nearly 40 functions are available (as of PHP 5.2). What might not be so obvious at first glance is that many of them are the procedural equivalents of two classes that were added to core PHP in version 5.2: DateTime and DateTimeZone.

It's worth taking a closer look at these classes to find out what methods they offer and whether they can be extended or overridden.

Examining the built-in date-related classes

At the time of this writing, the PHP Manual doesn't describe the DateTime and DateTimeZone classes. Instead, you need to look up the equivalent procedural function for each method. A quick way of inspecting the classes yourself is to use the Reflection application programming interface (API) introduced in PHP 5. **Reflection** is the process of examining the inner workings of functions, classes, and objects. The Reflection API comprises a set of specialized classes that can be used to extract information about a class. All the methods have descriptive names, so it's quite easy to use once you're familiar with OOP. You can find more details about the Reflection API, along with examples of its use at http://docs.php.net/manual/en/language.oop5.reflection.php. For the purposes of this chapter, I'm going to use the Reflection API in the simplest possible way by using the static Reflection::export() method to examine the DateTime and DateTimeZone classes.

To examine a class, you pass the name of the class you're interested in to the ReflectionClass constructor. Since the DateTime and DateTimeZone classes are part of core PHP, you can use them directly in a script without needing to include any external class files. The following code produces the output shown in Figure 3-1 (the code is in inspect_DateTime.php in the ch3_exercises folder; I have wrapped it in <pre> tags to make the display easier to read):

```
Reflection::export(new ReflectionClass('DateTime'));
```

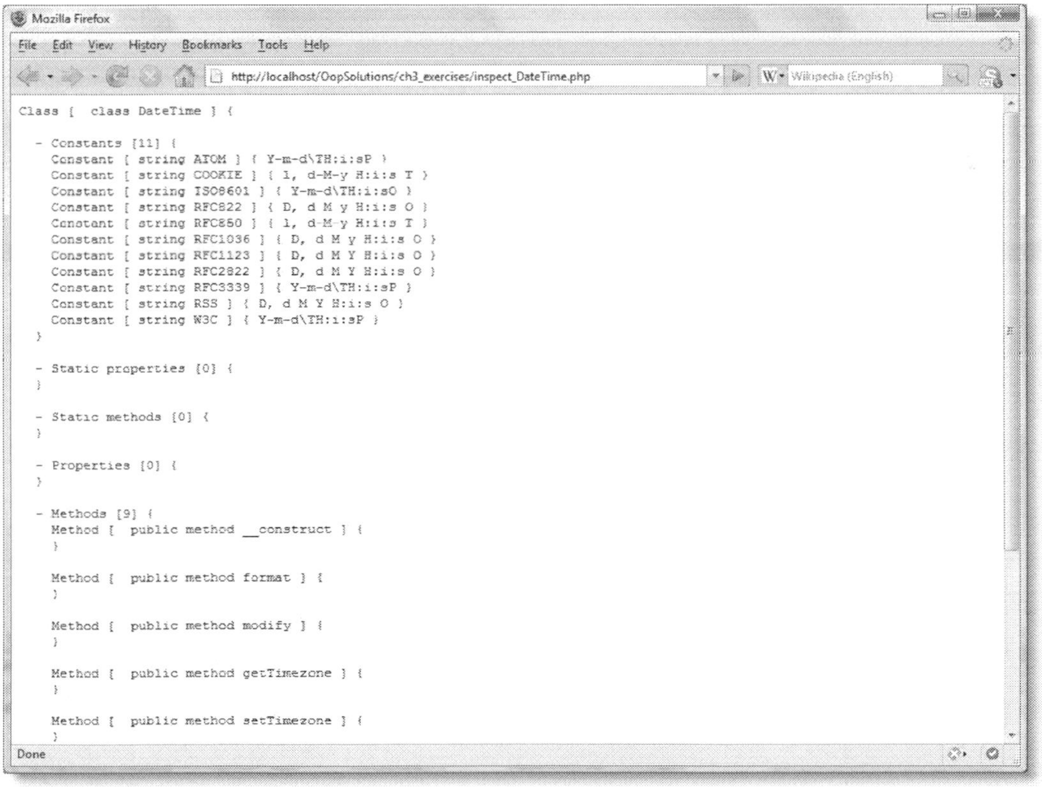

Figure 3-1. The Reflection API exposes a lot of detail about the methods and properties of a class.

At a glance, this tells you that the DateTime class has 11 constants, no static properties or methods, no properties, and nine methods, all of which are public. This means that everything can be inherited and, if necessary, overridden. I'll come back to the constants later. Let's take a look at the methods. Table 3-1 lists each method, the arguments it takes, and a description of its use.

Table 3-1. Methods of the PHP DateTime class

Method	Arguments	Description
__construct()	$date, $timezone	$date is a string in a format accepted by strtotime(). $timezone is a DateTimeZone object. Both arguments are optional. If no arguments are passed to the constructor, it creates a DateTime object representing the current date and time for the default time zone.
format()	$dateFormat	$dateFormat is a string consisting of the same date formatting characters accepted by the procedural date() function. The DateTime::format() method is simply an object-oriented version of date().
modify()	$relativeDate	$relativeDate is a string in a format accepted by strtotime(), e.g. '+1 week'. It modifies the date and time stored by the object by the duration specified.
getTimezone()		This takes no arguments. It returns a DateTimeZone object representing the time zone stored by the DateTime object, or false on failure.
setTimezone()	$timezone	$timezone must be a DateTimeZone object. This sets the time zone stored by the DateTime object, and returns null on success, or false on failure.
getOffset()		This takes no arguments. This returns the offset from Universal Coordinated Time (UTC, also known as GMT) in seconds on success, or false on failure.
setTime()	$hour, $minute, $second	This resets the time stored by the object. The arguments should be a comma-separated list of integers. The third argument is optional.

Method	Arguments	Description
setDate()	$year, $month, $date	This resets the date stored by the object. The arguments should be a comma-separated list of integers and must be in the specified order of year, month, date. This is different from the procedural function mktime(), which follows the American convention of month, date, year.
setISODate()	$year, $week, $dayOfWeek	This is a specialized way of representing the date using the "week date" format of ISO 8601, a standard laid down by the International Organization for Standardization (ISO). The arguments should be a comma-separated list of integers, as follows: $year is the calendar year, $week is the ISO 8601 week number, and $dayOfWeek is a number from 1 (Monday) to 7 (Sunday). So, to set a DateTime object to August 8, 2008, in this way, you need to pass the arguments like this: $olympics->setISODate(2008, 32, 5);.

Using the DateTime class

The way you use the DateTime class is like any other: instantiate an object, and store it in a variable like this:

```
$date = new DateTime();
```

You can then apply any of the methods listed in Table 3-1 (apart from __construct(), which is called automatically when you instantiate an object) by using the -> operator. To format the date, use the format() method with the standard PHP date formatting characters like this (the code is in date_test_01.php in the ch3_exercises folder):

```
$date = new DateTime();
echo $date->format('l, F jS, Y');
```

This creates a DateTime object representing the current date and time and displays it as shown in Figure 3-2.

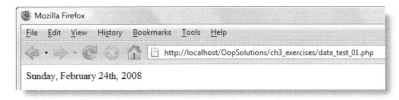

Figure 3-2. DateTime::format() displays the date in the same way as the standard date() function.

If you're familiar with the date() function that's been around since PHP 4, you're probably wondering what's the point of using a DateTime object. After all, you can produce exactly the same output as in Figure 3-2 with the following code:

```
echo date('l, F jS, Y');
```

It's much shorter and does exactly the same thing. Moreover, you need to use the same formatting characters, even if you choose the object-oriented approach.

> *Sometimes the procedural approach in PHP is quicker and simpler to implement. If it makes sense to use procedural code in a particular situation, don't feel obliged to go the object-oriented route because it's "more advanced." Choose the right solution for the job in hand.*

The DateTime class is more useful when you're working with dates other than the current date and time. Rather than juggle several different functions, such as mktime(), strtotime(), strftime(), and date(), everything is handled by the object and its methods. For example, you can display next Thursday's date by changing the previous code like this (it's in date_test_02.php):

```
$date = new DateTime('next Thursday');
echo $date->format('l, F jS, Y');
```

This produces the output shown in Figure 3-3 (obviously, the actual date will depend on when you run the script).

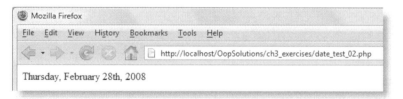

Figure 3-3. The DateTime class makes it easy to create dates based on natural language.

You can also use any of the eleven constants defined by the class to format a DateTime object. Because they are class constants, you need to prefix them with the class name and the scope resolution operator like this:

```
echo $date->format(DateTime::ATOM);
```

Figure 3-4 shows the output of each constant as applied to the same DateTime object. You can test the code yourself in date_test_03.php. Not only will the date and time be different, depending on when you view it, but the time zone offset will also change if your server is in a different part of the world.

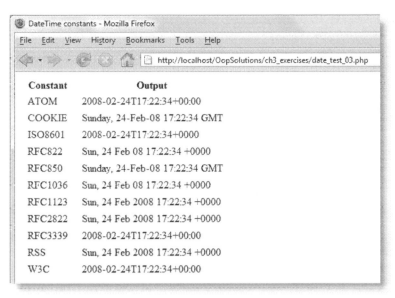

Constant	Output
ATOM	2008-02-24T17:22:34+00:00
COOKIE	Sunday, 24-Feb-08 17:22:34 GMT
ISO8601	2008-02-24T17:22:34+0000
RFC822	Sun, 24 Feb 08 17:22:34 +0000
RFC850	Sunday, 24-Feb-08 17:22:34 GMT
RFC1036	Sun, 24 Feb 08 17:22:34 +0000
RFC1123	Sun, 24 Feb 2008 17:22:34 +0000
RFC2822	Sun, 24 Feb 2008 17:22:34 +0000
RFC3339	2008-02-24T17:22:34+00:00
RSS	Sun, 24 Feb 2008 17:22:34 +0000
W3C	2008-02-24T17:22:34+00:00

Figure 3-4. The same DateTime object as formatted by each of the class constants

> *Because older date and time functions are not part of the* DateTime
> *class, global equivalents of these constants also exist. Just prefix the
> constant with* DATE_ *instead of the class name and scope resolution
> operator, for example,* DATE_ATOM *instead of* DateTime::ATOM. *You can
> use either version with the* DateTime *class. Use the global constants
> with other date and time functions.*

To change the date stored by a DateTime object after it has been created, you use DateTime::modify() with a natural language expression, or DateTime::setDate() with an actual date like this:

```
$date->modify('+2 months');   // adds two months to existing date
$date->setDate(2008, 8, 8);   // sets date to August 8, 2008
```

An important feature of the object-oriented way of handling dates in PHP is the ability to set the time zone of a DateTime object. You can set the time zone explicitly by passing a DateTimeZone object as the second argument to the constructor. I'll explain how to do this in "Using the DateTimeZone class" a little later in the chapter. However, this usually isn't necessary, as DateTime objects use the default time zone for your server.

Setting the default time zone in PHP

As its name suggests, the World Wide Web is international, and one of the biggest frustrations of handling dates in PHP scripts arises when your server is in a different time zone from your target audience. Since PHP 5.1, this is no longer a problem. The server administrator should set the default time zone in php.ini, using the date.timezone directive. You can check the value on your server by running phpinfo() and scrolling down to the date section. As you can see from Figure 3-5, Default timezone on my server is set to Europe/London.

date	
date/time support	enabled
"Olson" Timezone Database Version	2007.9
Timezone Database	internal
Default timezone	Europe/London

Directive	Local Value	Master Value
date.default_latitude	31.7667	31.7667
date.default_longitude	35.2333	35.2333
date.sunrise_zenith	90.583333	90.583333
date.sunset_zenith	90.583333	90.583333
date.timezone	no value	no value

Figure 3-5. It's a good idea to check the time zone being used by your server.

There are far too many time zones to list here, but you can find a list of all time zones supported by PHP at http://docs.php.net/manual/en/timezones.php. If the default time zone on your server doesn't suit your needs, never fear. There are several ways to reset it. If the server is under your own control, the best way to do it is to change the value of date.timezone in php.ini, and restart your web server. If you're on shared hosting and don't have access to php.ini, you can choose from one of the following methods (replace Europe/London in the following examples with the appropriate time zone from among those listed at the previous URL).

Resetting the time zone in .htaccess

If your server runs on Apache, and your hosting company has set the correct permissions for you to use an .htaccess file, add the following command to the .htaccess file in your site root (see http://en.wikipedia.org/wiki/Htaccess if you're not familiar with .htaccess files):

```
php_value date.timezone 'Europe/London'
```

This changes the default time zone for every page on the site.

Resetting the time zone in individual scripts

If you can't change the configuration for the whole site, or need to change the time zone only for a specific script, add the following line of code before using any date functions:

```
ini_set('date.timezone', 'Europe/London');
```

Alternatively, use this:

```
date_default_timezone_set('Europe/London');
```

Both do exactly the same. It doesn't matter which you use. It's a good idea to put configuration changes like this at the top of the script so that they are immediately obvious and
available.

Examining the DateTimeZone class

The DateTimeZone class is a close companion of the DateTime class, and it gives you much
greater control over the use of time zones, allowing you to create objects to represent
times in different parts of the world, regardless of the default time zone for your server.
Using the Reflection API to examine the DateTimeZone class with the following code (it's
also in inspect_DateTimeZone.php) produces the output shown in Figure 3-6:

```
Reflection::export(new ReflectionClass('DateTimeZone'));
```

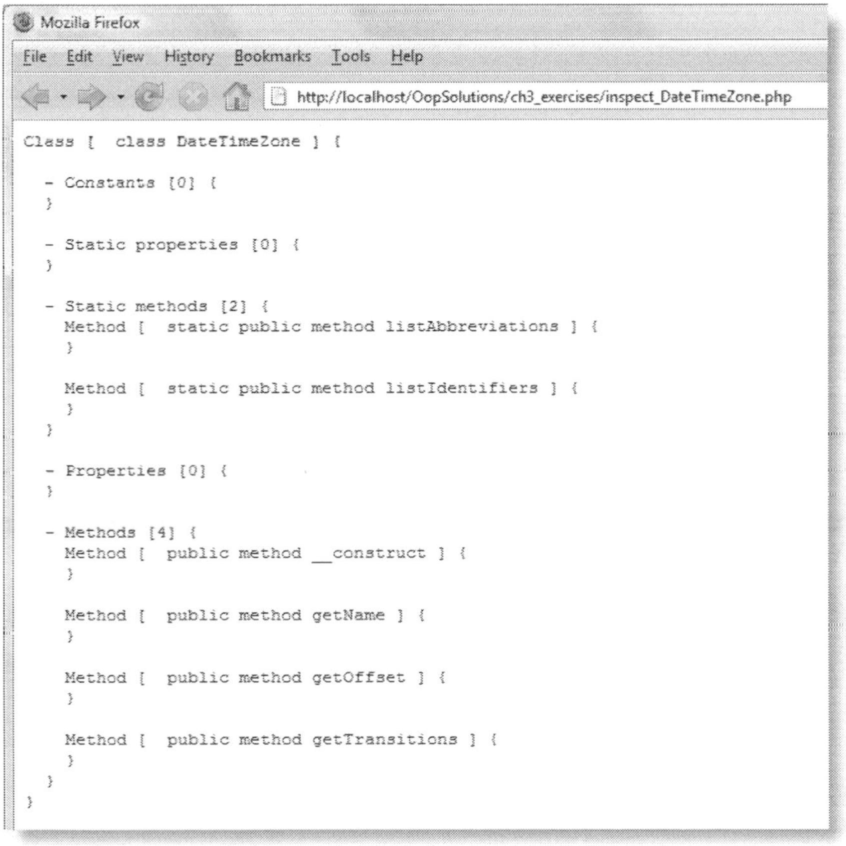

Figure 3-6. The details of the DateTimeZone class exposed by the Reflection API

As you can see from the output of the Reflection API, the DateTimeZone class has no constants or properties. It also has only six methods, but two of them are static. Table 3-2
describes each method.

Table 3-2. Methods of the PHP DateTimeZone class

Type	Method	Arguments	Description
Static			
	listAbbreviations()		This produces a huge multidimensional array listing the following elements for each time zone: daylight saving time (dst), offset from UTC in seconds (offset), and the name by which it is identified in PHP (timezone_id). The subarrays are grouped according to international time zone identifiers in lowercase characters. You can see the output in date_test_04.php.
	listIdentifiers()		This produces an array of all PHP time zone identifiers (there are more than 550) in alphabetical order. You can see the output in date_test_05.php.
Nonstatic			
	__construct()	$identifier	This creates a DateTimeZone object. $identifier must be a string consisting of one of the PHP time zone identifiers. You can find the supported identifiers by running the static function listed earlier or by going to http://docs.php.net/manual/en/timezones.php.
	getName()		This returns the name of the time zone represented by a DateTimeZone object on success or false on failure.
	getOffset()	$dateTime	This returns the offset from UTC in seconds of $dateTime, which must be a DateTime object. The calculation is based on the time zone stored in the DateTimeZone object, rather than that stored in $dateTime. One use is to calculate the time difference between two locations. For an example, study the code in date_test_06.php.
	getTransitions()		This outputs a multidimensional array listing past and future changes to the offset from UTC for a DateTimeZone object. This enables you to calculate whether daylight saving time is in force at a specific date and time. Each subarray contains the following elements: the Unix timestamp for the time of the transition to or from daylight saving time (ts), the date and time in ISO 8601 format (time), the offset from UTC in seconds (offset), whether daylight saving time is in force (isdst), and the official time zone abbreviation (abbr). Figure 3-7 shows part of the output for America/New_York (the code is in date_test_07.php).

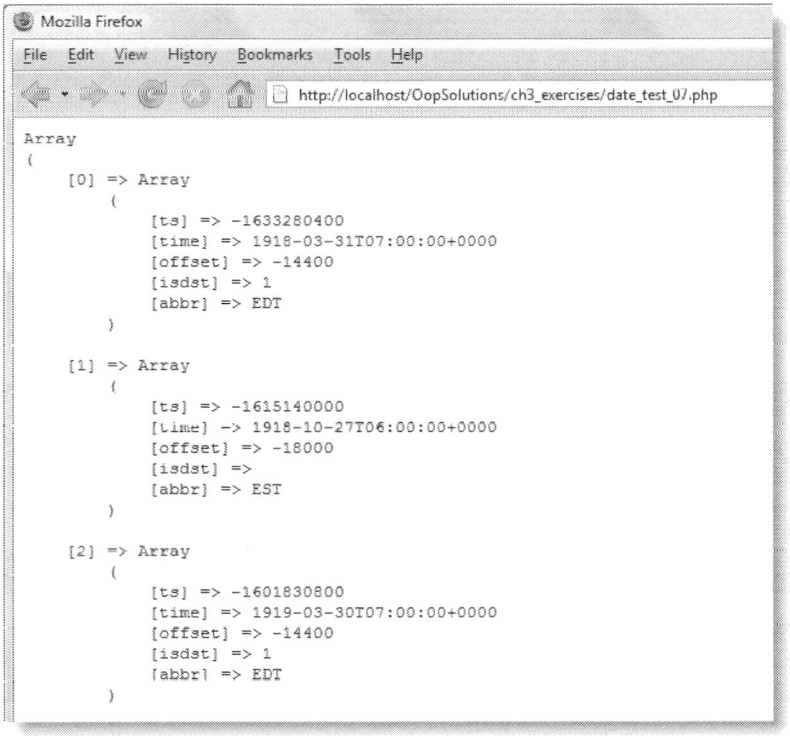
Mozilla Firefox
File Edit View History Bookmarks Tools Help
http://localhost/OopSolutions/ch3_exercises/date_test_07.php
Array
(
[0] => Array
(
[ts] => -1633280400
[time] => 1918-03-31T07:00:00+0000
[offset] => -14400
[isdst] => 1
[abbr] => EDT
)
[1] => Array
(
[ts] => -1615140000
[time] => 1918-10-27T06:00:00+0000
[offset] => -18000
[isdst] =>
[abbr] => EST
)
[2] => Array
(
[ts] => -1601830800
[time] => 1919-03-30T07:00:00+0000
[offset] => -14400
[isdst] => 1
[abbr] => EDT
)

Figure 3-7. DateTimeZone::getTransitions() provides historical and future data about daylight saving time for all time zones.

3

Using the DateTimeZone class

A quick glance at Table 3-2 reveals that most methods of the DateTimeZone class are rather specialized, so I don't intend to dwell on them at length. Use the files listed in Table 3-2 to see how they work. Take particular note of how `DateTimeZone::getOffset()` works in `date_test_06.php`. It uses the current time in New York to work out the time difference between New York and Los Angeles. The code is fully commented to explain how it works, and you can experiment by changing the time zone identifiers at the beginning of the script.

The most common use of the DateTimeZone class is to alter the time zone of a `DateTime` object. First, you create a `DateTimeZone` object by passing the time zone identifier to the constructor. Then you pass the `DateTimeZone` object as the second argument to the `DateTime` constructor like this (the code is in `date_test_08.php`):

```
$Tokyo = new DateTimeZone('Asia/Tokyo');
$now = new DateTime('now', $Tokyo);
echo "<p>In Tokyo, it's " . $now->format('g:i A') . '</p>';
```

This displays the current date and time in Tokyo, regardless of the time zone on your own server.

You can also use a DateTimeZone object to change the time zone of an existing DateTime object by passing it as an argument to DateTime::setTimezone(). The following code (it's also in date_test_09.php) displays the current time in different parts of the world by resetting the time zone of the DateTime object stored as $now:

```php
// create a DateTime object
$now = new DateTime();
echo '<p>My local time is ' . $now->format('l, g:i A') . '</p>';

// create DateTimeZone objects for various places
$Katmandu = new DateTimeZone('Asia/Katmandu');
$Moscow = new DateTimeZone('Europe/Moscow');
$Timbuktu = new DateTimeZone('Africa/Timbuktu');
$Chicago = new DateTimeZone('America/Chicago');
$Fiji = new DateTimeZone('Pacific/Fiji');

// reset the time zone for the DateTime object to each time zone in turn
$now->setTimezone($Katmandu);
echo "<p>In Katmandu, it's " . $now->format('l, g:i A') . '</p>';
$now->setTimezone($Moscow);
echo "<p>In Moscow, it's " . $now->format('l, g:i A') . '</p>';
$now->setTimezone($Timbuktu);
echo "<p>In Timbuktu, it's " . $now->format('l, g:i A') . '</p>';
$now->setTimezone($Chicago);
echo "<p>In Chicago, it's " . $now->format('l, g:i A') . '</p>';
$now->setTimezone($Fiji);
echo "<p>And in Fiji, it's " . $now->format('l, g:i A') . '</p>';
```

This script produces output similar to Figure 3-8.

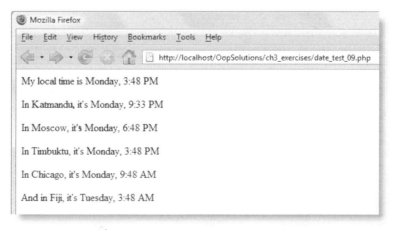

Figure 3-8. The DateTimeZone class makes it easy to display the time in different parts of the world.

This example uses the current time, but you can specify the date and time of a DateTime object, so using the DateTime and DateTimeZone classes in combination with each other makes it very easy to display the time of live events on a web site, showing the local time in various parts of the world where your target audience is likely to be. Remember, though, that if you need to maintain a reference to separate time zones in different parts of a script, it's better to create a DateTime object for each one like this:

```
$myTime = new DateTime();
$westCoast = new DateTimeZone('America/Los_Angeles');
$LAtime = new DateTime('now', $westCoast);
```

3

Now that you have got a good idea of the DateTime and DateTimeZone classes, you can set about deciding how to design a custom class that builds on the existing functionality.

Deciding how to extend the existing classes

That overview of the DateTime and DateTimeZone classes was deliberately detailed, as there's no point reinventing the wheel. The first decision is easy: the DateTimeZone class does all the work related to time zones. Unless you plan to do complex time zone calculations, it doesn't need extending. As long as the extended DateTime class doesn't override the DateTime::setTimezone() or DateTime::getTimezone() methods, everything to do with time zones will be taken care of by the existing classes.

That leaves the following methods of the DateTime class that you need to decide what to do with, if anything:

- __construct()
- format()
- modify()
- getOffset()
- setTime()
- setDate()
- setISODate()

It's easy to decide about getOffset() and setISODate(). They perform specialized tasks and don't need to be changed. All the others, however, present problems.

Although setTime() and setDate() accept arguments in a logical order, they accept out-of-range values. For instance, the minutes argument of setTime() quite happily accepts a value of 75 and silently converts it to 1 hour 15 minutes. Similarly, setDate() sets September 31 to October 1. Sometimes, that might be what you want, but changing values silently like this can lead to unexpected results. A date and time object that represents the wrong date or time is worthless.

The constructor and modify() methods suffer from the same drawback, as they both emulate strtotime(). Although strtotime() is extremely useful, it silently converts invalid dates to what PHP thinks you meant. For instance, it accepts February 29, 2007, without complaint, but the resulting timestamp is for March 1, 2007 (because 2007 wasn't a leap year). For this reason, I have decided to allow the constructor to instantiate objects only for the current date and time, although it will allow you to specify a time zone. This means you will need to go through two extra steps to reset the date and time, but I think this is a worthwhile tradeoff for accuracy. To prevent modify() from being used, I've gone for a more draconian solution: throw an exception.

That leaves just format(). The problem with this method is that it relies on the same mind-numbing formatting characters as date(). However, instead of trying to remember that F is used to format the name of the month, you can encapsulate the formatting process inside a method called getMonthName(). Because format() is a public method, it will remain accessible to objects created by the new class, should you still want to use it.

So, the only methods that will be inherited without any changes are format(), getOffset(), and setISODate(). The others will be overridden.

The main purpose of extending the DateTime class is to avoid the need to remember formatting characters, but there's no point replacing obscure characters with method names that are equally difficult to remember. One solution is to borrow function names from another Web technology; JavaScript springs to mind as a good candidate. Where a JavaScript equivalent doesn't exist, the names will be as descriptive as possible. Using descriptive names is one of the guidelines in the Zend Framework PHP Coding Standard; and if your IDE generates code hints from custom classes, there's no extra typing involved once the class has been defined.

It would also be useful to be able to perform calculations with dates, such as working out the number of days between two dates, and adding or subtracting a number of days or weeks from a specific point in time. In the original DateTime class, adding or subtracting a specific period is done with modify(); but I have decided to block its use in the extended class, so alternative methods are required.

So, in summary, the tasks required to extend the DateTime class are as follows:

- Methods to be overridden:
  - __construct()
  - modify()
  - setTime()
  - setDate()
- New methods for setting dates:
  - setMDY(): Accept a date in MM/DD/YYYY format
  - setDMY(): Accept a date in DD/MM/YYYY format
  - setFromMySQL(): Accept a date in MySQL format (YYYY-MM-DD)
- New methods for displaying dates:
  - getMDY(): Display a date in MM/DD/YYYY format
  - getDMY(): Display a date in DD/MM/YYYY format
  - getMySQLFormat(): Format a date as YYYY-MM-DD ready for insertion into MySQL

- New methods for displaying date parts:
  - Separate methods for displaying year, month, and date as numbers, words, and abbreviations
- New methods for doing date calculations:
  - Separate methods for adding and subtracting days, weeks, months, and years
  - A static method for calculating the number of days between two dates

> *Choosing names for methods is often subjective. I have used "MySQL" in the names of the methods that handle dates in the ISO format (YYYY-MM-DD) because MySQL is used so widely in conjunction with PHP. However, if you don't use MySQL, it might be more appropriate to change the names to* setFromISO() *and* getISOFormat().

That's quite a lot of coding ahead. If you don't relish the prospect of typing it all out yourself, you can find the finished class in the download files. Even if you take the lazy route, do read through the explanations in the following pages, as they will help you understand the process of extending an existing class. The finished class in the download files is also fully commented.

Building the class

At long last, it's time to roll your sleeves up and create your first custom class. Let's start with the basic shell and the constructor.

Creating the class file and constructor

Following the naming convention I explained in Chapters 1 and 2, all custom classes in this book are prefixed with Pos_, and the name maps to the location of the class file. I'm going to call this class Pos_Date, so you need to create an empty PHP file called Date.php in the Pos folder.

> *If you just want to review the final code along with the explanations in the text, copy* Date.php *from the* finished_classes *folder in the download files to the* Pos *folder.*

The Pos_Date class extends the DateTime class. Since DateTime is part of the PHP core, it's automatically available to any script, so there's no need to include it before the class definition (in fact, you can't; there's nowhere to include it from).

1. Declare the class name and use the extends keyword so that it inherits the existing methods of the DateTime class like this:

```
class Pos_Date extends DateTime
{
  // all code goes here
}
```

2. The purpose of a DateTime object is to store the date and time. It does so internally by storing a Unix timestamp, which represents the number of seconds elapsed since January 1, 1970. However, storing year, month, and date as properties within the class makes life easier. You don't want any of these properties to be changed arbitrarily, so they should be declared as protected. Add the properties between the curly braces of the class definition like this:

```
protected $_year;
protected $_month;
protected $_day;
```

Because they're protected properties, I have started each name with an underscore. Later, you'll set the values of these properties with arguments that use the same names *without* an underscore. This naming convention makes it easier to distinguish between values passed in from outside as arguments (no underscore) and values stored internally as properties (leading underscore).

3. The next step is to create the constructor method. To start off with, let's create an object that's identical to one created by the DateTime class and assign values to some of the properties declared in the previous step. Add the following code beneath the properties:

```
public function __construct($dateString, $timezone)
{
  // call the parent constructor
  parent::__construct($dateString, $timezone);

  // assign the values to the class properties
  $this->_year = (int) $this->format('Y');
  $this->_month = (int) $this->format('n');
  $this->_day = (int) $this->format('j');
}
```

This calls the parent constructor and passes the $dateString and $timezone arguments directly to it. As the code now stands, both arguments are required, so we'll need to fix this, but let's first have a look at the properties.

Each property uses the format() method inherited from the DateTime class to extract the numeric value for the year, month, and day, using the following date() formatting characters:

- Y: The year as a four-digit number
- n: The number of the month with no leading zero
- j: The day of the month as a number with no leading zero

TAKING THE PAIN OUT OF WORKING WITH DATES

The format() method returns a string, so each value is cast to an integer, using the casting operator (int). Most of the time, PHP automatically converts numeric strings to integers, but I have taken this precaution to ensure that calculations are handled correctly with no unpleasant surprises.

I have not assigned values to the time properties because I don't propose using them for any calculations. However, you might need to do so if you decide to add extra methods to the Pos_Date class later to handle time in greater detail.

Let's pause a moment to take a look at the arguments passed to the constructor. In the DateTime class, both are optional. However, the way DateTime handles invalid dates prompted me to allow this class to create an object only for the current date and time. So, instead of two arguments, I want only one—for the time zone—and it needs to be optional. There are two ways of handling optional arguments. One way is to assign a default value to the argument in the function definition like this:

```
public function __construct($timezone = null)
```

The other way is to leave out the arguments entirely, and to use func_get_args() and its related functions (see http://docs.php.net/manual/en/function.func-get-args.php) to find out how many arguments have been passed, and extract their values.

In this case, I'm going to take the first option, because leaving out the arguments prevents any automatic code hinting by an IDE. However, declaring $timezone as null also presents problems. Although a time zone is optional, if you choose to set it, the parent constructor expects it to be a DateTimeZone object. Anything else triggers an exception, so you need to check the value of $timezone before handing it off to the parent. With those points in mind, let's get back to the class definition.

4. Amend the constructor so it looks like this:

```
public function __construct($timezone = null)
{
  // call the parent constructor
  if ($timezone) {
    parent::__construct('now', $timezone);
  } else {
    parent::__construct('now');
  }

  // assign the values to the class properties
  $this->_year = (int) $this->format('Y');
  $this->_month = (int) $this->format('n');
  $this->_day = (int) $this->format('j');
}
```

If $timezone has a value other than its default (null) or anything that PHP treats as false (such as 0 or an empty string), the conditional statement equates to true and passes two arguments to the parent constructor. Even though both arguments are optional in the DateTime class, you can't call the parent constructor with only the second argument. So, the value now is hardcoded for the date and time, and

$timezone sets the time zone value passed as the sole argument to the Pos_Date constructor.

If no argument is passed to the Pos_Date constructor, $timezone is null, so the conditional statement fails, and runs the else clause instead. This passes the hard-coded value now to set the date and time. Since this is the default value used by DateTime, you could leave this out. However, you *must* call the parent constructor—even if you pass no arguments to it—because the extended class has defined a constructor of its own, overriding the parent. Without an explicit call to the parent constructor, an object to hold the date and time won't be created, defeating the purpose of extending the DateTime class.

Rather than omit the argument in the else block, I have chosen to hardcode the value now as a reminder of how I want the extended class to work. Explicit instructions remove any doubt.

You might be wondering why I don't check whether $timezone is a DateTimeZone object. The answer is simple: if anything other than a DateTimeZone object is passed to the parent constructor, the DateTime class throws an exception. In other words, the parent class performs the check on your behalf.

5. If you create an instance of the Pos_Date class now, it works in exactly the same way as a DateTime object, as it inherits all the public methods (apart from the constructor) listed in Table 3-1. Test it with the following code (in Pos_Date_test_01.php), which should produce output similar to Figure 3-9:

```php
require_once '../Pos/Date.php';
try {
  // create a Pos_Date object for the default time zone
  $local = new Pos_Date();
  // use the inherited format() method to display the date and time
  echo '<p>Local time: ' . $local->format('F jS, Y h:i A') . '</p>';

  // create a DateTimeZone object
  $tz = new DateTimeZone('Asia/Tokyo');
  // create a new Pos_Date object and pass the time zone as an argument
  $Tokyo = new Pos_Date($tz);
  echo '<p>Tokyo time: ' . $Tokyo->format('F jS, Y h:i A') . '</p>';
} catch (Exception $e) {
  echo $e;
}
```

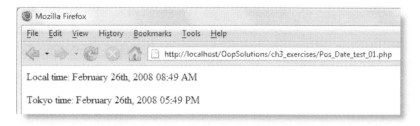

Figure 3-9. Confirmation that the Pos_Date class has inherited its parent's methods

Notice that I have wrapped the script in a try . . . catch block. You should get into the habit of doing this when using code that might trigger an exception (see "Handling errors with exceptions" in Chapter 2).

The only difference between the two classes so far is that the only way to create an object for a different time and date is to use the inherited setTime() and setDate() methods. But these methods accept out-of-range values, so let's improve the way they work.

Resetting the time and date

Apart from the way they handle out-of-range values, there's nothing wrong with the setTime() and setDate() methods. So all that's needed to override them in the Pos_Date class is to check the validity of the arguments, and then pass them directly to the parent method.

1. Let's start with setting the time. If you're typing out the code yourself, each method goes after the preceding one inside the curly braces of the class definition in Date.php. The code is very straightforward, so here is the complete listing for setTime():

```
public function setTime($hours, $minutes, $seconds = 0)
{
  if (!is_numeric($hours) || !is_numeric($minutes) || ➥
!is_numeric($seconds)) {
    throw new Exception('setTime() expects two or three numbers ➥
separated by commas in the order: hours, minutes, seconds');
  }
  $outOfRange = false;
  if ($hours < 0 || $hours > 23) {
    $outOfRange = true;
  }
  if ($minutes < 0 || $minutes > 59) {
    $outOfRange = true;
  }
  if ($seconds < 0 || $seconds > 59) {
    $outOfRange = true;
  }
  if ($outOfRange) {
    throw new Exception('Invalid time.');
  }
  parent::setTime($hours, $minutes, $seconds);
}
```

In the parent class, the third argument is optional. If omitted, it sets seconds to zero, so when overriding setTime(), it's necessary to set a default value for $seconds in the method definition.

The first conditional statement checks that all the arguments are numeric. If not, it throws an exception with a message informing users of the correct type and sequence of arguments. Strictly speaking, DateTime::setTime() expects each

3

argument to be an integer. However, in practice, it's much more lenient. As long as the input is numeric, it accepts strings and floating point numbers and converts them to the equivalent integers. So there's no need to perform a stricter check than is_numeric(). This is extremely helpful, because all input is transmitted through the $_POST and $_GET arrays as strings. If the parent class didn't take this approach, you would need to convert all input to integers before passing it to the parent method.

Before the next series of conditional statements, a variable called $outOfRange is set to false. Each conditional statement checks whether $hours, $minutes, and $seconds is in a valid range, and if not, $outOfRange is set to true. Since only one condition needs to fail, I could have put all six in a single statement. I have used three statements purely for readability. It involves a little extra typing, but I find the logic of the code is easier to follow when laid out like this.

If $outOfRange is reset to true, an exception is thrown. Since PHP jumps straight to a catch block when an exception is thrown, there's no need to wrap the call to the parent method in an else clause. If no exception has been thrown, the arguments are passed to the parent method, and the time is reset.

2. The code for setDate() is very similar, so here's the listing in full:

```php
public function setDate($year, $month, $day)
{
    if (!is_numeric($year) || !is_numeric($month) || ➥
!is_numeric($day)) {
        throw new Exception('setDate() expects three numbers separated ➥
by commas in the order: year, month, day.');
    }
    if (!checkdate($month, $day, $year)) {
        throw new Exception('Non-existent date.');
    }
    parent::setDate($year, $month, $day);
    $this->_year = (int) $year;
    $this->_month = (int) $month;
    $this->_day = (int) $day;
}
```

All three arguments are required for setDate(), so there's no need to set any default values. The first conditional statement again checks whether the submitted values are numeric. Although the parent class performs a similar check, you need to establish that you're working with numbers before checking they're in the correct range.

This time, you want to make sure the values submitted constitute a valid date, so you pass them to the PHP checkdate() function, which is smart enough to know there are only 30 days in September and when it's a leap year. Notice that the order of arguments expected by checkdate() follows the American convention of month, day, year, unlike DateTime, which follows the ISO standard of largest unit to smallest: year, month, day.

If no exception is thrown, the arguments are passed to the parent method. Finally, you need to reset the internal properties $_year, $_month, and $_day to their new values, casting them to integers in the process.

3. Test the overridden setTime() and setDate() methods with the following code (it's in Pos_Date_test_02.php):

```
require_once '../Pos/Date.php';
try {
  // create a Pos_Date object for the default time zone
  $local = new Pos_Date();
  // use the inherited format() method to display the date and time
  echo '<p>Time now: ' . $local->format('F jS, Y h:i A') . '</p>';
  $local->setTime(12, 30);
  $local->setDate(2008, 8, 8);
  echo '<p>Date and time reset: ' . $local->format('F jS, Y h:i A') .
'</p>';
} catch (Exception $e) {
  echo $e;
}
```

This code should display the current date and time, and show the reset date and time as August 8th, 2008 12:30 PM.

4. Change the date or time to an out-of-range value, and run the code again (there's an example in Pos_Date_test_03.php). It should catch the exception, and display details of the problem as shown in Figure 3-10.

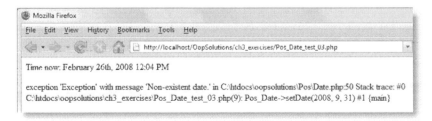

Figure 3-10. The overridden setTime() and setDate() methods reject out-of-range values.

As you can see from Figure 3-10, displaying the exception with echo provides a lot of information about the problem: the custom message (Non-existent date), the file and the line that caused the problem (Pos_Date_test_03.php(9)), and the arguments passed to the method that threw the exception (setDate(2008, 9, 31)).

5. The final step in closing the out-of-range loopholes in the parent class involves throwing an exception if anyone tries to use the modify() method inherited from DateTime. Add the following to the Pos_Date class definition:

```
public function modify()
{
  throw new Exception('modify() has been disabled.');
}
```

These simple changes make the Pos_Date class much more robust than the parent class. That completes overriding the inherited methods. All subsequent changes add new methods to enhance the class's functionality. You can either go ahead and implement all the new methods or just choose those that suit your needs. Let's start by adding some new ways to set the date.

Accepting dates in common formats

When handling dates in user input, my instinct tells me not to trust anyone to use the right format, so I create separate fields for year, month, and date. That way, I'm sure of getting the elements in the right order. However, there are circumstances when using a commonly accepted format can be useful, such as an intranet or when you know the date is coming from a reliable source like a database. I'm going to create methods to handle the three most common formats: MM/DD/YYYY (American style), DD/MM/YYYY (European style), and YYYY-MM-DD (the ISO standard, which is common in East Asia, as well as being the only date format used by MySQL). These methods have been added purely as a convenience. When both the month and date elements are between 1 and 12, there is no way of telling whether they have been inputted in the correct order. The MM/DD/YYYY format interprets 04/01/2008 as April 1, 2008, while the DD/MM/YYYY format treats it as January 4, 2008.

They all follow the same steps:

1. Use the forward slash or other separator to split the input into an array.

2. Check that the array contains three elements.

3. Pass the elements (date parts) in the correct order to Pos_Date::setDate().

I pass the elements to the overridden setDate() method, rather than to the parent method, because the overridden method continues the process like this:

4. It checks that the date parts are numeric.

5. It checks the validity of the date.

6. If everything is OK, it passes the date parts to the parent setDate() method and resets the object's $_year, $_month, and $_day properties.

This illustrates an important aspect of developing classes. When I originally designed these methods, all six steps were performed in each function. This involved not only a lot of typing; with four methods all doing essentially the same thing (the fourth is Pos_Date::setDate()), the likelihood of mistakes was quadrupled. So, even inside a class, it's important to identify duplicated effort and eliminate it by passing subordinate tasks to specialized methods. In this case, setDate() is a public method, but as you'll see later, it's common to create protected methods to handle repeated tasks that are internal to the class.

Accepting a date in MM/DD/YYYY format

This is the full listing for setMDY(), which accepts dates in the standard American format MM/DD/YYYY.

```
public function setMDY($USDate)
{
  $dateParts = preg_split('{[-/ :.]}', $USDate);
  if (!is_array($dateParts) || count($dateParts) != 3) {
    throw new Exception('setMDY() expects a date as "MM/DD/YYYY".');
  }
  $this->setDate($dateParts[2], $dateParts[0], $dateParts[1]);
}
```

The first line inside the setMDY() method uses preg_split() to break the input into an array. I have used preg_split() instead of explode(), because it accepts a regular expression as the first argument. The regular expression {[-/ :.]} splits the input on any of the following characters: dash, forward slash, single space, colon, or period. This permits not only MM/DD/YYYY, but variations, such as MM-DD-YYYY or MM:DD:YYYY.

> *Although Perl-compatible regular expressions are normally enclosed in forward slashes, I have used a pair of curly braces. This is because the regex contains a forward slash. Using braces avoids the need to escape the forward slash in the middle of the regex with a backslash. Regular expressions are hard enough to read without adding in the complication of escaping forward slashes.*

As long as $dateParts is an array with three elements, the date parts are passed internally to the overridden setDate() method for the rest of the process. If there's anything wrong with the data, it's the responsibility of setDate() to throw an exception.

Accepting a date in DD/MM/YYYY format

The setDMY() method is identical to setMDY(), except that it passes the elements of the $dateParts array to setDate() in a different order to take account of the DD/MM/YYYY format commonly used in Europe and many other parts of the world. The full listing looks like this:

```
public function setDMY($EuroDate)
{
  $dateParts = preg_split('{[-/ :.]}', $EuroDate);
  if (!is_array($dateParts) || count($dateParts) != 3) {
    throw new Exception('setDMY() expects a date as "DD/MM/YYYY".');
  }
  $this->setDate($dateParts[2], $dateParts[1], $dateParts[0]);
}
```

Accepting a date in MySQL format

This works exactly the same as the previous two methods. Although MySQL uses only a dash as the separator between date parts, I have left the regular expression unchanged, so that the setFromMySQL() method can be used with dates from other sources that follow the same ISO format as MySQL. The full listing follows:

```php
public function setFromMySQL($MySQLDate)
{
  $dateParts = preg_split('{[-/ :.]}', $MySQLDate);
  if (!is_array($dateParts) || count($dateParts) != 3) {
    throw new Exception('setFromMySQL() expects a date as "YYYY-MM-DD".');
  }
    $this->setDate($dateParts[0], $dateParts[1], $dateParts[2]);
}
```

Now let's turn to formatting dates, starting with the most commonly used formats.

Outputting dates in common formats

Outputting a date is simply a question of wrapping—or encapsulating, to use the OOP terminology—the format() method and its cryptic formatting characters in a more user-friendly name. But what should you do about leading zeros? Rather than create separate methods for MM/DD/YYYY and DD/MM/YYYY formats with and without leading zeros, the simple approach is to pass an argument to the method. The code is so simple; the full listing for getMDY(), getDMY(), and getMySQLFormat() follows:

```php
public function getMDY($leadingZeros = false)
{
  if ($leadingZeros) {
    return $this->format('m/d/Y');
  } else {
    return $this->format('n/j/Y');
  }
}

public function getDMY($leadingZeros = false)
{
  if ($leadingZeros) {
    return $this->format('d/m/Y');
  } else {
    return $this->format('j/n/Y');
  }
}

public function getMySQLFormat()
{
  return $this->format('Y-m-d');
}
```

I have assumed that most people will want to omit leading zeros, so I have given the $leadingZeros argument a default value of false. Inside each method, different formatting characters are passed to the format() method depending on the value of $leadingZeros. The ISO format used by MySQL normally uses leading zeros, so I have not provided an option to omit them in getMySQLFormat().

Because $leadingZeros has a default value, there's no need to pass an argument to getMDY() or getDMY() if you don't want leading zeros. If you do, anything that PHP treats as true, such as 1, will suffice. The following code (in Pos_Date_test_04.php) produces the output shown in Figure 3-11:

```php
require_once '../Pos/Date.php';
try {
  // create a Pos_Date object
  $date = new Pos_Date();
  // set the date to July 4, 2008
  $date->setDate(2008, 7, 4);
  // use different methods to display the date
  echo '<p>getMDY(): ' . $date->getMDY() . '</p>';
  echo '<p>getMDY(1): ' . $date->getMDY(1) . '</p>';
  echo '<p>getDMY(): ' . $date->getDMY() . '</p>';
  echo '<p>getDMY(1): ' . $date->getDMY(1) . '</p>';
  echo '<p>getMySQLFormat(): ' . $date->getMySQLFormat() . '</p>';
} catch (Exception $c) {
  echo $e;
}
```

Figure 3-11. The output methods make it easy to format a date in a variety of ways.

Outputting date parts

As well as full dates, it's useful to be able to extract individual date parts. Wherever possible, I have chosen method names from JavaScript to make them easy to remember. The following code needs no explanation, as it uses either the format() method with the appropriate formatting character or one of the class's properties:

```php
public function getFullYear()
{
  return $this->_year;
}

public function getYear()
{
  return $this->format('y');
}

public function getMonth($leadingZero = false)
{
  return $leadingZero ? $this->format('m') : $this->_month;
}

public function getMonthName()
{
  return $this->format('F');
}

public function getMonthAbbr()
{
  return $this->format('M');
}

public function getDay($leadingZero = false)
{
  return $leadingZero ? $this->format('d') : $this->_day;
}

public function getDayOrdinal()
{
  return $this->format('jS');
}

public function getDayName()
{
  return $this->format('l');
}

public function getDayAbbr()
{
  return $this->format('D');
}
```

You can check the output of these methods with Pos_Date_test_05.php in the download files. It displays results similar to Figure 3-12 for the current date.

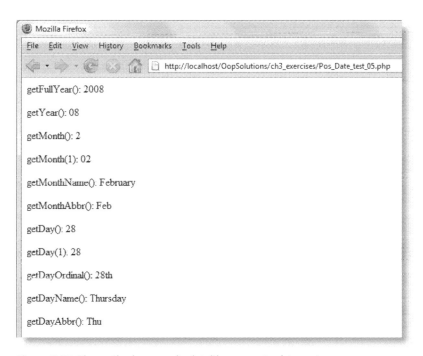

Figure 3-12. The method names give intuitive access to date parts.

Performing date-related calculations

The traditional way of performing date calculations, such as adding or subtracting a number of weeks or days, involves tedious conversion to a Unix timestamp, performing the calculation using seconds, and then converting back to a date. That's why strtotime() is so useful. Although it works with Unix timestamps, it accepts date-related calculations in human language, for example, +2 weeks, –1 month, and so on. That's probably why the developer of the DateTime class decided to model the constructor and modify() methods on strtotime().

As I have already mentioned, strtotime() converts out-of-range dates to what PHP thinks you meant. The same problem arises when you use DateTime::modify() to perform some date-related calculations. The following code (in date_test_10.php) uses modify() to add one month to a date, and then subtract it:

```
// create a DateTime object
$date = new DateTime('Aug 31, 2008');
echo '<p>Initial date is ' . $date->format('F j, Y') . '</p>';
```

```
// add one month
$date->modify('+1 month');
echo '<p>Add one month: ' . $date->format('F j, Y') . '</p>';
// subtract one month
$date->modify('-1 month');
echo '<p>Subtract one month: ' . $date->format('F j, Y') . '</p>';
```

Figure 3-13 shows the output of this calculation. It's almost certainly not what you want. Because September doesn't have 31 days, DateTime::modify() converts the result to October 1 when you add one month to August 31. However, subtracting one month from the result doesn't bring you back to the original date. The second calculation is correct, because October 1 minus one month is September 1. It's the first calculation that's wrong. Most people would expect that adding one month to the last day of August would produce the last day of the next month, in other words September 30. The same problem happens when you add 1, 2, or 3 years to the last day of February in a leap year. February 29 is converted to March 1.

Figure 3-13. DateTime::modify() produces unexpected results when performing some date calculations.

In spite of these problems, DateTime::modify() is ideal for adding and subtracting days or weeks. So, that's what I'll use for those calculations, but for working with months and years, different solutions will need to be found.

> *What about subtracting one month from September 30? Should the result be August 30 or 31? I have decided that it should be August 30 for the simple reason that August 30 is exactly one month before September 30. The problem with this decision is that you won't necessarily arrive back at the same starting date in a series of calculations that add and subtract months. This type of design decision is something you will encounter frequently. The important thing is that the class or method produces consistent results in accordance with the rules you have established. If arriving back at the same starting date is vital to the integrity of your application, you would need to design the methods differently.*

If you think I shot myself in the foot earlier on by overriding modify() to make it throw an exception, think again. Overriding modify() prevents anyone from using it with a

Pos_Date object, but that doesn't prevent you from using the parent method *inside* the class definition. You can still access it internally with the parent keyword. This is what encapsulation is all about. The end user has no need to know about the internal workings of a method; all that matters to the user is that it works.

Adding and subtracting days or weeks

Another problem with DateTime::modify() and strtotime() is that they accept any string input. If the string can be parsed into a date expression, everything works fine; but if PHP can't make sense of the string, it generates an error. So, it's a good idea to cut down the margin for error as much as possible. The four new methods, addDays(), subDays(), addWeeks(), and subWeeks() accept only a number; creation of the string to be passed to the parent modify() method is handled internally. The following listing shows all four methods:

```php
public function addDays($numDays)
{
  if (!is_numeric($numDays) || $numDays < 1) {
    throw new Exception('addDays() expects a positive integer.');
  }
  parent::modify('+' . intval($numDays) . ' days');
}

public function subDays($numDays)
{
  if (!is_numeric($numDays)) {
    throw new Exception('subDays() expects an integer.');
  }
  parent::modify('-' . abs(intval($numDays)) . ' days');
}

public function addWeeks($numWeeks)
{
  if (!is_numeric($numWeeks) || $numWeeks < 1) {
    throw new Exception('addWeeks() expects a positive integer.');
  }
  parent::modify('+' . intval($numWeeks) . ' weeks');
}

public function subWeeks($numWeeks)
{
  if (!is_numeric($numWeeks)) {
    throw new Exception('subWeeks() expects an integer.');
  }
  parent::modify('-' . abs(intval($numWeeks)) . ' weeks');
}
```

Each method follows the same pattern. It begins by checking whether the argument passed to it is numeric. In the case of addDays() and addWeeks(), I have also checked whether the number is less than 1. I did this because it seems to make little sense to accept a negative number in a method designed to add days or weeks. For some time, I toyed with the idea of creating just two methods (one each for days and weeks) and getting the same method to add or subtract depending on whether the number is positive or negative. In the end, I decided that an explicit approach was cleaner.

Since is_numeric() accepts floating point numbers, I pass the number to intval() to make sure that only an integer is incorporated into the string passed to parent::modify().

Another design problem that I wrestled with for some time was whether to accept negative numbers as arguments to subDays() and subWeeks(). The names of the methods indicate that they subtract a specified number of days or weeks, so most people are likely to insert a positive number. However, you could argue that a negative number is just as logical. One solution is to throw an exception if a negative number is submitted. In the end, I opted to accept either negative or positive numbers, but to treat them as if they mean the same thing. In other words, to subtract 3 days from the date regardless of whether 3 or -3 is passed to subDays(). So, the string built inside subDays() and subWeeks() uses abs() and intval() as nested functions like this:

```
'-' . abs(intval($numWeeks)) . ' weeks'
```

If you're not familiar with nesting functions like this, what happens is that the innermost function is processed first, and the result is then processed by the outer function. So, intval($numWeeks) converts $numWeeks to an integer, and abs() converts the result to its absolute value (in other words, it turns a negative number into a positive one). So, if the value passed to subWeeks() is -3.25, intval() converts $numWeeks to -3, and abs() subsequently converts it to 3. The resulting string passed to parent::modify() is '-3 weeks'.

You can test these methods in Pos_Date_test_06.php through Pos_Date_test_09.php in the download files.

Adding months

A month can be anything from 28 to 31 days in length, so it's impossible to calculate the number of seconds you need to add to a Unix timestamp—at least, not without some fiendishly complicated formula. The solution I have come up with is to add the number of months to the current month. If it comes to 12 or less, you have the new month number. If it's more than 12, you need to calculate the new month and year. Finally, you need to work out if the resulting date is valid. If it isn't, it means you have ended up with a date like February 30, so you need to find the last day of the new month, taking into account the vagaries of leap years.

It's not as complicated as it sounds, but before diving into the PHP code, it's easier to understand the process with some real figures.

Let's take February 29, 2008, as the starting date. In terms of the Pos_Date properties, that looks like this:

```
$_year = 2008;
$_month = 2;
$_day = 29;
```

Add 9 months:

```
$_month += 9;  // result is 11
```

The result is 11 (November). This is less than 12, so the year remains the same. November 29 is a valid date, so the calculation is simple.

Instead of 9 months, add 12:

```
$_month += 12;  // result is 14
```

There isn't a fourteenth month in a year, so you need to calculate both the month and the year. To get the new month, use modulo division by 12 like this:

```
14 % 12;  // result is 2
```

Modulo returns the remainder of a division, so the new month is 2 (February). To calculate how many years to add, divide 14 by 12 and round down to the nearest whole number using floor() like this:

```
$_year += floor(14 / 12);  // adds 1 to the current year
```

This works fine for every month except December. To understand why, add 22 months to the starting date:

```
$_month += 22;  // result is 24
$remainder = 24 % 12;  // result is 0
```

Dividing 24 by 12 produces a remainder of 0. Not only is there no month 0, division by 12 produces the wrong year as this calculation shows:

```
$_year += floor(24 / 12);  // adds 2 to the current year
```

Any multiple of 12 produces a whole number, and since there's nothing to round down, the result is always 1 greater than you want. Adding 2 to the year produces 2010; but 22 months from the starting date should be December 29, 2009. So, you need to subtract 1 from the year whenever the calculation produces a date in December.

Finally, you need to check that the resulting date is valid. Adding 12 months to the starting date produces February 29, 2009, but since 2009 isn't a leap year, you need to adjust the result to the last day of the month.

With all that in mind, you can map out the internal logic for addMonths() like this:

1. Add months to the existing month number ($_month), and call it $newValue.

2. If $newValue is less than or equal to 12, use it as the new month number, and skip to step 6.

3. If $newValue is greater than 12, do modulo division by 12 on $newValue. If this produces a remainder, use the remainder as the new month number, and proceed to step 4. If there is no remainder, you know the month must be December, so go straight to step 5.

4. Divide $newValue by 12, round down the result to the next whole number, and add it to the year. Jump to step 6.

5. Set the month number to 12, and divide $newValue by 12. Add the result of the division to the year, and subtract one.

6. Check that the resulting date is valid. If it isn't, reset the day to the last day of the month, taking into account leap year.

7. Pass the amended $_year, $_month, and $_day properties to setDate().

The full listing for addMonths(), together with inline comments, looks like this:

```php
public function addMonths($numMonths)
{
  if (!is_numeric($numMonths) || $numMonths < 1) {
    throw new Exception('addMonths() expects a positive integer.');
  }
  $numMonths = (int) $numMonths;
  // Add the months to the current month number.
  $newValue = $this->_month + $numMonths;
  // If the new value is less than or equal to 12, the year
  // doesn't change, so just assign the new value to the month.
  if ($newValue <= 12) {
    $this->_month = $newValue;
  } else {
    // A new value greater than 12 means calculating both
    // the month and the year. Calculating the year is
    // different for December, so do modulo division
    // by 12 on the new value. If the remainder is not 0,
    // the new month is not December.
    $notDecember = $newValue % 12;
    if ($notDecember) {
      // The remainder of the modulo division is the new month.
      $this->_month = $notDecember;
      // Divide the new value by 12 and round down to get the
      // number of years to add.
      $this->_year += floor($newValue / 12);
    } else {
      // The new month must be December
      $this->_month = 12;
      $this->_year += ($newValue / 12) - 1;
    }
  }
  $this->checkLastDayOfMonth();
  parent::setDate($this->_year, $this->_month, $this->_day);
}
```

The preceding explanation and the inline comments explain most of what's going on here. The result of the modulo division is saved as $notDecember and then used to control a conditional statement. Dividing $newValue by 12 produces a remainder for any month except December. Since PHP treats any number other than 0 as true, the first half of the conditional statement will be executed. If there's no remainder, $notDecember is 0, which PHP treats as false, so the else clause is executed instead.

All that remains to explain are the last two lines, the first of which calls an internal method called checkLastDayOfMonth(). This now needs to be defined.

Adjusting the last day of the month

The reason for not using DateTime::modify() is to prevent the date from being shifted to the first of the following month, so you need to check the validity of the resulting date before passing it to setDate() and reset the value of $_day to the last day of the month, if necessary. That operation is performed by the checkLastDayofMonth() method, which looks like this:

```
final protected function checkLastDayOfMonth()
{
  if (!checkdate($this->_month, $this->_day, $this->_year)) {
    $use30 = array(4 , 6 , 9 , 11);
    if (in_array($this->_month, $use30)) {
      $this->_day = 30;
    } else {
      $this->_day = $this->isLeap() ? 29 : 28;
    }
  }
}
```

The first thing to note about this method is that, unlike all other methods defined so far, this is both final and protected. This prevents anyone from either calling it directly or overriding it in a subclass. The reason I don't want it to be called directly is because it changes the value of the $_day property, so could result in arbitrary changes to your code. A protected method can be called only inside the class itself or a subclass. If it results in arbitrary changes to the date being stored, the only person to blame is yourself for making a mistake in the code.

The method passes the values of $_month, $_day, and $_year to checkdate(), which as you have seen before, returns false if the date is nonexistent. If the date is OK, the method does nothing. However, if checkdate() returns false, the method examines the value of $_month by comparing it with the $use30 array. April (4), June (6), September (9), and November (11) all have 30 days. If the month is one of these, $_day is set to 30.

If the month isn't in the $use30 array, it can only be February. In most years, the last day of the month will be 28, but in leap year, it's 29. The task of checking whether it's a leap year is handed off to another method called isLeap(), which returns true or false. If isLeap() returns true, the conditional operator sets $_day to 29. Otherwise, it's set to 28.

Checking for leap year

Leap years occur every four years on years that are wholly divisible by 4. The exception is that years divisible by 100 are not leap years unless they are also divisible by 400.

109

Translating that formula into a conditional statement that returns true or false produces the following method:

```
public function isLeap()
{
  if ($this->_year % 400 == 0 || ($this->_year % 4 == 0 && ➥
$this->_year % 100 != 0)) {
    return true;
  } else {
    return false;
  }
}
```

I've made this method public because it doesn't affect any internal properties and could be quite useful when working with Pos_Date objects. It bases its calculation on the value of $_year, so doesn't rely on the date being set to February.

Because checkLastDayOfMonth() has already checked the validity of the date, and the values of $_year, $_month, and $_day have already been adjusted, they can be passed directly to the parent setDate() method to save a little processing time.

Figure 3-14 shows the different results produced by Pos_Date::addMonths() and DateTime::modify() when simply changing the month number would produce an invalid date (the code is in Pos_Date_test_10.php).

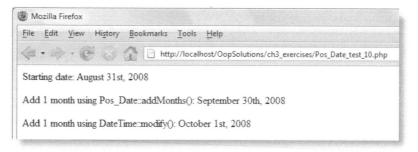

Figure 3-14. The addMonths() method adjusts the date automatically to the last day of the month if necessary.

Subtracting months

Subtracting months requires similar logic. You start by subtracting the number of months from the current month number. If the result is greater than zero, the calculation is easy: you're still in the same year, and the result is the new month number. However, if you end up with 0 or a negative number, you've gone back to a previous year.

Let's take the same starting date as before, February 29, 2008. Subtract two months:

```
$_month -= 2;  // result is 0
```

It's easy to work out in your head that subtracting two months from February 29, 2008, results in December 29, 2007. What about subtracting three months? That brings you to November, and a month number of –1. Deduct four months, and you get October and a month number of –2. Hmm, a pattern is forming here that should be familiar to anyone who has worked with PHP for some time. If you remove the minus signs, you get a zero-based array. So, that's the solution: create an array of month numbers in reverse, and use the absolute value of deducting the number of months from the original month number as the array key. You could type out all the numbers like this:

```
$months = array(12 , 11 , 10 , 9 , 8 , 7 , 6 , 5 , 4 , 3 , 2 , 1);
```

However, it's much simpler to use the range() function, which takes two arguments and creates an array of integers or characters from the first argument to the second, inclusive. If the first argument is greater than the second one, the values in the array are in descending order. The following line of code produces the same result as the previous one:

```
$months = range(12, 1);
```

PHP arrays begin from 0, so $months[0] is 12, $months[1] is 11, and so on.

Also, because you're working in reverse from addMonths(), the year calculations round up, rather than down.

The full listing follows:

```
public function subMonths($numMonths)
{
  if (!is_numeric($numMonths)) {
    throw new Exception('addMonths() expects an integer.');
  }
  $numMonths = abs(intval($numMonths));
  // Subtract the months from the current month number.
  $newValue = $this->_month - $numMonths;
  // If the result is greater than 0, it's still the same year,
  // and you can assign the new value to the month.
  if ($newValue > 0) {
    $this->_month = $newValue;
  } else {
    // Create an array of the months in reverse.
    $months = range(12 , 1);
    // Get the absolute value of $newValue.
    $newValue = abs($newValue);
    // Get the array position of the resulting month.
    $monthPosition = $newValue % 12;
    $this->_month = $months[$monthPosition];
    // Arrays begin at 0, so if $monthPosition is 0,
    // it must be December.
    if ($monthPosition) {
      $this->_year -= ceil($newValue / 12);
    } else {
```

```
            $this->_year -= ceil($newValue / 12) + 1;
        }
    }
    $this->checkLastDayOfMonth();
    parent::setDate($this->_year, $this->_month, $this->_day);
}
```

As Figure 3-15 shows, using DateTime::modify() can produce radically unexpected results with some date calculations (the code is in Pos_Date_test_11.php). Pos_Date::subMonths() gives the right answer.

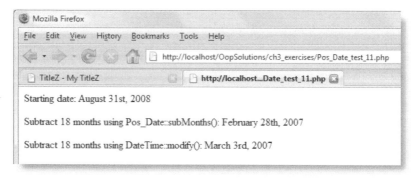

Figure 3-15. The subMonths() method correctly identifies the last day of the month when appropriate.

Adding and subtracting years

The code for addYears() and subYears() needs very little explanation. Changing the year simply involves adding or subtracting a number from $_year. The only date that causes a problem is February 29, but that's easily dealt with by calling checkLastDayOfMonth() before passing the $_year, $_month, and $_day properties to parent::setDate(). The full listing follows:

```
public function addYears($numYears)
{
  if (!is_numeric($numYears) || $numYears < 1) {
    throw new Exception('addYears() expects a positive integer.');
  }
  $this->_year += (int) $numYears;
  $this->checkLastDayOfMonth();
  parent::setDate($this->_year, $this->_month, $this->_day);
}

public function subYears($numYears)
{
  if (!is_numeric($numYears)) {
    throw new Exception('subYears() expects an integer.');
  }
```

```
    $this->_year -= abs(intval($numYears));
    $this->checkLastDayOfMonth();
    parent::setDate($this->_year, $this->_month, $this->_day);
  }
```

You can see examples of both methods in action in Pos_Date_test_12.php and Pos_Date_test_13.php.

Calculating the number of days between two dates

MySQL made calculating the number of days between two dates very easy with the introduction of the DATEDIFF() function in version 4.1.1. With PHP, though, you still need to do the calculation with Unix timestamps. The Pos_Date::dateDiff() method acts as a wrapper for this calculation. It takes two arguments, both Pos_Date objects representing the start date and the end date. Both dates are used to create Unix timestamps with gmmktime(). The difference in seconds is divided by 60 × 60 × 24 before being returned. The timestamps are set to midnight UTC to avoid problems with daylight saving time and make sure that deducting one from the other results in an exact number of days. If the date in the first argument is earlier than the second, a positive number is returned. If it's later, a negative number is returned. The code for the method looks like this:

```
static public function dateDiff(Pos_Date $startDate, Pos_Date $endDate)
{
  $start = gmmktime(0, 0, 0, $startDate->_month, $startDate->_day, ➥
$startDate->_year);
  $end = gmmktime(0, 0, 0, $endDate->_month, $endDate->_day, ➥
$endDate->_year);
  return ($end - $start) / (60 * 60 * 24);
}
```

An important thing to note about this method definition is that it's prefixed with the static keyword. This turns it into a static (or class) method. Instead of applying the method to a Pos_Date object, you call it directly using the class name and the scope resolution operator like this:

```
Pos_Date::dateDiff($argument1, $argument2);
```

The other thing to note is that the argument block uses type hinting (see Chapter 2 for details). Both arguments must be Pos_Date objects. If you try to pass anything else as an argument, the method throws an exception.

The following code (in Pos_Date_test_14.php) shows an example of how Pos_Date::dateDiff() might be used:

```
require_once '../Pos/Date.php';
try {
  // create two Pos_Date objects
  $now = new Pos_Date();
  $newYear = new Pos_Date();
  // set one of them to January 1, 2009
  $newYear->setDate(2009, 1, 1);
```

```
        // calculate the number of days
        $diff = Pos_Date::dateDiff($now, $newYear);
        $unit = abs($diff) > 1 ? 'days' : 'day';
        if ($diff == 0) {
            echo 'Happy New Year!';
        } elseif ($diff > 0) {
            echo "$diff $unit left till 2009";
        } else {
            echo abs($diff) . " $unit since the beginning of 2009";
        }
    } catch (Exception $e) {
        echo $e;
    }
```

This method poses another design dilemma. I have made it static because it works on two different Pos_Date objects. It also gives me an opportunity to demonstrate a practical example of creating and using a static method. You could argue, however, that it would be much simpler to compare two dates by passing one as an argument to the other. Both approaches are perfectly valid.

As an exercise, you might like to try your hand at modifying dateDiff() so that it works as an ordinary public method. The alternative solution is defined as dateDiff2() in Date.php, and Pos_Date_test_15.php demonstrates how it's used.

Creating a default date format

Finally, let's use the magic __toString()method to create a default format for displaying dates. The code is very simple, and looks like this:

```
public function __toString()
{
    return $this->format('l, F jS, Y');
}
```

Which format you use is up to you, but the one I have chosen displays a Pos_Date object as in Figure 3-16.

Figure 3-16. Defining the magic __toString() method makes it easy to display dates in a specific format.

With this method defined, you can use echo, print, and other string functions to display a Pos_Date object in a predefined format. The code that produced the output in Figure 3-16 looks like this (it's in Pos_Date_test_16.php):

```
$now = new Pos_Date();
echo $now;
```

The important thing to remember when defining __toString() is that it must *return* a string. Don't use echo or print inside __toString().

Creating read-only properties

The class definition is now complete, but before ending the chapter, I'd like to make a brief detour to look at an alternative way of accessing predefined formats and date parts. Because the $_year, $_month, and $_day properties are protected, you can't access them outside the class definition. The only way to access them is to change them from protected to public, but once you do that, their values can be changed arbitrarily. That's clearly unacceptable, so the class has defined a series of getter methods that give public access to the values, but prevent anyone from changing them except through the setDate() and setTime() methods, or one of the date calculation methods.

Many developers find getter methods inconvenient and prefer to use properties. Using the magic __get() method (see Chapter 2), in combination with a switch statement, it's possible to create read-only properties. As I explained in the previous chapter, a common way to use __get() is to store the properties as elements of an associative array. However, you can also use a switch statement to determine the value to return when an undefined property is accessed in an outside script.

The following listing shows how I have defined the __get() magic method for the Pos_Date class:

```
public function __get($name)
{
  switch (strtolower($name)) {
    case 'mdy':
      return $this->format('n/j/Y');
    case 'mdy0':
      return $this->format('m/d/Y');
    case 'dmy':
      return $this->format('j/n/Y');
    case 'dmy0':
      return $this->format('d/m/Y');
    case 'mysql':
      return $this->format('Y-m-d');
    case 'fullyear':
      return $this->_year;
```

```
            case 'year':
              return $this->format('y');
            case 'month':
              return $this->_month;
            case 'month0':
              return $this->format('m');
            case 'monthname':
              return $this->format('F');
            case 'monthabbr':
              return $this->format('M');
            case 'day':
              return $this->_day;
            case 'day0':
              return $this->format('d');
            case 'dayordinal':
              return $this->format('jS');
            case 'dayname':
              return $this->format('l');
            case 'dayabbr':
              return $this->format('D');
            default:
              return 'Invalid property';
        }
    }
```

You can probably recognize that this closely resembles the code in the getter methods in "Outputting date parts" earlier in the chapter. The switch statement compares $name to each case until it finds a match. I've passed $name to strtolower() to make the comparison case-insensitive. If it finds a match, it returns the value indicated. So, if it encounters MDY, it returns the date in MM/DD/YYYY format.

> *You don't need* break *statements after each* case *because* return *automatically prevents the* switch *statement from going any further.*

The value of creating this __get() method is that it simplifies code that uses the Pos_Date class. When used with a Pos_Date object called $date, the following two lines of code do exactly the same as each other:

```
    echo $date->getMDY();
    echo $date->MDY;
```

In most cases, I have used names based on the equivalent getter method. To indicate the use of leading zeros, I added 0 (zero) to the end of the name. So, DMY0 produces a date in DD/MM/YYYY format with leading zeros.

The disadvantages with using __get() like this are that the switch statement can easily become unwieldy, and it's impossible for an IDE to generate code hints for this sort of property.

You can see examples of these read-only properties in use in Pos_Date_test_17.php.

Organizing and commenting the class file

When developing a class, I normally create each new method at the bottom of the file, adding properties to the top of the file whenever necessary. Class files can become very long, so once I'm happy with the way the class works, I reorganize the code into logical groups in this order:

1. Constants
2. Properties
3. Static methods
4. Constructor
5. Overridden methods
6. New public methods grouped by functionality
7. Protected and private methods

The next job is to add comments in PHPDoc format to describe briefly what each property and method is for. Writing comments is most developers' least favorite task, but the time spent doing it is usually repaid many times over when you come to review code several months or even years later. Write the comments while everything is still fresh in your mind.

Not only do the comments generate code hints in specialized IDEs, as described in the previous chapter, you can also use PHPDocumentor to generate detailed documentation in a variety of formats, including HTML and PDF. PHPDocumentor is built into specialized IDEs, such as Zend Studio for Eclipse and PhpED. Alternatively, you can download it free of charge from the PHPDocumentor web site at www.phpdoc.org.

Once you have finished commenting the class file, it takes PHPDocumentor literally seconds to generate detailed documentation. It creates hyperlinked lists of properties and methods organized in alphabetical order with line numbers indicating where to find the code in the class file. The PHPDoc comments aren't shown in the code listings in this book, but the download versions of the class files are fully commented. The download files also include the documentation generated by PHPDocumentor for all the classes featured in this book. Double-click index.html in the class_docs folder to launch them in a browser (see Figure 3-17).

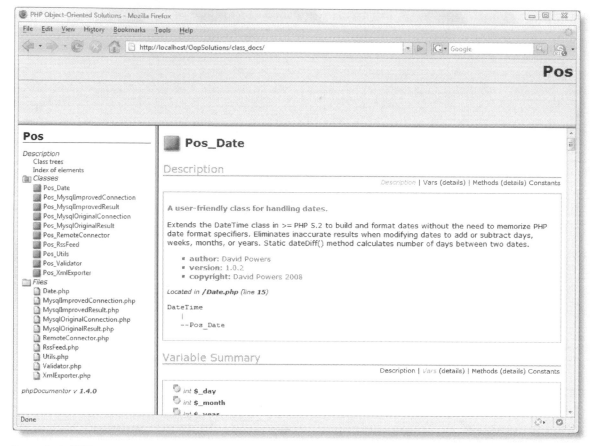

Figure 3-17. PHPDocumentor makes it easy to build online documentation for your custom classes.

> *Standards warriors will probably be horrified that PHPDocumentor doesn't generate 100 percent valid XHTML. However, it's much faster than attempting to type out all the documentation manually, and the coding errors don't affect the display in current browsers.*

Chapter review

If you have typed out all the code for the Pos_Date class, you might be thinking the chapter should be retitled "A Lot of Pain for Not Much in Return." Even without PHPDoc comments, the class definition file comes to more than 350 lines long. This is far from unusual in OOP. The idea is to create a library of tested and reusable code. When designing this class, I added new features only as I needed them. What you have seen here is the fruit of work over a much longer period of time than it has taken you to read this chapter.

I chose this class as the first practical exercise because, without getting too complex, it demonstrates the main features of OOP: inheritance, encapsulation, polymorphism, magic methods, and static methods. You might be surprised at how short the code is in many of the methods. That's not only because this class performs relatively simple tasks but also because a key concept in OOP is to break down code into discrete units: wherever possible, one task per method. If you attempt to do everything in a single method, your code becomes more rigid and more difficult to maintain.

One of the main purposes of this class is to avoid the need to use the unintuitive date formatting characters. The next chapter takes a similar approach: using encapsulation to hide the complexity of the PHP filter functions to create a class to validate and filter user input.

> As this book was about to go to press, details emerged of proposed changes to the DateTime *class in PHP 5.3, including the addition of* date_add(), date_sub(), *and* date_diff() *methods. When used in PHP 5.3 and above, the* Pos_Date *class will inherit these new methods alongside its own date calculation methods.*

3

4 USING PHP FILTERS TO VALIDATE USER INPUT

Failure to validate user input adequately—or even at all—is one of the main reasons that PHP is sometimes seen as having weak security. Part of the blame lies with the image PHP has often promoted of itself as being "easy to learn." Books and tutorials aimed at beginners often concentrate on the bare essentials of gathering input from an online form and sending it by email. As a result, inexperienced users find their web sites subject to malicious attacks from SQL injection or email header injection.

The problem with validation is that it's a tedious process, usually involving a lengthy series of conditional statements, not only checking whether a variable in the $_POST array has a value but also whether that value conforms to your criteria of acceptability. You need to make sure required fields are filled in; email addresses don't contain hidden code designed to inject additional headers; text fields don't contain more characters than your database can store; and so on.

In an attempt to improve security and simplify validation, PHP 5.2 introduced a new core extension called **filter functions** (http://docs.php.net/manual/en/book.filter.php). Although they're a welcome addition to PHP, they rely on the use of constants with unwieldy names like FILTER_SANITIZE_SPECIAL_CHARS, which are difficult to remember and a pain to type out. Not only that, setting options to fine-tune the filters is a complex process. This is where OOP can come to the rescue—encapsulating the filter functions in a custom class. Incidentally, this implements the Facade design pattern, which superimposes a simpler interface on a complex subsystem, making it easier to use.

In this chapter, you will

- Learn how the PHP filter functions work
- Hide the complexity of the filter functions behind the interface of a custom class
- Use the custom class to validate input from an online form
- Use the output of the custom class to display error messages

As in the previous chapter, the first stage in designing an OOP solution is to examine what PHP already has to offer. So, let's take a look at the PHP filter functions and see what they do.

Validating input with the filter functions

The filter functions are enabled by default in PHP 5.2 and higher. You can verify that your server supports them by running phpinfo() to display the configuration details. Scroll about halfway down the page, and you should see the section shown in Figure 4-1. If Input Validation and Filtering is listed as enabled, you're set to go.

If, for any reason, the filter functions aren't enabled, they can be installed separately from the PHP Extension Community Library (PECL). On shared hosting, this needs to be done by the server administrator.

filter	
Input Validation and Filtering	enabled
Revision	$Revision: 1.52.2.39 $

Directive	Local Value	Master Value
filter.default	unsafe_raw	unsafe_raw
filter.default_flags	no value	no value

Figure 4-1. Confirmation that the filter functions are enabled

If you're running your own server, type the following at the command line on Linux or Unix:

```
pecl install filter
```

On Windows, download php_filter.dll from http://pecl4win.php.net/ext.php/ php_filter.dll, and save it in the ext folder with the other PHP DLL files. Make sure the file matches the version of PHP that you're running.

After installing from PECL, restart the web server.

> There should be no need to install the filter functions from PECL in PHP 5.2 or higher, as they're part of core PHP and installed by default.

Understanding how the filter functions work

The PHP filter functions take a rather unconventional approach to validation. Instead of separate functions to test for specific data types or formats, there are just seven filter functions, only four of which actually do any filtering or validation. You control what's accepted or rejected by passing an array of PHP constants as arguments to the function. There are 50 constants associated with the filter functions, making them very versatile, but at the same time complex.

Although the purpose of this chapter is to hide that complexity, you need to understand how the filter functions work in order to be able to build a class that creates a simpler interface. The following sections contain a lot of reference material to guide you through the maze. I don't suggest committing it all to memory, but it should come in useful if you need to design validation methods to extend to the class that I have created.

Let's start by looking at the functions. Table 4-1 lists each function with a brief description of its purpose. The last four are the ones that do the actual filtering.

Table 4-1. The PHP filter functions

Function	Description
`filter_has_var()`	This checks whether a variable exists in one of the input superglobal arrays. It takes two arguments: one of the constants listed in Table 4-2 and the name of the variable you're looking for.
`filter_id()`	This returns the numerical value of the PHP constant for a named filter. It takes one argument: a string containing one of the filter names returned by `filter_list()` (see Figure 4-2).
`filter_list()`	This returns an array containing the names of supported filters (see Figure 4-2).
`filter_input()`	Use this function to apply a filter to a single variable from a superglobal array. It takes up to four arguments: one of the constants listed in Table 4-2, the name of the variable, the filter to be applied, and any options to be applied to the filter. The last two arguments are optional. If no filter is specified, PHP uses the default (see "Setting a default filter" later in the chapter).
`filter_input_array()`	This filters the contents of a superglobal array according to user-defined criteria. It takes two arguments: one of the constants listed in Table 4-2 and a multidimensional array that defines how each element of the superglobal array is to be filtered. The second argument is optional; if it's not supplied, the default filter is applied.
`filter_var()`	This handles a single variable that comes from an internal source, such as a database result or a calculation performed by the script (in other words, anywhere except from a superglobal array). It takes up to three arguments: the name of the variable, the filter to be applied, and any options. The last two arguments are optional. If no filter is specified, PHP applies the default.
`filter_var_array()`	This is identical to `filter_input_array()`, except that it filters an array of internal data, rather than external data from a superglobal array. The first argument is the name of the internal array.

Three functions—filter_has_var(), filter_input(), and filter_input_array()—are designed to work with superglobal arrays, such as $_POST and $_GET. Instead of using the superglobal variable, you need to refer to the array by its equivalent filter constant. The constants and their equivalents are listed in Table 4-2. At the time of this writing, two of the constants have not yet been implemented.

Table 4-2. Superglobal constants used by filter functions

Constant	Superglobal equivalent	Notes
INPUT_COOKIE	$_COOKIE variables	
INPUT_ENV	$_ENV variables	
INPUT_GET	$_GET variables	
INPUT_POST	$_POST variables	
INPUT_REQUEST	$_REQUEST variables	Not implemented yet
INPUT_SERVER	$_SERVER variables	
INPUT_SESSION	$_SESSION variables	Not implemented yet

Although our main interest is in the functions that do the actual filtering, let's take a quick look at the other three.

filter_has_var()

This function offers an alternative way to find out whether a variable exists in an input array. It takes as arguments one of the constants listed in Table 4-2 and the name of the variable. Use filter_has_var() to check whether the $_POST array contains a variable called component like this:

```
if (filter_has_var(INPUT_POST, 'component')) {
    // do something
}
```

This does exactly the same as array_key_exists('component', $_POST). Both test only whether the variable exists; they do not check whether it has a value.

> In practice, you can also use isset($_POST['component']) to check whether a $_POST variable exists. However, there's a subtle difference in that, unlike the other two, isset() returns false if the value being tested is null. Since $_POST variables are always transmitted as strings, the only way the value can be null is if it's reset after being received by the script. An empty string returns true.

filter_list()

This produces an array containing the names of the filters supported by the current server. The following code (it's in filter_list.php in the ch4_exercises folder) produces the output shown in Figure 4-2:

```
print_r(filter_list());
```

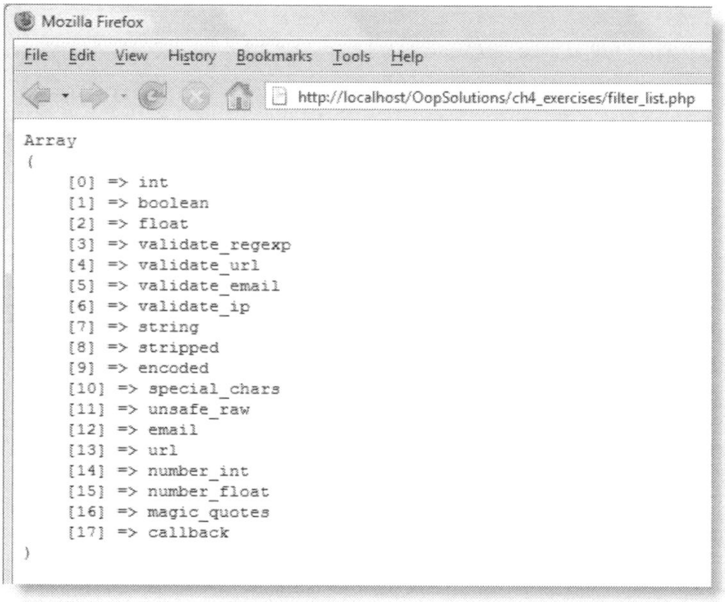

Figure 4-2. The filter_list() function produces an array of available filters.

The main purpose of these names is in combination with filter_id(), which is described next.

filter_id()

This takes as an argument one of the names displayed by filter_list(), and returns an integer representing one of the supported filters. For example, echo filter_id('int'); displays 257. You can see the values generated by filter_id() for each filter by running filter_id.php in the ch4_exercises folder.

You're probably thinking, "What on earth is the value in that?"

The main practical value for filter_id() is as a substitute for the PHP constants used by the main filter functions. Instead of using FILTER_VALIDATE_INT as an argument when filtering input, you can use filter_id('int'). I'll explain why this is useful later in the chapter in the "Testing other filter constants" exercise.

Setting filter options

The key to using the remaining four filter functions lies in setting the correct options for each filter (see Tables 4-3, 4-4, and 4-5). When you see how they work, you'll understand why this chapter is about wrapping them in a more user-friendly interface. At the time of this writing, PHP has support for 18 filters, which can be classified as follows:

- **Validation filters**: These check that the input is of a particular data type, such as integer or Boolean, or that it conforms to a specified format, such as email address. If the validation test succeeds, the filter normally returns the input unchanged (floating point numbers are treated slightly differently, as you'll learn shortly). If the test fails, the filter returns `false`.

- **Sanitizing filters**: These strip specific characters out of input and return the sanitized version. For example, you can use them to prevent someone from entering this into a comment in a blog page:

```
<a href="#" onclick="javascript:window.location = ➥
'http://example.com/dosomethingbad.php'">Freebies galore!</a>
```

The filter can either remove the `<a>` tags completely or convert the opening and closing brackets into HTML entities to prevent the link and script from working.

You need to be very careful when using sanitizing filters with numbers, as the decimal point is stripped out in certain circumstances, completely changing the value of the number.

- **Custom filter**: The `callback` filter accepts a user-defined function and filters the input according to its criteria.

Each filter is identified by a PHP constant. Most filters have options, flags, or both. These allow you to fine-tune how a filter works. Most flags can be used only with their related filters, but the flags listed in Table 4-3 can be used with any filter. The validating filters are listed in Table 4-4. Table 4-5 lists all the sanitizing filters.

Table 4-3. Flags that can be used with any filter

Flag	Description
FILTER_REQUIRE_ARRAY	This rejects any value that isn't an array. When this flag is set, the filter is applied to all elements of the array. It also works on multidimensional arrays, applying the filter recursively to each level.
FILTER_REQUIRE_SCALAR	This rejects any value that isn't scalar. In other words, the value must be one of the following data types: Boolean, integer, floating point number, resource (such as a database link or file handle), or string.

Table 4-4. Constants used by the PHP filter functions to validate data

Filter	Options	Flags	Description
FILTER_VALIDATE_BOOLEAN		FILTER_NULL_ON_FAILURE	When used without a flag, returns true for '1', 'true', 'on', and 'yes'; returns false otherwise. If the FILTER_NULL_ON_FAILURE flag is set, false is returned only for '0', 'false', 'off', 'no', and an empty string; NULL is returned for all non-Boolean values.
FILTER_VALIDATE_EMAIL			Checks that a value conforms to the email format.
FILTER_VALIDATE_FLOAT	decimal	FILTER_FLAG_ALLOW_THOUSAND	Checks for a floating point number or integer; returns false for any other data type. The decimal option permits the use of a comma as the decimal point. Setting the flag accepts numbers containing a thousands separator (comma is the default, but period is used when decimal is set to ','). The returned value is always stripped of the thousands separator, with a period as the decimal point.
FILTER_VALIDATE_INT	min_range max_range	FILTER_FLAG_ALLOW_OCTAL FILTER_FLAG_ALLOW_HEX	Checks for an integer; returns false for any other data type. Specify the minimum and maximum acceptable values as an associative array using min_range and max_range (you can set just one or both together). Flags permit octal and hexadecimal numbers. Rejects numbers with a decimal point, even if the fraction is 0, for example, 10.0.
FILTER_VALIDATE_IP		FILTER_FLAG_IPV4 FILTER_FLAG_IPV6 FILTER_FLAG_NO_PRIV_RANGE FILTER_FLAG_NO_RES_RANGE	Checks that a value is an IP address. Flags allow you to specify only IPv4 or IPv6, or not from private or reserved ranges.
FILTER_VALIDATE_REGEXP	regexp		Validates a value against a Perl-compatible regular expression. The whole value is returned, not just the part that matches the regular expression.
FILTER_VALIDATE_URL		FILTER_FLAG_SCHEME_REQUIRED FILTER_FLAG_HOST_REQUIRED FILTER_FLAG_PATH_REQUIRED FILTER_FLAG_QUERY_REQUIRED	Checks that a value conforms to the format of a URL, optionally with required components as specified by flags.

Table 4-5. Constants used by the PHP filter functions to sanitize data

Filter	Options	Flags	Description
FILTER_SANITIZE_EMAIL			Removes all characters except letters, digits, and !#$%&'*+-/=?^_`{|}~@.[].
FILTER_SANITIZE_ENCODED		FILTER_FLAG_STRIP_LOW FILTER_FLAG_STRIP_HIGH FILTER_FLAG_ENCODE_LOW FILTER_FLAG_ENCODE_HIGH	URL-encodes a string. Setting the flags optionally strips or encodes characters with an ASCII value of less than 32 (LOW) or greater than 127 (HIGH).
FILTER_SANITIZE_MAGIC_QUOTES			Escapes single and double quotes by inserting a backslash in front of them in the same way as the addslashes() function.
FILTER_SANITIZE_NUMBER_FLOAT		FILTER_FLAG_ALLOW_FRACTION FILTER_FLAG_ALLOW_THOUSAND FILTER_FLAG_ALLOW_SCIENTIFIC	Removes all characters except digits and the plus and minus signs. The flags optionally permit a decimal fraction, the thousands separator, and scientific notation (using uppercase or lowercase E). The decimal point and thousands separator are left untouched. If FILTER_FLAG_ALLOW_FRACTION is not set, the decimal point is removed, but not the fraction, for example, 10.5 becomes 105.
FILTER_SANITIZE_NUMBER_INT			Removes all characters except digits and the plus and minus signs. The decimal point is removed, if present, but not the fraction, for example, 10.0 becomes 100.
FILTER_SANITIZE_SPECIAL_CHARS		FILTER_FLAG_STRIP_LOW FILTER_FLAG_STRIP_HIGH FILTER_FLAG_ENCODE_HIGH	Converts into HTML entities single and double quotes, <, >, &, and characters with an ASCII value of less than 32. Setting the flags optionally strips characters with an ASCII value of less than 32 (LOW) or greater than 127 (HIGH), or encodes characters with an ASCII value greater than 127.
FILTER_SANITIZE_STRING		FILTER_FLAG_NO_ENCODE_QUOTES FILTER_FLAG_STRIP_LOW FILTER_FLAG_STRIP_HIGH FILTER_FLAG_ENCODE_LOW FILTER_FLAG_ENCODE_HIGH FILTER_FLAG_ENCODE_AMP	Strips all tags, including HTML, PHP, and XML. The flags set options to strip or encode special characters with an ASCII value of less than 32 (LOW) or greater than 127 (HIGH), leave quotes unencoded, and encode ampersands (&).

Continued

129

Table 4-5. Continued

Filter	Options	Flags	Description
FILTER_SANITIZE_STRIPPED			This is an alias of FILTER_SANITIZE_STRING.
FILTER_SANITIZE_URL			Removes all characters except letters, digits, and $-_.+!*'(), {}|\^~[]`<>#%";/?:@&=.
FILTER_UNSAFE_RAW		FILTER_FLAG_STRIP_LOW FILTER_FLAG_STRIP_HIGH FILTER_FLAG_ENCODE_LOW FILTER_FLAG_ENCODE_HIGH FILTER_FLAG_ENCODE_AMP	Do nothing. The flags set options to strip or encode special characters with an ASCII value of less than 32 (LOW) or greater than 127 (HIGH), and encode ampersands (&).
FILTER_CALLBACK	User-defined function or method		Calls a user-defined function to filter data.

Using a filter on its own is quite straightforward. It's when you start adding options and flags that life begins to get complicated. To keep things simple, let's start by looking at how to filter a single variable.

Filtering single variables

Two functions are designed to work with single variables: filter_input() and filter_var(). The difference between them is that filter_input() processes a variable that has come from one of the superglobal arrays, such as $_POST; filter_var() handles a variable that has come from any other source, for example, a database or an include file.

The filter_input() function takes four arguments, namely:

- **$source:** This indicates the superglobal array that contains the variable you want to filter. You must use one of the constants listed in Table 4-2, for example, INPUT_POST.
- **$variableName:** This is the name of the variable you want to filter.
- **$filter:** This is the filter you want to apply. You must use one of the filter constants listed in the first column of Tables 4-3 through 4-5. Alternatively, you can use filter_id() with the name of the filter. If this argument is omitted, PHP uses the default filter (see "Setting a default filter" later in the chapter).
- **$options:** This is an optional array containing any options or flags that you want to apply. The available options and flags are listed in Tables 4-3, 4-4, and 4-5.

The filter_var() function does not take the first of these arguments ($source), but the remaining three are the same as for filter_input().

Since both functions are very similar, let's experiment first with filter_var() by hard-coding some values.

Checking that a variable contains a number

The following exercise demonstrates how to use `filter_var()` to test whether a variable contains a number.

1. Create a file called `filter_var.php` in the ch4_exercises folder, and insert the following code (it's in `filter_var_01.php` in the download files):

```
$var = 10;
$filtered = filter_var($var, FILTER_VALIDATE_INT);
var_dump($filtered);
```

This assigns an integer to $var. This is passed to `filter_var()` with the filter constant for an integer, `FILTER_VALIDATE_INT`, and the result is stored in $filtered. The final line passes $filtered to `var_dump()` in order to display the data type and value returned by `filter_var()`.

2. Test the script in a browser, and you should see the same output as in Figure 4-3.

Figure 4-3. Using var_dump() displays both the data type and its value.

This confirms that $var is, indeed, an integer, and displays its value as 10.

3. Change the first line to enclose the number in quotes like this:

```
$var = '10';
```

4. Save the page, and test it again (you can use `filter_var_02.php`). The result should be the same. Even though $var is now a string, PHP interprets a string that contains only a whole number as an integer.

5. Change the value in the first line to a floating point number in a string like this:

```
$var = '10.5';
```

6. Save the page, and test it again (or use `filter_var_03.php`). This time you should see the result as shown in Figure 4-4.

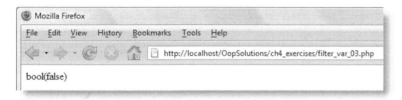

Figure 4-4. The filter function returns false when the variable fails the test.

The variable failed the test, so filter_var() returned the Boolean value false. To verify that it's because the number is no longer an integer, and not because it's a string, remove the quotes and test the page again (or use filter_var_04.php). The result should be the same.

7. Change the filter constant to test for a floating point number like this (the code is in filter_var_05.php):

```
$filtered = filter_var($var, FILTER_VALIDATE_FLOAT);
```

8. Test the page again. This time you should see confirmation that $var is a floating point number, together with its value, as shown in Figure 4-5.

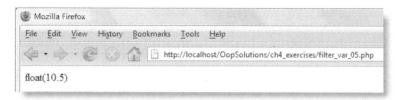

Figure 4-5. Confirmation that $var is a floating point number

9. Change the value of $var back to 10, and test the page again (or use filter_var_06.php). The result should look like Figure 4-6.

Figure 4-6. The filter for floating point numbers also accepts integers.

Even though $var is an integer, it's accepted by the filter. So, if you want to check for any number, use FILTER_VALIDATE_FLOAT. Use FILTER_VALIDATE_INT only when it's vital that the value must be an integer and nothing else.

10. Finally, replace the filter constant with a call to filter_id() like this (the code is in filter_var_07.php):

```
$filtered = filter_var($var, filter_id('float'));
```

11. Test the page. The result should be identical to before. This simply demonstrates that you can use filter_id() with the filter names if you find them easier to remember.

The only differences when using filter_input() are that you need to specify the source, and since the variable comes from an array, the variable name should be a string. To adapt the script in step 1 of the previous exercise to filter $_POST['var'], change it like this:

```
$var = 10;
$filtered = filter_var(INPUT_POST, 'var', FILTER_VALIDATE_INT);
var_dump($filtered);
```

Testing other filter constants

Rather than creating exercises to go through the remaining constants one by one, I have created a form that makes it easy to see the effect of each one.

1. Load filter_input.php in the ch4_exercises folder into a browser. As you can see in Figure 4-7, it's a simple form with a text area for you to enter the value you want to filter. The drop-down menu beneath the text area lets you select one of the filter constants. The only two that are missing from the list are FILTER_VALIDATE_REGEXP and FILTER_CALLBACK, both of which require the $options argument (adding options and flags is covered shortly). When you click the See filtered result button at the bottom of the form, the content of the text area and the selected filter are sent through the $_POST array.

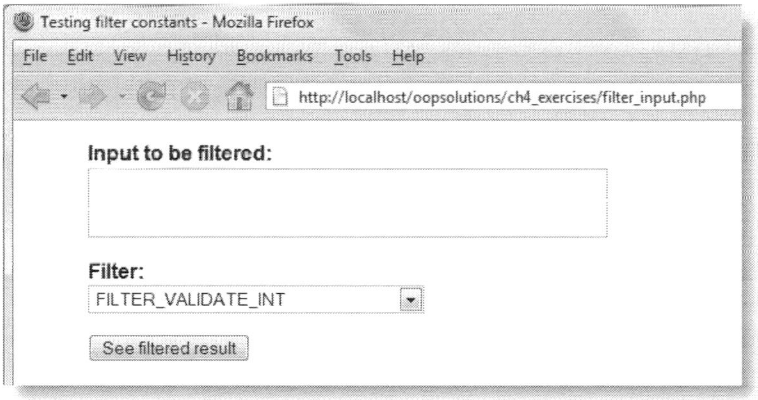

Figure 4-7. The form in filter_input.php makes it easy to see the effect of each filter.

If you study the code in filter_input.php, you'll see that I have created an array called $filters, which not only populates the drop-down menu but also controls the filter process when the form is submitted. The array looks like this:

```
$filters = array('int'              => 'FILTER_VALIDATE_INT',
                 'boolean'          => 'FILTER_VALIDATE_BOOLEAN',
                 'float'            => 'FILTER_VALIDATE_FLOAT',
                 'validate_url'     => 'FILTER_VALIDATE_URL',
                 'validate_email'   => 'FILTER_VALIDATE_EMAIL',
                 'validate_ip'      => 'FILTER_VALIDATE_IP',
                 'unsafe_raw'       => 'FILTER_UNSAFE_RAW',
                 'string'           => 'FILTER_SANITIZE_STRING',
                 'stripped'         => 'FILTER_SANITIZE_STRIPPED',
                 'encoded'          => 'FILTER_SANITIZE_ENCODED',
                 'special_chars'    => 'FILTER_SANITIZE_SPECIAL_CHARS',
                 'email'            => 'FILTER_SANITIZE_EMAIL',
                 'url'              => 'FILTER_SANITIZE_URL',
                 'number_int'       => 'FILTER_SANITIZE_NUMBER_INT',
                 'number_float'     => 'FILTER_SANITIZE_NUMBER_FLOAT',
                 'magic_quotes'     => 'FILTER_SANITIZE_MAGIC_QUOTES');
```

133

The key of each array element uses the name displayed by filter_list(), while the value is set to its equivalent filter constant. Here, the PHP constants are in quotes because I want to display them as labels in the drop-down menu, but in normal circumstances, they must not be enclosed in quotes. However, values passed through the $_POST and $_GET arrays are always treated as strings, so it's not possible to preserve the PHP constants when the form is submitted. To get around this, the code that does the actual filtering uses filter_id(), which takes one of the strings displayed by filter_list() and converts it to the equivalent constant, like this:

```
$filtered = filter_input(INPUT_POST, 'var', ➥
filter_id($_POST['filter']));
```

The result is the same as using the constant selected in the drop-down menu, but I have added this explanation in case you're confused by the code I have used.

2. Experiment with different types of input and filters to see the result. Pay particular attention to what happens when you use the sanitizing filters. Some results might come as a surprise. Figure 4-8 shows what happens when you apply FILTER_SANITIZE_NUMBER_FLOAT to 100.98.

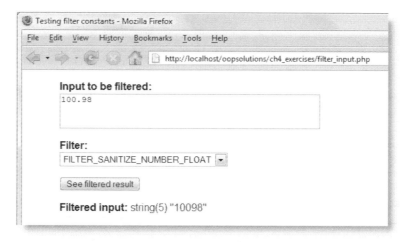

Figure 4-8. The sanitizing filters produce unexpected results when used without flags.

The decimal point is stripped out of the number, giving you a result 100 times greater than you probably expected.

This unexpected result happens because the sanitizing filters are concerned only with stripping out illegal or unwanted characters. To control them more precisely, you need to use the appropriate flags. So, let's take a look at how you add flags and options to a filter.

Setting flags and options when filtering a single variable

This is where things begin to get really complicated. The format of the optional final argument to filter_input() and filter_var() depends on whether you want to use flags, options, or both. The available options and flags are listed in Tables 4-3, 4-4, and 4-5. The following examples all use `filter_var()` so the variables can be hard-coded in the download files, but the syntax for options and flags is identical in `filter_input()`.

Flags only

A single flag can be passed directly to the function as the final argument. To preserve the decimal point in the example shown in Figure 4-8, pass FILTER_FLAG_ALLOW_FRACTION as the final argument like this (the code is in `filter_var_08.php`):

```
$var = 100.98;
$filtered = filter_var($var, FILTER_SANITIZE_NUMBER_FLOAT, ➥
    FILTER_FLAG_ALLOW_FRACTION);
```

To pass more than one flag, you need to create what's known as a **bitwise disjunction**. This compares the binary representation of each value. You don't need to concern yourself with the technical details. All that's necessary to know is that you insert a single vertical pipe (|) between each one like this:

```
FILTER_FLAG_ALLOW_FRACTION | FILTER_FLAG_ALLOW_THOUSAND
```

So, to preserve the thousands separator as well in the previous example, use FILTER_FLAG_ALLOW_THOUSAND in addition to FILTER_FLAG_ALLOW_FRACTION like this (the code is in `filter_var_09.php`):

```
$var = '100,000.98';
$filtered = filter_var($var, FILTER_SANITIZE_NUMBER_FLOAT, ➥
    FILTER_FLAG_ALLOW_FRACTION | FILTER_FLAG_ALLOW_THOUSAND);
```

Options only

Options must be presented as a multidimensional associative array, with the top-level array using the key `'options'`. For instance, FILTER_VALIDATE_INT accepts `min_range` and `max_range` as options. To accept integers only between 5 and 10 (inclusive), you pass the options like this (the code is in `filter_var_10.php`):

```
$var = 17;
$filtered = filter_var($var, FILTER_VALIDATE_INT, ➥
    array('options' => array('min_range' => 5,
                             'max_range' => 10)));
```

Even when there is only one option, it must still be presented as a multidimensional array. For example, to change the decimal point to a comma, as is commonly used in some parts of continental Europe, you need to set the `decimal` option for FILTER_VALIDATE_FLOAT like this (the code is in `filter_var_11.php`):

```
$var = '10,5';
$filtered = filter_var($var, FILTER_VALIDATE_FLOAT, ➥
    array('options' => array('decimal' => ',')));
```

Flags and options

When using a combination of flags and options, you add a `'flags'` array to the multidimensional associative array. So, to permit the use of the period as the thousands separator

4

with a continental European-style floating point number, you add FILTER_FLAG_ ALLOW_THOUSAND like this (the code is in filter_var_12.php):

```
$var = '100.789,5';
$filtered = filter_var($var, FILTER_VALIDATE_FLOAT, ➥
  array('options' => array('decimal' => ','),
        'flags'   => FILTER_FLAG_ALLOW_THOUSAND));
```

> *Although* FILTER_VALIDATE_FLOAT *accepts continental European-style numbers when the appropriate option and flag are set, the value returned by the filter always uses a period as the decimal point and strips the thousands separator. A space is not accepted as the thousands separator.*

Filtering multiple variables

Most of the time, filtering and validation operations need to handle multiple variables. To avoid the need to call filter_input() or filter_var() repeatedly, both functions have counterparts capable of processing many variables in a single operation: filter_input_array() and filter_var_array().

The filter_input_array() function takes the following arguments:

- **$source**: This indicates the superglobal array that contains the variables you want to filter. You must use one of the constants listed in Table 4-2, for example, INPUT_POST.
- **$instructions**: This is an optional multidimensional array indicating how the variables are to be filtered. If this argument is omitted, the default filter is applied (see "Setting a default filter" later in the chapter).

The filter_var_array() function takes the following arguments:

- **$data**: This is an array containing the variables you want to filter or validate.
- **$instructions**: This is the same as for filter_input_array().

The way you create the multidimensional array for the second argument is very similar to setting flags and options for filtering single variables, as described in the previous section. The top level of the array should contain an element for each of the variables to be processed. The value assigned to each variable should either be a filter constant or an array containing any combination of the following: 'filter', 'options', and 'flags'.

The following listing (the code is also in filter_var_13.php) shows examples of all variations:

```
$data = array('age'       => 21,
              'rating'    => 4,
              'price'     => 9.95,
              'thousands' => '100,000.95',
              'european'  => '100.000,95');
```

```
$instructions =
  array('age'       => FILTER_VALIDATE_INT,
        'rating'    => array('filter'  => FILTER_VALIDATE_INT,
                             'options' => array('min_range' => 1,
                                                'max_range' => 5)),
        'price'     => array('filter'  => FILTER_SANITIZE_NUMBER_FLOAT,
                             'flags'    => FILTER_FLAG_ALLOW_FRACTION),
        'thousands' => array('filter'  => FILTER_SANITIZE_NUMBER_FLOAT,
                             'flags'    => FILTER_FLAG_ALLOW_FRACTION |
                                           FILTER_FLAG_ALLOW_THOUSAND),
        'european'  => array('filter'  => FILTER_VALIDATE_FLOAT,
                             'options' => array('decimal' => ','),
                             'flags'    => FILTER_FLAG_ALLOW_THOUSAND)
       );
$filtered = filter_var_array($data, $instructions);
var_dump($filtered);
```

To filter the same variables coming from the $_POST array, build the $instructions array in exactly the same way, and use filter_input_array() and the INPUT_POST constant, instead of filter_var_array() and $data, like this:

```
$filtered = filter_input_array(INPUT_POST, $instructions);
```

Even with an IDE that has PHP code hints and code completion, constructing this sort of multidimensional associative array is time consuming and prone to error. That's why I decided to adopt the Facade design pattern to hide away all this complexity.

Before moving on to the class, there's just one final thing you might want to know about the filter functions: how to set a default filter.

Setting a default filter

If you use one type of filter predominantly, you can set a default filter and default flags. There are three places you can do this: in php.ini; or, if you're using an Apache server, in the Apache configuration file httpd.conf, or an .htaccess file.

The configuration directives that need to be changed are as follows:

- **filter.default**: This should be followed by a string containing one of the names generated by filter_list() (see Figure 4-2).
- **filter.default_flags**: This should be one of the flag constants from Tables 4-3, 4-4, and 4-5. To set more than one flag, separate each constant with a single vertical pipe (|).

To set the defaults in php.ini, remove the semicolon from the beginning of the line containing each directive, and put the value after the equal sign. The following directives set the default filter to convert into HTML entities single and double quotes, <, >, and &,

while the default flags strip all characters with an ASCII value of less than 32 or greater than 127:

```
filter.default = special_chars
filter.default_flags = FILTER_FLAG_STRIP_LOW | FILTER_FLAG_STRIP_HIGH
```

To set the values in `httpd.conf` or an `.htaccess` file, use `php_value`, followed by the directive and its value as a space-delimited list like this:

```
php_value filter.default special_chars
php_value filter.default_flags FILTER_FLAG_STRIP_LOW | ➥
  FILTER_FLAG_STRIP_HIGH
```

Building the validation class

In spite of the complexity of the filter functions, the ability to filter or validate many variables in a single operation is a huge benefit. It means that you can use a custom class to build the multidimensional array that determines how each variable should be treated. Once the array has been built, it's just a matter of passing it to the appropriate filter function and capturing the result. By encapsulating each stage of the process inside the class, you end up with a validation tool that is easy to use, but which leaves all the hard work to the filter functions.

First of all, let's consider what functionality the class should have.

Deciding what the class will do

Looking at the available filters in Tables 4-4 and 4-5, you can quickly come up with the following data types and formats the class should validate:

- Integer
- Floating point number
- Boolean
- Email
- URL
- Match against a regular expression

You also need to be able to strip HTML tags and convert special characters. Anything else? The following tasks are commonly required when validating input:

- Check that all required fields have a value
- Check for a numeric array
- Specify a minimum and maximum number of characters in text input

Finally, you want a method that does nothing. No, I haven't finally lost my senses. This simply adds an unchanged value to filtered results, which you can then process separately.

After the input has been validated, the class needs to produce three arrays as follows:

- The filtered results
- The names of required fields that are missing
- Any error messages generated by the validation process

I'm going to draw the line at this list, as it represents quite a lot of coding. Once you have seen how the class operates, you can add methods of your own.

Planning how the class will work

Once you have decided what a class will do, you need to plan how it will go about those tasks. Although there are four filter functions that perform validation tasks, two of them handle only single variables, so they're not suitable, as in most cases, you will need to deal with input from multiple fields. So that means the class needs to be based on either `filter_var_array()` or `filter_input_array()`. In the rare case that you want to validate only a single variable, you can still use these functions by passing the filter constants, flags, and options in a single-element array. Since filtering input from external sources is more commonly needed, I'm going to base this class on `filter_input_array()` and restrict it to handling input from the `$_POST` and `$_GET` arrays. If, at a later stage, you want to handle input from other sources, you can extend the base class and override the method that processes the input (I have called it `validateInput()`) and hand the variables to `filter_var_array()`.

The whole purpose of this class is to hide the complexity of the array of filter constants, flags, and options, so its core functionality lies in building that array behind the scenes, passing it to `filter_input_array()`, and capturing the results. So the class needs to follow these three stages:

1. **Instantiation (constructor)**
   - Retrieve the input from the `$_POST` or `$_GET` array.
   - Check whether any required fields are missing.

2. **Validation methods**
   - Create an array element for each field with the appropriate filter constants, flags, and options.
   - Generate error messages.

3. **Validation**
   - Check that a validation test has been set for each required field.
   - Pass the array of filter constants, flags, and options to `filter_input_array()`.
   - Store the filtered results, error messages, and names of required fields that haven't been filled in.

Now that you have a roadmap for the class, it's time to get down to the actual code.

139

Coding the validation class properties and methods

Following the naming convention I have adopted for this book, I have called the class Pos_Validator and am going to store it in Validator.php in the Pos folder. If you want to build the class yourself, follow the step-by-step instructions. Otherwise, you can find the completed class definition in the finished_classes folder. Just follow the code and the explanations. The code in the download files is fully commented, but I have left most of them out in the following pages, as all the important points are explained in the text.

Naming properties and defining the constructor

Deciding which properties to define isn't always practicable at the outset, but at a minimum, you'll need a way of referring inside the class to the following:

- Whether the input comes from the $_POST or $_GET array ($_inputType)
- The unfiltered input ($_submitted)
- A list of required fields ($_required)
- The array of filters, options, and flags to be passed to filter_input_array() ($_filterArgs)
- The filtered output ($_filtered)
- A list of required fields that haven't been filled in ($_missing)
- Error messages generated by the validator ($_errors)

The constructor needs to initialize the properties for the list of required items and the input type. It also needs to make sure that the filter functions are available on the server; without them, the class won't work.

1. Create a file called Validator.php in the Pos folder, and insert the following code:

```
class Pos_Validator
{
    protected $_inputType;
    protected $_submitted;
    protected $_required;
    protected $_filterArgs;
    protected $_filtered;
    protected $_missing;
    protected $_errors;

    public function __construct()
    {

    }
}
```

This defines the Pos_Validator class with its initial properties and an empty constructor. When validating data, it's important to prevent any outside influences from corrupting the data, so all the properties have been declared protected; and the names all begin with a leading underscore as a reminder.

2. Since the class is going to check that all required fields have a value, you need to pass an array containing the names of the required fields to the constructor and store it in the $_required property. The class is also going to be capable of handling either the $_POST or the $_GET array, so you need to pass that value to the constructor, too. However, it's possible that you might not want to make any fields required, so that should be an optional argument. And to save effort, let's make the input type an optional argument, too, by giving it a default value in the arguments block. Amend the constructor like this:

```
public function __construct($required = array(), $inputType = 'post')
{
  $this->_required = $required;
  $this->setInputType($inputType);
}
```

The two arguments, $required and $inputType, have the same names as their equivalent properties, but *without* the leading underscore. This is a reminder that their values come from outside the class. $required is set by default to an empty array, and $inputType is set to 'post'. This makes both arguments optional, but if other values are passed to the constructor, they will be used instead.

Setting the $_required property is straightforward; it just takes the value of the $required argument. However, the $_inputType property needs to be handled differently. As you might remember, filter_input_array() takes as its first argument one of the input constants listed in Table 4-2. I could have used INPUT_POST in the arguments block, but that means that you would need to pass INPUT_GET to the constructor if you want to validate the $_GET array instead. One of the main ideas behind the Pos_Validator class is to hide the unwieldy constants from view, so I have used a simple string as the argument. This means that the class needs to look up the correct constant to assign to the $_inputType property. That task is handed off to an internal method called setInputType(), which you'll define later.

3. The class relies on the filter functions to do all the hard work, so you need to make sure they're available. It's also a good idea to check that the $required argument contains an array. Amend the code like this to throw exceptions if either condition isn't met:

```
public function __construct($required = array(), $inputType = 'post')
{
  if (!function_exists('filter_list')) {
    throw new Exception('The Pos_Validator class requires the Filter ➥
Functions in >= PHP 5.2 or PECL.');
  }
  if (!is_null($required) && !is_array($required)) {
    throw new Exception('The names of required fields must be an array, ➥
even if only one field is required.');
  }
  $this->_required = $required;
  $this->setInputType($inputType);
}
```

141

The first conditional statement checks whether the filter_list() function exists. If it doesn't, you know that none of the filters is available, so an exception is thrown. The second conditional statement begins by checking that $required isn't null; in other words, that it contains a value of some sort. If it does contain a value, but it's not an array, the constructor throws an exception. Even if only one field is required, you need to make sure $required is an array; otherwise, dealing with it later will cause problems.

4. If an array of required fields has been passed to the constructor, you need to check that each field in the array has a value, so amend the code like this:

```php
public function __construct($required = array(), $inputType = 'post')
{
  if (!function_exists('filter_list')) {
    throw new Exception('The Pos_Validator class requires the Filter ➥
Functions in >= PHP 5.2 or PECL.');
  }
  if (!is_null($required) && !is_array($required)) {
    throw new Exception('The names of required fields must be an array, ➥
even if only one field is required.');
  }
  $this->_required = $required;
  $this->setInputType($inputType);
  if ($this->_required) {
    $this->checkRequired();
  }
  $this->_filterArgs = array();
  $this->_errors = array();
}
```

If the first argument isn't passed to the constructor, $this->_required will be an empty array, which PHP treats as false; otherwise, the constructor calls an internal method named checkRequired(), which you'll define in a moment.

The other new lines of code sets the $_filterArgs and $_errors properties to empty arrays.

That completes the constructor for the time being. A couple of other items will need to be added to it later, but it makes more sense to explain them in context when building the methods that need them.

The constructor makes calls to two internal methods, so the next task is to code them.

Setting the input type and checking required fields

The setInputType() and checkRequired() methods are both called from inside the constructor, so that gives you the option of hiding their existence from anyone using the class. In fact, with setInputType() it's essential to do so, because you don't want anybody to be able to change the input source arbitrarily once it has been set. So, both methods will be defined as protected, restricting access to inside the Pos_Validator class, but allowing it to be used by any child classes if you decide to extend the class later.

1. The purpose of the setInputType() method is twofold: as well as setting the input source, it assigns the variables from that source to the $_submitted property. This gives the class access to the variables you want to validate. The code is quite straightforward, so here's the entire code for the method:

```
protected function setInputType($type)
{
  switch (strtolower($type)) {
    case 'post':
      $this->_inputType = INPUT_POST;
      $this->_submitted = $_POST;
      break;
    case 'get':
      $this->_inputType = INPUT_GET;
      $this->_submitted = $_GET;
      break;
    default:
      throw new Exception('Invalid input type. Valid types are ➥
"post" and "get".');
  }
}
```

This is a simple switch statement. It takes the argument passed to setInputType() and passes it to strtolower(). This means that the second argument passed to the class constructor is case-insensitive. It doesn't matter if the user types 'Get' or 'GET', it's converted to lowercase. Depending on the value passed to setInputType(), the $_inputType property is set to the appropriate input constant (see Table 4-2). This will be needed later, when you pass the variables to filter_input_array() for processing. At the same time, the contents of the relevant superglobal array are assigned to the $_submitted property.

If a value other than post or get is submitted, the method throws an exception with a suitable message.

2. Now that you have populated the $_submitted property, you can compare it with the array of required fields. This is what the checkRequired() method looks like:

```
protected function checkRequired()
{
  $OK = array();
  foreach ($this->_submitted as $name => $value) {
    $value = is_array($value) ? $value : trim($value);
    if (!empty($value)) {
      $OK[] = $name;
    }
  }
  $this->_missing = array_diff($this->_required, $OK);
}
```

The method starts off by initializing a local variable $OK as an empty array. This array will be discarded once the checks have finished, so it doesn't need to be a property. A foreach loop then goes through each element of the $_submitted property, in other words, the $_POST or $_GET array, depending on the input type that has been selected.

You don't want people to get around a required field by just pressing the space bar a few times, so the following line strips whitespace from the value unless it's an array:

$value = is_array($value) ? $value : trim($value);

You can't pass an array to trim(), so this uses the conditional operator (?:) to check whether the value is an array. If it is, it reassigns it back to $value unchanged; otherwise, it passes it to trim() to strip off any whitespace before assigning it back to $value.

If $value is not empty, the name of the variable is added to the $OK array. By the time the loop comes to an end, $OK contains the names of all fields that contain a value.

There's a potential flaw in this approach. If an array contains nothing but empty strings, it will still pass the test. However, the purpose of the class is to process input from online forms. Values passed as arrays come from check box groups and multiple-selection lists. If your form is correctly set up, the only way an array of empty strings is likely to be transmitted through the $_POST or $_GET array is by someone spoofing your form. If that happens, other security measures, such as implementing a CAPTCHA (Completely Automated Turing Test to Tell Computers and Humans Apart, see www.captcha.net)*, are likely to be more effective than strengthening this test.*

All that remains is to find out whether there's any difference between the names in $OK and those in $_required. This is done by passing the $_required property and $OK to the array_diff() function, which returns an array containing all the values from the first array that are not present in the second array. So, any value in the $_required property absent from the $OK array is stored in the $_missing property.

If all the values in the $_required property are also in the $OK array, the $_missing property contains an empty array indicating that all the required fields have been filled in. It's quite likely that the $OK array might contain the names of optional fields that have been filled in, but this doesn't matter because array_diff() disregards any extra elements in the second array.

It might be difficult to grasp how this works, so here's a practical example. The $_required and $OK arrays are indexed arrays containing only the names of variables, not their values, so they might look something like this:

```
0 => 'name', 1 => 'email', 2 => 'comments'   // $_required
0 => 'name', 1 => 'comments'                 // $OK
```

When the array_diff() function returns an array of missing values, it preserves the original keys and values. In this case, the values are just the names of the variables. The preceding example would return an array containing the following single element:

```
1 => 'email'
```

The only array that contains both the names of the submitted fields and their values is the $_submitted property.

This is a good point to check the code so far, and testing the checkRequired() method should remove any doubts you might still have.

Testing the checkRequired() method

Testing your code at regular intervals makes it much easier to track down problems, rather than leaving everything to the end. I have created a simple form called test_validator_01.php in the ch4_exercises folder for you to use. Rename it test_validator.php, and add the code in the following steps. Alternatively, you can use any form of your own.

1. The form in test_validator.php contains three fields called name, email, and comments. The submit button is named send. The method attribute is set to post, and the action attribute has been left blank, so the form is self-processing.

   Insert the following code above the DOCTYPE declaration (or use test_validator_02.php):

   ```php
   <?php
   if (filter_has_var(INPUT_POST, 'send')) {
     require_once '../Pos/Validator.php';
     $required = array('name', 'email', 'comments');
     $val = new Pos_Validator($required);
   }
   ?>
   <!DOCTYPE html PUBLIC "-//W3C//DTD XHTML 1.0 Transitional//EN"
   ```

   This uses filter_has_var() to check whether the $_POST array contains a variable called send, so the code inside the braces runs only if the submit button has been clicked.

   The code includes the Pos_Validator class, creates an array called $required containing the names of all three form fields, and passes it as an argument to a new instance of the Pos_Validator class.

2. Open Validator.php, and amend the last few lines of the checkRequired() method by adding the line shown here in bold:

   ```php
       }
     $this->_missing = array_diff($this->_required, $OK);
     print_r($this->_missing);
   }
   ```

This displays the contents of the $_missing property. Don't worry about the fact that the output will appear above the DOCTYPE declaration. This is for testing purposes only.

3. Save both pages, load the form into a browser, and click the submit button without filling in any of the fields. If all your code is correct, you should see the names of the three fields at the top of the page, as shown in Figure 4-9.

Figure 4-9. Checking that the $_missing property contains the names of fields that weren't filled in

4. Fill in one of the fields, put some blank spaces in another, and click the submit button again. The array displayed at the top of the page should no longer contain the name of the field that had some real content, but the one with only blank spaces should still be listed.

5. Fill in each field, and click the submit button again. The top of the page should display Array ( ), indicating that $_missing is an empty array.

6. Remove the following line from checkRequired():

print_r($this->_missing);

Don't forget to do this. The line was required only for testing purposes.

This exercise confirms not only that checkRequired() is working but also that the constructor is populating the $_required property and setInputType() is populating the $_submitted property from the $_POST array.

Preventing duplicate filters from being applied to a field

Before moving on to the definition of the validation methods, there's one more internal method needed. Applying more than one filter to a variable could have unpredictable results, so it's a good idea to prevent users from doing so. The class needs to build a multidimensional array containing the name of each input field or variable, together with the filter, options, and flags you want to apply to it. This will be stored in the $_filterArgs property. If the field name has already been registered in the $_filterArgs array, you know a duplicate filter is being applied, so you need to throw an exception.

Rather than type out a similar message in every validation method, delegate the responsibility to a protected method called checkDuplicateFilter() like this:

```
protected function checkDuplicateFilter($fieldName)
{
  if (isset($this->_filterArgs[$fieldName])) {
    throw new Exception("A filter has already been set for the ➥
following field: $fieldName.");
  }
}
```

This method will be called by each validation method, passing it the name of the field that is to be validated. If the $_filterArgs array already contains an element for the field, the class throws an exception, displaying the field name in the error message.

Creating the validation methods

The filter functions offer a useful range of options and flags. One way to use them would be to create separate methods with names indicating exactly what they do. That has the advantage of being explicit, but it would result in a lot of coding, not to mention the danger of creating an interface just as complex as the one you're trying to hide. The solution that I have come up with is to control the options through optional arguments to each validation method. The first argument will be required: the name of the input field or variable that you want to validate. Where appropriate, the other arguments will have default values. Although this also runs the risk of complexity, using PHPDoc comments and an IDE capable of introspection solves this problem through code hints, as shown in Figure 4-10.

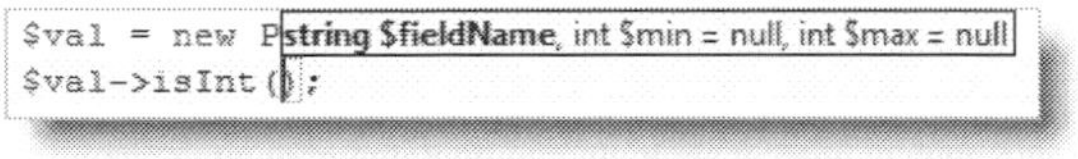

```
$val = new P string $fieldName, int $min = null, int $max = null
$val->isInt( );
```

Figure 4-10. Remembering each method's options is much easier if your IDE is capable of generating code hints.

The structure of each validation method is very similar. It begins by calling checkDuplicateFilter() to see if a filter has already been applied. If checkDuplicateFilter() doesn't throw an exception, the validation method adds the name of the field or variable to the top level of the $_filterArgs array, setting the filter and any flags or options. There's nothing complicated about the code; it simply builds an array similar to the one in "Filtering multiple values" earlier in the chapter, using the constants, options, and flags from Tables 4-3, 4-4, and 4-5. So, I'll keep my comments about each method relatively brief.

All validation methods need to be public. It doesn't matter where you put them inside the class definition, but my normal practice is to put public methods after the constructor and before any protected or private methods.

> *There's a lot of code over the next few pages. Typing it into the class definition yourself will help fix things in your mind more quickly, but if you can't face the prospect, you might prefer to use* Validator.php *in the* finished_classes *folder and just read through the explanations of how each method works.*

Validating integers

The filter constant for validating integers accepts an array of options to specify the minimum and maximum acceptable values. Since you won't always want to set these values, the arguments for both options need to be optional. The code for the isInt() method looks like this:

```php
public function isInt($fieldName, $min = null, $max = null)
{
  $this->checkDuplicateFilter($fieldName);
  $this->_filterArgs[$fieldName] = array('filter' => ➥
FILTER_VALIDATE_INT);
  if (is_int($min)) {
    $this->_filterArgs[$fieldName]['options']['min_range'] = $min;
  }
  if (is_int($max)) {
    $this->_filterArgs[$fieldName]['options']['max_range'] = $max;
  }
}
```

The default value of $min and $max is set to null. The min_range and max_range options are both optional, so you can set either, both, or neither. To set a minimum acceptable value on its own, simply omit the third argument. However, to set a maximum value without setting a minimum one, you need to pass null (without quotes) as the second argument to isInt().

Validating floating point numbers

The filter constant for validating floating point numbers accepts an option to set the character used for the decimal point and a flag for allowing numbers to use the thousands separator. Both options are given default values in the arguments block. The code for the isFloat() method looks like this:

```
public function isFloat($fieldName, $decimalPoint = '.', ➥
$allowThousandSeparator = true)
{
  $this->checkDuplicateFilter($fieldName);
  if ($decimalPoint != '.' && $decimalPoint != ',') {
    throw new Exception('Decimal point must be a comma or period in ➥
isFloat().');
  }
  $this->_filterArgs[$fieldName] = array(
    'filter'  => FILTER_VALIDATE_FLOAT,
    'options' => array('decimal' => $decimalPoint)
    );
  if ($allowThousandSeparator) {
    $this->_filterArgs[$fieldName]['flags'] = ➥
FILTER_FLAG_ALLOW_THOUSAND;
  }
}
```

The default value for $decimalPoint has been set to a period, and
$allowThousandSeparator defaults to true. This means that in the vast majority of cases
both arguments can be omitted.

Validating a numeric array

I have added this validation method mainly to demonstrate the use of one of the flags in
Table 4-3, FILTER_REQUIRE_ARRAY. The isNumericArray() function takes three optional
arguments: $allowDecimalFractions, $decimalPoint, and $allowThousandSeparator,
the names of which are self-explanatory. Here's what the function looks like:

```
public function isNumericArray($fieldName, $allowDecimalFractions = ➥
true, $decimalPoint = '.', $allowThousandSeparator = true)
{
  $this->checkDuplicateFilter($fieldName);
  if ($decimalPoint != '.' && $decimalPoint != ',') {
    throw new Exception('Decimal point must be a comma or period in ➥
isNumericArray().');
  }
  $this->_filterArgs[$fieldName] = array(
    'filter'  => FILTER_VALIDATE_FLOAT,
    'flags'   => FILTER_REQUIRE_ARRAY,
    'options' => array('decimal' => $decimalPoint)
    );
  if ($allowDecimalFractions) {
    $this->_filterArgs[$fieldName]['flags'] |= ➥
FILTER_FLAG_ALLOW_FRACTION;
  }
  if ($allowThousandSeparator) {
    $this->_filterArgs[$fieldName]['flags'] |= ➥
FILTER_FLAG_ALLOW_THOUSAND;
  }
}
```

The optional arguments are all set to the most commonly used values, so can normally be omitted. However, if you want the array to contain only integers, set the second argument ($allowDecimalFractions) to false.

An important thing to note about this method is the way the flags to allow decimal fractions and the thousands separator are added to the existing flags element with the combined assignment operator |=. The vertical pipe is a bitwise operator and can be combined with the equal sign in exactly the same way as arithmetic operators, for example, += or *=.

Validating an email

This method simply sets the email validation filter, which takes no options or flags.

```
public function isEmail($fieldName)
{
  $this->checkDuplicateFilter($fieldName);
  $this->_filterArgs[$fieldName] = FILTER_VALIDATE_EMAIL;
}
```

Validating a full URL

This method validates a full URL, requiring a scheme (such as http:// or ftp://). It takes one optional argument: $queryStringRequired, which is false by default. Validating a URL checks only that it is the correct format for a URL. It doesn't check whether the URL actually exists. The code looks like this:

```
public function isFullURL($fieldName, $queryStringRequired = false)
{
  $this->checkDuplicateFilter($fieldName);
  $this->_filterArgs[$fieldName] = array(
    'filter' => FILTER_VALIDATE_URL,
    'flags' => FILTER_FLAG_SCHEME_REQUIRED | FILTER_FLAG_HOST_REQUIRED ➥
| FILTER_FLAG_PATH_REQUIRED);
    if ($queryStringRequired) {
      $this->_filterArgs[$fieldName]['flags'] |= ➥
FILTER_FLAG_QUERY_REQUIRED;
    }
}
```

Validate a URL

This method is identical to isFullURL(), except that it omits the flags that require the URL to include a scheme and host:

```
public function isURL($fieldName, $queryStringRequired = false)
{
  $this->checkDuplicateFilter($fieldName);
  $this->_filterArgs[$fieldName]['filter'] = FILTER_VALIDATE_URL;
    if ($queryStringRequired) {
      $this->_filterArgs[$fieldName]['flags'] = ➥
FILTER_FLAG_QUERY_REQUIRED;
    }
}
```

Validate a Boolean value

The filter functions return the variable's value on success, and false on failure. However, this poses a problem when validating a Boolean, because—even though the validation test succeeds—the value of the Boolean might be false. To avoid this sort of false negative, you need to add a protected property called $_booleans to the class. You also need to initialize the property as an empty array in the constructor. Add protected $_booleans to the list of properties at the top of the class definition, and change the final lines of the constructor function like this:

```
    if ($this->_required) {
      $this->checkRequired();
    }
    $this->_filterArgs = array();
    $this->_errors = array();
    $this->_booleans = array();
  }
```

The isBool() method looks like this:

```
    public function isBool($fieldName, $nullOnFailure = false)
    {
      $this->checkDuplicateFilter($fieldName);
      $this->_booleans[] = $fieldName;
      $this->_filterArgs[$fieldName]['filter'] = FILTER_VALIDATE_BOOLEAN;
      if ($nullOnFailure) {
        $this->_filterArgs[$fieldName]['flags'] = FILTER_NULL_ON_FAILURE;
      }
    }
```

In addition to setting the appropriate filter arguments, this method adds the name of the Boolean field to the $_booleans property. This is used later by the validateInput() method to prevent Boolean fields from generating error messages.

See Table 4-4 for an explanation of FILTER_NULL_ON_FAILURE.

Validate against a regular expression

This matches a value against a Perl-compatible regular expression (PCRE). It takes two arguments, both of which are required: the name of the field or variable being tested and a PCRE. If the match succeeds, the entire value is returned, not just the matching portion.

```
    public function matches($fieldName, $pattern)
    {
      $this->checkDuplicateFilter($fieldName);
      $this->_filterArgs[$fieldName] = array(
        'filter'  => FILTER_VALIDATE_REGEXP,
        'options' => array('regexp' => $pattern)
        );
    }
```

Sanitize a string by removing tags

This method encapsulates one of the sanitizing filters. It removes all tags, including HTML, PHP, and XML, from input in a similar way to the PHP strip_tags(). A major difference is that, unlike strip_tags(), the filter constant, FILTER_SANITIZE_STRING, does not accept a list of acceptable tags. Instead, it offers a much tougher approach through options to strip or encode characters with an ASCII value of less than 32 or greater than 127. It also optionally encodes ampersands (&) and preserves quotes. With so many options, I have turned them all off, so using the removeTags() method with only the name of the field or variable to be sanitized results in tags being stripped, ampersands left intact, but double and single quotes converted to entities. The code looks like this:

```php
public function removeTags($fieldName, $encodeAmp = false, ➡
$preserveQuotes = false, $encodeLow = false, ➡
$encodeHigh = false, $stripLow = false, $stripHigh = false)
{
  $this->checkDuplicateFilter($fieldName);
  $this->_filterArgs[$fieldName]['filter'] = FILTER_SANITIZE_STRING;
  $this->_filterArgs[$fieldName]['flags'] = 0;
  if ($encodeAmp) {
    $this->_filterArgs[$fieldName]['flags'] |= FILTER_FLAG_ENCODE_AMP;
  }
  if ($preserveQuotes) {
    $this->_filterArgs[$fieldName]['flags'] |= ➡
FILTER_FLAG_NO_ENCODE_QUOTES;
  }
  if ($encodeLow) {
    $this->_filterArgs[$fieldName]['flags'] |= FILTER_FLAG_ENCODE_LOW;
  }
  if ($encodeHigh) {
    $this->_filterArgs[$fieldName]['flags'] |= FILTER_FLAG_ENCODE_HIGH;
  }
  if ($stripLow) {
    $this->_filterArgs[$fieldName]['flags'] |= FILTER_FLAG_STRIP_LOW;
  }
  if ($stripHigh) {
    $this->_filterArgs[$fieldName]['flags'] |= FILTER_FLAG_STRIP_HIGH;
  }
}
```

Note how the flags are handled. Behind the scenes, each flag constant represents an integer. So, when no flags are set, the flags subarray needs to be 0 (see the line of code highlighted in bold). If the argument for a flag is set to true, its value is added using the bitwise combined assignment operator |=.

> *The large number of options in the preceding method and the one that follows is impractical if you need to turn them on regularly. I could have created different methods for each combination of options, but that adds a new level of complexity, forcing users to remember what each method does. When designing a class, you need to decide how often a feature is likely to be used. There is no set formula for getting the balance right.*

Sanitize an array by removing tags

This method is identical to removeTags(), except that it processes the contents of an array. The code looks like this:

```
public function removeTagsFromArray($fieldName, $encodeAmp = false, ➥
$preserveQuotes = false, $encodeLow = false, ➥
$encodeHigh = false, $stripLow = false, $stripHigh = false)
{
  $this->checkDuplicateFilter($fieldName);
  $this->_filterArgs[$fieldName]['filter'] = FILTER_SANITIZE_STRING;
  $this->_filterArgs[$fieldName]['flags'] = FILTER_REQUIRE_ARRAY;
  if ($encodeAmp) {
    $this->_filterArgs[$fieldName]['flags'] |= FILTER_FLAG_ENCODE_AMP;
  }
  if ($preserveQuotes) {
    $this->_filterArgs[$fieldName]['flags'] |= ➥
FILTER_FLAG_NO_ENCODE_QUOTES;
  }
  if ($encodeLow) {
    $this->_filterArgs[$fieldName]['flags'] |= FILTER_FLAG_ENCODE_LOW;
  }
  if ($encodeHigh) {
    $this->_filterArgs[$fieldName]['flags'] |= FILTER_FLAG_ENCODE_HIGH;
  }
  if ($stripLow) {
    $this->_filterArgs[$fieldName]['flags'] |= FILTER_FLAG_STRIP_LOW;
  }
  if ($stripHigh) {
    $this->_filterArgs[$fieldName]['flags'] |= FILTER_FLAG_STRIP_HIGH;
  }
}
```

The default value of the flags subarray is set to FILTER_REQUIRE_ARRAY. This applies the filter function to every element of the array, including nested arrays. This recursive action makes it very powerful.

Sanitize a string by converting special characters to entities

This converts single and double quotes, <, >, &, and characters with an ASCII value of less than 32 into HTML entities. The optional arguments apply the method to an array, encode characters with an ASCII value greater than 127, or strip low and high special characters. The way the flags are set is identical to removeTags(). The code for the useEntities() method looks like this:

```
public function useEntities($fieldName, $isArray = false, ➥
$encodeHigh = false, $stripLow = false, $stripHigh = false)
{
  $this->checkDuplicateFilter($fieldName);
  $this->_filterArgs[$fieldName]['filter'] = ➥
FILTER_SANITIZE_SPECIAL_CHARS;
  $this->_filterArgs[$fieldName]['flags'] = 0;
```

4

```
    if ($isArray) {
      $this->_filterArgs[$fieldName]['flags'] |= FILTER_REQUIRE_ARRAY;
    }
    if ($encodeHigh) {
      $this->_filterArgs[$fieldName]['flags'] |= FILTER_FLAG_ENCODE_HIGH;
    }
    if ($stripLow) {
      $this->_filterArgs[$fieldName]['flags'] |= FILTER_FLAG_STRIP_LOW;
    }
    if ($stripHigh) {
      $this->_filterArgs[$fieldName]['flags'] |= FILTER_FLAG_STRIP_HIGH;
    }
  }
```

Check the length of text

This is the only validation method that doesn't use any of the filter functions or constants, so it can be used in combination with one of the other methods. It uses the PHP strlen() function to ascertain the number of characters in a string, and prepares appropriate error messages that are added to the $_errors property. Like all other validation methods, the first argument is the name of the field or variable that you want to check. Since you want to check the contents of the field or variable, it's necessary to get it from the $_submitted property, which contains an array of all submitted data. The second argument represents the minimum number of acceptable characters. The third argument is optional and sets the maximum number of characters. Because the second argument is required, it must be set to 0 if you only want to limit the maximum number of characters permitted. The following code is commented throughout, so the way the method works should be self-explanatory.

```
public function checkTextLength($fieldName, $min, $max = null)
{
  // Get the submitted value
  $text = trim($this->_submitted[$fieldName]);
  // Make sure it's a string
  if (!is_string($text)) {
    throw new Exception("The checkTextLength() method can be applied ➥
only to strings; $fieldName is the wrong data type.");
  }
  // Make sure the second argument is a number
  if (!is_numeric($min)) {
    throw new Exception("The checkTextLength() method expects a number ➥
as the second argument (field name: $fieldName)");
  }
  // If the string is shorter than the minimum, create error message
  if (strlen($text) < $min) {
    // Check whether a valid maximum value has been set
    if (is_numeric($max)) {
      $this->_errors[] = ucfirst($fieldName) . " must be between $min ➥
and $max characters.";
```

```
      } else {
        $this->_errors[] = ucfirst($fieldName) . " must be a minimum of ➥
$min characters.";
      }
    }
    // If a maximum has been set, and the string is too long
    if (is_numeric($max) && strlen($text) > $max) {
      if ($min == 0) {
        $this->_errors[] = ucfirst($fieldName) . " must be no more than ➥
$max characters.";
      } else {
        $this->_errors[] = ucfirst($fieldName) . " must be between $min ➥
and $max characters.";
      }
    }
  }
}
```

Filter for input that requires special handling

This method uses the FILTER_UNSAFE_RAW constant to handle input that you want to treat in a way not covered by the other validation methods. It has two options: to handle an array and encode ampersands (&). The reason for creating this seemingly useless method is to add the input to an array of filtered items. You can then loop through the filtered array confident that it contains only variables that you have specified. The code looks like this:

```
public function noFilter($fieldName, $isArray = false, ➥
$encodeAmp = false)
{
  $this->checkDuplicateFilter($fieldName);
  $this->_filterArgs[$fieldName]['filter'] = FILTER_UNSAFE_RAW;
  $this->_filterArgs[$fieldName]['flags'] = 0;
  if ($isArray) {
    $this->_filterArgs[$fieldName]['flags'] |= FILTER_REQUIRE_ARRAY;
  }
  if ($encodeAmp) {
    $this->_filterArgs[$fieldName]['flags'] |= FILTER_FLAG_ENCODE_AMP;
  }
}
```

Testing the $_filterArgs property

The validation methods described over the last few pages are responsible for populating the $_filterArgs property, which is an array specifying the filters, options, and flags that you want applied to each input variable. It's important to make sure that the array is being built correctly, so this short exercise applies some validation tests to a form to see what the $_filterArgs property contains.

1. Continue working with test_validator.php from the previous exercise. Amend the PHP code at the top of the page like this (or use test_validator_03.php):

```
$val = new Pos_Validator($required);
$val->checkTextLength('name', 3);
$val->removeTags('name');
$val->isEmail('email');
$val->checkTextLength('comments', 10, 500);
$val->useEntities('comments');
echo '<pre>';
print_r($val->_filterArgs);
print_r($val->_errors);
echo '</pre>';
```

This applies validation checks to the three fields in the form and then uses print_r() to display the contents of the $_filterArgs and $_errors properties. It doesn't matter which validation methods you use; just make sure you use checkTextLength() at least once. Again, don't worry that this produces output before the DOCTYPE declaration; this is only for testing.

2. The $_filterArgs and $_errors properties are protected, so you need to change their definition temporarily at the top of Validator.php like this:

```
public $_errors;
public $_filterArgs;
```

3. Save both pages, load the form into a browser, and click the submit button. You should see output similar to Figure 4-11.

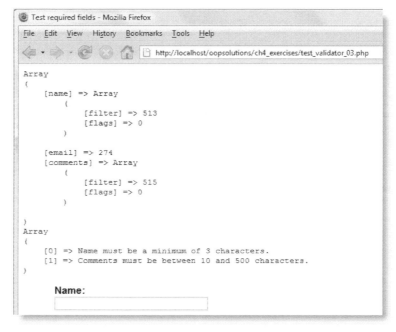

Figure 4-11. PHP turns the filter and flag constants into their numerical equivalents.

What might come as a surprise is that, instead of FILTER_SANITIZE_STRING, the value of the filter element for name is displayed as 513. This is confirmation that things are working correctly. If you see text for any of the filters or flags, it means that you have mistyped a PHP constant. Of course, if you get a parse error, it means there's a syntax error in your code.

Verify also that the $_errors property is displaying the correct error messages, as shown in Figure 4-11.

4. Apply another validation method to one of the fields like this (or use test_validator_04.php):

```
$val->checkTextLength('comments', 10, 500);
$val->useEntities('comments');
$val->removeTags('comments');
echo '<pre>';
```

5. Save the page, reload it in a browser, and click the submit button. This time, the class should throw an exception because you have applied two validation methods that use filters to the same field. This confirms that checkDuplicateFilter() is working correctly. The only validation method that can be used in combination with another is checkTextLength().

6. You can continue testing by using different validation methods and by entering some text in the fields that use checkTextLength() to see how it affects the error messages. When you have finished, change the visibility of $_errors and $_filterArgs back to protected:

```
protected $_errors;
protected $_filterArgs;
```

This is very important. The class will continue to work even if you don't change the visibility, but it will leave the properties open to arbitrary change.

> *Give yourself a bonus point if you noticed that I haven't been using* try . . . catch. *These exercises are intended just as quick tests of the code so far. Once the class is complete, it should always be used inside a* try *block because it is liable to throw an exception if something goes wrong.*

Creating the methods to process the tests and get the results

Now that you have built the array of filters, options, and flags, all that remains is to pass it to filter_input_array(), which takes two arguments: the input type (stored in this class as $_inputType) and the array of filters (stored as $_filterArgs). The function returns an array containing the filtered and validated input, which will be stored in the $_filtered property. So, all the hard work is done by this single command:

```
$this->_filtered = filter_input_array($this->_inputType, ➡
    $this->_filterArgs);
```

For the validator to produce useful results, though, a few more steps are necessary. First of all, the whole point of using a validator is to ensure that the rest of your script handles only data that you know has been filtered. So, after passing the $_POST or $_GET array to the validator, you should no longer access directly any data that it contains, but always take it from the filtered array. This means there is no point in specifying a field as required if you don't apply one of the validation methods to it.

The other thing that you need to do is to build a list of items that failed validation. In theory, this should be any element in the $_filtered array that returns false; but you need to exclude anything that has been passed to the isBool() validation method, since false could simply be the Boolean value contained by that variable. You also need to exclude items that have been added to the $_missing array to avoid reporting the same error twice. I have also decided to exclude items not marked as required, on the assumption that, if it's not required, you're not worried about the data failing validation. Such items will show up in the $_filtered array as false. If you disagree with this design decision, you can adjust the validateInput() method accordingly.

To summarize, the validateInput() method needs to perform these three tasks:

1. Verify that all required fields have been filtered.

2. Apply the filters to the input data, and store the result in the $_filtered property.

3. Build a list of items that failed validation, and store their names in the $_errors property.

The fully commented code for validateInput() follows:

```php
public function validateInput()
{
  // Initialize an array for required items that haven't been validated
  $notFiltered = array();
  // Get the names of all fields that have been validated
  $tested = array_keys($this->_filterArgs);
  // Loop through the required fields
  // Add any missing ones to the $notFiltered array
  foreach ($this->_required as $field) {
    if (!in_array($field, $tested)) {
      $notFiltered[] = $field;
    }
  }
  // If any items have been added to the $notFiltered array, it means a
  // required item hasn't been validated, so throw an exception
  if ($notFiltered) {
    throw new Exception('No filter has been set for the following ➥
required item(s): ' . implode(',', $notFiltered));
  }

  // Apply the validation tests using filter_input_array()
  $this->_filtered = filter_input_array($this->_inputType, ➥
$this->_filterArgs);

  // Now find which items failed validation
  foreach ($this->_filtered as $key => $value) {
```

```
        // Skip items that used the isBool() method
        // Also skip any that are either missing or not required
        if (in_array($key, $this->_booleans) || in_array($key, ➥
$this->_missing) || !in_array($key, $this->_required)) {
            continue;
        }
        // If the filtered value is false, it failed validation,
        // so add it to the $errors array
        elseif ($value === false) {
            $this->_errors[$key] = ucfirst($key) . ': invalid data supplied';
        }
    }

    // Return the validated input as an array
    return $this->_filtered;
}
```

4

All that remains is to provide public methods to give access to the protected $_missing, $_filtered, and $_errors properties. Each one simply returns the property, as you can see from the following code:

```
public function getMissing()
{
    return $this->_missing;
}

public function getFiltered()
{
    return $this->_filtered;
}

public function getErrors()
{
    return $this->_errors;
}
```

That completes the Pos_Validator class. It's a lot of code—more than 300 lines without the PHPDoc comments—but much of it follows a set pattern. The one-time pain of creating the class definition is more than repaid by encapsulating the complexity of the filter constants, flags, and options in methods with intuitive names. The final step is to put the validator to practical use.

Using the validation class

As I said at the beginning of the chapter, this class is an example of the Facade design pattern, which superimposes a simpler interface on a complex subsystem. In other words, it takes full advantage of encapsulation to hide the mind-bending complexities of the filter constants, flags, and options. One design decision I had to take was whether to create a large number of methods to deal with each possible combination of filters, flags, and options, or handle the flags and options as arguments. I decided on the latter course by making most arguments optional and choosing what I considered to be the most commonly used values as defaults. If your IDE generates code hints from custom classes, the PHPDoc comments make the arguments easy to use.

Validating user input with the Pos_Validator class involves the following steps:

1. Include the class definition with require_once or __autoload().
2. Create an array of the names of required fields or variables.
3. Instantiate a Pos_Validator object, and pass it the array of required fields (if any). If the values come from the $_GET array, set the input type to get.
4. Pass the name of each input variable to the appropriate validation method.
5. Call the validateInput() method, and capture the array of filtered values in a variable.
6. Call the getMissing() and getErrors() methods, and assign their results to variables.
7. If the getMissing() and getErrors() methods produce empty arrays, you know the input has passed all the validation tests and the filtered array is safe to use. Otherwise, use the error messages generated by getMissing() and getErrors() to alert the user to any mistakes.

You have already done the first four steps in the preceding exercises, so all that remains is to validate the input and display any error messages.

Validating form input

The following exercise uses the same basic form as in the rest of the chapter. Rather than test every method, I have kept it simple in order to demonstrate the basic principles of how to use the Pos_Validator class. If you have been updating test_validator.php throughout this chapter, continue using it. Alternatively, use test_validator_04.php in the ch4_exercises folder.

1. In the last exercise, you displayed the contents of the $_filterArgs and $_errors properties onscreen to test that they were working correctly. This time, you want to validate the form input, so those parts of the code are no longer needed. You also need to remove the duplicate validation test for the comments field. Delete the five lines highlighted in bold here:

```php
if (filter_has_var(INPUT_POST, 'send')) {
  require '../Pos/Validator.php';
  $required = array('name', 'email', 'comments');
  $val = new Pos_Validator($required);
  $val->checkTextLength('name', 3);
  $val->removeTags('name');
  $val->isEmail('email');
  $val->checkTextLength('comments', 10, 500);
  $val->useEntities('comments');
```

```
  $val->removeTags('comments');
  echo '<pre>';
  print_r($val->_filterArgs);
  print_r($val->_errors);
  echo '</pre>';
}
```

2. To validate the input, call the validateInput() method, and capture the result in a variable. To make it clear that it contains the filtered input, let's call it $filtered. Add the following line in place of the code you deleted in the previous step:

```
$filtered = $val->validateInput();
```

3. You also need to check whether any of the required fields are missing and if any of the fields failed validation. This involves calling the getMissing() and getErrors() methods and capturing the results in appropriately named variables. Add the following two lines immediately after the one you added in step 2:

```
$missing = $val->getMissing();
$errors = $val->getErrors();
```

4. Both getMissing() and getErrors() return arrays. PHP treats an array that contains any values as true; an empty array is treated as false. So, you can use $missing and $errors as conditions to determine how to treat the form input. If either of them evaluates to true, you need to display appropriate error messages in the form. If they both evaluate to false, you know the input has passed validation, and you can use the values in the $filtered array to send an email, input the values into a database, or display them onscreen.

Add the following conditional statement immediately below the code you entered in the previous step:

```
if (!$missing && !$errors) {
  // Everything passed validation.
  // The validated input is stored in $filtered.
}
```

This needs no explanation. If $missing and $errors are both *not* true, you can use $filtered in the knowledge that all the input met your validation criteria.

> It's important to remember the values in $filtered *are only as safe as the validation tests you subjected them to. If strings are likely to contain quotes or control characters, you need to pass them to* htmlentities() *before displaying them onscreen or use an escaping mechanism, such as* mysql_real_escape_string() *or prepared statements, before inserting them into a database. If you want to permit some HTML tags, you also need to use* strip_tags() *with a list of permissible tags as the second argument. Validation means passing a specific test; it does not automatically mean "safe."*

4

5. Since $missing and $errors tell you whether there has been a problem with the validation, it's a good idea to initialize them at the top of the script. By doing so, you can then use them in the body of the page to determine whether to display any error messages. If you don't understand why, all will become clear in a short while.

The Pos_Validator class throws exceptions, so you should also wrap the code that uses it in a try . . . catch block.

The complete validation code now looks like this:

```php
$missing = null;
$errors = null;
if (filter_has_var(INPUT_POST, 'send')) {
  try {
    require_once '../Pos/Validator.php';
    $required = array('name', 'email', 'comments');
    $val = new Pos_Validator($required);
    $val->checkTextLength('name', 3);
    $val->removeTags('name');
    $val->isEmail('email');
    $val->checkTextLength('comments', 10, 500);
    $val->useEntities('comments');
    $filtered = $val->validateInput();
    $missing = $val->getMissing();
    $errors = $val->getErrors();
    if (!$missing && !$errors) {
      // Everything passed validation.
      // The validated input is stored in $filtered.
    }
  } catch (Exception $e) {
    echo $e;
  }
}
```

6. How and where you display error messages is up to you, but a simple solution is to create an unordered list. Add the following code between the opening <body> and <form> tags in test_validator.php:

```php
<body>
<?php
if ($missing) {
  echo '<div class="warning">The following required fields have ➥
not been filled in:';
  echo '<ul>';
  foreach ($missing as $field) {
    echo "<li>$field</li>";
  }
  echo '</ul></div>';
}
?>
<form id="form1" name="form1" method="post" action="">
```

The condition tests whether $missing evaluates to true. When the form first loads into the browser, $missing is set to null (note that null should not be in quotes), so it equates to false, skipping the code inside the braces. However, when the form is submitted, the validation script runs, reassigning the result of getMissing() to $missing. If no required fields are missing, the value will be an empty array, which also equates to false; but if anything has been omitted from the required fields, $missing will contain at least one element, which equates to true. If the condition is true, the code inside the braces creates an unordered list of the fields that need to be filled in.

7. Save test_validator.php, and load it into a browser (or use test_validator_05.php from the download files). Leave all the form fields blank, and click the Send comments button. You should see the names of the fields displayed as shown in Figure 4-12.

Figure 4-12. The validator displays the names of required fields that have not been filled in.

8. The same technique can be used for error messages. Add this code inside the same PHP block as in step 6:

```php
if ($errors) {
  echo '<div class="warning">The following errors occurred:';
  echo '<ul>';
  foreach ($errors as $error) {
    echo "<li>$error</li>";
    }
  echo '</ul></div>';
}
```

9. Save test_validator.php, and load it into a browser (or use test_validator_06.php from the download files). Type fewer than three characters in the Name field; put anything except an email address into Email field; and leave the Comments field blank. Click the Send comments button, and you should see both sets of error messages, as shown in Figure 4-13.

Figure 4-13. The validator displays error messages for fields that fail validation.

10. The $_errors property of a Pos_Validator object not only stores the error messages but also uses the field name as the key (index) for each array element. So, instead of displaying list of errors at the top of the page, you can put the error messages alongside the appropriate fields.

Delete the code that you entered in step 8. Amend the code for the name text input field like this:

```
<p><label for="name">Name:
  <?php
  if (isset($errors['name'])) {
    echo '<span class="warning">' . $errors['name'] . '</span>';
  }
  ?>
</label>
<input name="name" type="text" class="textfield" id="name" /></p>
```

11. Do the same for the email and comments fields, using the field's name as the key of the $errors array.

12. Save the page, and test it in the same way as in step 9 (or use test_validator_07.php). This time you should see the error messages alongside the labels, as shown in Figure 4-14.

Figure 4-14. You can display the error messages alongside the relevant fields.

This brief exercise uses only a handful of the validation methods, but the way you use each of them is identical: the first argument is the name of the field being validated, followed by the arguments specific to each method. Apart from the first one, most arguments have a default value, so you need to set them explicitly only if you want to use a different value.

The class works in exactly the same way with the $_GET array, but you need to set the second argument to get, like this:

```
$val = new Pos_Validator($required, 'get');
```

If you want to use the class with the $_GET array without setting an array of required variables, set the first argument to null like this:

```
$val = new Pos_Validator(null, 'get');
```

Sticking to your design decisions

This chapter has presented you with some of the design choices that face the developer of a class. There is no single *right* way to design a class. I have made certain decisions and explained the reasoning behind them. You might come up with a completely different design that is equally valid, or even better. That's fully to be expected. In the process of writing this book, I have constantly refined my code, and I'm sure that I'll come up with new ideas even after the book has gone to the printers.

However, once you decide on a design, it's best to stick with it. Encapsulation leaves you free to change the internal workings of a method, but you should never change its name or the arguments it takes. Doing so breaks existing code that relies on the class. One of my design decisions was to use optional arguments to control the filter flags and options. Let's say I decide at some time in the future that this was a mistake. If I were to completely rewrite the Pos_Validator class, I would also need to amend every script that uses it. A better solution is to leave the existing methods as they are but to add new ones.

For instance, removeTags() has six optional arguments. It works just fine as it is, so there's no need to get rid of it, but I could add a new method called removeTagsEncodeAll() to encode ampersands, single and double quotes, and all characters with ASCII values less than 32 or greater than 127. Similarly, I could add another method called removeTagsStripAll() to strip all characters with ASCII values less than 32 or greater than 127. If I felt that one of the methods was so poorly implemented that it should be completely rewritten and take different arguments, I could use inheritance to solve the problem. By extending Pos_Validator to a new class called, say, Pos_ValidatorImproved, I could override the problem method in the new class. Existing scripts would continue to use Pos_Validator, but new ones would use Pos_ValidatorImproved.

You can make any changes you like to the internal workings of methods and classes, as long as they produce consistent results. When you need to change the way a user interacts with a class and its methods, or the results they produce, create a new class and/or methods, leveraging the advantages of inheritance where possible.

Chapter review

Validation of user input is one of the most important tasks in any web application, and the filter functions introduced in PHP 5.2 are intended to provide a reliable set of standard tests. But they come at the heavy price of complexity. So, I showed you how to implement the Facade design pattern to superimpose a more user-friendly interface on a complex subsystem. You can find full documentation for the Pos_Validator class and its methods in the class_docs folder of the download files.

Although the class file is more than 300 lines long (and twice that length when the PHPDoc comments are added), the validation script in the final exercise is just ten lines. Not only is it more compact and readable, the simpler script makes it easier to avoid mistakes. At the same time, this lays a heavy burden on the developer of the class. If there's an error in the internal logic of a class or its methods, the error remains hidden inside the class and affects all scripts that use it. So, it's important to test each section of code carefully before deploying a class in a live project.

In the next chapter, I'll show you how to solve a common problem: retrieve a file from a remote server, even if your hosting company has disabled allow_url_fopen.

5 BUILDING A VERSATILE REMOTE FILE CONNECTOR

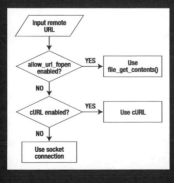

One of PHP's great strengths is its ability to access files on other servers, process them, and incorporate the results into your own output. For example, my web site (http:// foundationphp.com/) automatically runs a PHP script once an hour to send a request to Amazon.com to find the details of the current bestselling books on PHP and Dreamweaver. The results are stored in my database and then displayed on selected pages of my site. A similar technique can be used to display the contents of a news feed from another site. In the next chapter, I'll show you how to handle an incoming news feed, but before you can do so, you need to retrieve the remote file.

Including a remote file directly into your output without checking its content, however, leaves you vulnerable to malicious attacks. Hosting companies naturally perceive this as a major security risk in the hands of inexperienced users and frequently disable the PHP configuration setting that gives access to remote files, allow_url_fopen. To solve this problem, allow_url_fopen was modified in PHP 5.2 to prevent direct inclusion of remote files, and a new configuration directive, allow_url_include, was added. By default, allow_url_fopen is on, and allow_url_include is off. The intention is to close the security gap while still permitting access to remote files that will be processed before use. However, hosting companies are cautious by nature, so there's no guarantee that they will change their ingrained habit of turning off allow_url_fopen.

The PHP cURL (Client URL Library) extension provides an alternative way to retrieve the content of a remote file. It involves a bit more work but is efficient and convenient. The problem with cURL is that it's not enabled by default, so a cURL script won't work on every server. Fortunately, there is a final option to fall back on: using a socket connection. PHP supports socket connections by default, but the code is more complex. Instead of PHP doing all the work seamlessly for you in the background, you need to hand-code the connection to the remote server, send the request, capture the response, and extract the contents of the remote file.

It's a nuisance to have to check which method is available, particularly if you work for different clients on a variety of servers. So, to make life simple, I have created a class that automatically chooses the most direct way of retrieving the content of a remote text file. The advantage of using an object-oriented approach is that the class is entirely project neutral. You simply pass the URL of the remote file to the constructor and capture the result in a variable. In this chapter, you will learn how to

- Verify that a remote URL is valid and sends a response.
- Use PHP stream functions to communicate with a remote server.
- Use cURL or a socket connection if allow_url_fopen is disabled.
- Retrieve the headers returned by the remote server.
- Use regular expressions to separate the headers from the file content.

To keep things simple, the class doesn't handle binary files, such as images or PDF files. It's designed to retrieve web pages in HTML or XHTML, plain text files, and news feeds and other data services formatted in Extensible Markup Language (XML).

Designing the class

This class takes a very straightforward approach. It connects to the remote server, and if the file is readable, it grabs the contents and closes the connection. The simplest way to do this is with file_get_contents() if allow_url_fopen is enabled. The next best way is to use cURL, but again that's not always enabled, so the fallback scenario, as discussed previously, uses a socket connection. Figure 5-1 summarizes the decision process the class uses to find which method of connection is available.

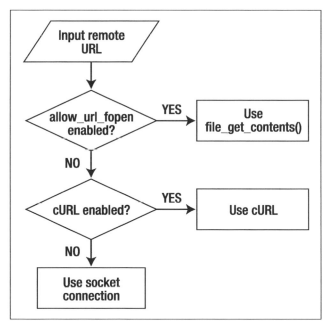

Figure 5-1. The class checks the availability of each connection method and chooses the first available.

Don't worry if you haven't used cURL or a socket connection before. They are just different ways of establishing a remote connection yourself and require only a few lines of code. By encapsulating the connection details inside the class, you write the code only once; thereafter the class handles everything seamlessly. Since the purpose of the class is to retrieve a remote text file, all that it needs to do is return the content of the file or an error message describing what has gone wrong.

The structure of the class is very simple. The constructor needs to accept a single argument: the URL of the remote file that you want to retrieve. It first needs to check that the argument is correctly formatted as a URL. The Pos_Validator class from the previous chapter processes only input from the $_POST or $_GET array, so you need to create a new method to process an internal variable. If the URL is correctly formatted, the constructor decides how to retrieve the remote file and hands off the task to the appropriate internal method. So, in addition to the constructor, you need the following methods, all of which should be hidden from view as protected:

- **checkURL()**: This checks that the URL of the remote file is formatted correctly. It adapts the code from the isFullURL() method from the previous chapter and passes it to filter_var() for validation.
- **accessDirect()**: This uses file_get_contents() to retrieve the remote file if allow_url_fopen is enabled.
- **useCurl()**: This retrieves the remote file when allow_url_fopen is disabled but cURL is enabled.
- **useSocket()**: This uses a socket connection to retrieve the remote file if no other method is available.

Once you have retrieved the contents of a remote file, you need a way of accessing it. Since the result should be a string, defining the __toString() magic method (see Chapter 2) offers an easy way to handle it. You also need a way to show what went wrong if the file cannot be retrieved. So, the class needs the following public methods:

- **__toString()**: This returns the contents of the file retrieved from the remote server.
- **getErrorMessage()**: This returns an error message if there is a problem with the remote file.

A couple of other methods are needed, but I'll explain them at the appropriate stage. Let's get coding.

Building the class

As always, the best way to understand code is to type it out yourself so you know what it contains; but if you want to just read the explanations, you can find the finished class, complete with comments, in RemoteConnector.php in the finished_classes folder of the download files.

Defining the constructor

There is no point attempting to connect to a remote server if the URL isn't correctly formatted, so the role of the constructor is to check the URL's format and then hand off the task of retrieving the file to the appropriate method. The class needs three internal properties to store the URL, the content of the remote file, and an error message.

Following the naming convention I have adopted for this book, I have called the class Pos_RemoteConnector.

1. Create a file called RemoteConnector.php in the Pos folder, and create the basic skeleton of the class definition like this:

```
class Pos_RemoteConnector
{
  protected $_url;
  protected $_remoteFile;
  protected $_error;

  public function __construct($url)
  {
    $this->_url = $url;
  }
}
```

This defines the three protected properties to hold the URL, the content of the remote file, and an error message. The constructor takes one argument, the URL of the file you want to retrieve, and assigns it to the $_url property.

2. Rather than putting all the code to check the URL format in the constructor, I am going to use a separate method called checkURL(), which you'll create shortly. Amend the constructor like this:

```
public function __construct($url)
{
  $this->_url = $url;
  $this->checkURL();
}
```

Notice that I haven't passed the URL as an argument to checkURL(). This is because it's already stored in the $_url property, so it can be accessed directly anywhere inside the class.

3. Now you need to check which method of connection is available. This is a simple series of conditional statements following the flow chart in Figure 5-1. The complete constructor looks like this:

```
public function __construct($url)
{
  $this->_url = $url;
  $this->checkURL();
  if (ini_get('allow_url_fopen')) {
    $this->accessDirect();
  } elseif (function_exists('curl_init')) {
    $this->useCurl();
  } else {
    $this->useSocket();
  }
}
```

The first condition uses ini_get() to check the value of the allow_url_fopen directive in the server's PHP configuration. The function ini_get() normally returns the value of a PHP configuration directive as a string; but when the value is on, it returns 1 (which equates to true), and when it's off, the function returns 0

5

(which equates to false). Consequently, if allow_url_fopen is enabled, the condition succeeds, and the constructor calls the accessDirect() method.

If allow_url_fopen is off, the condition fails, so the second condition is tested. This uses function_exists() to find out if curl_init(), the function that initiates a cURL session, is available. Note that function_exists() takes the name of the function as a string *without* the trailing parentheses. If this test succeeds, it means the cURL extension has been enabled on the local server, so the constructor calls the useCurl() method.

If neither of the previous two tests succeeds, the constructor calls the useSocket() method. PHP enables socket connections by default, so this method should normally always work.

> *I have added a note of caution by saying that* useSocket() *should* normally always work. System administrators can disable features within PHP, so it's possible that you might encounter a server that prevents you from using a socket connection. If that happens to you, it's probably time to look for a different hosting company.*

Checking the URL

The URL passed to the constructor doesn't come from the $_POST or $_GET array, so it cannot be checked with the Pos_Validator class from the previous chapter. To deal with an internal variable, you need to use the filter_var() function together with the appropriate filter constant and flags (see Table 4-4). If the URL isn't correctly formatted, there's no point in continuing, so the method needs to throw an exception.

1. The checkURL() method is very simple, so here it is in its entirety. Add it after the constructor.

```
protected function checkURL()
{
  $flags = FILTER_FLAG_SCHEME_REQUIRED | FILTER_FLAG_HOST_REQUIRED;
  $urlOK = filter_var($this->_url, FILTER_VALIDATE_URL, $flags);
  if (!$urlOK) {
    throw new Exception($this->_url . ' is not a valid URL');
  }
}
```

As you may recall from the previous chapter, the filter_var() function takes up to three arguments: the variable you want to validate or sanitize, the filter you want to apply, and any options or flags. To make sure a full URL is supplied, you need to use two flags separated by the bitwise | operator. I have assigned the flags to a variable to make the code easier to read.

The result of the test is captured in $urlOK. If the URL fails validation, $urlOK is false, triggering an exception with an appropriate message.

2. That's all there is to the checkURL() method, but this is a good point at which to test that you don't have any mistakes in your code so far. Before you can do the test, though, you need to add dummy versions of the three other methods called by the constructor. Add the following code after the definition for checkURL():

```
protected function accessDirect()
{
  echo 'allow_url_fopen is enabled';
}

protected function useCurl()
{
  echo 'cURL is enabled';
}

protected function useSocket()
{
  echo 'Will use a socket connection';
}
```

The echo inside each method simply confirms which access method is available on the local server. You will replace it later with the code that retrieves the remote file.

Testing the constructor and checkURL() method

This exercise tests the code so far. Although it might seem superfluous, testing small amounts of code is more efficient, as it helps identify problems early on. As you'll shortly see, the checkURL() method needs a few tweaks.

1. Create a page called test_connector.php in a new folder called ch5_exercises. Include the Pos_RemoteConnector class using require_once:

```
require_once '../Pos/RemoteConnector.php';
```

2. Assign the URL of a remote file to a variable. It doesn't matter which file you use, but for the purposes of this exercise, I have used the friends of ED news feed like this:

```
require_once '../Pos/RemoteConnector.php';
$url = 'http://friendsofed.com/news.php';
```

3. Inside a try block, create an instance of the Pos_RemoteConnector class, pass the URL to it as an argument, and create a catch block to catch and display any exception message, like this:

```
require_once '../Pos/RemoteConnector.php';
$url = 'http://friendsofed.com/news.php';
try {
  $output = new Pos_RemoteConnector($url);
} catch (Exception $e) {
  echo $e->getMessage();
}
```

5

4. Save `test_connector.php`, and load it into a browser. Alternatively, use `test_connector_01.php` in the download files. You should see a result similar to Figure 5-2. The actual message displayed depends on the configuration of your server. At this stage, `accessDirect()`, `useCurl()`, and `useSocket()` are only dummy methods, so you should see a text message even if the remote server is unavailable.

Figure 5-2. Confirmation that the URL is valid and that allow_url_fopen is enabled on the local server

5. Assuming everything went OK, this confirms that `checkURL()` is working. Before resting on your laurels, though, it's necessary to test it more thoroughly. Introduce a deliberate spelling mistake into the URL by changing `http` to `htp`. Test the page again (or use `test_connector_02.php`).

You probably expect that an exception will be thrown. Instead, you should see exactly the same result as before. Even though the URL is misspelled, the filter function has validated it!

The URL doesn't fail validation because PHP lets you define your own URL schemes. All the validation filter is concerned with is that the first part of the URL *looks* like a **scheme**. The scheme is the first part of the URL (always followed by a colon), which indicates the type of Internet resource it refers to. There are more than 60 official scheme names registered with the Internet Assigned Numbers Authority (IANA), so you need to make sure `checkURL()` accepts only those schemes you want to handle. To keep things simple, I am going to restrict the acceptable schemes to just one: `http`.

6. PHP provides an easy way to examine the different parts of a URL with the function `parse_url()`, which returns an array of its constituent parts. You'll need this array again later when coding the `useSocket()` method, so you should create a property for it.

In `RemoteConnector.php`, add a new protected property called `$_urlParts` to the existing list of properties at the beginning of the class definition like this:

```
protected $_url;
protected $_remoteFile;
protected $_error;
protected $_urlParts;
```

7. The array element that contains the scheme name is called, naturally enough, `scheme`. Amend the `checkURL()` method like this:

```
protected function checkURL()
{
```

```
$flags = FILTER_FLAG_SCHEME_REQUIRED | FILTER_FLAG_HOST_REQUIRED;
$urlOK = filter_var($this->_url, FILTER_VALIDATE_URL, $flags);
$this->_urlParts = parse_url($this->_url);
if (!$urlOK || $this->_urlParts['scheme'] != 'http') {
  throw new Exception($this->_url . ' is not a valid URL');
}
}
```

The new code highlighted in bold assigns to the $_urlParts property the array created by parse_url() and then checks whether the scheme element is http. So, if the URL fails validation or its scheme name is not http, checkURL() throws an exception.

8. Save RemoteConnector.php, and run test_connector.php (or test_connector_02.php) again. This time, you should see the output in Figure 5-3. The checkURL() method is now more robust.

Figure 5-3. The strengthened version of checkURL() detects the invalid scheme name.

9. Try introducing different mistakes in the URL. Removing the colon or one of the slashes preceding friendsofed triggers an exception, but removing the period in the domain name doesn't. Time for another refinement to checkURL().

The array produced by parse_url() contains an element called host, which contains the domain name of the URL. Trying to check for every valid top-level domain requires a lot of code that needs to be updated whenever new ones are approved, so let's keep the test as simple as possible. A domain name must contain at least one period, which cannot come at the beginning, and must be followed by at least two characters. You can test for this with the following Perl-compatible regular expression (PCRE):

```
/^[^.]+?\.\w{2}/
```

Regular expressions are a powerful way of matching patterns, but they can be difficult to master. A PCRE is always surrounded by delimiters, in this case, forward slashes. A caret (^) at the start of the PCRE means "begin at the start of the string." A caret inside square brackets means "match any character except those inside the brackets." So, [^.] matches anything other than a period. The +? means "match at least one, but as few as possible." A period preceded by a backslash looks for a literal period. This regular expression finishes with \w followed by 2 in braces, which means "look for any two alphanumeric characters or underscore." A full discussion of PCRE is beyond the scope of this book, but Table 5-1 lists the most common characters and modifiers used in building regular expressions.

To summarize, this PCRE looks for a string that does not begin with a period, but contains at least one period followed by at least two characters. It's a very crude check, because it accepts something like ?.a_, which doesn't resemble a domain name in the slightest. However, the idea is to catch simple typing errors, rather than to strive to create the perfect PCRE.

> *Creating a PCRE to match a valid domain name is remarkably complex, and there's a danger it could be made obsolete by the approval of new top-level domains. Fortunately, you don't always need to create your own regular expressions, as there are a number of regular expression libraries online. One of the most popular is at* http://regexlib.com/. *The URL is a reference to the other common abbreviation for regular expression—regex.*

Use this PCRE with preg_match() to find a match like this:

```
$domainOK = preg_match('/^[^.]+?\.\w{2}/', $this->_urlParts['host']);
```

The preg_match() function requires two arguments: a PCRE and the string that you want to search. As you'll see later in this chapter, it also takes an optional third argument, which captures an array of matches.

If the value of the host element of $_urlParts matches the pattern, preg_match() returns true. If there's no match, it returns false.

The revised version of checkURL() now looks like this:

```
protected function checkURL()
{
  $flags = FILTER_FLAG_SCHEME_REQUIRED | FILTER_FLAG_HOST_REQUIRED;
  $urlOK = filter_var($this->_url, FILTER_VALIDATE_URL, $flags);
  $this->_urlParts = parse_url($this->_url);
  $domainOK = preg_match('/^[^.]+?\.\w{2}/', $this->_urlParts['host']);
  if (!$urlOK || $this->_urlParts['scheme'] != 'http' || !$domainOK) {
    throw new Exception($this->_url . ' is not a valid URL');
  }
}
```

> *PHP 5 supports two types of regex: PCRE and Portable Operating System Interface (POSIX). Functions that begin with* preg_ *support PCRE, while functions that begin with* ereg *support POSIX. The* ereg *functions have been removed from core PHP 6. For future compatibility, you should always use PCRE with* preg_ *functions.*

> To learn more about regex, see Regular Expression Recipes: A Problem-Solution Approach *by Nathan A. Good (Apress, ISBN-13 978-1-59059-441-4). The standard work on regular expressions (not for faint hearts) is* Mastering Regular Expressions, Third Edition *by Jeffrey Friedl (O'Reilly, ISBN-13 978-0-59652-812-6).*

10. Test the revised class again. When you're happy that checkURL() is working correctly, change the URL in test_connector.php back to its correct value (http://friendsofed.com/news.php).

11. The only way to test the conditional statements that decide which method to call is to misspell allow_url_fopen in the constructor. When you run the test page again, it should display cURL is enabled or Will use a socket connection, depending on the configuration of your server. If cURL is enabled, but you get the wrong message, you know there's something wrong with your code. You can then misspell curl_init, and test the page again.

Misspelling the names doesn't generate any errors. PHP returns false if it doesn't recognize the name of a directive passed to ini_get() or a function passed to function_exists().

Make sure you change the spelling of allow_url_fopen *and* curl_init *back before continuing.* Otherwise, your class won't work as expected.

Table 5-1. Commonly used characters in Perl-compatible regular expressions

Character Sequence	Meaning	Character Sequence	Meaning
\n	New line	*	Match 0 or more times
\r	Carriage return	+	Match at least once
\w	Alphanumeric character or underscore	?	Match 0 or 1 times
		{n}	Match exactly *n* times
\d	Number	{n,}	Match at least *n* times
\s	Whitespace		
.	Any character, except new line	{x,y}	Match at least *x* times, but no more than *y* times
\.	Period (dot)	*?	Match 0 or more times, but as few as possible
^	Beginning of a string		
$	End of a string	+?	Match 1 or more times, but as few as possible

The next task is to access the remote file, using each of the three methods.

Retrieving the remote file

Now that you have confirmed that the constructor and checkURL() method are working, you can turn your attention to retrieving the remote file. The easiest way to do it is with file_get_contents(), so let's start with that.

Defining the accessDirect() method

Using file_get_contents() to retrieve a remote file relies on allow_url_fopen being enabled. I assume that you have a local testing environment with allow_url_fopen turned on. If not, you won't be able to test the code in this section. Even so, I recommend that you read through the explanations.

1. Retrieving a remote file with file_get_contents() couldn't be easier. It takes the URL of the remote file and returns the contents as a string. Remove the echo command from the accessDirect() method, and amend it as follows:

```
protected function accessDirect()
{
  $this->_remoteFile = file_get_contents($this->_url);
}
```

This assigns the result to the $_remoteFile property. Since this is a protected property, it's not accessible outside the class.

2. To give access to the contents of the remote file, define the __toString() magic property in the class file like this:

```
public function __toString()
{
  return $this->_remoteFile;
}
```

This is very straightforward: it returns the $_remoteFile property so you can use a Pos_RemoteConnector object directly in a string context. Let's test it.

Testing the accessDirect() and __toString() methods

These two methods look remarkably simple, so it's important to test them to see if they're robust enough. Continue working with test_connector.php from the previous exercise, or use test_connector_03.php in the download files.

1. Now that you have defined accessDirect() and __toString(), you can display the remote file with echo. Amend the code in test_connector.php like this:

```
require_once '../Pos/RemoteConnector.php';
$url = 'http://friendsofed.com/news.php';
try {
  $output = new Pos_RemoteConnector($url);
  echo $output;
} catch (Exception $e) {
  echo $e->getMessage();
}
```

2. Save `test_connector.phptest_connector.php`, and test it in a browser (or use `test_connector_03.php`). You should see output similar to Figure 5-4.

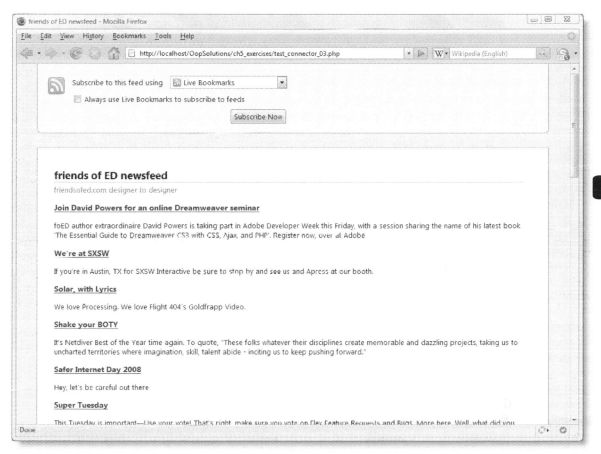

Figure 5-4. The friends of ED news feed looks exactly the same in the browser when retrieved with the class.

Although it looks the same as if you loaded the URL directly into your browser, the important difference is that it's also stored in a PHP variable, so you can later manipulate the content to extract only the information you want.

> *If you get a warning that PHP* `file_get_contents()` *failed, try to access the URL directly in your browser. It's possible that the remote server might be temporarily unavailable. If the script timed out after 30 seconds, it usually means that your firewall is preventing Apache or whichever web server you're using from accessing the Internet.*

3. Delete the "s" at the end of "news" in the URL so $url looks like this:

    $url = 'http://friendsofed.com/**new.php**';

4. This now points to a nonexistent page. Save test_connector.php, and reload the page into a browser (or use test_connector_04.php). This time you should see something similar to Figure 5-5.

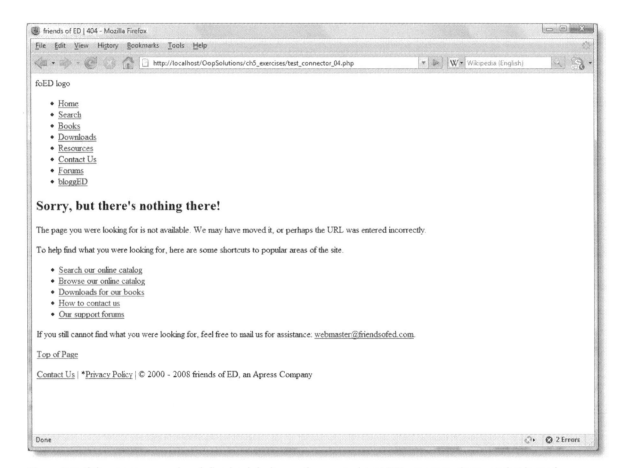

Figure 5-5. If the remote server has defined a default page for a nonexistent URL, you sometimes get that instead.

This isn't the page you intended to get, but there's not a great deal you can do about it. The Hypertext Transfer Protocol (HTTP) headers sent back by the remote server in this sort of case indicate that the page has been found, even if it's not the one you wanted.

5. What happens, though, if you misspell the domain name? Change it to fiendsofed.dom (or any other nonexistent domain name), and reload test_connector.php into a browser (or use test_connector_05.php). This time the result should look like Figure 5-6.

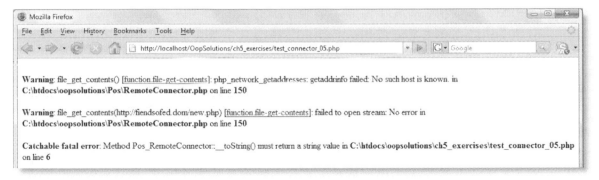

Figure 5-6. The class generates several errors if the URL contains a nonexistent domain name.

The rash of onscreen errors is unacceptable, so we'll need to do something about this.

6. As a final test, change the URL like this:

```
$url = 'http://foundationphp.com/notthere.php';
```

This points to a nonexistent file on my web site. Although I have defined a page to redirect visitors to if they enter a URL for a page that doesn't exist, it's set up in a different way from the friends of ED web site, so it is not loaded by file_get_contents().

7. Save test_connector.php, and reload it in a browser (or use test_connector_06.php). The result should look like Figure 5-7.

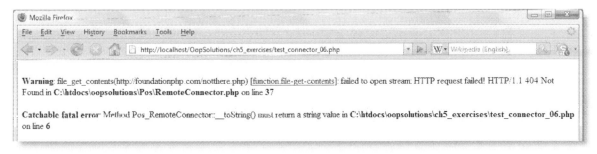

Figure 5-7. Depending on how the remote server is set up, you might get different error messages if the file doesn't exist.

This time, the warning message reports that the file wasn't found. The difference between my site and friends of ED is that mine immediately returns an HTTP status code of 404 ("Not Found") before loading the default page, whereas the friends of ED site uses a redirect command. Once file_get_contents() sees the 404 status, it gives up. You'll see the different status codes returned by both sites later in this chapter when building the useCurl() method.

183

Getting rid of the error messages

The warnings generated by file_get_contents() are easy to remedy. All that's needed is to add the error control operator (@) to that line of code. You can also get rid of the fatal error caused by __toString() by returning an empty string if file_get_contents() returns false. However, the class would be more helpful if it told you why you got an empty string. Let's fix those issues.

1. In RemoteConnector.php, amend the __toString() method like this:

```php
public function __toString()
{
  if (!$this->_remoteFile) {
    $this->_remoteFile = '';
  }
  return $this->_remoteFile;
}
```

This fixes the problem with __toString() if file_get_contents() returns false. However, it's quite possible that the operation succeeded, but the remote file contained nothing. You can check that by examining the HTTP response sent by the server. We'll do that in a moment.

2. Apply the error control operator to the line that calls file_get_contents():

```php
protected function accessDirect()
{
  $this->_remoteFile = @ file_get_contents($this->_url);
}
```

3. The function get_headers() fetches an array of HTTP headers sent in response to a request. It requires one argument: the URL of the request. You can also supply an optional, second argument to format the result as an associative array, instead of an indexed one. If used, the second argument is always 1. However, in both types of array, the header that contains the HTTP status is always contained in the 0 element, so there's no need for the second argument.

Like file_get_contents(), get_headers() displays error messages if the domain name is invalid, so you need to use the error control operator. Amend the accessDirect() method like this:

```php
protected function accessDirect()
{
  $this->_remoteFile = @ file_get_contents($this->_url);
  $headers = @ get_headers($this->_url);
  if ($headers) {
    echo $headers[0];
  }
}
```

I have used echo temporarily to display the header that contains the HTTP status. This is simply for testing purposes. It will be changed later.

4. Save RemoteConnector.php, and test it again with the URL to the nonexistent page on my site (the code is in test_connector_06.php). You should see the result shown in Figure 5-8.

Figure 5-8. Displaying the HTTP status reponse from a nonexistent file

5. This is quite useful, but the equivalent cURL function returns just the status code. An important principle of the object-oriented approach is to delegate tasks to other methods or objects that don't need to know anything about where the data comes from. So the method that deals with error messages needs to receive the HTTP status in a standard format. This means you need to extract the code—in this case 404—from the array element. You can do this with another PCRE. The HTTP status code is always the only three-digit number in the response, so the following PCRE should always find it:

```
/\d{3}/
```

To extract the status code, use preg_match(). As noted earlier, the first argument passed to preg_match() is the PCRE, and the second argument is the string you want to search. If you pass an optional, third argument to preg_match(), it captures an array of matching results. So, alter the accessDirect() method like this:

```php
protected function accessDirect()
{
  $this->_remoteFile = @ file_get_contents($this->_url);
  $headers = @ get_headers($this->_url, 1);
  if ($headers) {
    preg_match('/\d{3}/', $headers[0], $m);
    echo $m[0];
  }
}
```

There should be only one match, so the status code should be in the first element ($m[0]).

6. Save the class file, and test it again. This time you should see only the number 404 onscreen.

7. Displaying the status code was only for testing purposes, so add a new protected property called $_status to the list of properties at the top of the class file, and in accessDirect(), assign $m[0] to this new property. The final listing for accessDirect() looks like this:

```php
protected function accessDirect()
{
  $this->_remoteFile = @ file_get_contents($this->_url);
  $headers = @ get_headers($this->_url, 1);
  if ($headers) {
    preg_match('/\d{3}/', $headers[0], $m);
    $this->_status = $m[0];
  }
}
```

I'll come back later to dealing with the $_status property to handle error messages. Let's deal first with the other ways of retrieving the remote file.

Using cURL to retrieve the remote file

The cURL extension makes communication with remote servers very easy—although not as easy as using the built-in PHP functions such as file_get_contents(). It relies on an external library called "libcurl," which is why it's not enabled by default. You can check whether it's enabled on your server by running phpinfo() and looking for the section shown in Figure 5-9.

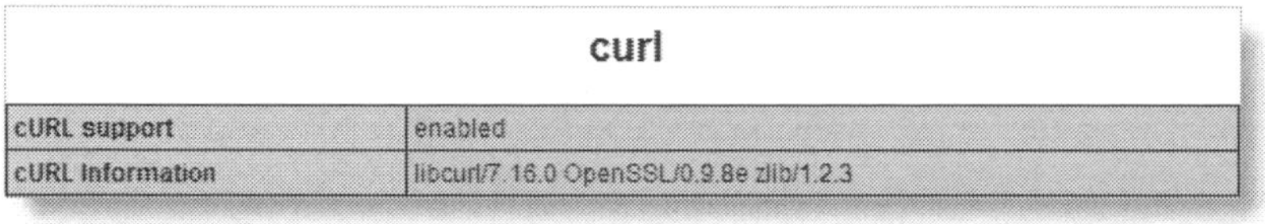

curl	
cURL support	enabled
cURL Information	libcurl/7.16.0 OpenSSL/0.9.8e zlib/1.2.3

Figure 5-9. This section is displayed by phpinfo() if cURL is enabled on your server.

cURL is enabled in the default version of PHP 5 in Mac OS X 10.5, but Windows users need to enable it explicitly. To enable cURL on Windows, select it from the options in the Windows PHP Installer. To do it manually, uncomment the following line in php.ini by removing the semicolon at the start of the line:

```
;extension=php_curl.dll
```

You also need to make sure that php_curl.dll, libeay32.dll, and ssleay32.dll are all in your Windows path.

> Don't confuse the word "session" in the following discussion with PHP session handling using session_start() and the $_SESSION superglobal array. It refers throughout to the session established by cURL to communicate with the remote server. The useCurl() method employs a local variable called $session, but there's no danger of conflict with $_SESSION for two reasons: variable names are case sensitive, and it doesn't begin with an underscore.

Using cURL to retrieve a remote file involves the following steps:

1. Initialize a cURL session with the remote server.

2. Set options for the way you want to retrieve the remote file.

3. Execute the session to get the contents of the remote file.

4. Gather information about the session (such as response headers), if required.

5. Close the session.

The useCurl() method implements each of these steps. The code is quite simple, so here is the listing in full, complete with comments to describe what's happening at each stage:

```
protected function useCurl()
{
  if ($session = curl_init($this->_url)) {
    // Suppress the HTTP headers
    curl_setopt($session, CURLOPT_HEADER, false);
    // Return the remote file as a string,
    // rather than output it directly
    curl_setopt($session, CURLOPT_RETURNTRANSFER, true);
    // Get the remote file and store it in the $remoteFile property
    $this->_remoteFile = curl_exec($session);
    // Get the HTTP status
    $this->_status = curl_getinfo($session, CURLINFO_HTTP_CODE);
    // Close the cURL session
    curl_close($session);
  } else {
    $this->_error = 'Cannot establish cURL session';
  }
}
```

You initiate a cURL session by passing the remote URL to curl_init(). This returns a PHP resource, captured here as $session, which needs to be passed as the first argument to all subsequent cURL functions. If cURL succeeds in establishing a session with the remote server, the conditional statement equates to true, and the code inside the braces is executed. Otherwise, an error message is stored in the $_error property.

To set options for the session, you pass special constants to curl_setopt(). Setting CURLOPT_HEADER to false suppresses the HTTP headers sent by the remote server, and setting CURLOPT_RETURNTRANSFER to true tells cURL that you want to capture the contents of the remote file, rather than outputting it directly to the browser.

Once the options have been set, you execute the session with curl_exec(), and the result is assigned to the $_remoteFile property. Before closing the session, the constant CURLINFO_HTTP_CODE is passed to curl_getinfo() to retrieve the HTTP status response from the remote server and store it in the $_status property. This will be a three-digit code, such as 200 for a file that's successfully retrieved or 404 for a nonexistent one. Finally, the cURL session is closed with curl_close().

> For details of all cURL functions and constants, see
> http://docs.php.net/manual/en/ref.curl.php.

If the session is successfully established, but there's a problem with the remote file, curl_exec() sets the $_remoteFile property to false in the same way as file_get_contents(). This is handled, as before, in the __toString() method. We'll deal later with error messages dependent on the $_status property.

Testing the useCurl() method

Before moving on, it's a good idea to test the class to make sure useCurl() is working correctly. Although you can continue working with test_connector.php from the previous exercises, you might find it easier to use the download files, as the different test URLs are in each file.

1. Assuming that allow_url_fopen is enabled on your local test server, you need to make a temporary change to the Pos_RemoteConnector constructor to prevent it from using the accessDirect() method. Locate the following line in the constructor method:

   ```
   if (ini_get('allow_url_fopen')) {
   ```

   Change it to this:

   ```
   if (ini_get('allow_url_open')) {
   ```

   This is a nonexistent PHP directive, so ini_get() returns false, and the condition fails. As long as cURL is enabled on your server, the constructor now invokes useCurl().

2. Repeat the tests you did in the previous exercise. Start with test_connector_03.php, which contains the correct URL for the friends of ED news feed (http://friendsofed.com/news.php). Assuming that the friends of ED server isn't temporarily unavailable, you should see the same result as in Figure 5-4.

3. Next, try test_connector_04.php, which attempts to access http://friendsofed.com/new.php, a nonexistent page. This time, you should see a blank screen. Unlike file_get_contents(), the cURL session doesn't retrieve the page that you were diverted to before.

4. You will also get a blank screen with test_connector_05.php, which attempts to connect to a nonexistent domain (fiendsofed.dom).

5. Now, try test_connector_06.php, which attempts to retrieve a nonexistent page on my web site (http://foundationphp.com/notthere.php). Instead of seeing the blank page you were probably expecting, you should see the page shown in Figure 5-10.

6. To understand why you get different results with nonexistent pages on different sites with cURL and file_get_contents(), you need to examine the HTTP status code. Amend the final section of the useCurl() method in RemoteConnector.php by adding a line to echo the value of the $_status property like this:

   ```
   $this->_status = curl_getinfo($session, CURLINFO_HTTP_CODE);
   echo $this->_status;
   // Close the cURL session
   curl_close($session);
   ```

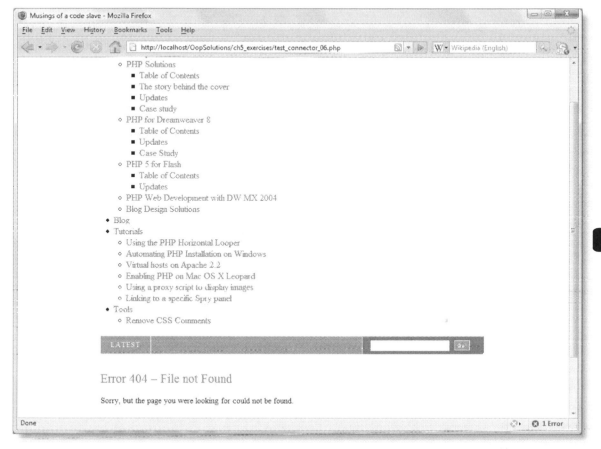

Figure 5-10. Using cURL displays a default page that file_get_contents() was unable to retrieve.

7. Save RemoteConnector.php, and run test_connector_06.php again. You should see the same output again, but with the HTTP status code 404 displayed in the top left corner, as shown in Figure 5-11. This is a number most web developers are familiar with; it means "Not Found."

HTTP status code →

Figure 5-11. Checking the HTTP status code returned by the remote server

8. Run `test_connector_04.php` to access the nonexistent page on the friends of ED web site. This time, you should see 302. This status code paradoxically means "found." According to the official definition (`www.w3.org/Protocols/rfc2616/rfc2616-sec10.html`), the requested page resides temporarily at a different location. For some reason, cURL doesn't follow the redirect. However, since it's pointing to a page that you don't want, it's not important.

> *One of the dangers of writing about the Internet is that web site configurations and URLs are constantly changing. It's possible that you won't get the same status codes from these pages at some stage in the future. It's not the status code returned by a particular page, but the principle of checking the status code that is the focus of attention here.*

9. Check the other test pages. You'll see a status code of 200 returned by the existing page. However, outputting the status code before the page's XML declaration prevents it from being formatted as in Figure 5-4. The page that attempts to access a nonexistent domain still displays a blank page, because there is no server to send an HTTP status code.

10. When you have finished, delete this line from the useCurl() method in RemoteConnector.php:

```
echo $this->_status;
```

There is no need to change back the line you amended in step 1, because you need it that way to test the useSocket() method later.

Using a socket connection to retrieve the remote file

Socket connections are the least user-friendly way of accessing a remote file, as you need to send the request to the remote server in the format it expects. Moreover, the HTTP headers and the body of the remote file are delivered as a single stream, so you need to split them apart. This makes socket connection an ideal candidate for encapsulation. Once the code has been wrapped in a method, you can forget about it and just use the URL in the same way as with file_get_contents().

Using a socket connection involves the following steps:

1. Open a socket connection to the remote server.

2. Prepare the HTTP headers to request the file from the remote server.

3. Send the headers over the socket connection.

4. Capture the response.

5. Close the connection.

6. Separate the HTTP response headers from the body of the file.

In many respects this is similar to using cURL. However, cURL makes things easier by handling the request and response headers cleanly. With a socket connection, you need to create your own code to deal with the headers. Fortunately, handling the request headers is quite easy, because the parse_url() function called in the checkURL() method earlier returns an array containing the following elements:

- **scheme**: This identifies the type of request, for example, http.
- **host**: Depending on the URL, this is the domain name (including subdomain, if appropriate) or IP address of the remote server.
- **port**: This specifies which port to connect on. The port number, if given, comes immediately after the domain name or IP address, separated by a colon, for example, localhost:8500 indicates that the URL uses port 8500 on localhost.
- **user**: Username, for example, in an FTP connection.
- **pass**: Password, for example, in an FTP connection.
- **path**: The path to the file.
- **query**: The query string, minus the leading question mark.
- **fragment**: The fragment identifier at the end of a URL, minus the leading #.

These elements are stored in the $_urlParts property. However, only those elements that exist in the URL are created, so you need to check whether they exist before attempting to use them.

The following instructions show you how to build the useSocket() method step by step and explain the process as you go along:

1. The fsockopen() function that PHP uses to create a socket connection needs to know which port on the remote computer the request must be sent to. Normally, web servers listen for requests on port 80, but if a different port is specified in the URL, it will be in the port element of the $_urlParts property. If the port element doesn't exist, you need to tell fsockopen() to use port 80. Amend the useSocket() method in RemoteConnector.php like this:

```
protected function useSocket()
{
  $port = isset($this->_urlParts['port']) ? $this->_urlParts['port'] ➥
    : 80;
}
```

This uses the conditional operator (?:) to set a local variable, $port, to the value in the $_urlParts property if it exists; otherwise, it's set to 80.

2. The fsockopen() function takes five arguments. Only the first one, the host (domain) name of the remote server, is required, but I'm going to use all five. Add the following line highlighted in bold to the useSocket() method:

```
protected function useSocket()
{
  $port = isset($this->_urlParts['port']) ? $this->_urlParts['port'] ➥
    : 80;
  $remote = fsockopen($this->_urlParts['host'], $port, $errno, ➥
    $errstr, 30);
}
```

5

191

The first two arguments tell fsockopen() the server and port you want to connect to. The next two arguments are used to capture any error messages; $errno captures an error number, and $errstr captures a string describing what went wrong. You don't need to supply any values to them, as they are populated automatically. The final argument sets a timeout limit in seconds for the remote server to respond. I have set it to 30 seconds.

The result is stored in $remote. If the connection is successful this contains a resource that refers to the socket connection. As you'll see shortly, the socket resource is passed to other functions so that PHP knows where to send and receive data. If the connection fails, $remote is set to false.

3. If the socket connection fails, you need to set the $_remoteFile property to false and use $errstr to create an error message in the $_error property. Add the following code to the useSocket() method:

```
protected function useSocket()
{
  $port = isset($this->_urlParts['port']) ? $this->_urlParts['port'] ➡
    : 80;
  $remote = fsockopen($this->_urlParts['host'], $port, $errno, ➡
    $errstr, 30);
  if (!$remote) {
    $this->_remoteFile = false;
    $this->_error = "Couldn't create a socket connection: $errstr";
  }
}
```

4. Assuming fsockopen() establishes a connection, you need to build the request headers to send to the remote server. You need to send the following headers, each followed by a carriage return and new line:

- GET /path/to/file HTTP/1.1

- Host: host_name

- Connection: close

The final header needs to be followed by two carriage returns and new lines.

The path to the file you want to retrieve is stored in the path element of $_urlParts, but you also need to add the query string, if it exists.

You send the request headers by using fwrite() with the socket resource as its first argument. The response is captured using stream_get_contents(), which is similar to file_get_contents(), except that it works with an independently established connection. It also returns the response headers, as well as the file contents. Finally, you close the connection with fclose().

The updated version of useSocket() implements each of these steps. The full listing follows, with the new code highlighted in bold, and inline comments to explain what's going on:

```
protected function useSocket()
{
  $port = isset($this->_urlParts['port']) ? $this->_urlParts['port'] ➡
    : 80;
```

```
$remote = fsockopen($this->_urlParts['host'], $port, $errno, ➥
  $errstr, 30);
if (!$remote) {
  $this->_remoteFile = false;
  $this->_error = "Couldn't create a socket connection: $errstr";
} else {
  // Add the query string to the path, if it exists
  if (isset($this->_urlParts['query'])) {
    $path = $this->_urlParts['path'] . '?' . ➥
      $this->_urlParts['query'];
  } else {
    $path = $this->_urlParts['path'];
  }
  // Create the request headers
  $out = "GET $path HTTP/1.1\r\n";
  $out .= "Host: {$this->_urlParts['host']}\r\n";
  $out .= "Connection: Close\r\n\r\n";
  // Send the headers
  fwrite($remote, $out);
  // Capture the response
  $this->_remoteFile = stream_get_contents($remote);
  fclose($remote);
}
}
```

5. As it now stands, useSocket() retrieves the remote file, but, as I mentioned earlier, it returns both the file and the HTTP response headers as a single stream. So, it's necessary to test the output to see what needs to be done to separate the headers from the body of the file. Before you can do that, you need to define the getErrorMessage() method to display the error message if the socket connection fails. Add this to the Pos_RemoteConnector class definition:

```
public function getErrorMessage()
{
  return $this->_error;
}
```

6. To test useSocket(), both accessDirect() and useCurl() need to be temporarily disabled. accessDirect() should still be disabled from when you tested useCurl(). To disable useCurl(), locate the following line in the Pos_RemoteConnector constructor:

```
} elseif (function_exists('curl_init')) {
```

Change it like this:

```
} elseif (function_exists('cur_init')) {
```

This is the name of a nonexistent function, forcing the condition to fail so the constructor selects useSocket().

7. Adapt test_constructor.php to call the getErrorMessage() method if the socket connection fails, or use the test_constructor_07.php in the download files. The script looks like this:

```
require_once '../Pos/RemoteConnector.php';
$url = 'http://friendsofed.com/news.php';
try {
  $output = new Pos_RemoteConnector($url);
  if (strlen($output)) {
    echo $output;
  } else {
    echo $output->getErrorMessage();
  }
} catch (Exception $e) {
  echo $e->getMessage();
}
```

The conditional statement passes $output to strlen(), which returns the number of characters in a string. Although $output is an object, since PHP 5.2, the __toString() magic method is called in any string context, so, if the $_remoteFile property contains anything, a number greater than zero is returned, equating to true. If the socket connection fails, the $_remoteFile property is an empty string, which equates to false, so the error message should be displayed instead.

8. Test the class by loading test_constructor.php or test_constructor_07.php into a browser. As long as the friends of ED site is accessible, you should see a mass of unformatted text. This is rather difficult to read, so right-click in your browser and view the page source. It should look similar to Figure 5-12.

Figure 5-12. When using a socket connection, you get everything returned by the remote server.

As you can see, the first few lines are the HTTP response headers sent by the remote server. Each header is always on a separate line, and the first blank line indicates the end of the headers. This makes them easy to separate from the rest of the output. Unfortunately, you occasionally get rogue characters before and after the body of the remote file. These will need to be cleaned up, if possible.

9. Run the tests with the other URLs. You can find the code in test_connector_08.php through test_connector_10.php. The results are similar to those with useCurl(). The nonexistent page on the friends of ED site (test_connector_08.php) produces response headers, but no page. The nonexistent domain (test_connector_09.php) generates error messages similar to Figure 5-6, so this means you need to use the error control operator with fsockopen(), which we'll cover in the next step. Finally, the nonexistent page on my site (test_connector_10.php) produces headers and the default "file not found" page.

10. Add the error control operator (@) to the line that calls fsockopen() in useSocket() like this:

```
$remote = @ fsockopen($this->_urlParts['host'], $port, $errno, ➥
    $errstr, 30);
```

11. Save the class file, and run test_connector_09.php again to attempt to connect to the nonexistent domain. This time, you should see the output shown in Figure 5-13.

Figure 5-13. An error message is generated when a socket connection cannot be made.

This certainly looks better than the unsightly PHP warnings, but it could be improved slightly.

12. Locate the following line in useSocket():

```
$this->_error = "Couldn't create a socket connection: $errstr";
```

Because the domain name fiendsofed.dom doesn't exist, fsockopen() fails to contact a remote server, so $errstr isn't populated. Make the error message more user-friendly by adding a conditional statement to the preceding code as follows:

```
$this->_error = "Couldn't create a socket connection: ";
if ($errstr) {
  $this->_error .= $errstr;
} else {
  $this->_error .= 'check the domain name or IP address.';
}
```

13. Run the code in test_connector_09.php again. This time, you should see the message shown in Figure 5-14.

Figure 5-14. The error message is now more informative.

Of course, if $errstr contains anything, the error message displays that instead.

Now let's turn our attention to separating the headers from the body of the remote file and cleaning up rogue characters where possible.

Handling the response headers from a socket connection

Before getting down to the code, let's work out how to handle the headers and the possibility of rogue characters. As I mentioned earlier, the headers are always followed by a blank line. So, you need to split the response from the remote server into an array, using blank lines as the separator between each element. Since the headers precede everything else, the first array element contains the headers. The remaining array elements constitute the body of the file and can be joined back together by inserting a blank line between each element.

Although you don't want to display the headers, they contain useful information. (You can see a typical set at the top of Figure 5-12.) The first header contains the status code, which you need to create an error message if there's a problem retrieving the file. Another useful header is Content-Type. This tells you what type of file is being sent: XML, HTML, plain text, and so on. However, the Content-Type header is present only if the file is successfully retrieved.

If you can find the Content-Type header, you not only know the file was retrieved, you can use the information it contains to determine how to eliminate any random characters, such as those shown in Figure 5-12. The Content-Type header from the friends of ED site looks like this:

```
Content-Type: application/xml
```

This indicates that it's an XML file. A typical HTML page usually sends this header:

```
Content-Type: text/html
```

Both XML and HTML files (assuming they're correctly formed) always begin with an opening angle bracket (<) and end with a closing angle bracket (>). So, all you need to do is look for the first < and last >, capture them and everything in between, and discard the rest. This is easy to do with the following PCRE:

```
/<.+>/s
```

The `.+` in this regular expression means "find any character at least once, but as many as possible." The angle brackets on either side mean that, to register as a match, the result must begin with an opening angle bracket, and end with a closing one. Normally, the period in a PCRE matches everything except new line characters, but adding s after the closing delimiter instructs the regular expression to include new lines. So, this simple but powerful pattern enables you to extract any XML or HTML file cleanly.

Unfortunately, this won't work for text files, so you need to use the Content-Type header to decide whether to use the PCRE. With a text file, there is no way of knowing whether any rogue characters exist, so the only option is to leave the remaining content untouched, apart from stripping whitespace from the beginning and end.

Figure 5-15 shows the decision process that needs to be followed after capturing the response from a socket connection. This is handed off to a new protected method called removeHeaders() that is called at the end of the useSocket() method.

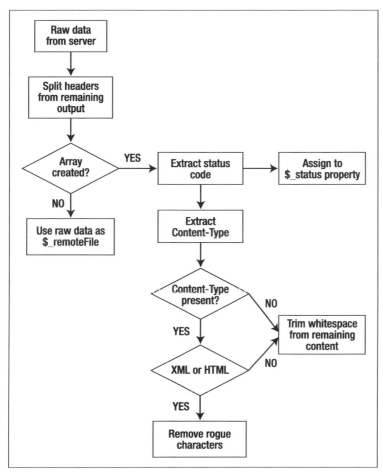

Figure 5-15. The decision process used in processing the raw output from a socket connection

Now that I have explained the underlying logic, let's get down to the code itself.

1. If the socket connection succeeds, the $_remoteFile property is populated with the response from the remote server. If it fails, the $_remoteFile property contains the Boolean value false. In the latter case, there's no point attempting to run removeHeaders(), because there's nothing to work with. So, you can use $_remoteFile to determine whether to call removeHeaders(). Amend the useSocket() method like this, adding the conditional statement highlighted in bold at the end of method (I have listed the entire method here to show the changes made in steps 10–12 of the previous section):

```php
protected function useSocket()
{
  $port = isset($this->_urlParts['port']) ? $this->_urlParts['port'] ➥
    : 80;
  $remote = @ fsockopen($this->_urlParts['host'], $port, $errno, ➥
    $errstr, 30);
  if (!$remote) {
    $this->_remoteFile = false;
    $this->_error = "Couldn't create a socket connection: ";
    if ($errstr) {
      $this->_error .= $errstr;
    } else {
      $this->_error .= 'check the domain name or IP address.';
    }
  } else {
    // Add the query string to the path, if it exists
    if (isset($this->_urlParts['query'])) {
      $path = $this->_urlParts['path'] . '?' . ➥
        $this->_urlParts['query'];
    } else {
      $path = $this->_urlParts['path'];
    }
    // Create the request headers
    $out = "GET $path HTTP/1.1\r\n";
    $out .= "Host: {$this->_urlParts['host']}\r\n";
    $out .= "Connection: Close\r\n\r\n";
    // Send the headers
    fwrite($remote, $out);
    // Capture the response
    $this->_remoteFile = stream_get_contents($remote);
    fclose($remote);
    if ($this->_remoteFile) {
      $this->removeHeaders();
    }
  }
}
```

2. Now let's define the removeHeaders() method, which needs to be protected, as it should only be called directly by the useSocket() method. Begin by adding the following code to RemoteConnector.php:

```
protected function removeHeaders()
{
  $parts = preg_split('#\r\n\r\n|\n\n#', $this->_remoteFile);
  if (is_array($parts)) {
    $headers = array_shift($parts);
    $file = implode("\n\n", $parts);
  }
}
```

This code uses preg_split() to convert the $_remoteFile property into an array, using the following PCRE:

```
#\r\n\r\n|\n\n#
```

This regular expression looks for a blank line by matching a carriage return (\r) and new line feed (\n) immediately followed by another pair, or for two new line feeds in succession. Be careful when typing this. Normally, a PCRE is surrounded by forward slashes as delimiters to mark the beginning and end of the regex, but you can use any nonalphanumeric, nonwhitespace character, such as # or a pair of curly braces. This regex contains a lot of backslashes, so I have used # instead of forward slashes to make it easier to read.

Notice there's a vertical pipe (|) after the second \n. This indicates an alternative pattern. I have added the alternative of two line feeds on their own in case a server doesn't send carriage returns. Another thing to note is that I have used single quotes around the PCRE. Unlike a PHP string, you don't need to enclose \r and \n in double quotes in a regular expression for them to be treated as a carriage return and line feed.

Since you have no idea what the remote server will return, it's important to check that preg_split() succeeds in creating an array. If it does, the code inside the conditional statement is executed. It begins by using array_shift() to remove the first element of the $parts array and reassigns it to $headers. The next line takes the remaining array elements, joins them back together with two new line characters between each element and stores them in a variable called $file. I have not used carriage returns when joining the remaining elements, as it might result in extra spacing on some operating systems.

If preg_split() fails to create an array, nothing happens. The value of $_remoteFile remains unchanged. It's probably unusable, but there's nothing you can do if you can't identify the server's response headers.

3. Following the flow chart in Figure 5-15, the next step, if an array has been created, is to extract the status code. This involves another regular expression:

```
#HTTP/1\.\d\s+(\d{3})#
```

The status code is always a three-digit number preceded by HTTP/1.0 or HTTP/1.1. This PCRE not only matches that pattern, it also contains a subexpression—the

5

199

PHP OBJECT-ORIENTED SOLUTIONS

section enclosed in parentheses—to isolate the status code itself. The regular expression is incorporated into the removeHeaders() method like this:

```
protected function removeHeaders()
{
  $parts = preg_split('#\r\n\r\n|\n\n#', $this->_remoteFile);
  if (is_array($parts)) {
    $headers = array_shift($parts);
    $file = implode("\n\n", $parts);
    if (preg_match('#HTTP/1\.\d\s+(\d{3})#', $headers, $m)) {
      $this->_status = $m[1];
    }
  }
}
```

This uses preg_match() to find the status code in the headers. The first argument is the PCRE; the second argument is the string you want to search; and the third argument is a variable that is used to catch any matches. If a match is found, the variable passed as the third argument contains an array, the first element of which is the match for the entire regular expression. If the PCRE contains subexpressions, the subsequent elements of the array contain the result of each subexpression in the order it appears in the regular expression.

The response headers shown in Figure 5-12 begin like this:

HTTP/1.1 200 OK

The regular expression matches this:

HTTP/1.1 200

This value is stored in the first element of the array, $m[0]. The subexpression matches 200, and its value is stored in the second element of the array, $m[1].

Again, you can't be sure there will be a match, so preg_match() is enclosed in a conditional statement. If it succeeds, the status code in $m[1] is assigned to the $_status property.

4. The next step is to find whether the headers contain Content-Type, using the following PCRE:

#Content-Type:([^\r\n]+)#i

This locates Content-Type, and the subexpression in parentheses captures everything after the colon to the end of the line. The i at the end of the PCRE performs a case-insensitive search. Amend removeHeaders() like this:

```
protected function removeHeaders()
{
  $parts = preg_split('#\r\n\r\n|\n\n#', $this->_remoteFile);
  if (is_array($parts)) {
    $headers = array_shift($parts);
    $file = implode("\n\n", $parts);
    if (preg_match('#HTTP/1\.\d\s+(\d{3})#', $headers, $m)) {
      $this->_status = $m[1];
    }
```

```
      if (preg_match('#Content-Type:([^\r\n]+)#i', $headers, $m)) {
        // Handle according to Content-Type
      } else {
        $this->_remoteFile = trim($file);
      }
    }
  }
}
```

If there's a match, you need to handle the body of the file according to the value of Content-Type. If there's no match, it usually means that the remote file couldn't be found, so the else clause removes any whitespace at the beginning and end of $file and assigns it to the $_remoteFile property. In most circumstances, this results in $_remoteFile containing an empty string.

5. There's one last section to add. This examines the value of Content-Type and decides whether to use the regular expression /<.+>/s to extract the body of an XML or HTML file, as explained at the beginning of this section. There are many possible values for Content-Type that can be used by XML and HTML files, but there's no need to check them all. Fortunately, the Content-Type for an XML file always contains the string "xml," and for an HTML file, it contains "html."

   To locate either string, you can use stripos(), which returns the position (counting from zero) of the first character of a matching string in a case-insensitive search. Although no current definitions of valid types begin with "xml" or "html," it's a good idea to use the "not identical" operator (!==) to make sure a result of 0 isn't interpreted as a false negative. The final version of removeHeaders() looks like this:

```
protected function removeHeaders()
{
  $parts = preg_split('#\r\n\r\n|\n\n#', $this->_remoteFile);
  if (is_array($parts)) {
    $headers = array_shift($parts);
    $file = implode("\n\n", $parts);
    if (preg_match('#HTTP/1\.\d\s+(\d{3})#', $headers, $m)) {
      $this->_status = $m[1];
    }
    if (preg_match('#Content-Type:([^\r\n]+)#i', $headers, $m)) {
      if (stripos($m[1], 'xml') !== false || stripos($m[1], 'html') ➥
        !== false) {
        if (preg_match('/<.+>/s', $file, $m)) {
          $this->_remoteFile = $m[0];
        } else {
          $this->_remoteFile = trim($file);
        }
      } else {
        $this->_remoteFile = trim($file);
      }
    }
  }
}
```

201

Because the PCRE for Content-Type uses a subexpression, the value you're looking for is contained in $m[1]; but the PCRE that extracts the XML or HTML contains no subexpression, so the value you're looking for is $m[0].

If the Content-Type contains "xml" or "html," the PCRE is used to extract the body of the file. Otherwise, it's likely to be a text file, so whitespace is removed from the beginning and end of $file, and the result assigned to the $_remoteFile property.

The removeHeaders() method is quite short but requires a good understanding of PCRE. Study it in conjunction with Figure 5-15, and you should be able to follow the logic, even if you don't understand the regular expressions.

There's just one thing left to do: use the status code to generate a suitable error message if the remote file can't be retrieved.

Generating error messages based on the status code

So far, the only time the class generates an error message is when the URL contains an invalid domain name. However, you need to be able to tell the user what has gone wrong if the class fails to retrieve the remote file. Regardless of which method is used to connect to the remote server, the HTTP status code is stored in the $_status property. You can use this to generate an appropriate error message.

1. Amend the getErrorMessage() method like this:

```
public function getErrorMessage()
{
  if (is_null($this->_error)) {
    $this->setErrorMessage();
  }
  return $this->_error;
}
```

The $_error property is set only if the class fails to connect to the remote server. Otherwise, $_error is null. So, if $_error is null when getErrorMessage() is invoked, you need to set a value by calling a new internal method, setErrorMessage().

2. The setErrorMessage() method checks the value of the $_status property and assigns a message to the $_error property. The messages are based on the status codes listed at www.w3.org/Protocols/rfc2616/rfc2616-sec10.html. If the status code is 200 (OK) and the $_remoteFile property contains a value, the error message is set to an empty string. Otherwise, a switch statement sets an appropriate message. Rather than using the official definition of each status code, I have grouped similar ones together. The case statements fall through until they hit a break. Here is the listing in full:

```php
protected function setErrorMessage()
{
  if ($this->_status == 200 && $this->_remoteFile) {
    $this->_error = '';
  } else {
    switch ($this->_status) {
      case 200:
      case 204:
        $this->_error = 'Connection OK, but file is empty.';
        break;
      case 301:
      case 302:
      case 303:
      case 307:
      case 410:
        $this->_error = 'File has been moved or does not exist.';
        break;
      case 305:
        $this->_error = 'File must be accessed through a proxy.';
        break;
      case 400:
        $this->_error = 'Malformed request.';
        break;
      case 401:
      case 403:
        $this->_error = 'You are not authorized to access this page.';
        break;
      case 404:
        $this->_error = 'File not found.';
        break;
      case 407:
        $this->_error = 'Proxy requires authentication.';
        break;
      case 408:
        $this->_error = 'Request timed out.';
        break;
      case 500:
        $this->_error = 'The remote server encountered an internal error.';
        break;
      case 503:
        $this->_error = 'The server cannot handle the request at the moment.';
        break;
      default:
        $this->_error = 'Undefined error. Check URL and domain name.';
        break;
    }
  }
}
```

5

Final testing

The final tests of the Pos_RemoteConnector class involve running test_connector_07.php through test_connector_10.php again. They should display the following results:

- test_connector_07.php: The friends of ED news feed, as shown in Figure 5-4
- test_connector_08.php: An error message reading "The file has been moved or does not exist"
- test_connector_09.php: The error message shown in Figure 5-14
- test_connector_10.php: The "file not found" page shown in Figure 5-10

After verifying that everything is working, you need to reenable the accessDirect() and useCurl() methods by correcting the spelling of allow_url_fopen and curl_init in the constructor method, as shown here:

```
public function __construct($url)
{
  $this->_url = $url;
  $this->checkURL();
  if (ini_get('allow_url_fopen')) {
     $this->accessDirect();
  } elseif (function_exists('curl_init')) {
     $this->useCurl();
  } else {
     $this->useSocket();
  }
}
```

As always, the class definition in the download files is fully commented, and the documentation generated by PHPDocumentor is in the class_docs folder.

Ideas for improving the class

The class is designed to work with nonbinary files only, but it makes no attempt to check whether the requested URL is for an image or other binary file, such as a PDF or Word document. To improve the class, you could check the filename extension in the checkURL() method. Alternatively, you could extend the class to handle binary files. The accessDirect() method uses file_get_contents(), which is binary safe. To override the useCurl() method for binary files, use the CURLOPT_BINARYTRANSFER constant with curl_setopt(). The removeHeaders() method also needs to be overridden and return the content on the basis of the value of the Content-Type header.

An extended class also needs a property to store the Content-Type header, getter methods for this property, and the content of the binary file. I'll leave that as a challenge for you to tackle on your own. By this stage, you should have the knowledge and confidence to start designing your own classes and extending existing ones.

Chapter review

The class you created in this chapter is an example of the **Proxy design pattern**. All you are interested in is retrieving the file on the remote server; the details of how to do it are left up to the class to decide. Using the __toString() magic method means you can use the Pos_RemoteConnector object directly in any string context without the need to call a separate getter method. The only time you need to invoke a method on the object is to display an error message if the class returns an empty string. All the error handling is performed inside the class, leaving you with clean, simple code in your main script.

Retrieving the remote file and HTTP status code with file_get_contents() and get_headers() or cURL is very easy, because you can access them individually. Working with a socket connection is more complicated, as everything is sent in a single stream, but you can extract all the relevant information with Perl-compatible regular expressions. Although creating regular expressions is difficult to master, it's a skill you need to acquire if you want to use PHP to its full potential.

In the next chapter, you'll put the Pos_RemoteConnector class to good use by retrieving a remote file and using SimpleXML to extract the information you want from it. SimpleXML has been a core part of PHP since version 5, so there are no class files to build; you just use it straight out of the box.

5

6 SIMPLEXML—COULDN'T BE SIMPLER

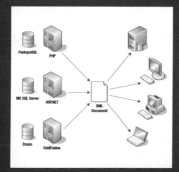

The main reason I migrated to PHP 5 within a month or two of its original release in July 2004 can be summed up in one word: SimpleXML. As the name suggests, it simplifies handling data stored in XML, which is frequently used for news feeds and transmitting data for web services, such as Google Maps and Amazon Web Services. Extracting data from an XML file in PHP 4 was so convoluted; my brain hurt just looking at the code. With SimpleXML, it became child's play.

In this chapter, you'll learn about:

- What XML is and what it's used for
- Extracting data from an XML document with SimpleXML
- How to modify the contents of an XML document
- Using SimpleXML with namespaces
- Locating data inside an XML document using XPath

SimpleXML is part of core PHP, so it's automatically available. It consists of a single built-in class called `SimpleXMLElement`, which has ten public methods and three helper functions. Before getting into the details of how to use SimpleXML, I think it would be helpful to explain briefly what XML is for and what it looks like. If you're already up to speed on XML, feel free to skip the next section.

A quick XML primer

Although Extensible Markup Language (XML) has been around since 1996, many web developers are still unclear about its purpose. Typical comments I have seen in online forums suggest that it's "the future of the Web," or "a new type of database." Both views are completely wrong, but, as often happens with misperceptions, they're based on a grain of truth.

What is XML?

XML, quite simply, is a platform-neutral way of storing data in a format that is easy for both humans and computers to understand. Let's say you wanted to get information from three different web sites: one runs a combination of PHP and the PostgreSQL database, another runs ASP.NET and Microsoft SQL Server, and the third uses ColdFusion and an Oracle database. Apart from the security implications of giving outsiders direct access to databases, this would require completely different coding for each one. However, XML gets around this problem very easily by using a simple, common format in plain text. As illustrated in Figure 6-1, an XML document acts as a bridge between computers, allowing them to share information even if they have completely different configurations and operating systems.

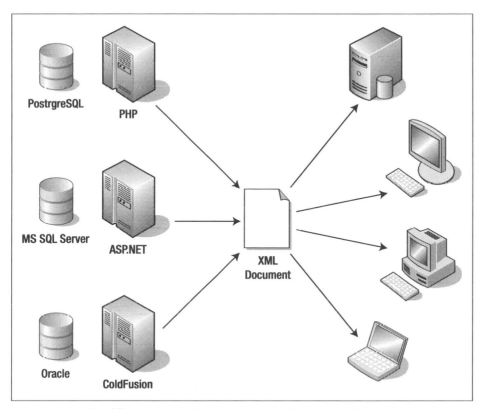

Figure 6-1. XML lets different systems share data by using a format they all understand.

The originating server generates the XML document either in response to a specific request or as a public feed. The recipient takes no interest in how it's generated by the originating server. Equally, the originator doesn't need to know anything about the technology used by the recipient. XML is a standard format; it's a common language that enables different systems to talk to each other. How the originator and recipient handle the data is left entirely up to them. In this chapter, I'll show you how to process XML with SimpleXML, and in Chapters 8 and 9, I'll show you how to generate your own XML for others to consume.

XML uses tags in the same way as HTML. However, unlike HTML, there isn't a fixed range of tags and attributes. As long as you follow certain basic rules, you can name tags and attributes whatever you want. So, if you want to store details of books, you can create tags for <author>, <publisher>, and so on.

The big difference between HTML and XML is that HTML tags tell you how a page is organized, by using tags like <h1>, <h2>, and <p>; an XML document contains no information about the layout or structure of a page. In fact, an XML document doesn't necessarily represent a page. What's more, it might not even exist as a physical file on the originating server. In practice, XML documents are frequently generated dynamically by a database in response to an incoming request. The server analyzes the request, queries the database to get the most up-to-date information, and sends the result to the recipient formatted as XML.

So, what does XML look like?

How XML documents are structured

The following is an example of a simple XML document with details of two books (you'll work with a longer version of this document in exercises later in the chapter; it's inventory.xml in the ch6_exercises folder):

```xml
<?xml version='1.0' encoding='utf-8'?>
<inventory>
  <book isbn13='978-1-43021-011-5'>
    <title>PHP Object-Oriented Solutions</title>
    <author>David Powers</author>
    <publisher>friends of ED</publisher>
    <description>A gentle introduction . . . </description>
  </book>
  <book isbn13='978-1-59059-819-1'>
    <title>Pro PHP: Patterns, Frameworks, Testing and More</title>
    <author>Kevin McArthur</author>
    <publisher>Apress</publisher>
    <description>Written for readers seeking . . . </description>
  </book>
</inventory>
```

The first line is the **XML declaration**, often also referred to as the **XML prolog**, which tells browsers and processors that it's an XML document. The XML declaration is recommended but not required. However, if you include it, the XML declaration *must* be the first thing in the document. There cannot be anything else before it—not even blank lines or comments. The version attribute in this example tells the recipient that it's XML 1.0. Although there is a later version (1.1), the World Wide Web Consortium (W3C) does *not* recommend using it unless you need its highly specialized features (www.w3.org/TR/2004/REC-xml11-20040204/#sec-xml11). Stick with XML 1.0. This example also contains an encoding attribute. This is required if you plan to use anything other than Unicode (utf-8 or utf-16). Since this document is encoded as utf-8, the encoding attribute could be omitted, but it's a good idea to include it to avoid ambiguity.

As you can see from this example, the tags give no indication as to how the document is intended to look. In fact, they normally shouldn't, because XML is intended primarily to store data in a hierarchical structure according to meaning and without any reference to presentation. Figure 6-2 shows the hierarchy inside the XML file.

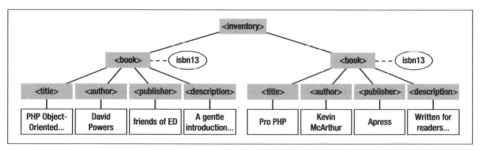

Figure 6-2. The XML document viewed as a tree diagram

At the top level is <inventory>, which contains everything else inside the document. This is known as the **root element**. At the next level are two <book> elements, each of which has an isbn13 attribute. Within each <book> element are four elements named <title>, <author>, <publisher>, and <description> that each contain a text element or **node**.

In descriptions of XML, "element" and "node" are frequently used interchangeably. For most purposes, you can regard them as the same, although there are subtle differences in some circumstances. XML defines seven types of nodes, namely:

- **The root node**: This contains everything in the XML document, including the root element.

- **Element nodes**: An element node can contain other element nodes, a text node, or be empty. The concept of an empty element is explained in the following section.

- **Attribute nodes**: An attribute node is a name/value pair in an element's opening tag.

- **Text nodes**: A text node is the literal text between an element's opening and closing tags. Take the following line from the previous example:

```
<publisher>friends of ED</publisher>
```

The whole line, including the opening and closing tags, is an element node. The text between the tags—in other words, friends of ED—is the text node.

- **Comment nodes**: These serve the same purpose as (X)HTML comments and use the same <!-- --> syntax, for example:

```
<!-- This is an XML comment -->
```

- **Processing instruction nodes**: These pass instructions to the application processing the XML document. They cannot occur inside an element. A processing instruction always begins with <? and ends with ?>. (Yes, it's exactly the same as the short form of PHP tags, which is why the short opening tag is no longer recommended in PHP.) Immediately following the opening question mark is a name identifying how the instruction should be processed. The following example shows a processing instruction to apply a style sheet to an XML document:

```
<?xsl-stylesheet href="styles.css" type="text/css"?>
```

211

- **Namespace nodes**: Namespaces are a way of preventing clashes between elements from different sources. This is done by associating a series of characters (usually two or three) with a URL as a unique identifier. The name of a namespace node is prefixed by these characters followed by a colon. The following example taken from the friends of ED news feed (http://friendsofed.com/news.php) shows a namespace node that uses the dc namespace to identify the date of an item:

```
<dc:date>2008-04-09T02:03:10-08:00</dc:date>
```

Namespaces are explained in more detail later in this chapter.

Unless you are working in a large collaborative project that needs to use a standardized vocabulary, you can make up your own tags, as I have done here. They can be made up not only of alphanumeric characters but also accented characters, Greek, Cyrillic, Chinese, and Japanese—in fact, any valid Unicode character. However, they cannot include any whitespace or punctuation other than the hyphen (-), underscore (_), and period (.), nor can they begin with xml in any combination of uppercase or lowercase letters.

The goals of XML include being human-legible, and terseness is considered of minimal importance. So, instead of using <pub>, which could mean publisher, publication date, or somewhere to get a drink, I have been specific and used <publisher>.

> An example of a standardized XML vocabulary that should be familiar to many web developers is MXML, which is used by the Flex framework (http://flex.org/) for creating rich Internet applications. friends of ED has published a series of books about Flex, including The Essential Guide to Flex 3 by Charles E. Brown (ISBN13: 978-1-59059-950-1). Other specialized vocabularies include Mathematic Markup Language, MathML (www.w3.org/Math/), and Scalable Vector Graphics, SVG (www.w3.org/Graphics/SVG/).

The rules of writing XML

The most important thing about an XML document is that it must be **well formed**. The main rules of what constitutes a well-formed document are as follows:

- There can be only one root element.
- Every start tag must have a matching closing tag.
- Empty elements can omit the closing tag, but, if they do so, must have a forward slash before the closing angle bracket (/>).
- Elements must be properly nested.
- Attribute values must be in quotes.
- In the content of an element or attribute value, < and & must be replaced by < and & respectively.

An empty element is one that doesn't have any content, although it can have attributes that point to content stored elsewhere. To borrow an example from XHTML, which is HTML 4.01 reformulated to adhere to XML rules, <img> is an empty element. The src attribute points to the location of the image, but the tag itself is empty. To comply with XML rules, it can be written as `<img src="mypic.jpg"></img>` or use the shorthand `<img src="mypic.jpg"/>`. (I have omitted the other attributes for brevity.) To avoid problems with older browsers, a space is normally inserted before the closing forward slash in XHTML, but this is *not* a requirement of XML.

If you look at the previous example, you will see that it has only one root element: `<inventory>`. All other elements are nested inside the root element, and the nesting follows an orderly pattern. This predictability is what makes it easy for a computer to process. It also makes it easy for humans to understand.

Using HTML entities in XML

Among the conditions of being well formed is the need to replace < and & with the HTML entities < and & in the content of an element or attribute value. This often leads to the misconception that XML supports the full range of HTML entities, such as é (for é). It doesn't. XML understands only the following five entities: < (<), & (&), > (>), " ("), and ' (').

When creating an XML document in an accented language, such as Spanish, French, or German, you should use accented characters in the same way as in ordinary text. A key principle of XML is that it should be human-readable.

Inserting HTML and other code in XML

A common mistake made by newcomers to XML is to try to insert an HTML link in a text node like this:

```
<publisher><a href="http://www.apress.com/">Apress</a></publisher>
```

It won't work. XML has no concept of what an `<a>` tag or `href` attribute means. Not only that, the `<a>` tag is treated as another element. "Apress" is no longer the text node of the `<publisher>` element. As Figure 6-3 shows, the hierarchy has changed; the `<a>` element is now a child of `<publisher>`, and "Apress" is the text node inside `<a>`.

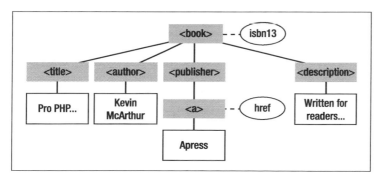

Figure 6-3. Inserting an HTML tag into a text node alters the hierarchy of the XML tree.

Although this is still valid XML, attempting to extract information from this type of hierarchy rapidly becomes an exercise in frustration. When embedding HTML code in a text node, you either need to convert the angle brackets of the tags into < and > or wrap the code in a CDATA section (CDATA stands for "character data"). Using a CDATA section is much simpler.

A CDATA section begins with the following opening tag:

```
<![CDATA[
```

To close a CDATA section, use the following tag:

```
]]>
```

To embed the `<a>` tag in a CDATA section, change the previous example like this:

```
<publisher><![CDATA[<a href="http://www.apress.com/">Apress</a>]]>
</publisher>
```

This restores the XML tree to the original hierarchy shown in Figure 6-2. Everything between the opening and closing tags of a CDATA section is treated as raw data. The `<a>` tag is no longer treated as a separate XML element, but as part of the `<publisher>` text node.

You can put anything inside a CDATA section; the only thing that cannot appear inside one is the same sequence of characters as the closing tag. An opening angle bracket is not treated as the start of a tag, and an ampersand is not regarded as the beginning of an HTML or numeric entity. This is particularly important when you want to include JavaScript in an XML text node, because converting the less-than (<) and greater-than (>) operators to < and > breaks the code. With a CDATA section, they are safe.

After that whirlwind tour of XML, let's take a look at how to extract information from an XML document with SimpleXML.

> *If you want to learn more about the basics of XML, a good starting place is the XML FAQ, edited by Peter Flynn, at* http://xml.silmaril.ie.

Using SimpleXML

As the name suggests, SimpleXML offers an easy way of accessing information in an XML document. The price you pay for that simplicity is that it's not capable of performing complex operations on XML. Nevertheless, what it does, it does very well, and is likely to be adequate for a wide range of operations. It's particularly suited to extracting data from news feeds, where you know in advance the structure of the XML document.

Table 6-1 lists the public methods in SimpleXML. You'll cover each one as you progress through the chapter.

Table 6-1. Public methods of the SimpleXMLElement class

Method	Arguments	Description
addAttribute()	$name, $value	Adds an attribute to the current element. Both arguments are required.
addChild()	$name, $value	Adds a new element to the current node. The second argument is optional and adds a text node to the new element. When only one argument is supplied, this creates an element node ready to receive new child nodes.
asXML()	$filename	The argument is optional. If supplied, the XML is saved to the designated file. When no argument is used, this method returns a string.
attributes()	$namespace, $is_prefix	Returns an array of attributes associated with the current node. Both arguments are optional and are used only when working with namespace nodes (see "Using SimpleXML with namespaces" later in this chapter).
children()	$namespace, $is_prefix	Returns an array of the current node's children. Both arguments are optional and are used only when working with namespace nodes.
getDocNamespaces()	$bool	Returns an array of namespaces declared in the document, regardless of whether they are used. If the optional Boolean argument is set to true, all declared namespaces are returned. Otherwise, it returns only those declared in the root element.
getName()		Returns the name of the current node. This applies to both element and attribute nodes.

6

Continued

Table 6-1. *Continued*

Method	Arguments	Description
getNamespaces()	$bool	Returns an array of namespaces actually used in the document. If the optional Boolean argument is set to true, all utilized namespaces are returned. Otherwise, it returns only the namespace used by the root element.
registerXPathNamespace()	$prefix, $url	Registers a namespace prefix for use with the xpath() method.
xpath()	$xpath	Locates XML elements using XPath (see "Using SimpleXML with XPath" later in this chapter).

For most of the examples in this chapter, I'm going to use a static XML file, inventory.xml, which you can find in the ch6_exercises folder of the download files. It contains details of six books published by friends of ED and its parent company, Apress. The basic structure of inventory.xml was shown in Figure 6-2 earlier in the chapter. Two of the books have more than one author. In those cases, multiple <author> elements are nested inside the <book> element like this:

```
<book isbn13="978-1-43020-991-1">
  <title>Foundation Web Standards: Design with CSS, XHTML, and ➥
    AJAX</title>
  <author>Lynn Kyle</author>
  <author>Jonathan Lane</author>
  <author>Joe Lewis</author>
  <author>Steve Smith</author>
  <publisher>friends of ED</publisher>
  <description>Introduces the key concepts . . . </description>
</book>
```

Multiple elements with the same tag are perfectly valid in XML, just as you can have as many <p> or <div> tags as you like in an ordinary web page. However, as you'll see shortly, multiple instances of the same element inside another element require special handling.

Figure 6-4 shows the web page you'll build over the next few pages using information extracted from inventory.xml. As you can see, the multiple authors from the third <book> element have been combined into a single line with the correct punctuation. I have kept the design simple, in order to concentrate on the mechanics of working with SimpleXML, but in a real application, this would probably be just part of a more complex page.

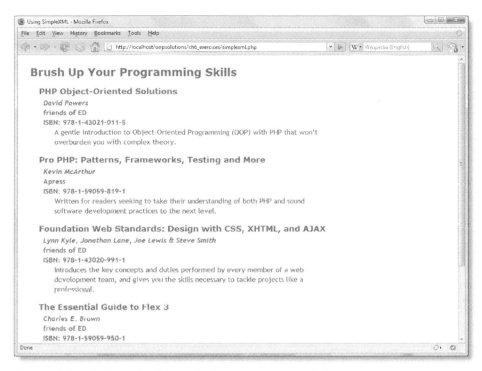

Figure 6-4. SimpleXML makes light work of incorporating an XML document into a web page.

Loading an XML document with SimpleXML

As I mentioned earlier, SimpleXML uses a built-in class called SimpleXMLElement. It converts an XML document into a SimpleXMLElement object. This contains an array of all the element, text, and attribute nodes, each of which is, in turn, a SimpleXMLElement object. What makes it so easy to use is that the name of each node becomes a property of the object, giving you direct access to it.

First, you need to load the XML document that you want to process. There are several ways of doing this, depending on whether the XML document is stored as a physical file (either locally or on a remote server) or as a string (e.g., after using the Pos_RemoteConnector class from the previous chapter).

Loading XML from a file

The easiest way to load an XML document from a file is to use the simplexml_load_file() function. This requires a single argument: a string containing either the path to a local file or the URL of the file on a remote server. You use it like this:

```
$xml = simplexml_load_file($location);
```

Alternatively, you can use the SimpleXMLElement class constructor. When used with a file, it requires two extra arguments, in addition to the file's path or URL, like this:

```
$xml = new SimpleXMLElement($location, null, true);
```

The second argument sets Libxml parameters (see http://docs.php.net/manual/en/libxml.constants.php), which are rarely used. Even though you don't normally want them, the argument needs to be set to null because the third argument is required when the XML document is stored as a physical file, rather than a string. The third argument is a Boolean value that needs to be set to true.

There's no advantage to using the SimpleXMLElement constructor unless you need the advanced features offered by the Libxml parameters. Keep things simple by using simplexml_load_file().

> To access a remote file with either simplexml_load_file() or the SimpleXMLElement constructor, allow_url_fopen must be enabled on the server submitting the request.

Loading XML from a string

If the XML document is stored as a string, the SimpleXMLElement constructor needs only the first argument:

```
$xml = new SimpleXMLElement($xmlAsString);
```

Alternatively, you can use the simplexml_load_string() function like this:

```
$xml = simplexml_load_string($xmlAsString);
```

Loading the XML document as a string comes in useful if allow_url_fopen is disabled. You can access the remote file with, for example, the Pos_RemoteConnector class from the previous chapter, store the result, and pass it either to the SimpleXMLElement constructor or to simplexml_load_string().

For the time being, though, let's work with a local XML file and simplexml_load_file().

> As you'll see in the next chapter, simplexml_load_file() and simplexml_load_string() can take optional arguments that make SimpleXML even more powerful, so it's generally better to use them in preference to the SimpleXMLElement constructor.

Creating and examining a SimpleXMLElement object

This brief exercise loads a local XML document, inventory.xml, converts it into a SimpleXMLElement object, and examines its contents. All the files are available in the ch6_exercises folder of the download files.

1. Create a page called simplexml.php in the ch6_exercises folder, and insert the following code (it's in simplexml_01.php):

```
$xml = simplexml_load_file('inventory.xml');
echo '<pre>';
print_r($xml);
echo '</pre>';
```

This is very straightforward. It loads inventory.xml into the page, and stores it as $xml. The contents of $xml is then displayed using print_r(). The pair of <pre> tags is there to make the output easier to read.

2. Save simplexml.php, and load it into a browser (or use simplexml_01.php). You should see the output shown in Figure 6-5.

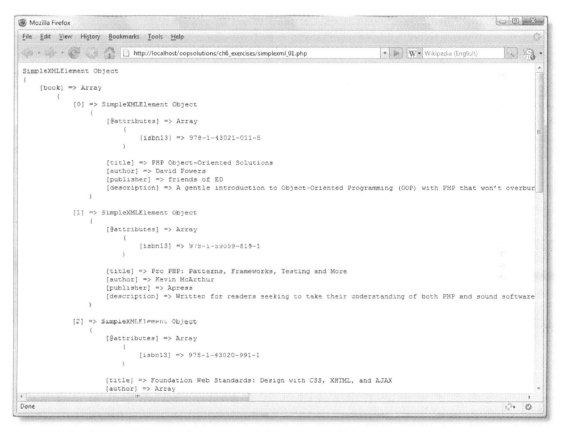

Figure 6-5. SimpleXML converts the XML document into an array of objects.

As you can see from Figure 6-5, the XML document has been converted into an array. But look carefully. It's no ordinary array. The first line of output from print_r() tells you it's a SimpleXMLElement object. That's followed by this line:

```
[book] => Array
```

This reflects the structure of inventory.xml, which consists of six <book> elements contained inside a root element called <inventory>. Notice that there's no sign of the root element in the output; SimpleXML goes directly to the element nodes. Also notice that each element of the book array in the output is labeled as another SimpleXMLElement object.

The fact that book is an array makes it easy to use a foreach loop to deal with the object stored in $xml. However, since each element of the array is, in itself, a SimpleXMLElement object, the array doesn't always work how you might expect. Scroll down to the third item, which looks like this:

```
[2] => SimpleXMLElement Object
(
  [@attributes] => Array
  (
    [isbn13] => 978-1-43020-991-1
  )

  [title] => Foundation Web Standards: Design with CSS, XHTML, and AJAX
  [author] => Array
  (
    [0] => Lynn Kyle
    [1] => Jonathan Lane
    [2] => Joe Lewis
    [3] => Steve Smith
  )

  [publisher] => friends of ED
  [description] => Introduces the key concepts . . .
)
```

This is one of the books with multiple authors. The author element of the SimpleXMLElement object is described here as an array, but as you'll see in the "Displaying the book details" exercise later, you can't use implode() to join the authors' names as a comma-separated string. In fact, you'll see that it isn't really an array at all.

So, let's see how you access the contents of an XML document with SimpleXML.

Extracting data with SimpleXML

As you have just seen, SimpleXML mirrors the tree hierarchy of the XML document just like a multidimensional array. This makes accessing the data very easy by iterating through the element nodes with a foreach loop. Each element node is treated as a property of the object.

Since there are multiple <book> elements in inventory.xml, you need to identify which one you want. You do this by counting from zero in the same way as with an array. So, the first book is $xml->book[0], and the third book is $xml->book[2].

Accessing text nodes

Each element node is a `SimpleXMLElement` object in its own right. If it has child nodes, you access them in the same way—as properties. The title of the first book is accessed like this: `$xml->book[0]->title`. If the element contains a text node, you can use the property in the same way as a string.

The following code displays the first book title from `inventory.xml` (the code is in `simplexml_02.php`):

```
$xml = simplexml_load_file('inventory.xml');
echo $xml->book[0]->title;
```

This displays onscreen as PHP Object-Oriented Solutions.

The following code (in `simplexml_03.php`) loops through each `<book>` element to access the text in its `<title>` element, and produces the output shown in Figure 6-6:

```
$xml = simplexml_load_file('inventory.xml');
foreach ($xml->book as $book) {
  echo $book->title . '<br />';
}
```

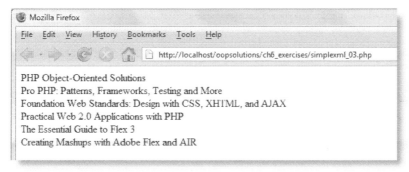

Figure 6-6. With SimpleXML, it takes just a few lines of code to extract the `<title>` element from each book.

> Although I am using echo in these examples, it's simply a convenient way of exposing the value. You can assign the value of a text node to another variable, or store it in an array for processing later. Alternatively, you can incorporate the value into a SQL query to insert it into a database.

Accessing attributes

The opening tag of each `<book>` element in `inventory.xml` contains an attribute called `isbn13`. To access an attribute by name, you use the same syntax as for an array element. The `isbn13` attribute of the fourth book is accessed like this: `$xml->book[3]['isbn13']`.

221

The following code (in simplexml_04.php) displays the title and ISBN of the fourth book, as shown in Figure 6-7:

```
$xml = simplexml_load_file('inventory.xml');
echo $xml->book[3]->title . ' (ISBN: ' . $xml->book[3]['isbn13'] . ')';
```

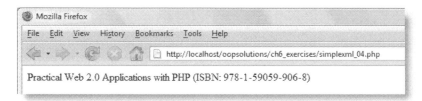

Figure 6-7. XML attributes are just as easy to extract with SimpleXML.

Accessing unknown nodes

Most of the time, when using SimpleXML, you know the structure of the XML document, so you can directly access the nodes you're interested in. However, SimpleXML provides two methods—one for element nodes, the other for attribute nodes—that give access to values without referring to them by name.

To access element nodes, use the children() method; and to access attributes, use the attributes() method. The getName() method reveals the name of the current node and can be used with both elements and attributes.

> *The children() and attributes() methods don't take any arguments in the following example, because the XML document doesn't use namespaces. Working with name-spaces is covered later in this chapter.*

The following code (in simplexml_05.php) loops through inventory.xml extracting the name and value of each element, and produces the output shown in Figure 6-8:

```
$xml = simplexml_load_file('inventory.xml');
// Get the element nodes at the top level of the XML document
$children = $xml->children();
// Loop through each top level node to display its name
foreach ($children as $child) {
  echo 'Node name: ' . $child->getName() . '<br />';
  // Get the attributes for the current node
  $attributes = $child->attributes();
  // Loop through the attributes of the current node
  foreach ($attributes as $attribute) {
    echo 'Attribute ' . $attribute->getName() . ": $attribute<br />";
  }
  // If the current node has no children, display its value
  if (false === $nextChildren = $child->children()) {
    echo "$child<br />";
```

```
  } else {
    // Otherwise loop through the next level
    foreach ($nextChildren as $nextChild) {
      echo $nextChild->getName() . ": $nextChild<br />";
    }
    echo '<br />';
  }
}
```

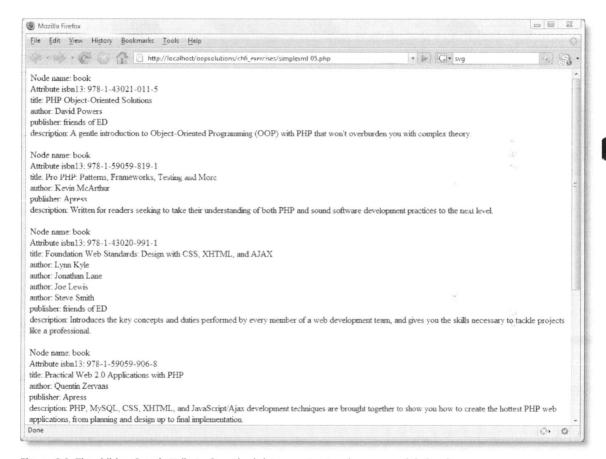

Figure 6-8. The children() and attributes() methods let you extract node names and their values.

An important thing to note is how the multiple authors are treated. As you can see in Figure 6-8, the output for the third book displays the names of all four authors. Remember that print_r() in the previous exercise listed them as an array numbered from zero, but here the element names are given simply as author. The children() method preserves the same hierarchy as in the XML document. You'll see how to handle multiple elements in the next exercise.

Using the children(), attributes(), and getName() methods results in code that is much harder to read. What's more, I have cheated somewhat because I know the structure of inventory.xml, so the code goes no further than a second level of element nodes, and it knows exactly where to look for the attributes. To probe an unknown XML document, you would need to write more complex code. However, SimpleXML is usually the wrong tool for working with an unknown XML document.

It's useful to know what these methods are for, but you rarely use them. SimpleXML is principally designed to work with XML documents that have a predictable structure. When working with a document the first time, access the raw XML in a browser and establish its hierarchy before using SimpleXML.

> *The Document Object Model (DOM) and Simple API (Application Programming Interface) for XML (SAX) extensions, or XMLReader are more suited to processing unpredictable XML documents. For a detailed discussion of the PHP DOM and SAX extensions and XMLReader, see* Pro PHP XML and Web Services *by Robert Richards (Apress, ISBN13: 978-1-59059-633-3).*

Now that you have seen the main ways of accessing data in an XML document, let's display the contents of inventory.xml as shown in Figure 6-4.

Displaying the book details

This exercise extracts the details from inventory.xml and displays them in a web page. Along the way, you'll see what happens when you try to treat multiple elements as an array. To make the page look slightly more attractive, I have created a style sheet called simplexml.css, which you can find in the ch6_exercises folder.

1. Open simplexml_06.php in the ch6_exercises folder. It contains the following code:

```
<!DOCTYPE html PUBLIC "-//W3C//DTD XHTML 1.0 Transitional//EN"
  "http://www.w3.org/TR/xhtml1/DTD/xhtml1-transitional.dtd">
<html xmlns="http://www.w3.org/1999/xhtml">
<head>
<meta http-equiv="Content-Type" content="text/html; charset=utf-8" />
<title>Using SimpleXML</title>
<link href="simplexml.css" rel="stylesheet" type="text/css" />
</head>

<body>
<h1>Brush Up Your Programming Skills</h1>
</body>
</html>
```

This is a basic XHTML skeleton, a link to the simplexml.css style sheet, and a heading.

2. You're going to display the details of the books after the heading. It doesn't matter where you put the code to load the XML document, as long as the SimpleXMLElement object is available before you attempt to use it. I find the best place to put code that doesn't send any output to the browser is out of the way above the DOCTYPE declaration. Load inventory.xml the same as in all previous exercise files like this:

```
$xml = simplexml_load_file('inventory.xml');
```

3. Insert the following PHP block after the heading in the main body of the page (the code is in simplexml_07.php):

```php
<h1>Brush Up Your Programming Skills</h1>
<?php
foreach ($xml->book as $book) {
  echo '<h2>' . $book->title . '</h2>';

  echo '<p class="author">';
  if (is_array($book->author)) {
    echo implode(', ', $book->author);
  } else {
    echo $book->author;
  }
  echo '</p>';

  echo '<p class="publisher">' . $book->publisher . '</p>';
  echo '<p class="publisher">ISBN: ' . $book['isbn13'] . '</p>';

  echo '<p>' . $book->description . '</p>';
}
?>
</body>
```

This uses a foreach loop to iterate through the <book> elements, accessing each text node as a property of $xml->book, and using the array square bracket syntax to access the isbn13 attribute.

The section of code I want to draw your attention to is the way $book->author is treated. As you saw earlier in the chapter, when the SimpleXMLElement object was examined with print_r(), multiple <author> elements in the same <book> element are shown as an array. So, it would seem logical to use is_array() to test whether $book->author is an array. If it is, implode() joins the array elements as a comma-separated list. If it isn't an array, the else clause simply displays $book->author unchanged.

4. Save the page, and load it into a browser. Alternatively, use simplexml_07.php. The output is shown in Figure 6-9. As you can see, only one author's name is displayed for each book. The is_array() test has failed.

6

225

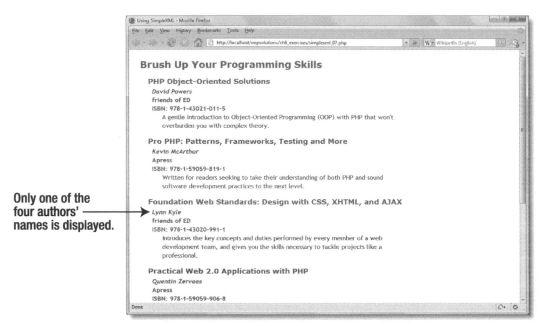

Figure 6-9. Treating the multiple authors as an array doesn't work.

5. Return to your script editor, delete the conditional statement that displays $book->author, and replace it with the following line highlighted in bold (the code is in simplexml_08.php):

```
echo '<p class="author">';
echo gettype($book->author);
echo '</p>';
```

This uses gettype() to find out the data type of $book->author.

6. Test the page in a browser again (or use simplexml_08.php). As Figure 6-10 shows, it doesn't matter whether $book->author contains one value or several, *it's always an object*.

Figure 6-10. Everything extracted from an XML file by SimpleXML is an object.

When used in a string context, SimpleXMLElement objects always display any text content. If there is no text content (in other words, the object represents an element node), it displays nothing—not even an error message. If the text content is held in an array, as in the case of the third book in inventory.xml, it displays only the first text element.

So, how do you display the remaining authors?

7. As you have already discovered, SimpleXMLElement objects can be used in a foreach loop to iterate through the element nodes. Contrary to what you might expect, it doesn't matter if the object contains only a single text node; it's still safe to use foreach. So, one way to handle this situation is to use a foreach loop to display each author with a trailing blank space like this (the code is in simplexml_09.php):

```
echo '<p class="author">';
foreach($book->author as $author) {
  echo $author . ' ';
}
echo '</p>';
```

This works, but it's not very elegant. You can't use a trailing comma instead, because you end up with an unwanted comma after the names of solo authors.

8. The answer is to use a different type of loop. You can use count() to find out how many elements a SimpleXMLElement object contains, and then use the value to control a for loop. Amend the section that displays the authors like this (the code is in simplexml_10.php):

```
$num_authors = count($book->author);
echo '<p class="author">';
for ($i = 0; $i < $num_authors; $i++) {
  echo $book->author[$i];
  // If there's only one author, break out of the loop
  if ($num_authors == 1) {
    break;
  } elseif ($i < ($num_authors - 2)) {
    // If there are more than one authors left, use a comma
    echo ', ';
  } elseif ($i == ($num_authors - 2)) {
    // Otherwise insert an ampersand
    echo ' &amp; ';
  }
}
echo '</p>';
```

The inline comments explain what's going on. The counter, $i, keeps track of the position in the loop and is used to identify the correct $book->author using array-style square bracket syntax and a series of conditional statements determine what, if anything, to insert after the author's name.

9. Save the page, and load it into a browser (or use simplexml_10.php). The result should now look the same as Figure 6-4.

6

Apart from the section of code needed to format multiple authors, the code required to extract and display the information from the XML document is very simple. The names of the element nodes give you direct access to the text they contain. The structure of inventory.xml is relatively shallow, but it doesn't matter how many levels are nested inside each other; you just daisy-chain the element names to get to the level you want. For example, inventory2.xml in the download files contains a new element called <price> with two nested elements: <paperback> and <ebook>. The XML document now looks like this (I have included only the first book to save space):

```
<inventory>
  <book isbn13='978-1-43021-011-5'>
    <title>PHP Object-Oriented Solutions</title>
    <author>David Powers</author>
    <publisher>friends of ED</publisher>
    <description>A gentle introduction . . . </description>
    <price>
      <paperback>$36.99</paperback>
      <ebook>$25.89</ebook>
    </price>
  </book>
</inventory>
```

To access the paperback price, you just move down the hierarchy like this: $book->price->paperback. You can see the code used to display the prices in simplexml_11.php. (The prices are for illustrative purposes only and might not be current.)

Saving and modifying XML with SimpleXML

Most of the time, you will probably want to use SimpleXML just to extract information from an XML document and display it, as in the preceding exercises, or use it to build a SQL query to insert it into a database. However, there are times when it's useful to access XML from a remote source and save it locally. For example, many web services update information only once an hour or once a day. Rather than accessing the remote XML every time someone views your web site, it makes more sense to create a local copy, and update it periodically. SimpleXML not only lets you save XML data, but you can also modify it.

Outputting and saving SimpleXMLElement objects

The asXML() method of the SimpleXMLElement class serves a dual purpose. When used without an argument, it returns a string containing the XML of the current object. However, if you pass a filename as an argument to asXML(), it saves the XML to the file (assuming the folder is writable).

The output is slightly different depending on whether asXML() is called on the object that contains the whole document or one of its properties. If called on the whole document, asXML() includes the XML declaration in its output. However, this is omitted when asXML() is called on an individual node. The examples in simplexml_12.php through simplexml_15.php should make things clear.

The code in simplexml_12.php looks like this:

```
$xml = simplexml_load_file('inventory.xml');
header('Content-Type: text/xml');
echo $xml->asXML();
```

It loads inventory.xml, stores it in $xml, and uses asXML() with echo to display it. The header() function in the second line tells the browser to expect XML. Figure 6-11 shows its output in a browser. As you can see from the source view, it includes the XML declaration, because asXML() is called on the object that contains the whole document.

The XML declaration is included.

Figure 6-11. The asXML() method includes the XML declaration when called on the full document.

In contrast, the code in simplexml_13.php, calls asXML() on the property that holds the details of the second book. It looks like this:

```
$xml = simplexml_load_file('inventory.xml');
header('Content-Type: text/xml');
echo $xml->book[1]->asXML();
```

As you can see from Figure 6-12, only the <book> element and its contents are output. The XML declaration is not included.

The XML declaration has not been added.

Figure 6-12. When used on an individual node, asXML() leaves out the XML declaration.

The code in simplexml_14.php and simplexml_15.php demonstrates how asXML() works when a filename is passed to it as an argument. The code in simplexml_14.php looks like this:

```
$xml = simplexml_load_file('inventory.xml');
if ($xml->asXML('inventory_copy.xml')) {
  echo 'XML saved';
} else {
  echo 'Could not save XML';
}
```

The asXML() method returns true if it succeeds in saving the XML to the file. So, if you load simplexml_14.php into a browser, it should display XML saved and create inventory_copy.xml in the same folder. Since $xml contains the whole document, the XML declaration is included at the top of the file.

> *If the target file supplied as an argument to asXML() already exists, it is silently overwritten. No warning is given. This is normally what you want, particularly when using asXML() to update a local version of an XML document from a remote source. If you want to preserve the existing version, you need to generate a new name, such as by appending a timestamp before the .xml filename extension.*

The code in simplexml_15.php creates an XML file called book2.xml containing the <book> node for the second book. The only difference is in the second line, which looks like this:

```
if ($xml->book[1]->asXML('book2.xml')) {
```

If you load simplexml_15.php into a browser, and then check book2.xml in the same folder, you'll see that it contains no XML declaration.

So, how do you add an XML declaration when you want to create an XML file from just part of a SimpleXMLElement object?

The answer is quite simple: use asXML() without an argument to return a string, and then use file_put_contents() to save both an XML declaration and the XML to a file like this (the code is in simplexml_16.php):

```
$xml = simplexml_load_file('inventory.xml');
$output = "<?xml version='1.0' encoding='utf-8'?>\n";
$output .= $xml->book[1]->asXML();
if (file_put_contents( 'book2_dec.xml', $output)) {
  echo 'XML saved';
} else {
  echo 'Could not save XML';
}
```

If you load `simplexml_16.php` into a browser, `book2_dec.xml` should be created in the same folder. Open it, and you should see the details of the second book stored as XML together with an XML declaration like this:

```
<?xml version='1.0' encoding='utf-8'?>
<book isbn13="978-1-59059-819-1">
  <title>Pro PHP: Patterns, Frameworks, Testing and More</title>
  <author>Kevin McArthur</author>
  <publisher>Apress</publisher>
  <description>Written for readers seeking . . . </description>
</book>
```

> *The examples in this section all rely on loading the PHP file manually into a browser. However, PHP can also be used for scripts scheduled to run automatically (as a cron job on Linux or a scheduled event on Windows). This involves running PHP from the operating system's command line. For details of the PHP Command Line Interface (CLI), see* `http://docs.php.net/manual/en/features.commandline.php`.

Modifying SimpleXMLElement objects

You can modify `SimpleXMLElement` objects in the following ways:

- Changing the values of text and attributes
- Removing text, attribute, or element nodes
- Adding new nodes and attributes

Let's take a brief look at each of them.

Changing the values of text and attributes

This is very easy. You simply assign the new value to the property you want to change. The following code (in `modify_xml_01.php`) loads `inventory2.xml`, reduces the price of the paperback version of each book by ten percent, and displays the modified XML onscreen:

```php
$xml = simplexml_load_file('inventory2.xml');
foreach ($xml->book as $book) {
  // Remove the dollar sign
  $reduced = substr($book->price->paperback, 1);
  // Multiply by .9 to give 10% discount
  $reduced *= .9;
  // Format the number, and reassign it to the original property
  $book->price->paperback = '$' . number_format($reduced, 2);
}
header ('Content-Type: text/xml');
echo $xml->asXML();
```

The inline comments explain what's going on here. The prices in the <paperback> nodes are formatted as U.S. currency, so the substr() function removes the dollar sign before the value is multiplied by 0.9. The dollar sign is then replaced, and the number formatted to two decimal places with number_format().

Removing nodes and values

This is also very easy: use unset(). The following code (in modify_xml_02.php) removes the isbn13 attribute, as well as the <publisher>, <price>, and <description> nodes:

```php
$xml = simplexml_load_file('inventory2.xml');
foreach ($xml->book as $book) {
  unset($book['isbn13']);
  unset($book->publisher);
  unset($book->price);
  unset($book->description);
}
header ('Content-Type: text/xml');
echo $xml->asXML();
```

As you can see in Figure 6-13, removing the <price> node also removes its child nodes, <paperback> and <ebook>, together with all the values they contained.

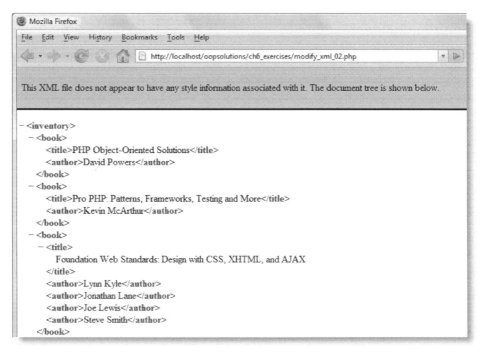

Figure 6-13. Using unset() removes nodes and their values.

If, for any reason, you want to preserve a node but remove its value, simply change its value to an empty string instead of using unset().

Adding attributes

The intuitively named addAttribute() method adds an attribute to an existing element tag. It takes two arguments: the name of the attribute and the value to be assigned. The following code (in modify_xml_03.php) shows addAttribute() in action, adding a category attribute to each <book> node:

```
$xml = simplexml_load_file('inventory2.xml');
foreach ($xml->book as $book) {
  if (strpos($book->title, 'PHP') !== false) {
    $book->addAttribute('category', 'PHP');
  } else {
    $book->addAttribute('category', 'Web design');
  }
}
header ('Content-Type: text/xml');
echo $xml->asXML();
```

This uses strpos() to detect whether the <title> node contains "PHP". Since "PHP" could be at the start of the title, which returns a value of 0, it's necessary to use false with the not identical operator (!==) to avoid getting a false negative. Figure 6-14 shows the output of this code (I have collapsed the <description> and <price> tags in the screenshot to save space).

Figure 6-14. The addAttribute() method has added a category attribute to each <book> tag.

Adding new elements

The addChild() method adds a new child element to the current node. It takes up to three arguments. The first one, the name of the new element, is required. The other two are optional. The first of these is the value you want to add to the new element; the other specifies the namespace to which you want the element to belong. I'll discuss namespaces later in the chapter. For the moment, let's just concentrate on the first two arguments.

You might be wondering, "What's the point of adding a new element without a value?" The answer is that you might want to add an element node that doesn't contain any text but acts as the parent to other elements. Examples of this in inventory2.xml are the <book> and <price> nodes.

The addChild() method returns the newly created element, so you can use it to add children to it. The following code (in modify_xml_04.php) first creates a <distributor> element as a child of each <book> element and then nests three new elements inside it:

```php
$xml = simplexml_load_file('inventory2.xml');
foreach ($xml->book as $book) {
  $distributor = $book->addChild('distributor');
  $distributor->addChild('company', 'Springer-Verlag New York, Inc.');
  $distributor->addChild('location', 'New York, NY');
  $distributor->addChild('country', 'USA');
}
header ('Content-Type: text/xml');
echo $xml->asXML();
```

Figure 6-15 shows the result of this code, as displayed in the first <book> element (as before, I have collapsed the <description> and <price> nodes in the screenshot).

The new <distributor> element has three child elements of its own. →

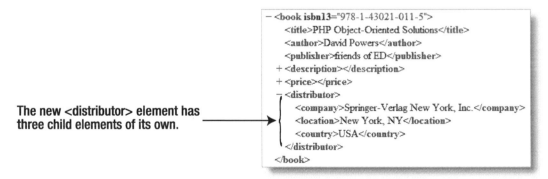

```
- <book isbn13="978-1-43021-011-5">
    <title>PHP Object-Oriented Solutions</title>
    <author>David Powers</author>
    <publisher>friends of ED</publisher>
  + <description></description>
  + <price></price>
  - <distributor>
      <company>Springer-Verlag New York, Inc.</company>
      <location>New York, NY</location>
      <country>USA</country>
    </distributor>
  </book>
```

Figure 6-15. The addChild() method can create new elements and text nodes, and nest them within each other.

Although I have modified an existing XML file to demonstrate the use of addChild() and addAttribute(), they can also be used in combination with the SimpleXMLElement constructor to generate a new XML document like this (the code is in createXML.php):

```
// Create the root element
$newXML = new SimpleXMLElement('<root></root>');
// Add an element node
$book1 = $newXML->addChild('book');
// Add child nodes with text nodes
$book1->addChild('title', 'Build Your Own XML');
$book1->addChild('author', 'All My Own Work');

// Add a second element node with child nodes
$book2 = $newXML->addChild('book');
$book2->addChild('title', 'Transcendental XML');
$book2->addChild('author', 'XML Guru');

// Send an XML header and output the XML to a browser
header('Content-Type: text/xml');
echo $newXML->asXML();
```

This produces the very basic XML document shown in Figure 6-16.

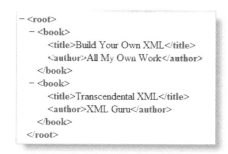

Figure 6-16. You can build XML from scratch with SimpleXML.

All the values are hard-coded in this example, but in a real application, they would probably be generated dynamically by looping through the results of a database query.

Using SimpleXML with namespaces

The ability to choose your own names for tags makes XML very flexible, but it presents a problem when XML from different sources is combined in a single document. Common tag names, such as <title>, are often used with very different meanings, so you need a way to tell which is which. XML solves this problem with a concept called namespaces.

How namespaces are used in XML

In XML, you give a set of tags a unique identity by declaring a **namespace** in the root element's opening tag with the xmlns attribute. One namespace that you're probably familiar with, even if you didn't know what it's for, is in the opening <html> tag of every XHTML document, which looks like this:

```
<html xmlns="http://www.w3.org/1999/xhtml">
```

The URL in the xmlns attribute doesn't need to point to a real document. Its sole purpose is to give the namespace a unique identity.

In the previous chapter, you worked with the friends of ED news feed at http://friendsofed.com/news.php (see Figures 5-4 and 5-12). The root element tag is much more complicated, and looks like this:

```
<rdf:RDF xmlns:dc="http://purl.org/dc/elements/1.1/"
         xmlns:h="http://www.w3.org/1999/xhtml"
         xmlns:hr="http://www.w3.org/2000/08/w3c-synd/#"
         xmlns:rdf="http://www.w3.org/1999/02/22-rdf-syntax-ns#"
         xmlns="http://purl.org/rss/1.0/">
```

In addition to the xmlns attribute, there are four others that begin with xmlns followed by a colon and one or more letters. The xmlns on its own defines the **default namespace**. The others define **namespace prefixes**; the letter or letters after the colon are prefixes that can be prepended to element or attribute names to identify which namespace they belong to. The name of the opening tag itself (rdf:RDF) is an example of a namespace prefix in use; the tag name is RDF, and it belongs to the rdf namespace. Tags in the default namespace have no prefix.

Declaring a namespace in an XML document is optional. There's no need for one if the document stands alone and there's no danger of conflicts. However, when you come across XML documents that use namespace prefixes, you need to know how to handle them, because SimpleXML doesn't treat namespace prefixes in the same way as tags without a prefix.

Handling namespace prefixes in SimpleXML

Figure 6-17 shows the basic XML structure of the friends of ED news feed. The root element <rdf:RDF> has one child element called <channel> and a large number of elements called <item>. The <channel> element contains several child nodes with information about the feed; the news items are in the series of <item> elements, each of which contains the following children: <title>, <description>, <link>, and <dc:date>.

SimpleXML treats the root element differently from all other nodes. The root element is loaded automatically, regardless of whether the tag has a namespace prefix, so the <rdf:RDF> root element of the friends of ED feed needs no special treatment. However, child elements that use a namespace prefix, such as <dc:date>, need to be handled differently. The simplest way to show you is through a practical exercise.

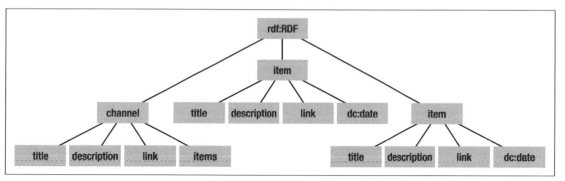

Figure 6-17. The basic structure of the friends of ED news feed

Displaying the friends of ED feed

This exercise demonstrates the difference in the way SimpleXML handles elements in the default namespace and those in a different namespace. It uses the Pos_RemoteConnector class from the previous chapter to access a remote news feed. If you didn't build the class yourself, you can find a copy in the finished_classes folder. You need to copy it to the Pos folder for the following code to work.

1. For testing purposes, it's a good idea to create a local version of the remote feed to avoid the need for repeated connections to the Internet. Insert the following code into a PHP file (or use get_feed.php in ch6_exercises):

```php
require_once '../Pos/RemoteConnector.php';
try {
  $foed = new Pos_RemoteConnector('http://friendsofed.com/news.php');
  if ($foed) {
  $xml = simplexml_load_string($foed);
  if ($xml->asXML('foed.xml')) {
    echo 'XML saved';
  } else {
    echo 'Could not save XML';
  }
  } else {
    echo $foed->getErrorMessage();
  }
} catch (Exception $e) {
  echo $e->getMessage();
}
```

237

This combines code from the previous chapter with code from "Outputting and saving SimpleXMLElement objects" earlier in this chapter. The important thing to note is that the fifth line of code uses simplexml_load_string(), *not* simplexml_load_file(). This is because a Pos_RemoteConnector object returns the remote file *as a string*.

2. Save the page, and load it into a browser. As long as the friends of ED site is available, you should see XML saved onscreen and a local copy of the news feed saved as foed.xml. (The existing copy of foed.xml in ch6_exercises will be overwritten with the latest version of the feed. If you can't connect to friends of ED, just use the old version for the remaining steps.)

3. Open namespace_01.php in ch6_exercises, and save it as namespace.php. It contains an HTML skeleton, a heading, and a link to the simplexml.css style sheet. Above the DOCTYPE declaration, add a PHP block with the following code to load the XML document:

```
$xml = simplexml_load_file('foed.xml');
```

Note that, this time, you use simplexml_load_file(), not simplexml_load_string(), because the news feed is now saved as a file.

4. Beneath the heading in the main body of the page, create a foreach loop to display the children of the <item> elements like this:

```
foreach ($xml->item as $item) {
    echo '<h2>' . $item->title . '</h2>';
    echo '<p>' . $item->description . '</p>';
    echo '<p>Date: ' . $item->dc:date . '</p>';
}
```

5. Save namespace.php, and load it into a browser, or use namespace_02.php from the download files. Don't be alarmed if you get a parse error. You should see an error message similar to Figure 6-18. The colon in the namespace prefix (dc:date) gives PHP severe indigestion.

Figure 6-18. The colon in the namespace prefix triggers a parse error in PHP.

6. Try removing the namespace prefix like this:

```
echo '<p>Date: ' . $item->date . '</p>';
```

7. Save the page, and test it again (or use namespace_03.php). As long as you don't have any other errors in your page, it should display correctly this time, but as Figure 6-19 shows, the date is missing.

updatED

Adobe TV

Adobe TV launches today, and very useful it looks too.

Date:

Time to get nekkid again

Well it doesn't seem like 12 months since the last one, but we're getting our CSS off again for CSS Naked Day. We'll be covering ourselves up again tomorrow.

Date:

Here's lookin' at you kid

An rather unnerving mouse driven moving portrait thing at cubo.cc

Date:

The date is not displayed.

Figure 6-19. Leaving out the namespace prefix doesn't work either.

6

8. There are two ways to access elements that have a namespace prefix. One is by passing the URL that identifies the namespace as an argument to the children() method. This works in all versions of PHP 5. The second way was added in PHP 5.2 and involves passing two arguments to the children() method: the namespace prefix and a Boolean true to indicate that the first argument is a prefix, not a URL. In both cases, you assign the result to a variable that stores a SimpleXMLElement object that you can use in the ordinary way.

Although the way of handling namespaces added in PHP 5.2 uses two arguments, it's a lot easier to type the prefix than the URL, so that's how we'll do it. This requires a minimum of PHP 5.2. If you're using PHP 5.0 or 5.1, read the following explanation, but use the code in step 9.

If you refer to Figure 6-17, you can see that <dc:date> is a child of the repeating <item> element, so you apply the children() method to <item> inside the foreach loop like this:

```
foreach ($xml->item as $item) {
  echo '<h2>' . $item->title . '</h2>';
  echo '<p>' . $item->description . '</p>';
  $dc = $item->children('dc', true);
  echo '<p>Date: ' . $dc->date . '</p>';
}
```

This creates a SimpleXMLElement object called $dc that contains all child elements in the dc namespace, so <dc:date> for the current <item> can be accessed as $dc->date.

> The dc namespace is widely used in news feeds on other online XML sources. The initials stand for "Dublin Core," a standardized set of terms for describing the content of documents. You can find a full list of Dublin Core terms at http://dublincore.org/documents/dcmi-terms/.

9. *This step applies only if you're using PHP 5.0 or 5.1.*

You need to pass the namespace URL as an argument to the children() method. Get the URL from the opening tag of the root element. The dc namespace is highlighted here in bold:

```
<rdf:RDF xmlns:dc="http://purl.org/dc/elements/1.1/"
         xmlns:h="http://www.w3.org/1999/xhtml"
         xmlns:hr="http://www.w3.org/2000/08/w3c-synd/#"
         xmlns:rdf="http://www.w3.org/1999/02/22-rdf-syntax-ns#"
         xmlns="http://purl.org/rss/1.0/">
```

Replace the line highlighted in bold in step 8 with the following:

```
$dc = $item->children('http://purl.org/dc/elements/1.1/');
```

10. Save the page, and load it in a browser (or use namespace_04.php). The date should now be displayed, as shown in Figure 6-20.

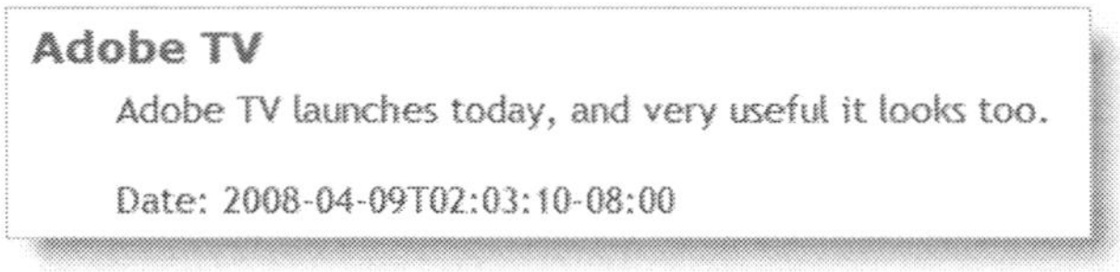

Adobe TV

Adobe TV launches today, and very useful it looks too.

Date: 2008-04-09T02:03:10-08:00

Figure 6-20. The date is now displayed, although it still needs formatting.

11. All that remains to be done now is to format the date. This is a job for the Pos_Date class from Chapter 3. Load the Pos_Date class with require_once (if you don't have a copy of the class, copy it from the finished_classes folder in the download files to the Pos folder). Amend the code above the DOCTYPE declaration like this:

```
require_once '../Pos/Date.php';
$xml = simplexml_load_file('foed.xml');
```

12. The friends of ED news feed uses the ISO 8601 format to represent the date and time (http://www.w3.org/TR/NOTE-datetime). The "T" in the middle separates the date from the time, so you can use this to split the string in two with explode(). The first element of the resulting array contains the date element presented as YYYY-MM-DD, the format used by Pos_Date::setFromMySQL(). The amended code inside the foreach loop looks like this (it's in namespaces_05.php):

```
foreach ($xml->item as $item) {
  echo '<h2>' . $item->title . '</h2>';
  echo '<p>' . $item->description . '</p>';
  $dc = $item->children('dc', true);
```

```
    try {
      $dateParts = explode('T', $dc->date);
      $date = new Pos_Date();
      $date->setFromMySQL($dateParts[0]);
      echo '<p>Date: ' . $date . '</p>';
    } catch (Exception $e) {
      echo $e->getMessage();
    }
  }
```

13. Save the page, and test it in a browser (or use namespace_05.php). The formatted date for each item should be displayed as shown in Figure 6-21.

Adobe TV

Adobe TV launches today, and very useful it looks too.

Date: Wednesday, April 9th, 2008

Time to get nekkid again

Well it doesn't seem like 12 months since the last one, but we're getting our CSS off again for CSS Naked Day. We'll be covering ourselves up again tomorrow.

Date: Tuesday, April 8th, 2008

Figure 6-21. The dates are now formatted in a user-friendly way.

Handling namespaced attributes

Attributes can also be prefixed with a namespace. You handle them in the same way as namespaced tags by extracting the values to a SimpleXMLElement object. The only difference is that you use the attributes() method instead of children(). The attributes() method takes the same arguments, namely:

- A single argument containing the namespace URL. This works in all versions of PHP 5.0 and above.

- Alternatively, the namespace prefix and a Boolean true. This works in PHP 5.2 and above.

Since the principle is exactly the same as handling namespaced tags, I won't bore you with another exercise. You can see an example of handling namespaced attributes in namespace_06.php and inventory3.xml in the download files. These files have been adapted from simplexml_10.php and inventory.xml from one of the exercises earlier in the chapter.

The file inventory3.xml adds a namespace to the isbn13 attributes of inventory.xml like this (only the first two lines are shown here):

```
<inventory xmlns:pos="http://foundationphp.com/ns/pos/">
  <book pos:isbn13='978-1-43021-011-5'>
```

241

In the original exercise, the following line in `simplexml_10.php` displays the `isbn13` attribute:

```
echo '<p class="publisher">ISBN: ' . $book['isbn13'] . '</p>';
```

To display the namespaced `pos:isbn13` attribute, this has been replaced in `namespace_06.php` by the following:

```
$attributes = $book->attributes('pos', true);
echo '<p class="publisher">ISBN: ' . $attributes['isbn13'] . '</p>';
```

This passes the namespace prefix (pos) to the `attributes()` method, together with a Boolean `true` to indicate that it's a prefix, and stores the result in $attributes. The `pos:isbn13` attribute is then accessed as $attributes['isbn13'].

If you need to be compatible with PHP 5.0 or 5.1, the first of these two lines should use the URL instead, like this:

```
$attributes = $book->attributes('http://foundationphp.com/ns/pos/');
```

If you test `namespace_06.php` in a browser, you should see the same output as in Figure 6-4.

> *The change to the arguments accepted by the `children()` and `attributes()` methods demonstrates an important OOP principle. When originally designed, the methods took only one optional argument: the URL namespace. They were improved in PHP 5.2 to accept the namespace prefix instead. However, to avoid breaking existing code, a second optional argument was added to indicate whether the first argument is a namespace prefix. By default, the argument is* false, *so if only one argument is passed to `children()` or `attributes()`, it's treated as a namespace URL—in other words, as the methods were originally designed. To indicate that the first argument is a namespace prefix, you must explicitly set the second argument to* true.*
>
> *What this means is that code written for PHP 5.0 or 5.1 continues to work. When making changes to classes and methods, you must always ensure that you don't break existing code. In this case, it has been done by adding an optional argument. In other circumstances, you might need to create a new method or extend the original class.*

Finding out which namespaces a document uses

The `SimpleXMLElement` class has two methods that reveal details about namespaces, namely:

- `getNamespaces()`: This returns an array of namespaces used in a document.
- `getDocNamespaces()`: This returns an array of namespaces declared in a document.

At first glance, both methods appear to do the same thing. The difference is that getDocNamespaces() tells you all the namespaces that have been declared, even if they're not used, whereas getNamespaces() returns only those namespaces actually used in the document.

Both methods take a Boolean value (true or false) as an optional argument. If true, the method reports on namespaces in all elements. If omitted, the argument defaults to false, and the method restricts its report to namespaces in the root element.

Figure 6-22 helps make the distinction clearer. It shows the results of applying getNamespaces() and getDocNamespaces() with and without the optional argument on a SimpleXMLElement object that contains the output of the friends of ED news feed. You can find the code in namespaces_07.php in the ch6_exercises folder of the download files.

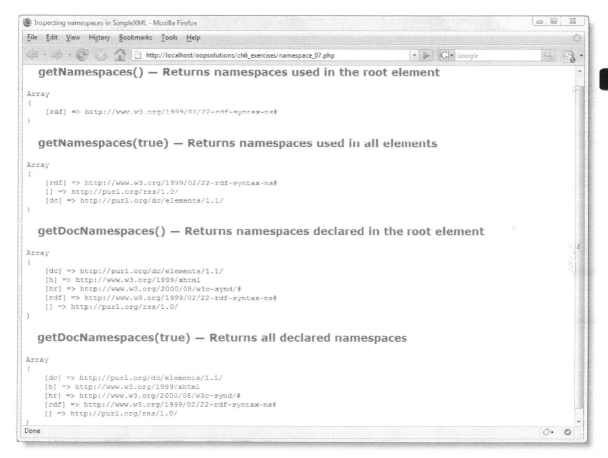

Figure 6-22. The SimpleXMLElement class provides different ways to inspect a document's namespaces.

As you can see from Figure 6-22, getNamespaces() returns only the rdf namespace, which is used by the root element, whereas getNamespaces(true) returns the rdf, dc, and default namespaces (the default namespace is indicated by an empty pair of square brackets).

However, getDocNamespaces() returns two more namespaces (h and hr), which are declared in the root element but never used. The results produced by getDocNamespaces() and getDocNamespaces(true) are identical, because no namespaces are declared in other parts of the document.

> *This analysis applies to the original version of* foed.xml *supplied in the* ch6_exercises *folder of the download files. If you have overwritten* foed.xml *with a more recent version of the friends of ED news feed, it's possible that namespaces have been used in a different way.*

Using SimpleXML with XPath

The XML Path Language (XPath) is a W3C standard (www.w3.org/TR/xpath) for identifying elements and attributes in an XML document. It shares many similarities with the pathnames you are familiar with from web design but is much more powerful. A detailed discussion of XPath is beyond the scope of this book, but the next section describes some of its main features.

A quick introduction to XPath

A leading forward slash (/) indicates the root element of the XML document, and the path moves down through the hierarchy from parent to child until the target element is reached. So, the XPath to the <paperback> element in inventory2.xml looks like this:

```
/inventory/book/price/paperback
```

Because the path begins with a leading slash, this always identifies the correct element. However, XPath also uses relative paths dependent on the current context. So, if the script processing the XML is currently inside a <book> node, you can refer to <paperback> nodes like this:

```
price/paperback
```

Other features XPath shares with ordinary pathnames are the use of a single period (.) to represent the current node, two periods (..) to represent the parent of the current node, and an asterisk (*) to represent any element.

A useful shortcut is a double forward slash (//), which selects all descendants of the current node, as well as the current node itself. So, instead of typing the full path to paperback, you can use this instead:

```
//paperback
```

To identify an attribute, you prefix the attribute's name with @.

> *XPath has many more features. For an in-depth look at what you can do with XPath, see* Pro PHP XML and Web Services *by Robert Richards (Apress, ISBN13: 978-1-59059-633-3).*

Using XPath to drill down into XML

Because XPath has the ability to burrow down into the XML hierarchy to identify elements, the xpath() method is more suited to extracting specific information, rather than displaying everything as in previous examples.

The following code (in xpath_01.php) uses the xpath() method with the shorthand //title to extract all the book titles from inventory.xml and then displays them in an unordered list, as shown in Figure 6-23:

```
$xml = simplexml_load_file('inventory.xml');
$titles = $xml->xpath('//title');
echo '<ul>';
foreach ($titles as $title) {
  echo "<li>$title</li>";
}
echo '</ul>';
```

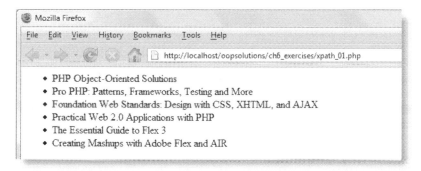

Figure 6-23. Using XPath with SimpleXML is more suited to extracting just one part of the data.

The next example uses a fully qualified path to access the isbn13 attributes and displays them in a similar manner (the code is in xpath_02.php):

```
$xml = simplexml_load_file('inventory.xml');
$isbn13 = $xml->xpath('/inventory/book/@isbn13');
echo '<ul>';
foreach ($isbn13 as $isbn) {
  echo "<li>$isbn</li>";
}
echo '</ul>';
```

Using XPath expressions for finer control

XPath really comes into its own when you use more advanced selectors. The following XPath identifies <publisher> nodes that have the value "Apress":

```
//publisher[. = "Apress"]
```

This matches the <publisher> node of two books in inventory.xml. You can then use XPath to climb back up the XML tree to find the <title>, <author>, and <description> nodes of the same book. The xpath() method always returns an *array* of matching SimpleXMLElement objects, so even if you know there's only one match, you either need to loop through the results or use array syntax to access the result. The following code (in xpath_03.php) finds the two books published by Apress, and then uses ../ to find the related details:

```php
$publishers = $xml->xpath('//publisher[. = "Apress"]');
foreach ($publishers as $pub) {
  $title = $pub->xpath('../title');
  $author = $pub->xpath('../author');
  $description = $pub->xpath('../description');
  echo "<h2>$title[0]</h2>";
  echo "<p class='author'>$author[0]</p>";
  echo "<p>$description[0]</p>";
}
```

This produces the output shown in Figure 6-24.

Figure 6-24. A knowledge of XPath selectors makes it easy to drill down into XML to find the data you want.

Using XPath with namespaces

All the examples so far work without problem. However, things are very different if the XML document uses namespaces. Even a default namespace affects the operation of the xpath() method. The download files for this chapter contain an XML document called inventory_ns.xml. It's identical to inventory.xml, except that the opening tag of the root element contains a default namespace like this:

```
<inventory xmlns="http://foundationphp.com/ch6/">
```

The file xpath_04.php contains the same code as the first XPath example (in xpath_01.php), except that it loads the version of the XML document with a default namespace. If you load xpath_04.php into a browser, all you'll see is a blank screen. To use the xpath() method with a namespace, you must first register the namespace.

Registering namespaces to work with XPath

To register a namespace to work with the SimpleXMLElement::xpath() method, use the registerXPathNamespace() method. This takes two arguments: a prefix to identify the namespace and the namespace's URL.

As I explained earlier, the default namespace of an XML document doesn't use a prefix. So, what should you use for the first argument when dealing with a default namespace? The answer is simple, but it might come as a bit of a surprise: you make one up.

The following code shows the amended script to work with inventory_ns.xml (it's in xpath_05.php):

```
$xml = simplexml_load_file('inventory_ns.xml');
$xml->registerXPathNamespace('ch6', 'http://foundationphp.com/ch6/');
$titles = $xml->xpath('//ch6:title');
echo '<ul>';
foreach ($titles as $title) {
  echo "<li>$title</li>";
}
echo '</ul>';
```

This code now displays the same result as in Figure 6-23.

Handling attributes in an XML document with a default namespace requires a slightly different approach, as the code in xpath_06.php shows:

```
$xml = simplexml_load_file('inventory_ns.xml');
$xml->registerXPathNamespace('ch6', 'http://foundationphp.com/ch6/');
$books = $xml->xpath('//ch6:book');
echo '<ul>';
foreach ($books as $book) {
  $isbn = $book->attributes();
  echo "<li>$isbn</li>";
}
echo '</ul>';
```

247

Instead of selecting the attribute directly with the xpath() method, select the element that contains the attribute, and then apply the attributes() method to each node as you loop through them.

You register namespace prefixes in the same way. The following script accesses all the <dc:date> nodes in foed.xml (the code is in xpath_07.php):

```
$xml = simplexml_load_file('foed.xml');
$xml->registerXPathNamespace('dc', 'http://purl.org/dc/elements/1.1/');
$dates = $xml->xpath('//dc:date');
echo '<ul>';
foreach ($dates as $date) {
  echo "<li>$date</li>";
}
echo '</ul>';
```

At the time of this writing, there doesn't seem to be a way to access attributes that are governed by a namespace prefix with the xpath() method.

Chapter review

If you have any experience of working with XML in PHP 4 or older versions of ActionScript, you'll appreciate how much easier SimpleXML makes access to XML data. Once you have loaded the XML document, you can go straight to the nodes you're interested in, identifying them by name. If you want finer control—and have a good knowledge of XPath—you can drill down to the target information with the xpath() method.

SimpleXML does have limitations. It's best suited to handling XML documents that have a predictable structure. It gives you access only to text nodes and attributes. Admittedly, this is usually all you want, but if you do need to examine comments and processing instructions, then you need to use the more powerful—and therefore complex—DOM and SAX extensions. SimpleXML treats the XML source in a linear fashion, so it's not capable of sorting the data. There are several ways you can get around this problem, but I find the easiest is to use SimpleXML to extract the data and insert it into a database. You can then use SQL to sort and filter the data however you want.

In the next chapter, I'll show how you can use the Standard PHP Library (SPL) in conjunction with SimpleXML and other classes to exercise greater control over looping through their contents.

Window 1 (Mozilla Firefox):

1. PHP Object-Oriented Solutions
2. Pro PHP: Patterns, Frameworks, Testing and More
3. Foundation Web Standards: Design with CSS, XHTML, and AJAX
4. Practical Web 2.0 Applications with PHP
5. The Essential Guide to Flex 3
6. Creating Mashups with Adobe Flex and AIR
7. The Essential Guide to Open Source Flash Development
8. Beginning PHP and MySQL: From Novice to Professional, Third Edition
9. Pro Web 2.0 Mashups: Remixing Data and Web Services
10. AdvancED AIR Application
11. Beginning PHP and MySQL E-Commerce: From Novice to Professional, Second Edition

Window 2 (What happens after moving the file pointer? - Mozilla Firefox):

Pointer moved to line 13

- $file->fgets(): I never writ, nor no man ever loved.

Pointer moved to line 13

- $file->getCurrentLine(): I never writ, nor no man ever loved.

Pointer moved to line 13

- $file->current(): If this be error and upon me proved

Window 3 (Mozilla Firefox):

name: David
city: London
country: United Kingdom

The Standard PHP Library (SPL) was added to PHP in version 5.0 and is enabled by default. In fact, since PHP 5.3, you cannot disable SPL. Yet, in spite of being part of PHP since 2004, it's still poorly documented at the time of this writing. There have been calls within the PHP development team for better documentation, so the situation might have improved by the time you read this.

The name gives the impression that SPL is a framework similar to the Zend Framework (http://framework.zend.com/), CakePHP (www.cakephp.org), or CodeIgniter (www.codeigniter.com). However, SPL is more narrowly focused—at least, it is at the moment. SPL is still evolving. Most of its existing features are concerned with sophisticated types of looping. What sets SPL apart from other frameworks is that it's written in C. SPL classes are part of the PHP core engine, so they run much faster than frameworks written in PHP code. However, you don't need to know C to be able to use SPL. You use SPL classes in exactly the same way as other PHP classes, but as they're part of the core language, you don't need to include any external files to use them.

It's impossible to cover the whole of the SPL in this chapter, but I'll show you some of its most useful features. In particular, this chapter covers the following:

- Converting arrays and SimpleXML objects for use with SPL iterators
- Controlling the start of a loop and the number of times it runs
- Filtering loops with a regular expression
- Combining XML data from multiple sources and processing them in a single operation
- Examining files and directories with directory iterators and the SplFileInfo class
- Reading and writing files with the SplFileObject class
- Creating your own filters

In order to use SPL, you need to understand the role of abstract classes and interfaces in OOP. If you're new to these concepts or need to brush up your knowledge, I recommend that you read "Exploring advanced OOP features" in Chapter 2 before going any further. Many of the examples use SimpleXML and the XML documents from the previous chapter, so you should also be familiar with the contents of Chapter 6.

Introducing iterators

Most of what is currently available in SPL implements the **Iterator design pattern**. The purpose of this design pattern is to make it easy to traverse a structure, such as an array or set of database results, one at a time. In other words, it's basically all about loops—one of the most common aspects of working with a language such as PHP. SPL provides a series of specialized tools that affect the behavior of the loop. For example the LimitIterator sets the starting point of the loop and the number of times it will run, and the FilterIterator lets you filter acceptable values. Not only that, you can combine iterators, so you can filter and limit in a single operation. However, to use SPL iterators, the array or object you're using must implement the Iterator interface.

Using an array with SPL iterators

One of the first things you learn about PHP is that you can iterate through an array with a loop. To take a simple example, the following code loops through the array of numbers, and displays each one on a separate line:

```
$numbers = array(5, 10, 8, 35, 50);
foreach ($numbers as $number) {
  echo $number . '<br />';
}
```

You don't need to do anything special to use a loop with an array; it's an inherent part of the way arrays work. However, if you try to use an array with any of the SPL iterators, you end up with a fatal error, as shown in Figure 7-1. (You can find the code in limit_iterator_01.php in the ch7_exercises folder of the download files, but it probably won't mean very much to you until you have read the next section.) Although you can iterate through an array on its own, you need to prepare it before passing it to an iterator.

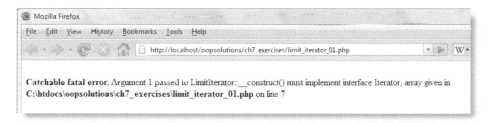

Figure 7-1. Trying to use an ordinary array with an SPL iterator won't work.

As the error message in Figure 7-1 shows, the argument passed to the iterator must implement the Iterator interface. This is a built-in interface that provides the necessary methods to interact with an iterator. I'll come back to the interface later in the chapter, but for the moment let's concentrate on using an iterator with an array.

To prepare an array to work with an iterator, pass it to the ArrayIterator constructor like this:

```
$iterator = new ArrayIterator($array);
```

That's all that's necessary. The array continues to work like an array, but it's also ready to use with an iterator, such as the LimitIterator.

Limiting the number of loops with the LimitIterator

The LimitIterator is one of the easiest SPL iterators to use. It determines where to start the loop and how many times it should run. The LimitIterator constructor takes three arguments: the array or object you want to loop through, the starting point (counting from zero), and the number of times the loop is to run. The first argument must be an object that implements the Iterator interface, so when using it with an array, the array needs to be passed first to the ArrayIterator constructor. The following code (in limit_iterator_02.php in the ch7_exercises folder) shows how it works:

```
$numbers = array(5, 10, 8, 35, 50);

// Prepare the array for use with an iterator
$iterator = new ArrayIterator($numbers);

// Pass the converted array to the LimitIterator
$limiter = new LimitIterator($iterator, 0, 2);

// Loop through the LimitIterator object
foreach ($limiter as $number) {
  echo $number . '<br />';
}
```

This displays the first two numbers from the array, as shown in Figure 7-2. If you change the second argument to 2, it displays the third and fourth numbers from the array (8 and 35).

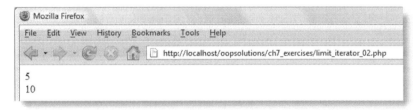

Figure 7-2. The LimitIterator controls the number of times a loop runs.

You have probably realized that the preceding example achieves exactly the same as this:

```
$numbers = array(5, 10, 8, 35, 50);
for ($i = 0; $i < 2; $i++) {
  echo $numbers[$i] . '<br />';
}
```

The for loop is much shorter, and more familiar, so why bother with LimitIterator? The reason is because SPL iterators aren't designed to work with arrays; they're designed to make *objects* work like arrays. Passing $numbers to ArrayIterator converts it to an object. Using an array as the starting point to demonstrate LimitIterator is simply a convenience. It makes sense to see what iterators can do before explaining all the details of the Iterator interface.

Now that you have seen how LimitIterator works, let's use it with a real object: a SimpleXML object from the previous chapter. But first, you need to prepare it for use with an iterator.

Using SimpleXML with an iterator

As you saw in the previous chapter, SimpleXML makes it easy to iterate through the contents of an XML document with a foreach loop. However, like an array, a SimpleXMLElement object does not implement the Iterator interface, so it needs to be converted before you can use it with an SPL iterator. Not surprisingly, you do this with the SimpleXMLIterator class.

> Most of the examples in this chapter use inventory.xml or inventory2.xml from the previous chapter. For convenience, I have copied them to the ch7_exercises folder in the download files.

Creating a SimpleXMLIterator object is easy, but you need to be careful because the constructor expects a string. The Pos_RemoteConnector class from Chapter 5 implements the __toString() magic method, which converts the object to a string whenever used in a string context, so you can pass the result directly to the SimpleXMLIterator constructor. However, if you're accessing a local file, instead of simplexml_load_file(), you need to use file_get_contents() like this:

```
$xml = file_get_contents('inventory.xml');
$iterator = new SimpleXMLIterator($xml);
```

An alternative and very elegant way of creating a SimpleXMLIterator object is by passing the class name as a string to either simplexml_load_file() or simplexml_load_string() like this:

```
$xml = simplexml_load_file('inventory.xml', 'SimpleXMLIterator');
```

The SimpleXML is now ready to use with an iterator.

The following code (in simplexml_iterator_01.php) loads inventory.xml as a SimpleXMLIterator object and passes it to LimitIterator to display three titles starting from the third one, as shown in Figure 7-3:

```
$xml = simplexml_load_file('inventory.xml', 'SimpleXMLIterator');
$limiter = new LimitIterator($xml, 2, 3);
foreach ($limiter as $book) {
  echo $book->title . '<br />';
}
```

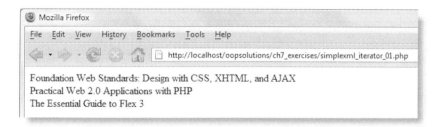

Figure 7-3. The SimpleXMLIterator class lets you use XML with the SPL iterators.

> *The important concept to grasp is that an iterator turns an object that contains a collection of values into something that can be used in a loop just like an array. Once an object has been converted to an iterator (or implements the* Iterator *interface), you can wrap it in other iterators. It's the outermost iterator that you use in the loop.*
>
> *In the previous example, the* SimpleXMLElement *object is first wrapped in a* SimpleXMLIterator, *which is then wrapped in a* LimitIterator. *The loop is applied to the outermost wrapper—the* LimitIterator.

Filtering a loop with a regular expression

The RegexIterator class lets you apply a Perl-compatible regular expression (PCRE) to an iterator to filter the results of the loop. The class has two required arguments: an iterator and a PCRE. Table 5-1 in Chapter 5 lists the most common characters and modifiers used in building regular expressions, but a PCRE can also simply be literal text between a pair of delimiters, so /PHP/ searches for the string "PHP."

The following code (in regex_iterator_01.php) produces the output shown in Figure 7-4:

```php
$xml = simplexml_load_file('inventory.xml', 'SimpleXMLIterator');
foreach ($xml as $book) {
  $match = new RegexIterator($book->title, '/PHP/');
  foreach ($match as $title) {
    echo $title . '<br />';
    echo $book->description . '<br /><br />';
  }
}
```

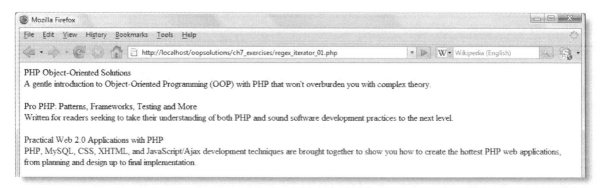

Figure 7-4. The RegexIterator has selected all books with "PHP" in the title.

Let's take a closer look at what's happening in this example. Figure 7-5 summarizes the process.

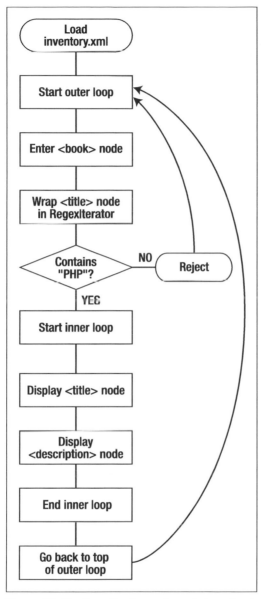

Figure 7-5. The RegexIterator works on just one book at a time inside the inner loop.

First of all, inventory.xml is loaded as a SimpleXMLIterator object and stored as $xml. The first foreach loop (the outer loop) iterates through each <book> element of inventory.xml one at a time.

To search for "PHP" in the current book's title, $book->title is wrapped in a RegexIterator, and the PCRE /PHP/ is passed as the second argument to the constructor. The second argument must be a string, so the PCRE is wrapped in quotes.

The RegexIterator is stored as $match, so a second foreach loop (the inner loop) iterates through $match, which contains only those titles with the string "PHP." However, the outer loop goes through only one book at a time, so the code in the inner loop runs only if the current title matches the regular expression. Since the inner loop is nested inside the first, you can still access other properties associated with the current book through $book. So, the appropriate <description> node is displayed by accessing $book->description. The inner loop comes to an end, and the outer loop moves onto the next book. If the regular expression doesn't match, the inner loop never runs.

One thing you need to be careful about is that even when there is no match, $match contains a RegexIterator object, so you can't use the negative operator, empty(), or is_null() to detect a nonmatch. The for loop automatically takes care of nonmatches by skipping them.

If you still find this difficult to grasp, load regex_iterator_02.php into a browser. It displays onscreen the entry and exit points of both loops, together with the ordinary output, as shown in Figure 7-6.

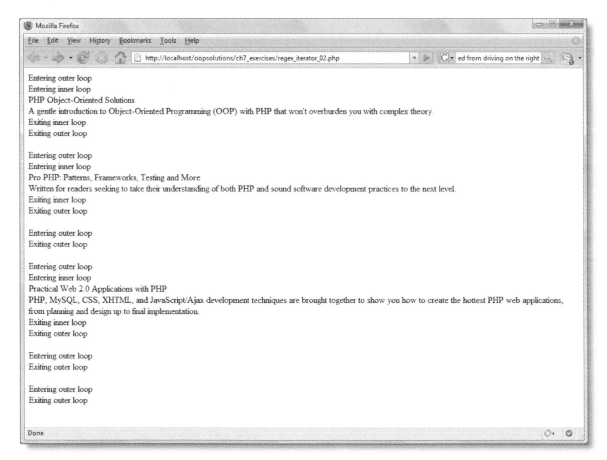

Figure 7-6. Displaying the entry and exit points of each loop shows how the RegexIterator filters the XML data.

Displaying messages identifying the current location in a loop is a good way of understanding the flow of a script, and it can help with debugging when things don't turn out as expected.

Setting options for RegexIterator

In addition to the two required arguments, the `RegexIterator` constructor accepts three optional arguments, namely:

- **Mode**: This controls how the regular expression is used by emulating the PCRE functions `preg_match()` and `preg_match_all()`. The default is to find a match for the regular expression.

- **Flags**: There is currently only one flag: `RegexIterator::USE_KEY`. This applies the regular expression to the key (or index) of each element, rather than the value.

- **PREG_* flags**: These are global PHP constants that control the way the regular expression is applied. They work the same way as with `preg_match()`, `preg_match_all()`, and `preg_split()`. Their use is rather specialized, so I don't plan to cover them in this book. You can find a full list of the constants and their uses at http://docs.php.net/manual/en/pcre.constants.php.

To set the mode and flags arguments, you need to use the class constants listed in Table 7-1.

Table 7-1. RegexIterator class constants

Constant	Type	Description
MATCH	Mode	This returns true when there is a match for the regular expression. This is the default setting and doesn't normally need to be used unless you set the other optional arguments.
GET_MATCH	Mode	This returns the first match and captures any subexpressions.
ALL_MATCHES	Mode	This emulates `preg_match_all()` and captures any subexpressions.
SPLIT	Mode	This uses the regular expression to split the value and returns the resulting array.
REPLACE	Mode	Currently not used.
USE_KEY	Flag	This applies the regular expression to the key of each element, rather than the value.

7

The best way to understand how these constants work is to see them in action. It also helps if you have a good understanding of the PCRE functions, preg_match(), preg_match_all(), and preg_split(). See the PHP Manual at http://docs.php.net/manual/en/book.pcre.php if you need to refresh your memory.

> The following examples use the function iterator_to_array(), which returns an array containing all the data in an iterator. This is useful for testing and debugging.

Finding the first match and subexpressions

Using the GET_MATCH mode constant emulates using preg_match() with the third argument to capture any matches. It returns an array, the first element of which contains the entire string that matches the regular expression. Any subsequent array elements contain matching subexpressions.

In the following example, the PCRE /(\w+?)e/ looks for as few as possible alphanumeric characters or the underscore followed by the letter "e." The parentheses capture them as a subexpression (the code is in regex_iterator_03.php):

```
$files = array('inventory.xml', 'createXML.php', 'modify_xml_03.php');
$iterator = new ArrayIterator($files);
$regex = new RegexIterator($iterator, '/(\w+?)e/', ➥
  RegexIterator::GET_MATCH);
print_r(iterator_to_array($regex));
```

This produces the output shown in Figure 7-7. The third filename in the original array doesn't contain the letter "e," so results are produced only for the first two. Note that because GET_MATCH is a class constant, it needs to be preceded by the class name and the scope resolution operator (::).

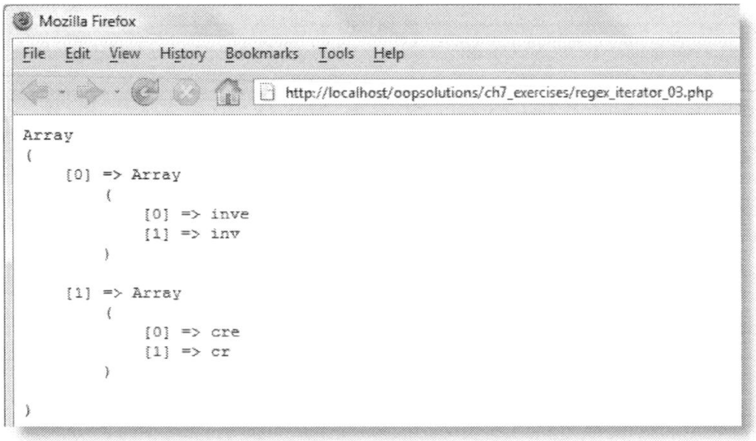

Figure 7-7. Using GET_MATCH produces an array of the first match and any subexpressions.

Finding all matches

The ALL_MATCHES constant emulates preg_match_all(). Changing the mode in the previous example to ALL_MATCHES produces the output shown in Figure 7-8 (the code is in regex_iterator_04.php).

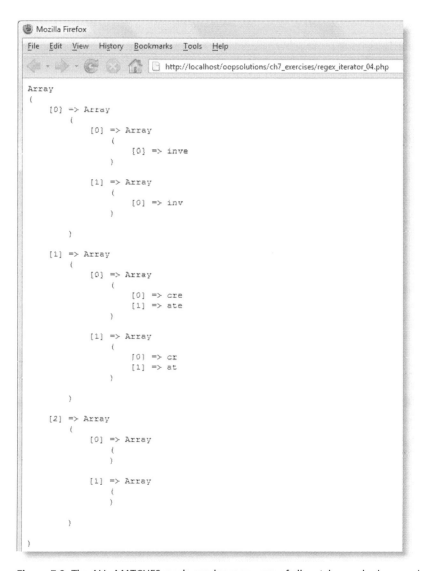

Figure 7-8. The ALL_MATCHES mode produces an array of all matches and subexpressions.

The interesting thing to note here is that ALL_MATCHES produces an empty array for the third filename, which doesn't contain the letter "e." In other words, it produces an array for each iteration, but the array is empty if there's no match.

Splitting with a regular expression

The SPLIT mode uses a regular expression to split the data in each element into an array. The regular expression /_|\./ in regex_iterator_05.php looks for an underscore or period and uses it as the separator on which to split the filenames, as shown in Figure 7-9. The code looks like this:

```
$files = array('inventory.xml', 'createXML.php', 'modify_xml_03.php');
$iterator = new ArrayIterator($files);
$regex = new RegexIterator($iterator, '/_|\./', RegexIterator::SPLIT);
print_r(iterator_to_array($regex));
```

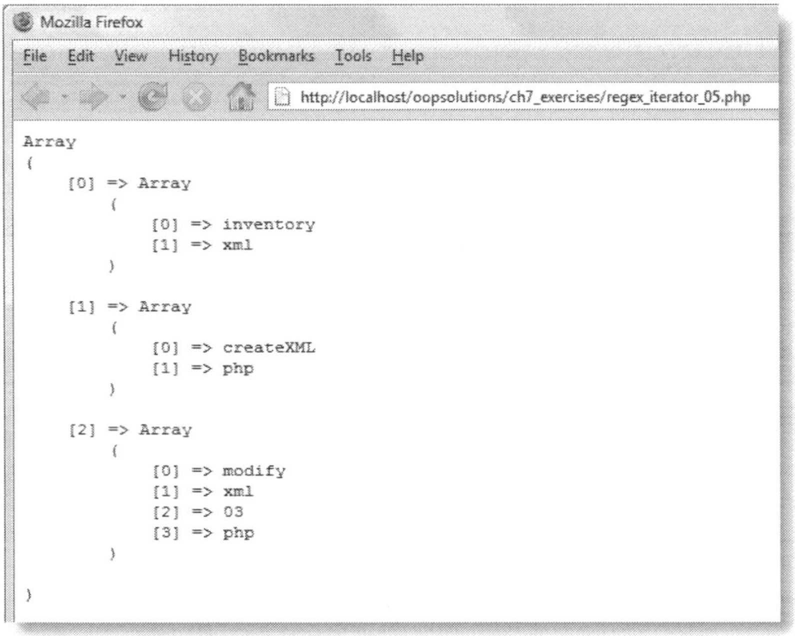

Figure 7-9. The SPLIT mode creates individual arrays of elements split on whatever matches the regular expression.

The third filename contains two underscores and a period; both characters are used as the basis for the split.

Applying the regular expression to the element keys

By default, RegexIterator applies the PCRE to the *value* of each item in the iterator. However, setting the USE_KEY flag changes this behavior and applies the regular expression to the items' keys instead. Because the USE_KEY flag must be passed to the constructor as the fourth argument, you must always set a value for the third argument when using it.

The following code (in regex_iterator_06.php) uses the PCRE /^c/ to find strings that begin with the letter "c." Although MATCH is the default mode for RegexIterator, it needs to be set explicitly, so that USE_KEY can be passed to the constructor as the fourth argument.

```
$author = array('name'    => 'David',
                'city'    => 'London',
                'country' => 'United Kingdom');
$iterator = new ArrayIterator($author);
$regex = new RegexIterator($iterator, '/^c/', RegexIterator::MATCH, ➥
  RegexIterator::USE_KEY);
print_r(iterator_to_array($regex));
```

As you can see from Figure 7-10, the iterator selects the two keys that begin with "c."

Figure 7-10 The USE_KEY flag applies the regular expression to the key of each element instead of its value.

Looping sequentially through more than one set of data

The AppendIterator lets you append one or more iterators to another, and loop through them in one operation. Using it is very simple. You create an instance of the AppendIterator class and use its append() method to add each iterator in sequence. This can be very useful for processing data from different sources, as the following exercise shows.

Displaying book details from two sources

This exercise takes two XML documents with details of books published by friends of ED and its parent company, Apress. It combines them with AppendIterator and displays the titles in a single operation. It also shows how iterators can be chained to limit the number of items selected from each source.

1. Create a file called append_iterator.php in the ch7_exercises folder, and add the following code to load inventory.xml and more_books.xml as SimpleXMLIterator objects:

```
$books = simplexml_load_file('inventory.xml', 'SimpleXMLIterator');
$moreBooks = simplexml_load_file('more_books.xml', ➥
'SimpleXMLIterator');
```

The structure of more_books.xml is identical to inventory.xml (see Figure 6-2 in the previous chapter). It contains details of five books; inventory.xml contains six.

2. Create an instance of `AppendIterator`, and then add each `SimpleXMLIterator` in turn by applying the append() method to the `AppendIterator` object like this:

```
$books = simplexml_load_file('inventory.xml', 'SimpleXMLIterator');
$moreBooks = simplexml_load_file('more_books.xml', ➥
'SimpleXMLIterator');
$combined = new AppendIterator();
$combined->append($books);
$combined->append($moreBooks);
```

3. You can now loop through the `AppendIterator` object to display the titles from both sources in a single operation. Add the following code immediately below the code in the previous step:

```
echo '<ol>';
foreach ($combined as $book) {
  echo "<li>$book->title</li>";
}
echo '</ol>';
```

4. Save the page, and load it into a browser (or use append_iterator_01.php). You should see 11 titles displayed, as shown in Figure 7-11.

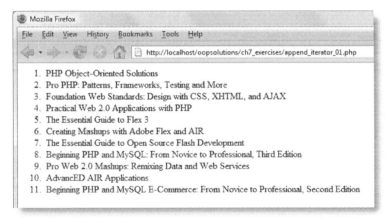

Figure 7-11. Data from two separate sources is handled seamlessly by the AppendIterator class.

5. What happens, though, if each XML source contains a much larger number of items, and you want to show only the first few? The answer is simple: combine this operation with the `LimitIterator` class.

Add the following lines highlighted in bold to select the first two items from each `SimpleXMLIterator` object:

```
$moreBooks = simplexml_load_file('more_books.xml', ➥
'SimpleXMLIterator');
$limit1 = new LimitIterator($books, 0, 2);
$limit2 = new LimitIterator($moreBooks, 0, 2);
$combined = new AppendIterator();
```

6. You now need to change the iterator objects passed to the append() method of the AppendIterator like this:

```
$combined->append($limit1);
$combined->append($limit2);
```

7. Instead of $books and $moreBooks, which contain all the data, the $combined object now works with $limit1 and $limit2, which contain just the first two from each source. Prove it by saving the page, and loading it into a browser (or use append_iterator_02.php). You should see the same output as shown in Figure 7-12. Leave the file open, as I'll come back to it in the next section.

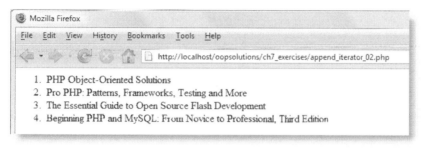

Figure 7-12. A combination of LimitIterator and AppendIterator makes it possible to select the first two from each source.

Looking ahead with the CachingIterator

Several of the books in inventory.xml and more_books.xml are written by multiple authors. In Chapter 6, I got around the problem of displaying their names by using a for loop with a series of conditional statements to insert commas between each name and an ampersand before the last one. The CachingIterator class makes it easy to do a similar thing in a foreach loop without the need for all the conditional statements.

The CachingIterator provides a hasNext() method to look ahead to see if there's another element to process after the current one. If there is, it returns true; otherwise, it returns false. You can use this to insert a comma after every name except the last one—not as elegant as adding the ampersand before the last name, but certainly a useful feature.

> *If you're thinking you can use* implode() *or* join() *to insert a comma between array elements, don't forget that it won't work with* SimpleXMLElement *or* SimpleXMLIterator *objects. As you saw in the previous chapter, the* <author> *nodes of books with multiple authors are stored as an object, and not as an ordinary array. The* implode() *and* join() *functions won't work on an object.*

So, let's use the CachingIterator to fix the author's names.

Inserting commas between authors' names

This continues the exercise in the previous section, and uses the CachingIterator to display the names of multiple authors with a comma between each one. If you don't have the file from the previous exercise, use append_iterator_02.php in the ch7_exercises folder of the download files.

1. Amend the foreach loop like this:

```
echo '<ol>';
foreach ($combined as $book) {
  echo "<li>$book->title";
  $authors = new CachingIterator($book->author);
  echo '<ul><li>';
  foreach ($authors as $name) {
    echo $name;
    if ($authors->hasNext()) {
      echo ', ';
    }
  }
  echo '</li></ul></li>';
}
echo '</ol>';
```

Note that the closing </li> tag has been removed after $book->title, so that the authors' names can be displayed as an indented bullet beneath the title.

The third line in the foreach loop wraps $book->author in a CachingIterator and saves it as $authors. Then an inner loop iterates through $authors, using $name as the alias for each element, and displaying it with echo.

The conditional statement calls the hasNext() method on the $authors object. If it returns true, it means there's another name, so a comma followed by a space is inserted. If there is no other name, the condition equates to false, and the comma is omitted.

2. Save the page, and load it in a browser (or use caching_iterator_01.php). You should see the output in Figure 7-13.

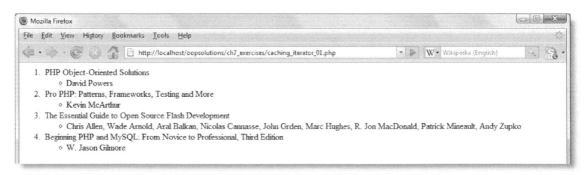

Figure 7-13. The CachingIterator makes it easy to add a comma between each author's name.

Not bad, but what if you don't want to show all nine names for the third book on the list? Yes, you've guessed it: a `LimitIterator`.

3. Amend the foreach loop like this:

```
echo '<ol>';
foreach ($combined as $book) {
  echo "<li>$book->title";
  $moreThan3 = false;
  if (count($book->author) > 3) {
    $limit3 = new LimitIterator($book->author, 0, 3);
    $authors = new CachingIterator($limit3);
    $moreThan3 = true;
  } else {
    $authors = new CachingIterator($book->author);
  }
  echo '<ul><li>';
  foreach ($authors as $name) {
    echo $name;
    if ($authors->hasNext()) {
      echo ', ';
    }
  }
  if ($moreThan3) {
    echo ' et al';
  }
  echo '</li></ul></li>';
}
echo '</ol>';
```

It's common to abbreviate long lists of authors' names by showing just the first three and adding "et al." or "and others" at the end of the list. The first new line highlighted in bold creates a flag called $moreThan3, which is initially set to `false`. The conditional statement passes $book->author to the count() function.

> I tend to use the count() *function out of habit, but* SimpleXMLIterator *and* ArrayIterator *objects also have a* count() *method. So, you could use* $book->author->count() *instead of* count($book->author). *Both do exactly the same thing. Use whichever you like.*

If the result is more than 3, the code inside the braces is executed. This wraps $book->author in a LimitIterator that selects the first three names, and assigns it to $limit3. This, in turn, is wrapped in a CachingIterator and assigned to $authors. Finally, $moreThan3 is set to true.

If the result is 3 or fewer, $book->author is wrapped directly in a CachingIterator and assigned to $authors.

In either case, the iterator that displays the names is always called $authors.

7

267

The second new block of code simply adds "et al" to the end of the list of names if the original list contained more than three.

4. Save the page, and load it in a browser (or use caching_iterator_02.php). The list of names for the third book should now be reformatted as shown in Figure 7-14.

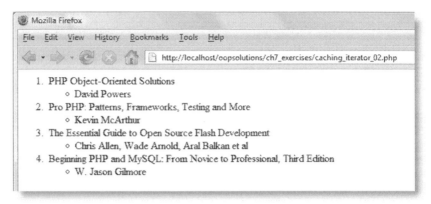

Figure 7-14. Combining a LimitIterator with a CachingIterator results in a nicely formatted list of names.

Using anonymous iterators as shorthand

Throughout these examples, I have declared each iterator as a separate statement and assigned it to a variable, as I think it makes the code a lot easier to read and understand. However, some developers prefer to create anonymous iterators, since creating a variable and storing it requires slightly more processing cycles.

To create an anonymous iterator, you pass the constructor directly to the iterator you want to wrap it in or to the foreach loop. For example, this is the code in limit_iterator_02.php from the beginning of this chapter:

```
$numbers = array(5, 10, 8, 35, 50);

// Prepare the array for use with an iterator
$iterator = new ArrayIterator($numbers);

// Pass the converted array to the LimitIterator
$limiter = new LimitIterator($iterator, 0, 2);

// Loop through the LimitIterator object
foreach ($limiter as $num) {
  echo $num . '<br />';
}
```

Neither the $iterator nor the $limiter variable is necessary. The code can be rewritten like this (it's in anonymous_iterator_01.php):

```
$numbers = array(5, 10, 8, 35, 50);

foreach (new LimitIterator(new ArrayIterator($numbers), 0, 2) as $num)
{
  echo $num . '<br />';
}
```

Equally, the code in the previous exercise can be rewritten using anonymous iterators. This is how the iterators are initialized at the start of caching_iterator_02.php:

```
$books = simplexml_load_file('inventory.xml', 'SimpleXMLIterator');
$moreBooks = simplexml_load_file('more_books.xml', ➥
'SimpleXMLIterator');
$limit1 = new LimitIterator($books, 0, 2);
$limit2 = new LimitIterator($moreBooks, 0, 2);
$combined = new AppendIterator();
$combined->append($limit1);
$combined->append($limit2);
```

Those seven lines of code can be reduced to just three with anonymous iterators like this (I have had to split two of the lines to fit them onto the printed page):

```
$combined = new AppendIterator();
$combined->append(new LimitIterator(simplexml_load_file( ➥
    'inventory.xml', 'SimpleXMLIterator'), 0, 2));
$combined->append(new LimitIterator(simplexml_load_file( ➥
    'more_books.xml', 'SimpleXMLIterator'), 0, 2));
```

In the same script, these two lines are also candidates for modification:

```
$limit3 = new LimitIterator($book->author, 0, 3);
$authors = new CachingIterator($limit3);
```

They can be merged like this (the revised script is in anonymous_iterator_02.php):

```
$authors = new CachingIterator(new LimitIterator($book->author, 0, 3));
```

In limited testing, I discovered that using anonymous iterators resulted in anonymous_iterator_02.php running 0.16 milliseconds faster than caching_iterator_02.php. That's a tiny fraction of a second. In a large, complex application, such savings might add up to make a difference in performance. However, there's a considerable loss in readability of the script. Choose whichever style suits your circumstances and preferences.

Examining files and directories

SPL makes looping through the contents of your computer's file system much easier than with procedural code. Currently, there are two classes: DirectoryIterator, which loops through a single directory or folder, and RecursiveDirectoryIterator, which burrows

7

down into subdirectories. As they progress through the file system, these iterators return an SplFileInfo object that gives access to a wealth of detail about the current item.

Using DirectoryIterator

You use DirectoryIterator just like any other iterator. The constructor takes just one argument: a string containing the path to the directory or folder that you want to examine. You can then loop through the contents of the directory with a foreach loop. The following code in directory_iterator_01.php examines the current directory (accessed using the shorthand .), and displays results similar to those shown in Figure 7-15:

```php
$dir = new DirectoryIterator('.');
foreach ($dir as $file) {
  echo $file . '<br />';
}
```

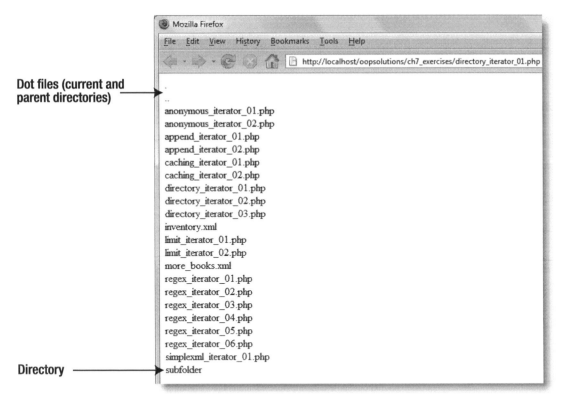

Figure 7-15. The DirectoryIterator reveals everything inside a directory, including dot files and subdirectories.

> *The purpose of Figures 7-15 and 7-16 is to show the type of output pro-*
> *duced by directory iterators, rather than the actual filenames. You will see*
> *a longer list when you run the scripts in this section.*

As you can see from Figure 7-15, the results include not only all the files in the current directory, but also the dot files (. and ..), which represent the current and parent directories and any subdirectories (there's just one dummy folder called subfolder in the ch7_exercises folder). Although each item in the foreach loop has been displayed using echo, it's not a string but an SplFileInfo object. The object's __toString() magic method conveniently displays its name.

One of the SplFileInfo class's many public methods is isDir(), which returns true if the object is a directory. The DirectoryIterator class also has a public method called isDot(), which identifies whether the current object is a dot file. So, you can use both of these methods to eliminate dot files and subdirectories like this (the code is in directory_iterator_02.php):

```
$dir = new DirectoryIterator('.');
foreach ($dir as $file) {
  if (!$file->isDot() && !$file->isDir()) {
    echo $file . '<br />';
  }
}
```

> *The isDot() method identifies only the special files . . . that identify the*
> *current and parent directories. It does not return true for files, such as*
> *.htaccess, that begin with a period. If you want to eliminate such files*
> *when looping through a directory, you need to do so with a conditional*
> *statement or wrap the DirectoryIterator in a RegexIterator. The PCRE*
> *to recognize a file or directory name beginning with a period looks like*
> *this: /^\./.*

Including subdirectories in a single operation

The DirectoryIterator examines only one directory. If you want to burrow down into subdirectories, you need to use a different class: RecursiveDirectoryIterator. This automatically enters any subdirectory and loops through its contents. It keeps going down until it reaches the lowest level of the file hierarchy that is descended directly from the starting point.

However, you can't use RecursiveDirectoryIterator on its own. All SPL iterators that begin with Recursive need to be wrapped in the oddly named RecursiveIteratorIterator (the name's not so odd when you realize it's an iterator for recursive iterators).

The following code (in `directory_iterator_03.php`) shows how you use these two itera-tors in combination:

```
$dir = new RecursiveIteratorIterator(new ➥
  RecursiveDirectoryIterator('.'));
foreach ($dir as $file) {
  echo $file . '<br />';
}
```

This produces output similar to that shown in Figure 7-16. As you can see, the RecursiveDirectoryIterator no longer needs to check isDot() and isDir(). It ignores dot files and prefixes each filename with its path. Because the code in `directory_iterator_03.php` uses the shorthand for the current directory (.), files in the current directory are prefixed with `.\`; the two text files in the subdirectory are prefixed with `.\subfolder\`. (On Linux and Mac OS X, forward slashes are used as the directory separators.)

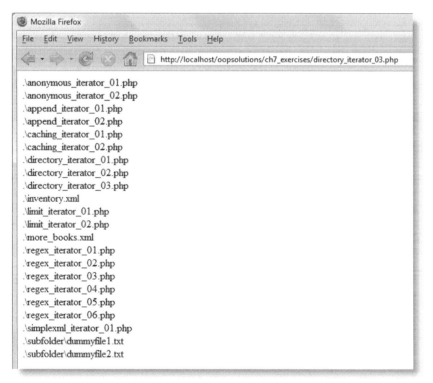

Figure 7-16. The RecursiveDirectoryIterator includes the contents of subdirectories in the results.

The pathname generated by the iterator is dependent on the string passed to the RecursiveDirectoryIterator constructor. On my computer, the ch7_exercises folder is located at `C:\htdocs\oopsolutions\ch7_exercises`. If I use that instead of the shorthand form, the full path is displayed like this:

```
C:\htdocs\oopsolutions\ch7_exercises\anonymous_iterator_01.php
C:\htdocs\oopsolutions\ch7_exercises\anonymous_iterator_02.php
C:\htdocs\oopsolutions\ch7_exercises\append_iterator_01.php
. . .
```

The ability to loop through an entire directory structure with so few lines of code is very convenient, but what if you don't want the path? One way would be to use strrpos() to find the last directory separator, but the public methods of the SplFileInfo class make it a lot easier and provide a lot of useful information. So, let's take a quick look at them.

Extracting file information with SplFileInfo

The SplFileInfo class reveals the properties of a file or directory. SplFileInfo objects are created automatically when you examine the contents of a directory with DirectoryIterator or RecursiveDirectoryIterator, but you can also create one directly by passing the filename or path to the SplFileInfo constructor. Table 7-2 describes information returned by SplFileInfo methods. You can see the output of each method in fileinfo.php in the ch7_exercises folder.

Table 7-2. File information accessible through SplFileInfo methods

Method	Description
getATime()	Returns a Unix timestamp indicating when the file was last accessed.
getCTime()	Returns a Unix timestamp indicating when any changes were last made to the file. This includes changing permissions or ownership, even if the contents are not updated.
getMTime()	Returns a Unix timestamp indicating when the contents of the file were last modified.
getFilename()	Returns the name of the file.
getGroup()	Returns the ID of the group that owns the file or directory. On Windows, this is 0.
getInode()	Returns the number of the inode that stores the ownership and permissions of the file or directory. On Windows, this is 0.
getLinkTarget()	Returns the target path of a symbolic link or alias.
getOwner()	Returns the ID of the owner of the file or directory. On Windows, this is 0.
getPath()	Returns the path minus the filename. If the current object is a directory, the directory name is omitted. The path is based on the argument passed to the constructor. To get the full path, use getRealPath().

Continued

Table 7-2. *Continued*

Method	Description
getPathname()	Returns the path and file or directory name. The path is based on the argument passed to the constructor. To get the full path, use getRealPath().
getRealPath()	Returns the full path, including the filename, if appropriate.
getPerms()	Returns the permissions as a base-ten number. See text for explanation of how to convert this to an octal number (such as 0755).
getSize()	Returns the size of the file or directory in bytes.
getType()	Returns a string indicating the current object is a file, directory, or link.
isDir()	Returns true if the current object is a directory.
isExecutable()	Returns true if the current object is executable.
isFile()	Returns true if the current object is a file.
isLink()	Returns true if the current object is a symbolic link or alias.
isReadable()	Returns true if the current object is readable.
isWritable()	Returns true if the current object is writable.

So, to access only the filenames with RecursiveDirectoryIterator, you need to use getFilename() like this (the code is in directory_iterator_04.php):

```
$dir = new RecursiveIteratorIterator(new ➥
  RecursiveDirectoryIterator('.'));
foreach ($dir as $file) {
  echo $file->getFilename() . '<br />';
}
```

The methods and the information they reveal are self-explanatory. The only method that produces a rather user unfriendly result is getPerms(), which returns the permissions of a file or directory as a base-ten integer, rather than in the more familiar octal format, such as 0755 or 0777. The following formula converts $file->getPerms() to an octal figure:

```
$octalPermissions = substr(sprintf('%o', $file->getPerms()), -4);
```

Finding files of a particular type

SPL directory iterators can easily be combined with other iterators. To find an XML filename extension when looping through a list of files, use this case-insensitive PCRE: /\.xml$/i. So, you can wrap $dir from the previous example in a RegexIterator like this (the revised code is in directory_iterator_05.php):

```
$dir = new RecursiveIteratorIterator(new ➥
  RecursiveDirectoryIterator('.'));
$xmlFiles = new RegexIterator($dir, '/\.xml$/i');
foreach ($xmlFiles as $file) {
  echo $file->getFilename() . '<br />';
}
```

If you run this script in ch7_exercises, it displays the names of three XML files: inventory.xml, inventory2.xml, and more_books.xml.

Reading and writing files with SplFileObject

Looping through directories to find information about files is all very well, but the reason you examine the contents of a directory is usually because you want to do something with the files you find. No problem. The SplFileInfo class has a handy method called openFile(), which opens the file ready for reading or writing, and returns it as an instance of the SplFileObject class. What's really nice about SplFileObject is that it combines the convenience of SPL iteration with the familiarity of existing PHP functions for reading and writing files.

> SplFileObject *inherits from* SplFileInfo, *so both classes have many features in common. Since the names are very similar, take care not to get them mixed up.*

Let's start by using the openFile() method with SplFileInfo objects created by DirectoryIterator. The following code (in read_file_01.php) uses DirectoryIterator to loop through the subfolder directory of ch7_exercises. The conditional statement makes sure that the code inside the first foreach loop deals only with files, opens the file, and processes it line by line with another foreach loop.

```
$dir = new DirectoryIterator('subfolder');
foreach ($dir as $file) {
  // Make sure it's not a dot file or directory
  if (!$file->isDot() && !$file->isDir()) {
    // Open the file
    $currentFile = $file->openFile();
    // Loop through each line of the file and display it
    foreach ($currentFile as $line) {
      echo $line . '<br />';
    }
  echo '<br />';
  }
}
```

As you can see from Figure 7-17, the inner foreach loop has displayed the contents of each file in the subfolder directory. By default, openFile() returns the file as an

SplFileObject in read-only mode with each line of the file treated as an iterator element, so you can loop through the file's contents with foreach.

Figure 7-17. You can read the contents of files while exploring the contents of a directory.

The other way to create an SplFileObject is by passing the filename (with path, if necessary) to the SplFileObject constructor. By default, this also opens the file in read-only mode. You can loop through the lines of the file in exactly the same way, as shown by this example in read_file_02.php:

```php
$file = new SplFileObject('sonnet116.txt');
foreach ($file as $line) {
  echo $line . '<br />';
}
```

Figure 7-18 shows the output of read_file_02.php both in a browser and the underlying source code. Note the way that the <br /> characters are at the beginning of each line, rather than at the end, as you might have expected. This is because the foreach loop puts a new line character at the end of each line. (As you know, browsers ignore new line characters; the <br /> is simply required for display in a browser.) A new line character at the end of each line is usually what you want, but you might need to strip the new line characters if they interfere with the way you process the contents of a file.

However, that's not all. An SplFileObject can be opened with any of the read/write modes that you're probably already familiar with from using the standard PHP function fopen(). Table 7-3 lists the modes and what they're used for. When setting the mode, you need to bear in mind the following:

- The mode needs to be enclosed in quotes.
- The openFile() method takes the mode as its first argument.
- The SplFileObject constructor takes the mode as its second argument (after the filename).
- You can't read a nonexistent file, so the SplFileObject constructor throws an exception if passed an incorrect filename when used without a mode.
- SplFileObject inherits from SplFileInfo, so both support the openFile() method.
- The file must already exist before an SplFileInfo object can be created, so the x and x+ modes do not work with SplFileInfo::openFile().

276

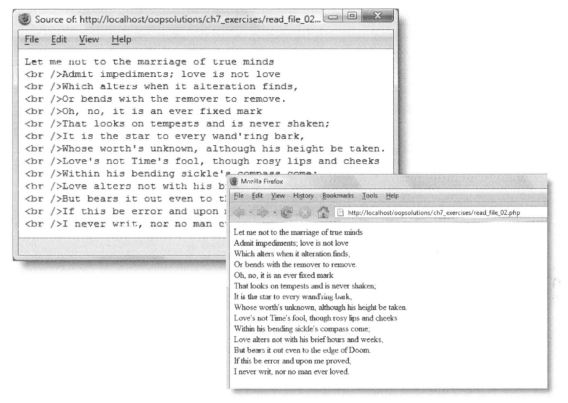

Figure 7-18. A new line character is kept at the end of each line when looping through the contents of a file.

Table 7-3. Read/write modes used with SplFileInfo::openFile() and SplFileObject

Type	Mode	Description
Read-only	r	This is the default mode, and specifying it is optional. It opens the file at the first line in read-only mode. When used with the SplFileObject constructor, the file must already exist.
Write-only	w	Existing data is deleted before writing. When used with the SplFileObject constructor, this creates the file if it doesn't already exist.
	a	Append mode. New data is added at end of file. When used with the SplFileObject constructor, this creates a file if it doesn't already exist.
	x	This creates a file only if it doesn't already exist and prevents existing data from being overwritten by accident.

Continued

Table 7-3. *Continued*

Type	Mode	Description
Read/write	r+	Read/write operations can take place in either order and begin wherever the internal pointer is at the time. The pointer is initially placed at beginning of file. The file must already exist.
	w+	Existing data is deleted. Data can be read back after writing. When used with the SplFileObject constructor, this creates a file if it doesn't already exist.
	a+	This opens a file ready to add new data at the end. It also permits data to be read back after the internal pointer has been moved. When used with the SplFileObject constructor, this creates a file if it doesn't already exist.
	x+	This creates a new file but fails if a file of the same name already exists. Data can be read back after writing.

Read and write operations use an internal pointer that keeps track of the current position inside the file in the same way as a cursor in a word processor. You can move the pointer to the beginning of a specific line by using the seek() method and passing it the number of the line (counting from 0). If you want more precise control over the position of the pointer, you can use fseek(), which calculates the new position as an offset measured in bytes. Many SplFileObject methods like fseek() have been adapted from the PHP file system functions used with fopen(), and work the same way. Table 7-4 describes the read/write methods that you can use with an SplFileObject and provides the URL for the online documentation of the equivalent file system function where appropriate.

Table 7-4. SplFileObject read/write methods

Method	Arguments	Description
eof()		Returns true when the end of the file is reached; otherwise false.
fflush()		Flushes current data. Returns true on success, false on failure.
fgetc()		Returns the next character from the file. If the character is a new line character, the object's internal line counter is *not* updated.

Method	Arguments	Description
fgetcsv()	$delimiter, $enclosure	Gets the next line from a CSV (comma-separated values) file, and returns it as an array. Both arguments are optional. $delimiter sets the field delimiter, and defaults to a comma. $enclosure sets the field enclosure character and defaults to a double quotation mark.
fgets()		Gets the next line from the file, and increases the object's internal line number.
fgetss()	$allowable_tags	Gets the next line from the file, and strips all HTML and PHP tags. At the time of this writing, you must set a maximum line length with setMaxLineLen() before calling fgetss(). The $allowable_tags optional argument lists those tags that you want to preserve. They should be presented as a string like this: '<strong><em>'.
flock()	$operation, $wouldblock	This works the same way as the PHP flock() function and uses the same constants (see http://docs.php.net/manual/en/function.flock.php).
fpassthru()		Outputs the remaining part of the file, and returns the size of the remaining part passed through.
fscanf()	$format	Outputs the current line formatted as specified in the $format argument, which uses the same formatting characters as sprintf() (see http://docs.php.net/manual/en/function.sprintf.php).
fseek()	$pos, $whence	Moves the file's internal pointer. It works the same way as the PHP function fseek() and uses the same constants (see http://docs.php.net/manual/en/function.fseek.php).
fstat()		Outputs an array of statistics about the file (see http://docs.php.net/manual/en/function.stat.php).
ftell()		Returns the current position of the file's internal pointer.
ftruncate()	$size	Truncates the file to the number of bytes specified in the $size argument.
fwrite()	$string, $length	Writes the string passed as the first argument. Writing begins at the current position of the file's internal pointer and overwrites existing content. The optional $length argument specifies the maximum length of the string to write. Returns the number of bytes written, or false on failure.

7

Continued

279

Table 7-4. *Continued*

Method	Arguments	Description
getCurrentLine()		Moves to the *next* line and returns it. To get the current line, use current().
seek()	$line	Moves the file's internal pointer to the beginning of the line specified (counting from zero).
setMaxLineLen()	$length	Sets the maximum line length (in bytes) for read operations. This method must be used to set a line length before calling the fgetss() method.

Most of the methods work exactly as you would expect. They duplicate their procedural counterparts but don't need a reference to a file handle because that's already stored in the SplFileObject. For example, the code in write_file_01.php and write_file_02.php opens a file called newfile.txt in the subfolder directory in append mode and writes a line of text. If the newfile.txt doesn't already exist, it's automatically created. Both files do the same thing, but write_file_01.php uses the object-oriented approach with SplFileObject like this:

```
$file = new SplFileObject('subfolder/newfile.txt', 'a');
$written = $file->fwrite("This was written by an SplFileObject\n");
echo $written . ' bytes written to ' . $file->getFilename();
```

The code in write_file_02.php uses the procedural approach, and looks like this:

```
$file = fopen('subfolder/newfile.txt', 'a');
$written = fwrite($file, "This was written using procedural code\n");
fclose($file);
echo $written . ' bytes written to file';
```

With the procedural approach, you need to pass the reference to the file as the first argument to fwrite(). You also need to close the file afterward. There's no real difference between the two, but the object-oriented approach is arguably cleaner and easier to read. Load write_file_01.php and write_file_02.php into a browser. As long as there are no problems with file permissions, newfile.txt will be created in the subfolder directory. If you open the file, it should contain the following:

```
This was written by an SplFileObject
This was written using procedural code
```

Each time you reload write_file_01.php or write_file_02.php, the relevant string will be added to newfile.txt.

You should have no difficulty using the methods in Table 7-4 if you're familiar with their procedural equivalents. However, you need to be careful about the following points:

- Using seek() takes you to the beginning of the designated line. However, both the fgets() and getCurrentLine() methods move to the *next* line before reading the content. To get the current line after moving the file's internal pointer, you need to use current(), one of the Iterator interface methods listed in Table 7-5 and described in the next section. The difference is demonstrated in Figure 7-19 (the code is in read_file_03.php).

- Before using the fgetss() method to strip HTML and PHP tags, you must set a maximum line length with setMaxLineLen(). The procedural function takes this value as a direct argument, but the object-oriented method needs it to be set separately.

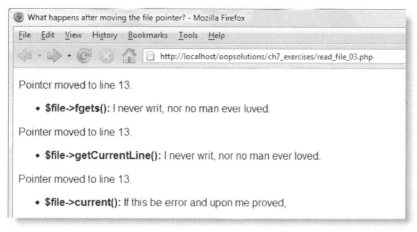

Figure 7-19. To get the current line after moving the file's internal pointer, you must use current().

To round out this whirlwind tour of the Standard PHP Library, let's take a quick look at extending SPL iterators.

Extending iterators

All the iterators discussed so far are built-in, but some SPL iterators, such as FilterIterator, exist only as abstract classes, so you need to extend them before you can use them. Also, all the classes in the Standard PHP Library are extensible, allowing you to create your own custom iterators.

Understanding the Iterator interface

All iterators implement the internal Iterator interface, which comprises the five methods in Table 7-5.

Table 7-5. Iterator interface methods

Method	Description
rewind()	Moves the iterator back to the first element.
key()	Returns the key of the current element. This can be a string or an index number, depending on the object.
current()	Returns the value of the current element.
next()	Moves to the next element.
valid()	Checks if there is a current element after calls to next() or rewind(). Returns true if one is found; otherwise, false.

The following code shows the methods listed in Table 7-5 in action by using a while loop instead of foreach (the code is in iterator_interface.php):

```
$author = array('name'    => 'David',
                'city'    => 'London',
                'country' => 'United Kingdom');
$iterator = new ArrayIterator($author);

// Move the iterator to the first item
$iterator->rewind();
// Loop through each element while the valid() method returns true
while ($iterator->valid()) {
    // Display the key and value of each element
    echo $iterator->key() . ': ' . $iterator->current() . '<br />';
    // Move to the next element
    $iterator->next();
}
```

The output of this code is shown in Figure 7-20. Strictly speaking, it's not necessary to use the rewind() method with a new iterator, but I have included it here to show all five methods in operation. It goes without saying that a foreach loop is much simpler, but it's useful to know how these methods work if you need greater control over the flow of a loop either with an existing iterator or when extending one.

In the next chapter, you'll see a fully worked example of implementing the Iterator interface in a custom class that returns the results of a database query that you can iterate through with a foreach loop.

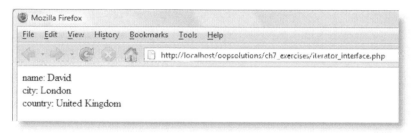

Figure 7-20. Using the methods of the Iterator interface directly produces the same results as a foreach loop.

Extending the FilterIterator class

The FillerIterator class is abstract, so you can't instantiate a FilterIterator object directly. You need to extend the class by defining the accept() method, which should return true when the current element meets whatever conditions you set. The following exercise demonstrates how it works.

Creating a price filter

This exercise shows how to create a FilterIterator class to set the maximum price of books to be displayed from inventory2.xml. It begins by hard-coding the accept() method to limit the maximum price to $40. The class is then improved by overriding the constructor so that it accepts the maximum price as an argument. To keep things simple, the class is defined in the same file as the script that uses it.

1. Create a file called filter_iterator.php in the ch7_exercises folder, and insert the following class definition:

```
class PriceFilter extends FilterIterator
{
  public function accept()
  {
    return substr($this->current(), 1) <= 40;
  }
}
```

The FilterIterator abstract class defines all the Iterator interface methods listed in Table 7-5, so the only thing you need to do is extend the FilterIterator class and create your own accept() method. The PriceFilter class will be used to iterate through the <paperback> node of inventory2.xml.

The accept() method needs to see whether the value of the current <paperback> node is less than or equal to 40. If it is, it should return true; otherwise, false.

$this->current() gives you the value of the current element, but the prices in inventory2.xml begin with a dollar sign, so you need to strip that off by passing $this->current() to substr() and beginning the substring at the second

283

character counting from 0. This leaves you with the raw number to make the comparison. All you're interested in is whether it's true or false, so the result is returned in the same line.

2. That's all that's needed to define the PriceFilter class. You can now use it like this (the code is in filter_iterator_01.php):

```
$xml = simplexml_load_file('inventory2.xml', 'SimpleXMLIterator');
foreach ($xml->book as $book) {
  foreach (new PriceFilter($book->price->paperback) as $price) {
    echo "$book->title ($price)<br />";
  }
}
```

This uses an inner loop in the same way as in "Filtering a loop with a regular expression" earlier in the chapter (see Figure 7-5). The inner loop passes $book->price->paperback to the PriceFilter. If the price is $40 or less, the book title and its price are displayed. All other books are filtered out, as shown in Figure 7-21.

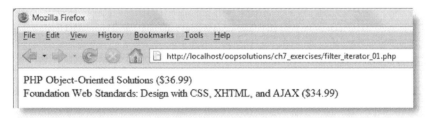

Figure 7-21. The filter has excluded all books that cost more than $40.

3. Hard-coding the maximum price into the PriceFilter class makes this very inflexible, so let's improve it by turning the maximum price into a property and setting its value by passing an argument to the constructor. The revised code (in filter_iterator_02.php) looks like this:

```
class PriceFilter extends FilterIterator
{
  protected $_max;

  public function __construct($iterator, $maxPrice)
  {
    parent::__construct($iterator);
    $this->_max = (float) $maxPrice;
  }

  public function accept()
  {
    return substr($this->current(), 1) <= $this->_max;
  }
}
```

When overriding the constructor of a parent class, unless you want to replace the functionality of the parent constructor completely, you must always call the parent constructor and pass it any arguments it expects. A basic `FilterIterator` takes just one argument: the iterator that you want to filter. So, the constructor of the revised `PriceFilter` takes that argument, and just passes it directly to `parent::__construct()`.

The second argument, $maxPrice, is cast to a floating point number and assigned to the protected property $_max. Casting the value to a floating point number avoids any problems with invalid arguments. If the string "fifty" is passed as the second argument, it's converted to 0.

The final change is to the `accept()` method, which now uses $this->_max instead of the hard-coded value.

4. The `PriceFilter` class now expects two arguments, so change the code in step 2 like this (the finished code is in `filter_iterator_02.php`):

```
$xml = simplexml_load_file('inventory2.xml', 'SimpleXMLIterator');
foreach ($xml->book as $book) {
  foreach (new PriceFilter($book->price->paperback, 40) as $price) {
    echo "$book->title ($price)<br />";
  }
}
```

If you run the script now, it produces the same result as shown in Figure 7-18, but you can control the display by altering the value of the second argument passed to PriceFilter. Because both scripts are in the same file, it makes no real difference in this exercise, but building an adaptable filter like this with the class in a separate file is potentially very useful in a large application.

You might be wondering if there's much to be gained by creating a `FilterIterator` like this. After all, the same effect could be achieved by using a simple conditional statement inside the outer foreach loop. The `accept()` method in this exercise performs a very simple calculation, but you might want to run a series of tests on the value of the current element. Encapsulating them in a `FilterIterator` would certainly be worthwhile, resulting in cleaner code that is easy to maintain and debug.

Chapter review

The Standard PHP Library is still a work in progress. In this chapter, I have covered ten of the most useful iterators, namely:

- `ArrayIterator`: Converts an array into an object that can be used with an iterator
- `LimitIterator`: Restricts the number of loops by setting start and end points
- `SimpleXMLIterator`: Allows you to combine SimpleXML with other iterators
- `RegexIterator`: Filters the loop using a Perl-compatible regular expression
- `AppendIterator`: Combines multiple iterable objects so they can be processed in a single loop

- CachingIterator: Looks ahead to see if any more elements remain in the loop
- DirectoryIterator: Iterates through a single directory of files
- RecursiveDirectoryIterator: Iterates recursively through a directory hierarchy
- RecursiveIteratorIterator: Required to loop through a recursive iterator
- FilterIterator: Abstract class that lets you create your own filters

More iterators are planned, including a search iterator, which stops after finding a matching element. Although you can emulate these iterators with procedural code, one of the main advantages lies in the fact that they are part of core PHP and are implemented in C code, which runs much faster. The other important advantage is that you can wrap iterators within each other. Although this concept takes a little getting used to, it results in much cleaner code than a series of nested loops interspersed with conditional statements. We also looked at the SplFileInfo and SplFileObject classes, which provide a lot of useful information about files.

In the next two chapters, we'll continue our journey with XML by generating it on the fly from a database and using it to create a news feed similar to the one on the friends of ED web site. The next chapter builds on this one by showing you how to create your own iterators.

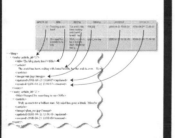

XML is a highly efficient way of sharing information between computers. It's platform-neutral and widely used for web services, such as news feeds. But typing out XML documents manually is both tedious and prone to mistakes. It's far better to store the information in a database and generate XML dynamically. That way, you can always be sure that the content is the most recently available. Moreover, all it takes to customize the structure of the XML is a change to the query you send to the database.

Because XML is intended for processing by computers, you need to be very careful to get the syntax right. Browsers are forgiving of mistakes in HTML, but a missing quote, misplaced tag, or invalid tag name can render XML unreadable to a program intended to process it. XMLWriter, which was added to PHP in version 5.1.2, takes the doubt out of generating XML dynamically. It's easy to use and guarantees valid XML.

But this chapter isn't only about XML; it's about improving the way you retrieve results from a database by implementing the Iterator interface from the Standard PHP Library (SPL). This enables you to wrap a database result in any of the iterators covered in the previous chapter, resulting in much more versatile code.

This chapter covers

- Creating a class to query a MySQL database
- Implementing the Iterator interface to return a database result that's easy to loop through
- Using specialized exceptions for greater control over error handling
- Using XMLWriter to generate valid XML
- Outputting the generated XML directly and storing it in a file

I assume that you have access to a MySQL database and that you are familiar with at least the basics of Structured Query Language (SQL) for creating database queries. If you need to get up to speed with MySQL and SQL, I suggest studying my earlier book *PHP Solutions: Dynamic Web Design Made Easy* (friends of ED, ISBN-13: 978-1-59059-731-6) or *Beginning PHP and MySQL: From Novice to Professional, Third Edition* by W. Jason Gilmore (Apress, ISBN-13: 978-1-59059-862-7).

The class that converts the database result into an XML document forms the basis of a more specialized news feed that you'll build in Chapter 9.

Designing the application

The first stage in building any application is to decide what it's for and what features it will have. Although generating your own XML from a database sounds cool, there's not much point in doing so unless it's going to be used for something that can't be done by accessing the database directly. It might be more efficient to query the database and display the results within a web page without going through the extra step of generating XML.

Defining the application's purpose

A common use for XML is to provide data for Ajax (Asynchronous JavaScript and XML) widgets that update part of a web page's content without the need to reload the whole page. Another is for news feeds. Unless you have been on Mars for the past few years, you should be familiar with the initials RSS that seem to have sprung up everywhere on web sites large and small. The initials refer to several different formats: Really Simple Syndication, RDF Site Summary, and Rich Site Summary. (RDF, incidentally, stands for Resource Description Framework.) In spite of the different formats, RSS feeds all have one thing in common: they're based on XML.

So, that's what we're going to build: a class that generates XML from information in a database. The XML will be suitable for use with Ajax widgets or can also be extended to create XML that conforms to one of the RSS formats. I'll discuss the RSS requirements in the next chapter, but the basic structure needs to be similar to the friends of ED news feed that you worked with in Chapters 5 and 6 (see Figure 6-17). In other words, you need a series of repeating nodes, each containing a single level of child elements where the actual data is stored. In the friends of ED news feed, each top-level node represents an article, but the same structure can be used for an image gallery (filename, caption, and description) or a product catalog (name, description, price, etc.)

This makes it very easy to extract data from a database. Each row of results becomes a top-level node, and the individual fields in each row populate the child elements, as shown in Figure 8-1. The root element in this example is called <blog>, and each top-level node is called <entry>. The child nodes have the same names as their respective database columns, but the table's primary key has been added as an attribute in the opening tag of each <entry> node.

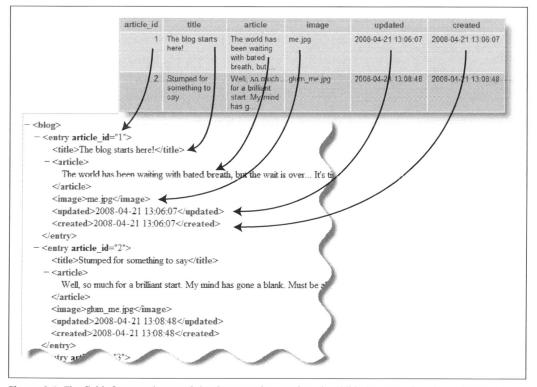

Figure 8-1. The fields from each row of database results populate the child elements of each top-level node.

Setting the requirements

The example in Figure 8-1 draws data from a single table, but the class that creates the XML must be flexible enough to cope with data drawn from multiple tables, rather than just grabbing all the data from one table. This means the class needs to pass a SQL query to the database, instead of just a table name. Handling the result from multiple tables won't be any different, because it's just a question of processing one row of the database result at a time. Let's draw up a list of other requirements.

- Default names will be set for the root and top-level nodes, but there must be a way to specify custom names.
- The names and order of the child nodes will be taken from the column names. This is another advantage of using a SQL query, making it possible to assign aliases to column names.
- There must be a way of designating which primary key (if any) is used as an attribute in the opening tag of the top-level nodes.
- The class must be capable of outputting the XML directly in response to a request from a browser.
- There must also be a way of saving the XML to a local file.

It's also important to define the limitations of the application. To keep things simple, I have made the following decisions:

- The only database supported is MySQL.
- Each top-level node replicates a row in the results from the database query, so there is only one level of child nodes.
- Multiple child nodes of the same name are not permitted in the same top-level node.

This final restriction means that the class can't generate XML documents similar to inventory.xml in Chapters 6 and 7, where some <book> nodes have multiple <author> child nodes. I made this decision because allowing multiple child nodes of the same name involves either multiple queries or looping through the database result set to associate the multiple values with the correct parent node. My aim in this book is to provide generic solutions for use in a wide range of situations. Building more complex XML is probably better suited to a custom solution.

Building the application

In keeping with good OOP practice, the database side of things needs to be kept separate from the XML generation. The database class can be used in other projects, and if you decide to use a different database later on, all that's necessary is to call a different database connection class. (That's a separate project for you. As I said before, this chapter deals only with MySQL.)

The class that generates the XML has no interest in how the data is retrieved; all it cares about is receiving the data in a consistent format. Handing off the creation of a database connection like this is an example of the **Factory design pattern**. The concept of a "factory" is that it's an object or method that creates another object. If you want to use a different database, you just use a different factory. Delegating a task like this avoids the need to rewrite a substantial part of a class whenever requirements change. All it involves is changing the call to the factory. Of course, the other factory has to exist or be created before you can use it, but because it's not closely coupled with anything else, it can be used with other classes.

In fact, I'm going to split the database side of things into two classes. The first handles the connection and submits the query to the second class, which implements the SPL Iterator interface (see Chapter 7) and prepares the result set so that it can be accessed with a foreach loop. So, there are three classes, namely:

- Pos_XmlExporter
- Pos_MysqlImprovedConnection
- Pos_MysqlImprovedResult

> *There are three ways of connecting to a MySQL database: the original MySQL extension, MySQL Improved, and PHP Data Objects (PDO). However, not all hosting companies install the PDO drivers for MySQL, so I have based the classes on MySQL Improved, which requires MySQL 4.1 or above. For the benefit of readers using an older version of MySQL, the download files include two classes based on the original MySQL extension. The underlying design is the same, so they are not described in the text.*

Since everything depends on the database result, let's deal with the two database classes first. As with previous chapters, the complete code for each class is in the finished_classes folder of the download files. If you want to build your own versions, create each class in a separate file in the Pos folder, and give the file the same name as the section after the underscore (e.g., define Pos_MysqlImprovedConnection in MysqlImprovedConnection.php).

Creating the database connection

The MySQL Improved extension (http://docs.php.net/manual/en/book.mysqli.php) has both procedural functions and object-oriented methods, but since this book is dedicated to OOP, I'm using the object-oriented approach except where there is no alternative to a procedural function.

The code for the Pos_MysqlImprovedConnection class is very simple, so here it is in full:

```
class Pos_MysqlImprovedConnection
{
  protected $_connection;
```

8

```php
    public function __construct($host, $user, $pwd, $db)
    {
      $this->_connection = @new mysqli($host, $user, $pwd, $db);
      if (mysqli_connect_errno()) {
        throw new RuntimeException('Cannot access database: ' ➥
          . mysqli_connect_error());
      }
    }

    public function getResultSet($sql)
    {
      $results = new Pos_MysqlImprovedResult($sql, $this->_connection);
      return $results;
    }

    public function __destruct()
    {
      $this->_connection->close();
    }
  }
```

The class has one protected property that stores a reference to the database connection. The connection is created in the constructor by passing the server name, username, password, and database name as arguments, and passing them directly to a mysqli constructor. To avoid ugly error messages being displayed onscreen, I have used the error control operator (@) and checked for errors with mysqli_connect_errno(). This, along with mysqli_connect_error(), is one of the few cases where only a procedural function is available. Although this might seem odd, it's because the mysqli object can't be created if connection to the database fails. Without an object, there's nothing to apply a method to.

If the connection fails, the constructor throws a RuntimeException. This is one of several specialized exception classes defined in the SPL (see Chapter 7). You use it in exactly the same way as an ordinary exception. The advantage of using specialized exception classes is they give you greater control over error handling routines, as you'll see later.

The getResultSet() method takes a SQL query as its single argument, creates a Pos_MysqlImprovedResult object, and returns it. You'll see how the Pos_MysqlImprovedResult class works in a moment.

Finally, the __destruct() magic function closes the database connection. The destructor is called automatically when the Pos_MysqlImprovedConnection object is no longer needed.

Getting the database result

The MySQL Improved object-oriented interface has a query() method that submits the SQL to the database and returns the result. So, why create a separate class to handle this simple operation? The answer is because it makes life a lot easier if you can iterate through the results with a foreach loop. This has been made possible by the SPL Iterator interface that was described in the previous chapter. Classes that implement this interface must define five methods. For convenience, they're listed again in Table 8-1.

Table 8-1. Iterator interface methods

Method	Description
rewind()	Moves the iterator back to the first element.
key()	Returns the key of the current element. This can be a string or an index number, depending on the object.
current()	Returns the value of the current element.
next()	Moves to the next element.
valid()	Checks if there is a current element after calls to next() or rewind(). Returns true if one is found; otherwise, false.

It's also important to be able to count the number of rows in a database result. As I explained in Chapter 2, although a class cannot inherit from more than one parent, it can implement as many interfaces as you want. In addition to Iterator, I'm going to implement another SPL interface called Countable. This requires the definition of just one method: count(), which returns the number of elements in the object.

So, the basic structure of the Pos_MysqlImprovedResult class needs to look like this:

```
class Pos_MysqlImprovedResult implements Iterator, Countable
{
  public function __construct($sql, $connection)
  {
    // Submit the query and capture the result
  }
  public function rewind() {}
  public function valid() {}
  public function current() {}
  public function key() {}
  public function next() {}
  public function count() {}
}
```

Defining the properties and constructor

The class needs the following properties, all of which need to be protected:

- **$_key**: The key of the current element
- **$_current**: The value of the current element
- **$_valid**: Keeps track of whether the loop has moved beyond the end of the list
- **$_result**: The database resource containing the result of the SQL query

The constructor submits the SQL query and stores the result in the $_result property. It's also a good idea to throw a RuntimeException if the query fails. So, the first part of the class definition now looks like this:

```
class Pos_MysqlImprovedResult implements Iterator, Countable
{
  protected $_current;
  protected $_key;
  protected $_valid;
  protected $_result;

  public function __construct($sql, $connection)
  {
    if (!$this->_result = $connection->query($sql)) {
      throw new RuntimeException($connection->error . '. The actual ➥
        query submitted was: ' . $sql);
    }
  }

  // other methods
}
```

The SQL query and the connection object are passed to the constructor by the getResultSet() method of the Pos_MysqlImprovedConnection object. The constructor passes the SQL to the mysqli::query() method and stores the result in the $_result property.

If the query fails, the RuntimeException builds a message using the mysqli::error property and the SQL query. I have included the query in the message as an aid to debugging. The error messages returned by MySQL often tell you there is a syntax error "near" something. That "near" means "immediately preceding," so seeing the whole SQL query is vital to understanding what went wrong. Exposing the SQL query to outside users is a serious security risk, so this should be used only for debugging. In a real application, you need to handle this exception in such a way that the error is logged or emailed to you, but the user sees a neutral error message.

Up to this point, the Pos_MysqlImprovedResult class adds little advantage over using mysqli::query(). What makes the real difference is implementing the Iterator interface.

Implementing the Iterator interface

Coding the five methods required by the Iterator interface is a lot less scary than you might imagine. The purpose of the interface is to make it possible to loop through the results of a database query. A common way is to use a while loop like this:

```
while ($row = $result->fetch_assoc()) {
  // extract each field from $row
}
```

The condition uses `mysqli_result::fetch_assoc()` to grab the next row, stores it as $row, and keeps on running until it returns false. Inside the loop, $row gives you access to the current element.

In terms of the Iterator interface, this performs the same role as the next() method. The main difference is that the Iterator interface has explicit ways of keeping track of the current position in the loop. So, the next() method needs to set the values of the three protected properties like this:

- $this->_result->fetch_assoc() gets the next available row of results and assigns it to the $_current property.

- If you have reached the end of the result set, $this->_result->fetch_assoc() returns null. So, if $_current is null, the $_valid property is set to false; otherwise, it's set to true.

- The $_key property is incremented by 1. (Its initial value is set to 0 by the rewind() method.)

All that boils down to just a few of lines of code:

```
public function next()
{
  $this->_current = $this->_result->fetch_assoc();
  $this->_valid = is_null($this->_current) ? false : true;
  $this->_key++;
}
```

The $_current, $_key, and $_valid properties now have values, so each property's corresponding method simply returns its value like this:

```
public function current()
{
  return $this->_current;
}

public function key()
{
  return $this->_key;
}

public function valid()
{
  return $this->_valid;
}
```

All that remains to be done is to define the rewind() method. It's very similar to the next() method in that it uses $this->_result->fetch_assoc() to set the values of the $_current and $_valid properties. However, it fulfils two other important roles: setting the value of the $_key property to 0 and rewinding the result set if the loop has

8

already been accessed. You can tell if the loop has already been run if the $_key property has a value. So, if $_key is not null, the loop is reset to the first row by calling mysqli_result::data_seek() and passing it 0 as an argument. The rewind() method looks like this:

```
public function rewind()
{
  if (!is_null($this->_key)) {
    $this->_result->data_seek(0);
  }
  $this->_key = 0;
  $this->_current = $this->_result->fetch_assoc();
  $this->_valid = is_null($this->_current) ? false : true;
}
```

That's all there is to implementing the Iterator interface. The Countable interface is even easier.

Implementing the Countable interface

The Countable interface consists solely of the count() method, which needs to return the number of countable elements in the object. Since the Pos_MysqlImprovedResult class is a wrapper for a mysqli_result object, the count() method returns the value of the mysqli_result->num_rows property like this:

```
public function count()
{
  return $this->_result->num_rows;
}
```

That completes the Pos_MysqlImprovedConnection and Pos_MysqlImprovedResult class definitions. Now it's time to make sure they work as expected.

Testing the database classes

This brief exercise tests the Pos_MysqlImprovedConnection and Pos_MysqlImprovedResult classes. If you haven't created your own versions, you can find fully commented versions of both classes in the finished_classes folder of the download files. You can use any MySQL database of your own for this test. Alternatively, you can load the blog table from blog.sql (or blog40.sql for MySQL 4.0) in the download files.

1. Create a file called test_iterator.php in the ch8_exercises folder. You need both the Pos_MysqlImprovedConnection and Pos_MysqlImprovedResult classes, so include them at the top of the script like this:

   ```
   require_once '../Pos/MysqlImprovedConnection.php';
   require_once '../Pos/MysqlImprovedResult.php';
   ```

2. In a try block, create an instance of Pos_MysqlImprovedConnection, and pass it the database login details:

```
try {
  $conn = new Pos_MysqlImprovedConnection('localhost', 'user', ➥
    'password', 'db_name');
}
```

Replace the arguments with the appropriate values for your own database.

3. Call the getResultSet() method by passing it a SQL query, and assign the result to a variable called $result like this:

```
try {
  $conn = new Pos_MysqlImprovedConnection('localhost', 'user', ➥
    'password', 'db_name');
  $result = $conn->getResultSet('SELECT * FROM blog');
}
```

The blog table has only a few columns and a handful of records, so I'm just selecting everything. If you're working with a bigger table, you might want to add a LIMIT clause to your SQL query to get just three or four results.

4. Because the result from the database implements the Iterator interface, you can access each row with a foreach loop. Then use a nested foreach loop to display the name of each field in the row and its value. The amended code should look like this:

```
try {
  $conn = new Pos_MysqlImprovedConnection('localhost', 'user', ➥
    'password', 'db_name');
  $result = $conn->getResultSet('SELECT * FROM blog');
  foreach ($result as $row) {
    foreach ($row as $field => $value) {
      echo "$field: $value<br />";
    }
  echo '<br />';
  }
}
```

5. To complete the code, add *two* catch blocks like this:

```
try {
  $conn = new Pos_MysqlImprovedConnection('localhost', 'user', ➥
    'password', 'db_name');
  $result = $conn->getResultSet('SELECT * FROM blog');
  foreach ($result as $row) {
    foreach ($row as $field => $value) {
      echo "$field: $value<br />";
    }
  echo '<br />';
  }
} catch (RuntimeException $e) {
  echo 'This is a RuntimeException: ' . $e->getMessage();
} catch (Exception $e) {
  echo 'This is an ordinary Exception: ' . $e->getMessage();
}
```

299

If a RuntimeException is triggered, the first catch block handles it. Any other exception is caught by the second catch block. It's important to put the catch blocks for specialized exceptions *before* a generic catch block. All specialized exceptions inherit from the base Exception class, so if you put the catch blocks the other way round, a specialized exception never gets to the catch block intended for it.

Because this is a test script, the catch blocks simply display error messages, but in a real application, you can fine-tune the way different types of errors are handled. For example, for an exception that indicates a major problem, you can redirect the user to a general error page, but for one that's caused by invalid input, you could invite the user to resubmit the data. Using exceptions and try . . . catch blocks makes it easier to centralize such error handling logic.

6. Save test_iterator.php, and load it into a browser. Alternatively, use test_iterator_01.php in the download files, but make sure you change the database login details and SQL to access one of your own database tables. You should see something similar to Figure 8-2, with the contents of each row from the database query displayed onscreen.

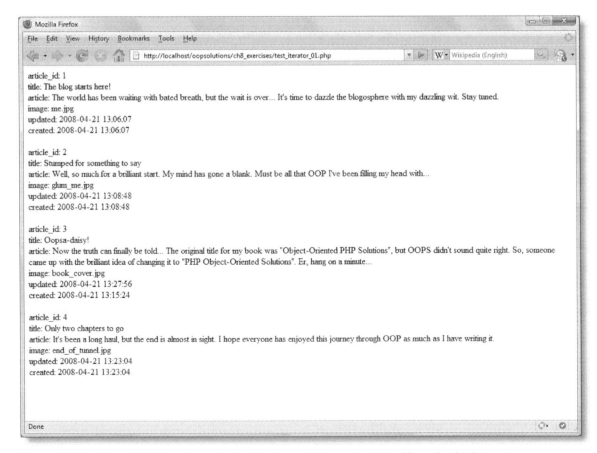

Figure 8-2. The test script displays the contents of each row of the result obtained from the database query.

7. Assuming everything went OK, it's now time for the real test of the iterator. Copy the nested foreach loops that you inserted in step 4, and paste the copy immediately below the original loops like this:

```
foreach ($result as $row) {
  foreach ($row as $field => $value) {
    echo "$field: $value<br />";
  }
  echo '<br />';
}
foreach ($result as $row) {
  foreach ($row as $field => $value) {
    echo "$field: $value<br />";
  }
  echo '<br />';
}
```

8. Save the page, and test it again (or use test_iterator_02.php). This time, you should see the results repeated immediately below the original ones. This is something you can't do with a normal database result without resetting it to the first item. With the Iterator interface, though, using a foreach loop automatically calls the rewind() method, so you can loop through the database results as many times as you need.

9. Because Pos_MysqlImprovedResult implements the Iterator interface, you can use it with any of the SPL iterators that you learned about in Chapter 7. For example, you can pause the display of the database results, insert some text, and then resume from where you left off.

Amend the code in the foreach loops like this:

```
foreach (new LimitIterator($result, 0, 1) as $row) {
  foreach ($row as $field => $value) {
    echo "$field: $value<br />";
  }
  echo '<br />';
}
echo '<p><strong>This is outside both loops.
    Now, back to the database results.</strong></p>';
foreach (new LimitIterator($result, 1, 3) as $row) {
  foreach ($row as $field => $value) {
    echo "$field: $value<br />";
  }
  echo '<br />';
}
```

This uses the LimitIterator to restrict the first loop to displaying just one row of results. This allows a paragraph of text to be displayed before the second loop, which uses LimitIterator again to display the remaining results, as shown in Figure 8-3. Converting the database result to an iterator makes it much more versatile.

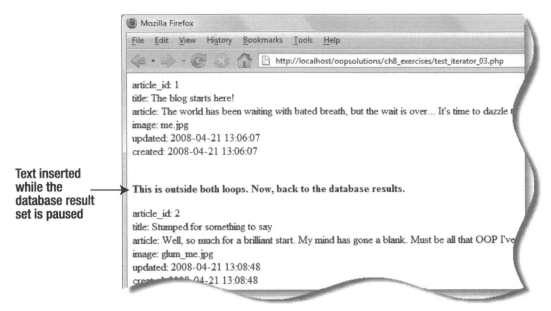

Text inserted while the database result set is paused

Figure 8-3. Implementing the Iterator interface gives you much greater control over the display of database results.

Generating the XML output

Looking back at the requirements laid down at the beginning of the chapter, you can begin to define a skeleton structure for the Pos_XmlExporter class. To start with, it needs to connect to the database and submit a SQL query. You could perform both operations in the constructor, but I think it makes the class easier to use if the database connection and SQL query are handled separately.

Other requirements are the ability to select custom names for the root element and top-level nodes, to use the primary key of a selected table as an attribute of the top-level nodes, and to save the XML to a file. That means the class needs the following methods:

- **__construct()**: This creates the database connection.
- **setQuery()**: This sets the SQL query to be submitted to the database.
- **setTagNames()**: This method sets custom names for the root and top-level nodes. If it's not set, default values are used.
- **usePrimaryKey()**: This defines which table's primary key is used as an attribute in the opening tag of the top-level nodes. If it's not set, no attribute is added.

- **setFilePath()**: This sets the path, filename, and formatting options of the output file. If it's not set, the XML is output to a string.
- **generateXML()**: This does all the hard work, checking the settings, and looping through the database result with XMLWriter to generate the XML.

Defining the properties and constructor

With this list of methods in mind, you can now define the properties for the class as follows:

- **$_dbLink**: This holds a reference to the database connection, which the constructor creates.
- **$_sql**: This is the SQL query set by the setQuery() method.
- **$_docRoot and $_element**: These are the names for the root and element nodes set by setTagNames().
- **$_primaryKey**: This is the name of the table designated by usePrimaryKey().
- **$_xmlFile, $_indent, and $_indentString**: These are all set by the setFilePath() method.

The constructor takes four arguments—the database server, username, password, and database name—which are passed directly to the Pos_MysqlImprovedConnection constructor. An up-to-date server should have XMLWriter, MySQL Improved, and a minimum of MySQL 4.1 installed. Checking the first two is easy, because they're part of PHP. However, checking the version of MySQL involves querying the database, and doing so every time a Pos_XmlExporter object is instantiated is wasteful of resources. Consequently, the constructor limits itself to the first two.

The initial structure of the class looks like this:

```
class Pos_XmlExporter
{
  protected $_dbLink;
  protected $_sql;
  protected $_docRoot;
  protected $_element;
  protected $_primaryKey;
  protected $_xmlFile;
  protected $_indent;
  protected $_indentString;

  public function __construct($server, $username, $password, $database)
  {
    if (!class_exists('XMLWriter')) {
      throw new LogicException('Pos_XmlExporter requires the PHP core ➥
        class XMLWriter.');
    }
```

8

```
      if (!class_exists('mysqli')) {
        throw new LogicException('MySQL Improved not installed. Check ➥
          PHP configuration and MySQL version.');
      }
      $this->_dbLink = new Pos_MysqlImprovedConnection($server, ➥
        $username, $password, $database);
    }

    public function setQuery() {}
    public function setTagNames() {}
    public function usePrimaryKey() {}
    public function setFilePath() {}
    public function generateXML() {}
  }
```

Both conditional statements in the constructor use class_exists() with the negative operator to throw exceptions if the necessary class is not enabled on the server. Notice that I have used LogicException, which is another SPL extension of the base Exception class. A logic exception should be thrown when something is missing that prevents the class from working. Like RuntimeException, which was used in the database connection classes, the idea of throwing a specialized exception is to give you the opportunity to handle errors in different ways depending on what causes them. Since specialized exceptions all inherit from the base class, a generic catch block handles any that are not dealt with separately.

If your server throws an exception because MySQL Improved isn't installed, first check which version of MySQL is running by submitting the following SQL query: SELECT VERSION() (do this using your normal method of connection to MySQL). If the version number is 4.1 or higher, your PHP configuration needs updating to enable MySQL Improved. On shared hosting, Linux, and Mac OS X, there's no easy way to do this, as MySQL Improved needs to be compiled into PHP. On Windows, add extension=php_mysqli.dll to php.ini, make sure that php_mysqli.dll is in the PHP ext folder, and restart the web server.

If you cannot install MySQL Improved or you're using an older version of MySQL, amend the constructor like this:

```
    public function __construct($server, $username, $password, $database)
    {
      if (!class_exists('XMLWriter')) {
        throw new LogicException('Pos_XmlExporter requires the PHP core ➥
          class XMLWriter.');
      }
      $this->_dbLink = new Pos_MysqlOriginalConnection($server, ➥
        $username, $password, $database);
    }
```

The Pos_MysqlOriginalConnection and Pos_MysqlOriginalResult class definitions are in the finished_classes folder of the download files. I have included them as a convenience for readers stuck with an outdated system, but they are not discussed further in this book.

> MySQL ended all support for version 3.23 in 2006, and support for MySQL 4.0 ends on December 31, 2008 (www.mysql.com/about/legal/lifecycle/). If you're still using either version, it's time to upgrade.

The constructor simply establishes the database connection; the SQL query is set and submitted by other methods of the Pos_XmlExporter class.

Setting the SQL query

The SQL query is passed to the setQuery() method as an argument and assigned to the $_sql property like this:

```
public function setQuery($sql)
{
  $this->_sql = $sql;
}
```

Setting the root and top-level node names

You could do the same with the setTagNames() method and assign the value of the arguments to the properties like this:

```
public function setTagNames($docRoot, $element)
{
  $this->_docRoot = $docRoot;
  $this->_element = $element;
}
```

However, this runs the risk of using an invalid XML name. The names of XML tags cannot begin with a number, period, hyphen, or "xml" in either uppercase or lowercase. Punctuation inside a name is also invalid, with the exception of periods, hyphens, and underscores. Trying to remember these rules can be difficult, so let's get the class to check the validity by creating a method called checkValidName(). The amended version of setTagNames() looks like this:

```
public function setTagNames($docRoot, $element)
{
  $this->_docRoot = $this->checkValidName($docRoot);
  $this->_element = $this->checkValidName($element);
}
```

The checkValidName() method is required only internally, so should be protected. I have created a series of Perl-compatible regular expressions to detect illegal characters and thrown different runtime exceptions with helpful messages about why the name is

8

rejected. If no exception is thrown, the method returns the value of the name passed to it. The method looks like this:

```php
protected function checkValidName($name)
{
  if (preg_match('/^[\d\.-]/', $name)) {
    throw new RuntimeException('XML names cannot begin with a number, ⟶
      period, or hyphen.');
  }
  if (preg_match('/^xml/i', $name)) {
    throw new RuntimeException('XML names cannot begin with "xml".');
  }
  if (preg_match('/[\x00-\x2c\x2f\x3b-\x40\x5b-\x5e\x60\x7b-\xbf]/', ⟶
    $name)) {
    throw new RuntimeException('XML names cannot contain spaces or ⟶
      punctuation.');
  }
  if (preg_match('/:/', $name)) {
    throw new RuntimeException('Colons are permitted only in a
      namespace prefix. Pos_XmlExporter does not support namespaces.');
  }
  return $name;
}
```

The rather horrendous PCRE in the third conditional statement uses hexadecimal notation to specify a range of characters. It looks incomprehensible, but is actually a lot easier than attempting to list all the illegal punctuation characters. Trust me. It works.

The final conditional statement prevents the use of colons in the node names. A colon is permitted in an XML name only to separate a node name from a namespace prefix. To keep things simple, I have decided not to support the use of namespaces in this class.

Obtaining the primary key

Adding one of the database primary keys as an attribute in the opening tag of each top-level element in the XML document is a good way of identifying the data in the child elements. Rather than relying on the user's memory to set the name of the column that holds the primary key, it makes the class more error-proof by getting the usePrimaryKey() method to look it up by querying the database like this:

```php
public function usePrimaryKey($table)
{
  $getIndex = $this->_dbLink->getResultSet("SHOW INDEX FROM $table");
  foreach ($getIndex as $row) {
    if ($row['Key_name'] == 'PRIMARY') {
      $this->_primaryKey[] = $row['Column_name'];
    }
  }
}
```

This accepts the name of the table whose primary key you want to use and submits a query to the database to find all indexed columns in the table. The result is returned as a Pos_MysqlImprovedResult object, so you can use a foreach loop to go through it. Lookup tables use a composite primary key (two or more columns designated as a joint primary key), so the $_primaryKey property stores the result as an array.

Setting output file options

To save the XML output to a file, you need to specify where you want to save it. XMLWriter also lets you specify whether to indent child nodes. Indentation makes the file easier to read, so it's a good idea to turn it on by default. I have chosen to use a single tab character as the string used to indent each level. The setFilePath() method assigns the values passed as arguments to the relevant properties like this:

```
public function setFilePath($pathname, $indent = true, ➥
  $indentString = "\t")
{
  $this->_xmlFile = $pathname;
  $this->_indent = $indent;
  $this->_indentString = $indentString;
}
```

Using XMLWriter to generate the output

The final public method, generateXML(), brings everything together by submitting the SQL query to the database, setting the various options, and using XMLWriter to output the XML. Three of the public methods (setTagNames(), usePrimaryKey(), and setFilePath()) are optional, so generateXML() needs to make the following series of decisions, summarized in Figure 8-4:

1. Has the SQL query been set? If not, throw an exception; otherwise, submit the query to the database.

2. Extract the first row of the database result, and pass the key of each field to the internal checkValidName() method. This ensures that column names don't contain spaces or characters that would be illegal in the name of an XML tag. The checkValidName() method throws an exception if it encounters an invalid name.

3. Check if the $_docRoot and $_element properties have been set by setTagNames(). If so, use them; otherwise, use the default values (root and row).

4. Check if usePrimaryKey() has set a value for the $_primaryKey key property. If so, set a Boolean variable to insert its value as an attribute into the opening tag of each top-level node.

5. Check if file options have been set by the setFilePath() method. If so, generate the XML, and save it to the designated file; otherwise, return the XML as a string.

8

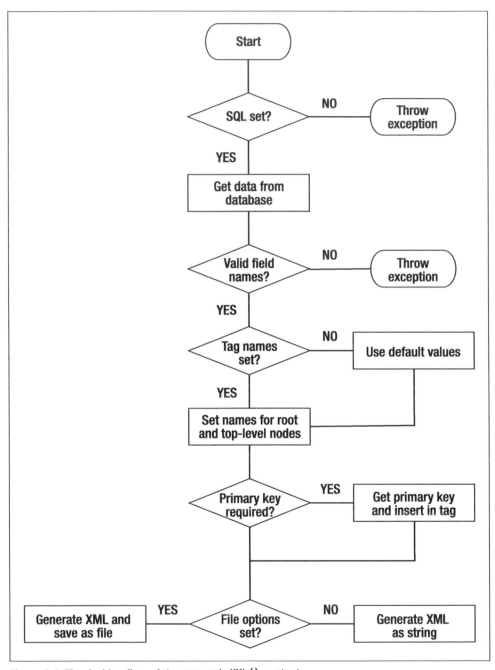

Figure 8-4. The decision flow of the generateXML() method

Steps 1 through 4 look like this:

```
public function generateXML()
{
  // Step 1: Check that the SQL query has been defined
  if (!isset($this->_sql)) {
    throw new LogicException('No SQL query defined! Use setQuery() ➥
before calling generateXML().');
  }
  // Submit the query to the database
  $resultSet = $this->_dbLink->getResultSet($this->_sql);

  // Step 2: Check first row of result for valid field names
  foreach (new LimitIterator($resultSet, 0, 1) as $row) {
    foreach ($row as $field => $value) {
      $this->checkValidName($field);
    }
  }

  // Step 3: Set root and top-level node names
  $this->_docRoot = isset($this->_docRoot) ? $this->_docRoot : 'root';
  $this->_element = isset($this->_element) ? $this->_element : 'row';

  // Step 4: Set a Boolean flag to insert primary key as attribute
  $usePK = (isset($this->_primaryKey) && !empty($this->_primaryKey));

  // Step 5: Generate and output the XML
}
```

The code in the first four steps should need little explanation. The $_dbLink property submits the SQL query to the database and captures the result, which is a Pos_MysqlImprovedResult object. Because the object implements the Iterator interface, the first row can be extracted by using LimitIterator. The name of each field is passed to the internal method checkValidName(). Although this method returns the name, there's no need to capture it; all you're interested in is whether it throws an exception.

If $_docRoot and $_element have already been set by setTagNames(), those values are preserved. Otherwise, the default values of root and row are assigned to them as strings. Finally, $usePK is set to true or false, depending on whether a primary key has been specified by usePrimaryKey().

The rest of the generateXML() method loops through the database result set, using XMLWriter to generate and output the data as XML. XMLWriter is easy to use, as long as you keep track of unclosed elements. The following is an outline of how it works:

1. Instantiate an XMLWriter object.
2. If the XML is to be saved to file, pass the filename (and path if necessary) to the openUri() method, and set the file indentation preferences with setIndent() and setIndentString().

8

309

Alternatively, if the output is not being written to file, use openMemory() instead of openUri().

3. Start the document with a call to startDocument(). You must remember to close the document after all the XML has been generated.

4. Create the root element by passing its name to startElement(). You must remember to close this element before closing the document.

5. Loop through the data you want to include in the XML document.

- If an opening tag contains any attributes or child elements, use startElement().
- After opening a tag, create attributes by passing the name of the attribute and its value as arguments to writeAttribute().
- To create elements that contain only text nodes, pass the name of the element and the value of the text node as arguments to writeElement().
- Close any open tags with endElement().

6. Close the root element with endElement().

7. Close the XML document with endDocument().

8. Output the XML by calling flush(). This applies to all XML documents, regardless of whether being written to file or as a string.

Before moving onto the rest of the code for the generateXML() method, let's take a look at XMLWriter using hard-coded values. Seeing a concrete example makes it easier to visualize with dynamically generated values. The following code generates an XML document with details of two books and outputs it to the browser (it's also in generateXML_01.php):

```
$xml = new XMLWriter();
$xml->openMemory();
$xml->startDocument();
$xml->startElement('inventory'); // open root element
$xml->startElement('book');      // open top-level node
$xml->writeAttribute('isbn13', '978-1-43021-011-5');
$xml->writeElement('title', 'PHP Object-Oriented Solutions');
$xml->writeElement('author', 'David Powers');
$xml->endElement();              // close first <book> node
$xml->startElement('book');      // open next <book> node
$xml->writeAttribute('isbn13', '978-1-59059-819-1');
$xml->writeElement('title', 'Pro PHP: Patterns, Frameworks, Testing ➥
  and More');
$xml->writeElement('author', 'Kevin McArthur');
$xml->endElement();              // close second <book> node
$xml->endElement();              // close root element
$xml->endDocument();
header('Content-Type: text/xml');
echo $xml->flush();
```

The key thing to remember when using XMLWriter is that you need to close open elements with endElement() in the correct place. Unlike startElement(), which takes the element's name as an argument, endElement() doesn't take any arguments, so it can be tricky to keep track of which element is being closed. There's no such problem with attributes and elements that don't have children. Both writeAttribute() and writeElement() complete the operation in one go, taking two arguments: the name of the attribute or element and its value.

If you load generateXML_01.php into a browser, you should see the output shown in Figure 8-5.

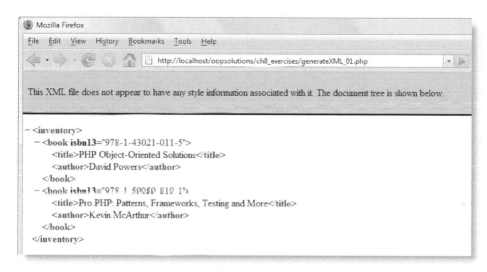

Figure 8-5. An example of XML output by XMLWriter

The code in generateXML_02.php outputs the same XML document to a file called test.xml. The differences are highlighted here in bold.

```
$xml = new XMLWriter();
$xml->openUri('test.xml');
$xml->setIndent(true);
$xml->setIndentString("\t");
$xml->startDocument();
$xml->startElement('inventory');
$xml->startElement('book');
$xml->writeAttribute('isbn13', '978-1-43021-011-5');
$xml->writeElement('title', 'PHP Object-Oriented Solutions');
$xml->writeElement('author', 'David Powers');
$xml->endElement();
$xml->startElement('book');
$xml->writeAttribute('isbn13', '978-1-59059-819-1');
$xml->writeElement('title', 'Pro PHP: Patterns, Frameworks, Testing ➥
    and More');
$xml->writeElement('author', 'Kevin McArthur');
$xml->endElement();
$xml->endElement();
$xml->endDocument();
```

```php
if ($xml->flush()) {
    echo 'XML created';
} else {
    echo 'Problem with XML';
}
```

If you load generateXML_02.php into a browser, you should see XML created displayed onscreen, and the same XML as in Figure 8-5 saved to test.xml in the ch8_exercises folder.

XMLWriter really comes into its own when used to generate XML from dynamic content. Now that you have seen how XMLWriter works, here's the rest of the code for the generateXML() method, fully commented to explain what happens at each stage (if you're typing out the code yourself, this goes inside the method definition under the Step 5 comment):

```php
// Instantiate an XMLWriter object
$xml = new XMLWriter();

// Set the output preferences
if (isset($this->_xmlFile)) {
  // Open the output file
  $fileOpen = @$xml->openUri($this->_xmlFile);
  if (!$fileOpen) {
    throw new RuntimeException("Cannot create $this->_xmlFile. Check ➥
      permissions and that target folder exists.");
  } else {
    // Set indentation preferences
    $xml->setIndent($this->_indent);
    $xml->setIndentString($this->_indentString);
  }
} else {
  // If the output is being sent to a string, open memory instead
  $xml->openMemory();
}

// Start the document and create the root element
$xml->startDocument();
$xml->startElement($this->_docRoot);

// Loop through each row of the database result set
foreach ($resultSet as $row) {
  // Create the opening tag of the top-level node
  $xml->startElement($this->_element);
  // Add the primary key(s) as attribute(s)
  if ($usePK) {
    foreach ($this->_primaryKey as $pk) {
      $xml->writeAttribute($pk, $row[$pk]);
    }
  }
```

```
    // Inside each row, loop through each field
    foreach ($row as $field => $value) {
      // Skip the primary key(s) if used as attribute(s)
      if ($usePK && in_array($field, $this->_primaryKey)) {
        continue;
      }
      // Create a child node for each field
      $xml->writeElement($field, $value);
    }
    // Create the closing tag for the top-level node
    $xml->endElement();
  }

  // Create the closing tag for the root element
  $xml->endElement();
  // Close the XML document
  $xml->endDocument();
  // Output the generated XML
  return $xml->flush();
```

This starts off by instantiating an XMLWriter object called $xml. If the $_xmlFile property has been defined, it's passed to the openUri() method to open the file ready for writing. Otherwise, the openMemory() method is called. Since failure to open the file would trigger PHP error messages, I have used the error control operator (@) with openUri() and thrown an exception so the problem can be handled more elegantly elsewhere.

The code then initializes the XML with the startDocument() method and passes the $_docRoot property to startElement() to create the opening root element tag.

Building the contents of the XML document is done by two foreach loops, one nested inside the other. The outer loop handles the top-level nodes, while the inner one handles the child nodes of each top-level one. In terms of the database result, each row of the result becomes a top-level node, and the individual fields of the current row populate the child nodes.

The outer loop begins by creating the opening tag of a top-level node and inserting the primary key as an attribute inside the tag if $usePK is true.

The inner loop then iterates through each field in the current row of the database result. To prevent creating a child node for the primary key if it has already been used as an attribute in the top-level opening tag, it's necessary to check $usePK and if the current field contains the primary key. If both equate to true, the continue keyword skips the current iteration of the inner loop. All remaining field names and values are passed to the writeElement() method, which wraps the text node in opening and closing tags in a single operation.

When each field in the current row has been processed, the inner loop comes to an end, and the outer loop uses the endElement() method to create the closing tag for the current top-level node, before going back to the top of the loop to process the next row of the database result.

8

When the outer loop finally comes to an end, you need to call endElement() again to close the root element, before closing the document with endDocument() and outputting the XML with the flush() method.

That completes the code for the Pos_XmlExporter class. All that remains is to test it.

Using the Pos_XmlExporter class

This brief exercise shows how to generate XML from a database, first by sending the output to a browser and then saving it to a local file. You can use any database of your own. If you want to use the same test database table as me, load blog.sql from the download files for this chapter into a MySQL database. If you haven't created your own versions of Pos_XmlExporter, Pos_MysqlImprovedConnection, and Pos_MysqlImprovedResult, you can find them in the finished_classes folder.

1. Create a page called generateXML.php in the ch8_exercises folder. You need to include all three classes from this chapter, so add the following code to the top of the script:

```
require_once '../Pos/MysqlImprovedConnection.php';
require_once '../Pos/MysqlImprovedResult.php';
require_once '../Pos/XmlExporter.php';
```

2. In a try block, create an instance of Pos_XmlExporter, passing it as arguments the server name, username, password, and database that you want to use.

```
try {
    $xml = new Pos_XMLExporter('host', 'user', 'password', 'dbName');
}
```

3. Use the setQuery() method to define the SQL query like this:

```
try {
    $xml = new Pos_XMLExporter('host', 'user', 'password', 'dbName');
    $xml->setQuery('SELECT * FROM blog');
}
```

4. The setTagNames() and usePrimaryKey() methods are optional, so let's leave them out for the moment. Generate the XML, capture it in a variable, and output it to the browser with an XML header like this:

```
try {
    $xml = new Pos_XMLExporter('host', 'user', 'password', 'dbName');
    $xml->setQuery('SELECT * FROM blog');
    $output = $xml->generateXML();
    header('Content-Type: text/xml');
    echo $output;
}
```

5. The classes use runtime and logic exceptions, so you can capture each type of exception in its own catch block like this:

```
try {
  $xml = new Pos_XMLExporter('host', 'user', 'password', 'dbName');
  $xml->setQuery('SELECT * FROM blog');
  $output = $xml->generateXML();
  header('Content-Type: text/xml');
  echo $output;
} catch (LogicException $e) {
  echo 'This is a logic exception: ' . $e->getMessage();
} catch (RuntimeException $e) {
  echo 'This is a runtime exception: ' . $e->getMessage();
}catch (Exception $e) {
  echo 'This is a generic exception: ' . $e->getMessage();
}
```

6. Save the page, and load it into a browser. Alternatively use generateXML_03.php from the download files after adjusting the database login details and SQL query. You should see output similar to that shown in Figure 8-6.

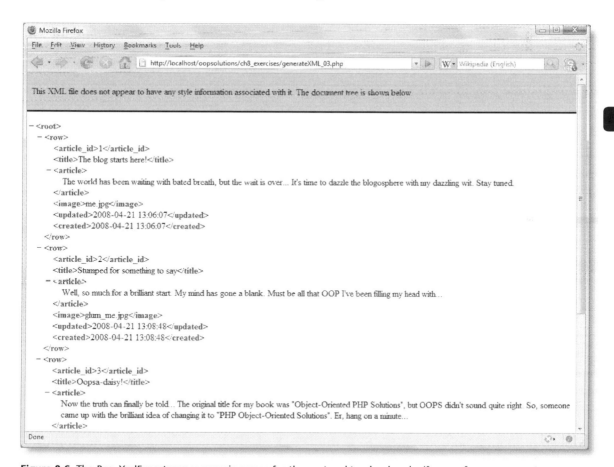

Figure 8-6. The Pos_XmlExporter uses generic names for the root and top-level nodes if no preferences are set.

As you can see, the root node is called <root>, and each top-level node is called <row>. The primary key (article_id) is displayed as an independent child node of each <row> element.

7. Amend the code in the try block to set custom names for root and top-level nodes, and to use the primary key from the blog table like this:

```
try {
  $xml = new Pos_XMLExporter('host', 'user', 'password', 'dbName');
  $xml->setQuery('SELECT * FROM blog');
  $xml->setTagNames('blog', 'entry');
  $xml->usePrimaryKey('blog');
  $output = $xml->generateXML();
  header('Content-Type: text/xml');
  echo $output;
}
```

The setTagNames() method takes two arguments: the names you want to give the root and top-level nodes. The usePrimaryKey() method takes the name of the table whose primary key you want to use.

8. Save the page, and load it into a browser (or use an amended version of generateXML_04.php). This time, the root and top-level tags should have custom names, and the primary key is inserted inside each top-level tag as an attribute, as shown in Figure 8-7.

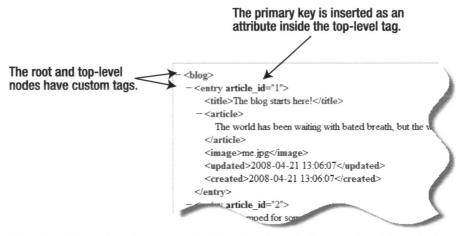

The primary key is inserted as an attribute inside the top-level tag.

The root and top-level nodes have custom tags.

Figure 8-7. The tags have been customized by setting the setTagNames and usePrimaryKey() methods.

9. Test the error handling by using illegal names for the tags, comment out the line that sets the SQL query, or make a mistake in the SQL. Figure 8-8 shows what happened when I supplied the name of a nonexistent table to usePrimaryKey().

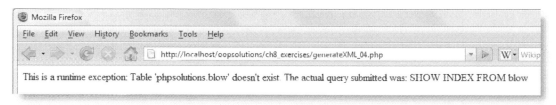

Figure 8-8. It's important to test what happens when invalid values are supplied.

10. After testing error handling, delete the lines that send the XML header and output the document to the browser, and use setFilePath() to save the XML to file. The amended try block should look like this:

```
try {
  $xml = new Pos_XMLExporter('host', 'user', 'password', 'dbName');
  $xml->setQuery('SELECT * FROM blog');
  $xml->setTagNames('blog', 'entry');
  $xml->usePrimaryKey('blog');
  $xml->setFilePath('blog.xml');
  $output= $xml->generateXML();
  if ($output) {
    echo 'XML file saved.';
  } else {
    echo 'A problem occurred.';
  }
}
```

11. Save the file, and load it into a browser (or use an amended version of generateXML_05.php). You should see XML file saved onscreen, and the XML document saved to blog.xml in the same folder.

12. Experiment with different options for the second and third arguments to setFilePath() to change the indentation of the XML output. By default, indentation is turned on and uses a single tab for each level. To turn indentation off, set the second argument to false (without quotes). To change the indentation style, define the spacing you want as a string. For example, to use three spaces, type an opening quote, press the space bar three times, followed by a closing quote. To use tabs, type \t between double quotes as many times as you want tabs.

In this exercise, I have used the setQuery(), setTagNames(), and usePrimaryKey() methods in the same order as the Pos_XmlExporter class definition. However, they can be in any order, as long as you instantiate a Pos_XmlExporter object first and call generateXML() last.

Chapter review

This chapter has brought together three classes working in cooperation with each other. The Pos_XmlExporter class is dependent on the other two, but the Pos_MysqlImprovedConnection and Pos_MysqlImprovedResult classes can be redeployed in any application that requires a database result set. It's not tightly coupled to the generation of XML. The implementation of the Iterator interface makes the result set much more versatile. As it stands, the Pos_MysqlImprovedConnection class has only the getResultSet() method, but you can add further methods to improve it. Wrapping other database routines in custom methods that incorporate error checking greatly cuts down on the amount of code needed in your applications.

In addition to demonstrating how to implement the SPL Iterator interface, this chapter has also introduced you to some of the SPL exceptions. Using a different type of exception for each type of error has both advantages and disadvantages. The main advantage is that separate catch blocks can handle the exceptions in different ways. The disadvantages lie in the need to set up those catch blocks and keep track of all the different types of exception that you have used. However, this becomes less of a problem when you realize that all exceptions descend from the base class, so a single catch block can handle them all, as long as its type hint is set to Exception. By using specialized exceptions inside your classes, you give yourself greater freedom to choose how each type of error is handled in the final application.

In the next—and final—chapter, I'll show you how to extend the Pos_XmlExporter class to create your own RSS feed.

9 CASE STUDY: CREATING YOUR OWN RSS FEED

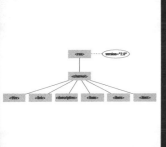

This chapter builds on the previous one by extending the Pos_XmlExporter class to create an RSS feed. There are several RSS formats, but the one I have chosen is RSS 2.0 (www.rssboard.org/rss-specification). As the specification says, RSS stands for Really Simple Syndication, it's a dialect of XML, and it's a format for Web content syndication. The Pos_XmlExporter class does a good job of generating XML from a database, but the content and node names are entirely dependent on the SQL query submitted by the user, making it too generic for RSS. Browsers and newsreaders expect RSS to be in a specific format, so the SQL query needs to be built internally by the extended class.

This chapter covers

- Understanding the requirements of the RSS 2.0 format
- Extending the Pos_XmlExporter class to create an RSS feed from any MySQL database
- Building a utility to extract a specified number of sentences from the beginning of text

As always when designing a class, the first priority is to set out its requirements. Since the purpose of the class is to generate an RSS feed, the main requirements are to be found in the RSS 2.0 specification.

Understanding the RSS 2.0 format

The friends of ED news feed (http://friendsofed.com/news.php) that you used in Chapters 5 and 6 follows the RSS 1.0 format. It's still perfectly valid, but it's complicated by the use of namespaces. The newer RSS 2.0 format eliminates the need for namespaces, making it easier to generate.

> *I have avoided namespaces in the XML generated by the classes in this chapter and the previous one purely out of a desire to keep things relatively simple. XMLWriter is capable of generating namespaced elements and attributes. For details, see* http://docs.php.net/manual/en/book.xmlwriter.php *(the relevant methods all end in NS).*

RSS 2.0 lives up to the name Really Simple Syndication. There are very few rules, and they're quite simple.

The structure of an RSS 2.0 feed

RSS 2.0 is a specialized XML format, so the first requirement is that an RSS feed must be a valid XML document. The root element is always called <rss> and contains the attribute version="2.0". The root element must have a single child element called <channel>. Inside the <channel> element are at least three required elements (<title>, <link>, and

<description>) that contain information about the feed, plus any number of elements called <item>. As their name suggests, these contain the individual items that make up the RSS feed. Although there's no limit on the number of <item> elements, it's common to limit them to no more than 30 and often much fewer. Figure 9-1 illustrates the basic structure of an RSS 2.0 feed.

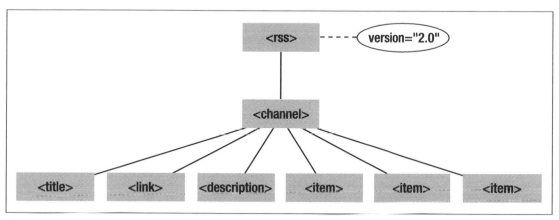

Figure 9-1. The <channel> element of an RSS 2.0 feed contains information about the feed in addition to individual items.

> *This structure differs from the friends of ED feed that you used in Chapters 5 and 6. In RSS 2.0 (and most other RSS specifications), the <channel> element contains the entire contents of the feed, not just the elements that describe it. The friends of ED feed uses RSS 1.0, which is the odd one out in that it puts the <item> elements outside the <channel> element and at the same level of the XML hierarchy. Although RSS 1.0 remains a valid format, I recommend that you use RSS 2.0 for new feeds.*

What the <channel> element contains

The role of the <channel> element is to identify the feed and give a brief description. It has three required and 16 optional child elements, which are described in Table 9-1.

Table 9-1. Allowable child elements in an RSS 2.0 <channel> element

Element	Required	Description
<title>	Yes	The name of the feed. This should be the same as the title of the web site.
<link>	Yes	The URL of the web site that the feed refers to.
<description>	Yes	A brief phrase or sentence describing the feed. Don't write an essay here.

Continued

Table 9-1. *Continued*

Element	Required	Description
`<category>`	No	Used to specify one or more categories that the feed belongs to. The optional attribute domain specifies the URL of the category system.
`<cloud>`	No	Allows registration with a cloud (see `www.rssboard.org/rsscloud-interface`).
`<copyright>`	No	Copyright notice.
`<docs>`	No	The URL of the RSS 2.0 specification (`http://www.rssboard.org/rss-specification`). This must include the leading `http://`.
`<generator>`	No	The program used to generate the feed.
`<image>`	No	An image (GIF, JPEG, or PNG) that can be displayed with the feed. Often this is a company logo.
`<language>`	No	The language used by the feed (see `www.rssboard.org/rss-language-codes`). You can also follow the W3C rules at `www.w3.org/TR/REC-html40/struct/dirlang.html#langcodes`.
`<lastBuildDate>`	No	The last time the content changed. This must conform to RFC 822 (the PHP constant, DATE_RSS, handles this for you).
`<managingEditor>`	No	The editor's email address.
`<pubDate>`	No	This is for feeds that publish on a regular basis, e.g., daily, weekly, or monthly. The `<pubDate>` indicates the date of original publication, whereas `<lastBuildDate>` indicates the most recent change, say for a correction.
`<rating>`	No	The feed's PICS (Platform for Internet Content Selection) rating (see `www.w3.org/PICS/`).
`<skipDays>`	No	The days aggregators can skip (see `www.rssboard.org/skip-hours-days`).
`<skipHours>`	No	The hours aggregators can skip (see `www.rssboard.org/skip-hours-days`).
`<textInput>`	No	A text input box that can be displayed with the feed (see `www.rssboard.org/rss-specification#lttextinputgtSubelementOfLtchannelgt`).

Element	Required	Description
`<ttl>`	No	"Time to live"—the number of minutes a feed can be cached by the user's browser or a proxy server. This is useful if the feed is updated at fixed times. If the feed is generated dynamically each time it's requested, your script could calculate the number of minutes to the next scheduled update and insert the value here. This reduces the traffic load on your web server.
`<webMaster>`	No	The technical contact's email address. As with `<managingEditor>`, this is optional, so it's left up to the originator of the feed to decide how to use this tag, if at all. There's no guarantee that human beings or spambots will make any distinction between the two.

Most information in the nodes listed in Table 9-1 is intended for consumption by feed aggregators and doesn't normally appear when the feed is displayed in a browser. The interesting information (we hope) is in the `<item>` elements, which are also direct children of the `<channel>` element.

What the `<item>` elements contain

Although this is where the "meat" of an RSS feed can be found, all child elements of an `<item>` node are optional. However, each `<item>` must contain at least one of the following: `<title>` or `<description>`. Table 9-2 lists all the elements that can be included in an `<item>` element.

Table 9-2. Allowable child elements of RSS 2.0 <item> elements

Element	Description
`<title>`	A brief title describing the item.
`<description>`	The body of the item. This is usually kept brief and is used as a "taster" inviting the recipient to read the full item on the main web site. The `<description>` element can contain HTML markup, but it must either be entity encoded (see later in this chapter) or in a CDATA section (see Chapter 6).
`<link>`	The URL of the item on the main web site.
`<author>`	The author's email address.

Continued

Table 9-2. *Continued*

Element	Description
`<category>`	This is the same as for `<channel>` elements (see Table 9-1).
`<comments>`	The URL of a page for comments relating to the item.
`<enclosure>`	A media object, such as an MP3 file, attached to the item (see `www.rssboard.org/rss-specification#ltenclosuregtSubelementOfLtitemgt`).
`<guid>`	A string that uniquely identifies the item. This is frequently the same as `<link>`. However, if `<link>` points to a longer version of the item, `<guid>` should be a permalink to the summary.
`<pubDate>`	When the item was published. This must be in RFC 822 format (use the PHP constant, DATE_RSS).
`<source>`	The RSS feed that the item came from. This tag has one required attribute, `url`, which should contain the feed's URL.

> *The descriptions in Tables 9-1 and 9-2 summarize version 2.0.10 of the RSS 2.0 specification. You can see the full specification at* `www.rssboard.org/rss-specification`. *A more detailed set of best practices can be found at* `www.rssboard.org/rss-profile`.

Deciding what the feed will contain

The number of optional elements offers considerable choice, but most RSS feeds seem to use a relatively small subset. For the purposes of this case study, I'm going to do the same. Once you have seen the basic principles underlying the class, you can extend or adapt it to incorporate other options.

The class, which I have called Pos_RssFeed, creates an RSS 2.0 feed using the following elements to describe the feed:

- `<title>`
- `<link>`
- `<description>`
- `<lastBuildDate>`
- `<docs>`

Each `<item>` element contains the following child nodes:

- `<title>`
- `<description>`

- <pubDate>
- <link>

The resulting XML tree is shown in Figure 9-2 (for space reasons, the figure shows only one <item> element).

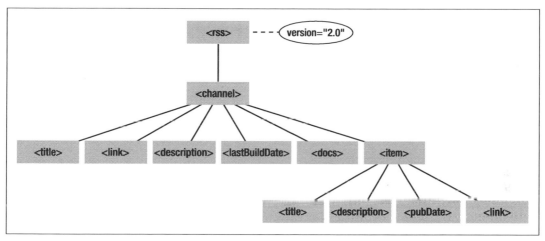

Figure 9-2. Each <item> element must contain at least <title> or <description>.

The <channel> element and each <item> element contain three identically named child nodes: <title>, <link>, and <description>, so it's important to make sure they don't get mixed up when generating the XML.

Building the class

The Pos_XmlExporter class in the previous chapter uses the names of the database columns for the child nodes of the top-level elements. However, that won't work for an RSS feed. The tag names are fixed. This time, the SQL needs to be built automatically by the class, using information supplied through setter methods. Since most RSS feeds carry news items or blog entries, I have assumed that all the data used in the feed comes from a single table.

The Pos_RssFeed class extends Pos_XmlExporter, so it inherits all its methods and properties. However, the generateXML() method needs to be overridden, and the setQuery() method is reduced to minor importance. The use of setQuery() becomes optional and is left in purely in case the need arises to build the SQL manually. This might happen if the database query needs to join multiple tables. However, in such a case, it would probably be better to redesign the class. Another significant change is that the usePrimaryKey() method is used internally, but to prevent it from being used accidentally, it needs to be overridden. I'll explain what's happening and the thinking behind it as we get to each section of the code.

9

Populating the elements that describe the feed

With the exception of `<lastBuildDate>`, all elements that describe the feed have fixed values, so all that's necessary is to create a series of properties and setter methods.

I plan to test the Pos_RssFeed class at various stages of construction, so I suggest you roll up your sleeves and start typing. If you just want to look at the finished code, you can find a fully commented version in the finished_classes folder of the download files. I have also provided versions of the class at different stages of construction in the ch9_exercises folder.

1. Create a file called RssFeed.php in the Pos folder. The class extends the Pos_XmlExporter class, so you need to include it at the top of the script like this:

```php
require_once 'XmlExporter.php';
class Pos_RssFeed extends Pos_XmlExporter
{

}
```

2. The URL used by the `<docs>` element is fixed, so you don't need a property to store a user-specified value. However, the other four all need properties and setter methods. Define the following protected properties:

```php
require_once 'XmlExporter.php';
class Pos_RssFeed extends Pos_XmlExporter
{
  protected $_feedTitle;
  protected $_feedLink;
  protected $_feedDescription;
  protected $_useNow;
}
```

The meaning of the first three properties is self-explanatory. The fourth one, $_useNow, stores a Boolean value to determine how to set the value of `<lastBuildDate>`. If set to true, the current time is used. Otherwise, the time of the most recently updated item is used instead.

3. Create a setter method for each property. Add the following code inside the class definition below the property definitions:

```php
public function setFeedTitle($title)
{
  $this->_feedTitle = $title;
}

public function setFeedLink($link)
{
  $this->_feedLink = $link;
}

public function setFeedDescription($description)
{
```

```
    $this->_feedDescription = $description;
  }

  public function setLastBuildDate($useNow = true)
  {
    $this->_useNow = $useNow;
  }
```

These methods need no explanation, apart from the fact that the argument passed to setLastBuildDate() has a default value of true.

4. If any of the first three properties is not set, you can't generate the feed, so the overridden generateXML() method needs to check each one. Add the following code immediately after the code in the previous step:

```
public function generateXML()
{
  $error = array();
  if (!isset($this->_feedTitle)) {
    $error[] = 'feed title';
  }
  if (!isset($this->_feedLink)) {
    $error[] = 'feed link';
  }
  if (!isset($this->_feedDescription)) {
    $error[] = 'feed description';
  }
  if ($error) {
    throw new LogicException('Cannot generate RSS feed. Check the ➥
      following item(s): ' . implode(', ', $error) . '.');
  }
}
```

This initializes a local variable, $error, as an empty array. A series of conditional statements checks whether the $_feedTitle, $_feedLink, and $_feedDescription properties have been set. If an error is encountered, the name of the property is added to the $error array, and a LogicException is thrown. Using an array like this makes sure that all missing elements are identified, rather than throwing an exception at the first problem.

5. At this stage, the code hasn't been added to query the database, so the value for <lastBuildDate> needs to use the default value, the current time formatted according to RFC 822. PHP has a handy constant (DATE_RSS) that works with the date() function and produces the date in the correct format. Add the code highlighted in bold to the generateXML() method to assign the formatted date to a local variable, $lastBuildDate:

```
public function generateXML()
{
  $error = array();
  if (!isset($this->_feedTitle)) {
    $error[] = 'feed title';
  }
```

9

```
      if (!isset($this->_feedLink)) {
        $error[] = 'feed link';
      }
      if (!isset($this->_feedDescription)) {
        $error[] = 'feed description';
      }
      if ($error) {
        throw new LogicException('Cannot generate RSS feed. Check the ➥
          following item(s): ' . implode(', ', $error) . '.');
      }
      if ($this->_useNow) {
        $lastBuildDate = date(DATE_RSS);
      }
    }
```

The conditional statement sets a value for $lastBuildDate only if the $_useNow property equates to true. Later, you'll add an else clause to retrieve the time of the most recently updated item in the feed. Until then, $_useNow must not be set to false when testing the code.

6. You can now begin to generate the XML for the RSS feed with XMLWriter. The code is very similar to the previous chapter, so refer to Chapter 8 if you need to refresh your memory.

```
public function generateXML()
{
  $error = array();
  if (!isset($this->_feedTitle)) {
    $error[] = 'feed title';
  }
  if (!isset($this->_feedLink)) {
    $error[] = 'feed link';
  }
  if (!isset($this->_feedDescription)) {
    $error[] = 'feed description';
  }
  if ($error) {
    throw new LogicException('Cannot generate RSS feed. Check the ➥
      following item(s): ' . implode(', ', $error) . '.');
  }
  if ($this->_useNow) {
    $lastBuildDate = date(DATE_RSS);
  }
  $rss = new XMLWriter();
  if (isset($this->_xmlFile)) {
    $fileOpen = @$rss->openUri($this->_xmlFile);
    if (!$fileOpen) {
      throw new RuntimeException("Cannot create $this->_xmlFile. Check ➥
        permissions and that target folder exists.");
    }
```

```
$rss->setIndent($this->_indent);
$rss->setIndentString($this->_indentString);
} else {
  $rss->openMemory();
}
$rss->startDocument();
$rss->startElement('rss');
$rss->writeAttribute('version', '2.0');
$rss->startElement('channel');
$rss->writeElement('title', $this->_feedTitle);
$rss->writeElement('link', $this->_feedLink);
$rss->writeElement('description', $this->_feedDescription);
$rss->writeElement('lastBuildDate', $lastBuildDate);
$rss->writeElement('docs', ➡
  'http://www.rssboard.org/rss-specification');

// Code to generate <item> elements goes here

$rss->endElement();
$rss->endElement();
$rss->endDocument();
return $rss->flush();
}
```

Note that I have inserted a comment indicating where the code for the <item> elements will be added later. The first call to endElement() after that comment closes the <channel> node, while the second one closes the root node (<rss>).

7. It's time to test your handiwork. Create a page called generate_rss.php in the ch9_exercises folder. In addition to the Pos_RssFeed class, you need Pos_MysqlImprovedConnection and Pos_MysqlImprovedResult, so include all three at the top of the script like this:

```
require_once '../Pos/RssFeed.php';
require_once '../Pos/MysqlImprovedConnection.php';
require_once '../Pos/MysqlImprovedResult.php';
```

8. The Pos_RssFeed class inherits the parent constructor, so you instantiate an object in the same way as Pos_XmlExporter by passing the connection details to the constructor like this:

```
$xml = new Pos_RssFeed('host', 'user', 'password', 'dbName');
```

9. Next, set the properties for the <channel> element:

```
$xml->setFeedTitle('OOP News');
$xml->setFeedLink('http://www.example.com/oop_news.xml');
$xml->setFeedDescription('Get the lowdown on OOP and PHP.');
$xml->setLastBuildDate(true);
```

9

As I mentioned in step 5, the $_useNow property must not be set to false until the else clause is added to the conditional statement that sets the value for $lastBuildDate. By default, the setLastBuildDate() method sets $_useNow to true, so the argument is optional. However, I have passed a Boolean true as a reminder of how the <lastBuildDate> element is being handled in the current test.

10. The class also inherits setFilePath() from its parent, so let's save the RSS feed to a file called oop_news.xml. The file doesn't need to exist yet; the class automatically creates it (as long as it has permission to write to the specified location). Finally, wrap everything in a try . . . catch block. The finished code should look like this (it's in generate_rss_01.php):

```php
try {
  $xml = new Pos_RssFeed('host', 'user', 'password', 'dbName');
  $xml->setFeedTitle('OOP News');
  $xml->setFeedLink('http://www.example.com/oop_news.xml');
  $xml->setFeedDescription('Get the lowdown on OOP and PHP.');
  $xml->setLastBuildDate(true);
  $xml->setFilePath('oop_news.xml');
  $result = $xml->generateXML();
  if ($result) {
    echo 'XML file created';
  }
  else {
    echo 'Error';
  }
}
catch (Exception $e) {
  echo $e->getMessage();
}
```

11. Load the file into a browser (or use generate_rss_01.php). If all goes well, you should see XML file created onscreen, and oop_news.xml should have been created in the ch9_exercises folder. The content of oop_news.xml should look similar to Figure 9-3.

```xml
<?xml version="1.0"?>
<rss version="2.0">
    <channel>
        <title>OOP News</title>
        <link>http://www.example.com/oop_news.xml</link>
        <description>Get the lowdown on OOP and PHP.</description>
        <lastBuildDate>Fri, 25 Apr 2008 19:55:11 +0100</lastBuildDate>
        <docs>http://www.rssboard.org/rss-specification</docs>
    </channel>
</rss>
```

Figure 9-3. Most elements that describe the feed have fixed values, so they are easy to generate.

> *If you open the file in Windows Notepad, the formatting will look chaotic. This is because Notepad expects both a carriage return and new line character for each new line. Open the file in a dedicated text editor, and the formatting should be preserved.*

If you encounter any problems, there's a copy of the class definition so far in RssFeed_01.php in the ch9_exercises folder.

Populating the <item> elements

The <item> elements are what the RSS feed is all about. Whenever new articles or posts are published on the web site, the <item> elements change. So, the Pos_RssFeed class needs to query the database table that stores the items the feed is based on in order to build the <item> elements. However, it's highly unlikely that the database columns use the same names as required by the RSS 2.0 specification. As you can see in Figure 9-4, only one of the columns (title) in the blog table that I used in the previous chapter has a name that matches the RSS specification.

article_id	title	article	image	updated	created
1	The blog starts here!	The world has been waiting with bated breath, but ...	me.jpg	2008-04-21 13:06:07	2008-04-21 13:06:07
2	Stumped for something to say	Well, so much for a brilliant start. My mind has g...	glum_me.jpg	2008-04-21 13:08:48	2008-04-21 13:08:48

Figure 9-4. The database column names don't match the tag names required by the RSS 2.0 specification.

What this means is that the SQL query needs to pair the right column name with the tag name and assign it an alias in the SQL query. I'm going to use the article column for the <description> node, updated column for the <pubDate> node, and article_id as the query string of the URL for the <link> node. An RSS feed normally orders items with the most recently updated one first, and limits the number to 15. So, I need to build a query that looks like this:

```
SELECT title AS title, article AS description,
updated AS pubDate, article_id AS link FROM blog
ORDER BY updated DESC LIMIT 15
```

Once the query has been submitted, the generateXML() method loops through the result creating each <item> element and its four child elements: <title>, <description>, <pubDate>, and <link>.

To keep the class flexible I can't hard-code the query, so the challenge is to build it dynamically. If you study the SQL query, you'll see there's an obvious pattern like this:

columnName AS *tagName*

Since the tag names are fixed, all that's needed is to create an associative array with an element for each tag. The appropriate column name can be assigned to each element through setter methods following this pattern:

$_itemArray['*tagName*'] = *columnName*;

So, you end up with an array like this:

```
$_itemArray['title']        = 'title';
$_itemArray['description']  = 'article';
$_itemArray['pubDate']      = 'updated';
$_itemArray['link']         = 'article_id';
```

You can then loop through this array to generate the SQL query. This array and its role in building the SQL query for the <item> child elements lie at the heart of the class.

Building the SQL query

Let's get back to the code. Generating the SQL query dynamically requires a considerable amount of forethought, so I have broken up the process into several stages. To start, you'll concentrate on the <title> and <description> tags, as well as the table name. Once you have seen how the values from the $_itemArray property are mapped to the column aliases, dealing with the more complex code for the <pubDate> and <link> tags should be easier to understand.

Continue working with the class definition from the previous section, or if you want to jump in at this point, copy RssFeed_01.php from ch9_exercises to the Pos folder, and rename the file RssFeed.php.

1. Add the $_itemArray property shown here in bold to the definitions at the top of the page:

   ```
   protected $_feedTitle;
   protected $_feedLink;
   protected $_feedDescription;
   protected $_useNow;
   protected $_itemArray;
   ```

2. The setter method for the <title> nodes of each <item> is very simple. It takes one argument: the name of the database column you want to use and assigns it to the title element of the $_itemArray property. It doesn't matter where you put this method in the class definition, but I prefer to keep methods in the same order as they're used, so put the following definition between setLastBuildDate() and generateXML():

```
public function setItemTitle($columnName)
{
  $this->_itemArray['title'] = $columnName;
}
```

3. The setter method for the <description> element is similar, but the RSS 2.0 specification suggests that this element should be a summary, so you don't want to include the entire article if it's more than a couple of lines long. After all, the idea of an RSS feed is to attract visitors to a site; the <description> element should be a teaser. Unless you have a separate database column for this element, you need to extract the first couple of sentences only. Add the following definition after the one for setItemTitle():

```
public function setItemDescription($columnName, $numSentences = 2)
{
  $this->_itemArray['description'] = $columnName;
  $this->_numSentences = $numSentences;
}
```

This takes two arguments: the name of the database column to be used for the <description> element, and the number of sentences you want to extract from the beginning of the text. I have given the second argument a default value of 2, so it becomes optional. The value is assigned to a new protected property called $_numSentences, which you need to add to the list of property definitions at the top of the page. I'll come back later to the extraction of the sentences from the beginning of the text.

4. Building the <link> and <pubDate> nodes is relatively complex, so before dealing with them, let's turn our attention to building the SQL query. Once you see how the query is built, the code in the remaining methods will make more sense. The query needs to know which table to draw the data from, so you need to create a property for the table name and a setter method for it. You also need to set the maximum number of records to be retrieved.

Add $_tableName and $_maxRecords as protected properties to the list of definitions at the top of the page, and insert the combined setter method for both properties after the definition for setItemDescription(). The code looks like this:

```
public function setTable($tableName, $maxRecords = 15)
{
  $this->_tableName = $tableName;
  $this->_maxRecords = is_numeric($maxRecords) ? ➥
    (int) abs($maxRecords) : 15;
}
```

The conditional operator (?:) tests the value passed in as the second argument. If it's a number, the value is assigned to the $_maxRecords property. Since is_numeric() accepts fractions and negative numbers, the value of the second argument is cast to an integer and passed to the abs() function, which converts a negative number into its positive equivalent. If the second argument isn't a number, the default value of 15 is used.

9

5. You're now ready to build the SQL query. This method is used internally by the class, so it needs to be protected. I usually keep all protected methods together after the public ones. Add the following code to the bottom of the class definition, just inside the closing brace:

```
protected function buildSQL()
{
  if (!isset($this->_tableName)) {
    throw new LogicException('No table defined. Use setTable().');
  }
  if (!isset($this->_itemArray['description']) && ➥
    !isset($this->_itemArray['title'])) {
    throw new LogicException('RSS items must have at least a ➥
      description or a title.');
  }
  // Initialize an empty array for the column names
  $select = array();
  // Loop through the $_itemArray property to build the list of aliases
  foreach ($this->_itemArray as $alias => $column) {
    $select[] = "$column AS $alias";
  }
  // Join the column/alias pairs as a comma-delimited string
  $select = implode(', ', $select);
  // Build the SQL
  $this->_sql = "SELECT $select FROM $this->_tableName";
  // Add a LIMIT clause if $_maxRecords is not 0
  if ($this->_maxRecords) {
    $this->_sql .= " LIMIT $this->_maxRecords";
  }
  // Display the SQL for testing purposes
  echo $this->_sql;
}
```

The foreach loop and the following line highlighted in bold do all the hard work for you. The loop iterates through the elements in the $_itemArray property, assigning the key to $alias and the value to $column. Inside the loop, the order of the variables is reversed, and they're inserted into a double-quoted string with the SQL keyword AS before being added to an array called $select. If the current element of the $_itemArray property looks like this:

```
$this->_itemArray['description'] = 'article';
```

it's added to $select in this form:

```
article AS description
```

$select is then joined as a comma-delimited string by implode() before being incorporated into the $_sql property.

The query is built in two parts: the first part selects the columns from the table, while the second part adds a LIMIT clause if the $_maxRecords property is not 0. Separating the LIMIT clause like this means you can retrieve all records by setting the second argument of setTable() to 0. Make sure you leave a space at the beginning of the LIMIT clause to avoid a SQL syntax error when both halves of the query are joined together.

Finally, the buildSQL() method displays the $_sql property onscreen for testing purposes.

6. Before you can test the revised class, the generateXML() method needs to call the buildSQL() method. Insert it after the series of conditional statements that check for errors and just before the code that gets the last build date. The code is shown here in bold with the surrounding lines for context:

```
if ($error) {
  throw new LogicException('Cannot generate RSS feed. Check the ➥
    following item(s): ' . implode(', ', $error) . '.');
}
if (is_null($this->_sql)) {
  $this->buildSQL();
}
if ($this->_useNow) {
  $lastBuildDate = date(DATE_RSS);
}
```

I have wrapped the call to the buildSQL() method in a conditional statement that checks whether the $_sql property is null. This allows you to set the SQL manually using the setQuery() method inherited from the parent class. The only reason you might want to do this is if you need to join two or more tables in the query.

> If you prefer to disable the setQuery() method, override it with an empty definition in the same way as usePrimaryKey() in "Creating the <link> elements" later in the chapter.

9

7. Save RssFeed.php, and amend the try block in generate_rss.php like this (the code is in generate_rss_02.php):

```
try {
  $xml = new Pos_RssFeed('localhost', 'psadmin', 'kyoto', 'phpsolutions');
  $xml->setFeedTitle('OOP News');
  $xml->setFeedLink('http://www.example.com/oop_news.xml');
  $xml->setFeedDescription('Get the lowdown on OOP and PHP.');
  $xml->setLastBuildDate(true);
  $xml->setFilePath('oop_news.xml');
  $xml->setItemTitle('title');
  $xml->setItemDescription('article');
  $xml->setTable('blog');
  $result = $xml->generateXML();
  if ($result) {
    // echo 'XML file created';
  }
  else {
    echo 'Error';
  }
}
```

This sets the columns that you want to use for the <title> and <description> nodes, as well as the table from which they are to be drawn. If you are using your own database, substitute the names of the columns and tables with the ones you want to use.

Note also that I have commented out the line that displays XML file created. This is because I want to display only the $_sql property.

8. Save generate_rss.php, and load it into a browser (or use generate_rss_02.php). You should see the SQL query displayed onscreen as shown in Figure 9-5. Make sure that the column names and aliases are correct.

Figure 9-5. The SQL query uses aliases to give each column the right name for use in the RSS feed.

9. Change the arguments to the setTable() method by adding 0 as the second argument like this:

```
$xml->setTable('blog', 0);
```

10. Save the page, and test it again. This time, the LIMIT clause should be omitted.

11. Change the second argument to a number other than 15, and test the page again. The LIMIT clause should be restored, but with the new number.

    If anything goes wrong, you can compare your class definition so far with RssFeed_02.php in the ch9_exercises folder.

Don't remove the echo command at the end of the buildSQL() method just yet. You need it for testing other parts of the class.

Now that you have seen how the SQL query is built, you can turn your attention to setting the <pubDate> and <link> elements. First, <pubDate>.

Creating the <pubDate> element

The <pubDate> element needs to be formatted in the RFC 822 format like this:

```
Sat, 26 Apr 2008 10:06:59 +0100
```

The +0100 at the end is the time zone offset from UTC (Universal Coordinated Time). Getting this information from MySQL is complicated, but the PHP DateTime class can normally do the job for you if provided with the date and time in the same format without the time zone offset. So, the setter method for the <pubDate> nodes needs to wrap the name of the column that provides the item's date and time in a MySQL function to format it correctly. The setter method also needs to take into account that MySQL timestamps are based on the calendar date, whereas Unix timestamps represent the number of seconds elapsed since January 1, 1970. Consequently, you need to pass two arguments: the column name and the type of timestamp. I have assumed that most people use MySQL timestamps in their databases, so the default value of the second argument is set to MySQL.

Continue working with the class definition file from the previous section. If you want to jump in at this stage, copy RssFeed_02.php from ch9_exercises to the Pos folder, and rename the file RssFeed.php.

1. Insert the following code in the Pos_RssFeed class definition between the setItemDescription() and setTable() methods:

```php
public function setItemPubDate($columnName, $type = 'MySQL')
{
    $this->_itemPubDate = $columnName;
    $rssFormat = '%a, %d %b %Y %H:%i:%S';
    if (stripos($type, 'MySQL') === false) {
        $this->_itemArray['pubDate'] = "FROM_UNIXTIME($columnName, ➥
          '$rssFormat')";
    } else {
        $this->_itemArray['pubDate'] = "DATE_FORMAT($columnName, ➥
          '$rssFormat')";
    }
}
```

If the second argument is anything other than its default value, the pubDate element of the $_itemArray property wraps the column name in the MySQL FROM_UNIXTIME() function; otherwise, it uses the DATE_FORMAT() function. Both functions use the same formatting characters, which are stored in $rssFormat to format the output in the way stipulated by the RSS 2.0 specification minus the time zone offset.

2. Because the value of $_itemArray['pubDate'] contains more than just the column name, the setter method needs to store the column name separately in another property: $_itemPubDate. Add this as a protected property to the list of properties at the top of the page.

3. You can now use this property to add an ORDER clause inside the first half of the SQL query. Amend the section of the buildSQL() method shown here in bold:

```php
$select = implode(', ', $select);
// Build the SQL
$this->_sql = "SELECT $select FROM $this->_tableName
              ORDER BY $this->_itemPubDate DESC";
// Add a LIMIT clause if $_maxRecords is not 0
if ($this->_maxRecords) {
    $this->_sql .= " LIMIT $this->_maxRecords";
}
```

9

4. To test the setItemPubDate() method, amend generate_rss.php by calling it between the setItemDescription() and setTable() methods like this (the code is in generate_rss_03.php):

```
$xml->setItemDescription('article');
$xml->setItemPubDate('updated');
$xml->setTable('blog');
```

5. Save both pages, and load generate_rss.php (or generate_rss_03.php) into a browser. You should see output similar to Figure 9-6.

The column containing the <pubDate> is
wrapped in a MySQL date formatting function.

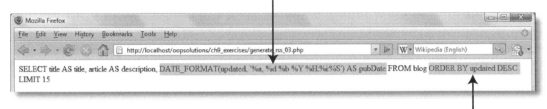

Storing the column name separately
allows you to add it to an ORDER clause.

Figure 9-6. The column used for <pubDate> requires special handling in the SQL query.

Make sure that the SQL query is formatted correctly. This is one area where things are likely to go wrong if you get the wrong combination of single and double quotes. A common mistake is to leave a gap between the MySQL function and the opening parenthesis. The problem won't show up until you attempt to run the query, but now is the time to track down any errors.

6. Amend the code in step 4 to add a second argument to setItemPubDate(). It doesn't matter what you add, but I used 'ts' (for timestamp) like this:

```
$xml->setItemPubDate('updated', 'ts');
```

7. Save the page, and test it again. This time, the updated column should be wrapped in the FROM_UNIXTIME() function.

If anything goes wrong, you can compare your code with RssFeed_03.php in ch9_exercises.

Creating the <link> elements

There are two ways to create <link> elements: one is to store the URL in a database column. You might do this if the RSS feed links to long articles with dedicated pages. The other way is to use the item's primary key in the database. You can then create a page that gets the primary key from a query string in the URL, and uses it to display the item. Since both are legitimate ways of creating <link> elements, the Pos_RssFeed class needs separate methods to handle each scenario.

Continue working with the class definition file from the previous section. If you want to jump in at this stage, copy RssFeed_03.php from ch9_exercises to the Pos folder, and rename the file RssFeed.php.

1. As with the \<pubDate\> elements, you need a separate property to refer to the \<link\> column name. You also need a Boolean property that indicates whether the \<link\> column contains a URL, or whether the class needs to build one. Begin by adding the two protected properties highlighted in bold to the list at the top of the class definition:

```
protected $_feedTitle;
protected $_feedLink;
protected $_feedDescription;
protected $_useNow;
protected $_itemArray;
protected $_numSentences;
protected $_maxRecords;
protected $_itemPubDate;
protected $_itemLink;
protected $_useURL;
```

2. The setter method for a link that's stored in a database column is very similar to those for the \<title\> and \<description\> elements. Add the following code after the setItemPubDate() method that you defined in the previous section:

```
public function setItemLink($columnName)
{
  if (isset($this->_useURL)) {
    throw new LogicException('The methods setItemLink() and ➥
      setItemLinkURL() are mutually exclusive. Use one or the other.');
  }
    $this->_itemArray['link'] = $columnName;
    $this->_useURL = false;
}
```

The method begins by checking whether the $_useURL property has been set. Although the property is defined at the top of the script, it has no value, so isset() returns false unless a value has been assigned elsewhere. The only time this would happen is if you use both setItemLink() and setItemLinkURL() (you'll define the second method in the next step). Since they're mutually exclusive, you need to throw an exception if this happens.

Then the column name is assigned to the link element of the $_itemArray property, and the $_useURL property is set to false.

3. The method that builds a URL with the primary key is, naturally, more complex. Insert the following code immediately after the preceding method, and I'll explain how it works.

```
public function setItemLinkURL($url)
{
  if (isset($this->_useURL)) {
    throw new LogicException('The methods setItemLink() and ➥
      setItemLinkURL() are mutually exclusive. Use one or the other.');
```

9

341

PHP OBJECT-ORIENTED SOLUTIONS

```
  }
  if (!isset($this->_tableName)) {
    throw new LogicException('You must set the table name with ➥
      setTable() before calling setItemLinkURL().');
  }
  parent::usePrimaryKey($this->_tableName);
  if (is_array($this->_primaryKey)) {
    $this->_primaryKey = $this->_primaryKey[0];
  } else {
    throw new RuntimeException("Cannot determine primary key for ➥
      $this->_tableName.");
  }
  $this->_itemArray['link'] = $this->_primaryKey;
  $this->_itemLink = $url . "?$this->_primaryKey=";
  $this->_useURL = true;
}
```

The method takes one argument: the URL that you want to use in combination with the record's primary key. Two conditional statements check that it's OK to proceed. The first is the same conditional statement as in setItemLink(), and it prevents the mutually exclusive methods from being used in the same script. The second conditional statement checks that the $_tableName property has been set by the setTable() method. This is necessary because you need the table name to find its primary key.

Assuming everything is OK, the method passes $_tableName to parent::usePrimaryKey(). Although usePrimaryKey() is inherited from the parent class, I plan to disable it in this class to prevent the wrong primary key from being selected by accident.

As you might recall from Chapter 8, the usePrimaryKey() method returns the name(s) of the primary key column(s) as an array. In the case of a blog or news site, the table should not have a composite primary key, so you're interested in only the first array item.

Once the name of the primary key column has been found and assigned to the $_primaryKey property, the final section of the method prepares the SQL query and builds the URL. These lines are important, so let's take a look at them individually. The following line assigns the name of the primary key column to the link element of the $_itemArray property:

```
$this->_itemArray['link'] = $this->_primaryKey;
```

This passes the name of the primary key column to the SQL query with link as its alias.

The next line builds the URL and assigns it to the $_itemLink property like this:

```
$this->_itemLink = $url . "?$this->_primaryKey=";
```

$url is the URL passed as an argument to the method. The rest of the line concatenates a query string on the end of the URL. Let's say the argument passed to setItemLinkURL() is this:

http://www.example.com/detail.php

342

If the primary key column is called article_id, the value of $_itemLink evaluates to this:

http://www.example.com/detail.php?article_id=

The value of article_id is later added dynamically to this URL when the generateXML() method loops through the database results.

The final line sets the Boolean $_useURL property to true. This tells the generateXML() method to use the base URL stored in $_itemLink.

Quite a lot is going on in those few lines!

4. As I said earlier, I want to prevent anyone from setting the wrong primary key by accident, so add this code immediately after the setItemLinkURL() method:

```
public function usePrimaryKey()
{}
```

This is an empty method. It accepts no arguments and does nothing. The reason for creating it is that you can't change the visibility of an inherited public method. Ideally, I would have liked to make usePrimaryKey() protected in the child class, but doing so triggers a fatal error. Overriding the method like this renders it harmless, but the parent method is still accessible through the parent keyword.

5. Save the class definition, and test the setItemLinkURL() method by adding the following line to generate_rss.php (the code is in generate_rss_04.php):

```
$xml->setTable('blog');
$xml->setItemLinkURL('http://www.example.com/detail.php');
$result = $xml->generateXML();
```

6. Save generate_rss.php, and load it into a browser (or use generate_rss_04.php). You should see output similar to Figure 9-7. You can't see the URL, but the table's primary key column has been added to the SQL query with link as its alias.

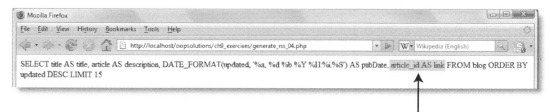

The primary key column name is
detected automatically.

Figure 9-7. The SQL query is now ready to generate the data for the <item> child elements.

7. Test the setItemLink() method by commenting out the line you added in step 5 and adding the following code:

```
$xml->setTable('blog');
// $xml->setItemLinkURL('http://www.example.com/detail.php');
$xml->setItemLink('url');
$result = $xml->generateXML();
```

343

This time, the SQL should contain url AS link.

8. Check that the SQL query is being built correctly, and then comment out this line at the end of the buildSQL() method:

```
// echo $this->_sql;
```

I recommend disabling the line rather than removing it completely, because you might need to display the SQL query later for debugging.

If you encounter any problems, compare your code with RssFeed_04.php in ch9_exercises.

The SQL query gathers all the information needed to populate the child elements of each <item>. However, the <description> and <pubDate> elements need a little extra work before you can include them in the RSS feed. The <description> element should normally be relatively short; say, two or three sentences. The <pubDate> also needs the time zone offset to conform to the RSS 2.0 specification. This calls for a couple of helper methods.

Creating helper methods to format <item> child elements

Normally, helper methods go inside the class definition as protected or private methods. That's fine for handling the <pubDate> time zone offset, but extracting a specified number of sentences from the beginning of a longer piece of text is something that could be useful in many other situations. So, I'm going to put that in an external class called Pos_Utils. Although it sounds extravagant to have a separate class for a single method, you can add other utility methods to it as you build your own class library.

Extracting sentences from the beginning of text

If you're building all the files yourself, create a file called Utils.php in the Pos folder, and insert the following code (alternatively use the version in the finished_classes folder):

```php
class Pos_Utils
{

  public static function getFirst($text, $number = 2)
  {
    $result = array();
    if ($number == 0) {
      $result[0] = $text;
      $result[1] = false;
    } else {
      // regular expression to find typical sentence endings
      $pattern = '/([.?!]["\']?)\s/';
      // use regex to insert break indicator
      $text = preg_replace($pattern, '$1bRE@kH3re', $text);
      // use break indicator to create array of sentences
      $sentences = preg_split('/bRE@kH3re/', $text);
      // check relative length of array and requested number
      $howMany = count($sentences);
      $number = $howMany >= $number ? $number : $howMany;
```

```
        // rebuild extract and return as single string
        $remainder = array_splice($sentences, $number);
        $result[0] = implode(' ', $sentences);
        $result[1] = empty($remainder) ? false : true;
    }
    return $result;
    }
}
```

You might recognize most of this code from some of my earlier books. I make no apology for repeating it here. OOP is all about reusable code.

The getFirst() method is static, so you call it by using the class name and the scope resolution operator (::). It takes two arguments: the text from which you want to extract the first few sentences and the number of sentences to extract. The default value for the second argument is set to 2, so its use is optional. The method returns an array of two elements: the first contains the extracted sentences, and the second is a Boolean value indicating whether any more text remains.

This method is called automatically by the generateXML() method, so I have modified the code from my earlier books to allow the option of displaying all text by setting the second argument to 0. If the second argument is 0, the first element of the returned array contains the whole text, and the second element is set to false.

What I didn't do in my earlier books was explain in detail how the rest of the code works, so here goes. The regular expression /([.?!]["\']?)\s/ searches for a period, question mark, or exclamation mark, followed by space, with an optional double or single quotation mark in between. In other words, the pattern is looking for the end of a sentence. Everything within the regular expression, apart from the final space, is enclosed in parentheses, making it a subexpression. This captures the punctuation mark(s) at the end of the sentence, but not the space. The text and the regular expression are passed to preg_replace(), which replaces the punctuation mark(s) and space at the end of each sentence with $1bRE@kH3re. The $1 at the beginning of the replacement string is a nifty way of representing the first subexpression. So, in effect, preg_replace() preserves the punctuation at the end of the sentence, but replaces the space with bRE@kH3re, a combination of characters that's highly unlikely to occur in normal text.

This combination of characters is then used with preg_split() to break the text into an array of sentences. The number of sentences is counted and stored in $howMany. This is compared with the number passed as the second argument to the getFirst() method, and the smaller of the two is assigned to $number. This is then passed to array_splice() to split the array of sentences in two. The first half of the array remains in $sentences; the remaining sentences are stored in $remainder. Arrays are numbered from zero, so if $number is 2, array_splice() moves the third and any subsequent sentences into $remainder, leaving just the first two in $sentences.

Finally, the selected number of sentences from the beginning of the text are glued back together with implode() and assigned to $result[0]. The second element of $result is a Boolean value indicating whether the selected sentences contain the full text, or if there is

9

any more. This second element isn't needed for the Pos_RssFeed class, but it comes in useful if you want to display the selected sentences followed by a More link pointing to the full text.

My design discards the remaining sentences. If you want to preserve them, change the last few lines of the method like this:

```
$result[0] = implode(' ', $sentences);
if (!empty($remainder)) {
  $result[1] = implode(' ', $remainder);
} else {
  $result[1] = '';
}
return $result;
```

However, it's not a good idea to do this unless you really want the remaining sentences, as they will occupy memory unnecessarily.

Getting the time zone offset

The date and time are formatted the right way for an RSS 2.0 feed, except for the time zone offset. You can add this easily by passing the date and time to the format() method of the PHP DateTime class with the DATE_RSS constant. The DateTime class has been part of core PHP since version 5.2, so it should always be available. Just in case it isn't, it's worth checking to avoid a fatal error. Add the following protected method to the bottom of the Pos_RssFeed class definition:

```
protected function getTimezoneOffset($pubDate)
{
  if (class_exists('DateTime')) {
    $date = new DateTime($pubDate);
    return $date->format(DATE_RSS);
  } else {
    return $pubDate;
  }
}
```

Everything is now ready to finish the Pos_RssFeed class.

Generating the XML for the <item> elements

All that remains is to execute the SQL query and loop through the result set to generate the XML for the <item> elements.

1. To use the Pos_Utils::getFirst() static method, you need access to the class definition, so include it at the top of the Pos_RssFeed definition.

```
require_once 'XmlExporter.php';
require_once 'Utils.php';
class Pos_RssFeed extends Pos_XmlExporter
```

2. The remaining changes all go inside the generateXML() method. First, you need to run the SQL query. Add the following line highlighted in bold immediately after the query has been built:

```
if (is_null($this->_sql)) {
  $this->buildSQL();
}
$resultSet = $this->_dbLink->getResultSet($this->_sql);
if ($this->_useNow) {
  $lastBuildDate = date(DATE_RSS);
}
```

This is the same as in the parent class, so should need no explanation.

3. The $_useNow property determines whether the <channel> element <lastBuildDate> uses the current time or the time of the most recently updated <item>. Now that you have the results from the database, you can use LimitIterator to inspect the first row and get the time from the most recent item. Add an else clause to the conditional statement that assigns the value of $lastBuildDate like this:

```
$resultSet = $this->_dbLink->getResultSet($this->_sql);
if ($this->_useNow) {
  $lastBuildDate = date(DATE_RSS);
} else {
  foreach (new LimitIterator($resultSet, 0, 1) as $row) {
    $lastBuildDate = $row['pubDate'];
  }
}
$rss = new XMLWriter();
```

The SQL query orders the results with the most recently updated item first, so this takes the value of the pubDate field from the first result and assigns it to $lastBuildDate. Because the result set implements the Iterator interface, you can inspect the first row like this without needing to reset it manually before looping through the entire set of results later.

4. Create the loops to generate the XML for the <item> elements. Locate the following comment:

```
// Code to generate <item> elements goes here
```

Replace it with this code:

```
foreach ($resultSet as $row) {
  $rss->startElement('item');
  foreach ($row as $field => $value) {
    if ($field == 'pubDate') {
      $value = $this->getTimezoneOffset($value);
    } elseif ($field == 'link' && $this->_useURL) {
      $value = $this->_itemLink . $value;
    } elseif ($field == 'description') {
```

9

347

```
      $extract = Pos_Utils::getFirst($value, $this->_numSentences);
      $value = $extract[0];
    }
    $rss->writeElement($field, $value);
  }
  $rss->endElement();
}
```

The outer foreach loop iterates through each row of the result set and opens an
<item> element. The inner foreach loop iterates through each field of the current
row. Before creating the child node, a series of conditional statements checks the
name of the field and formats the value according to the following criteria:

- If the field name is pubDate, the value is formatted by getTimezoneOffset().

- If the field name is link and the $_useURL property is true, the value is prefixed
  by the URL and query string stored in the $_itemLink property.

- If the field name is description, the value is passed to the Pos_Utils::getFirst()
  static method along with the $_numSentences property to extract the specified
  number of sentences from the beginning of the text.

After the child node is created from the current field name and value, the inner
loop continues until it reaches the end of the row. The outer loop then closes the
<item> element before moving onto the next row in the result set.

That completes the Pos_RssFeed class definition. This section involved changes to several
different parts of the generateXML() method, so here is the final version of the method
in full:

```
public function generateXML()
{
  $error = array();
  if (!isset($this->_feedTitle)) {
    $error[] = 'feed title';
  }
  if (!isset($this->_feedLink)) {
    $error[] = 'feed link';
  }
  if (!isset($this->_feedDescription)) {
    $error[] = 'feed description';
  }
  if ($error) {
    throw new LogicException('Cannot generate RSS feed. Check ➡
      the following item(s): ' . implode(', ', $error) . '.');
  }
  if (is_null($this->_sql)) {
    $this->buildSQL();
  }
  $resultSet = $this->_dbLink->getResultSet($this->_sql);
  if ($this->_useNow) {
    $lastBuildDate = date(DATE_RSS);
```

```php
  } else {
    foreach (new LimitIterator($resultSet, 0, 1) as $row) {
      $lastBuildDate = $row['pubDate'];
    }
  }
  $rss = new XMLWriter();
  if (isset($this->_xmlFile)) {
    $fileOpen = @$rss->openUri($this->_xmlFile);
    if (!$fileOpen) {
      throw new RuntimeException("Cannot create $this->_xmlFile. ➡
        Check permissions and that target folder exists.");
    }
    $rss->setIndent($this->_indent);
    $rss->setIndentString($this->_indentString);
  } else {
    $rss->openMemory();
  }
  $rss->startDocument();
  $rss->startElement('rss');
  $rss->writeAttribute('version', '2.0');
  $rss->startElement('channel');
  $rss->writeElement('title', $this->_feedTitle);
  $rss->writeElement('link', $this->_feedLink);
  $rss->writeElement('description', $this->_feedDescription);
  $rss->writeElement('lastBuildDate', $lastBuildDate);
  $rss->writeElement('docs', ➡
   'http://www.rssboard.org/rss-specification');
  foreach ($resultSet as $row) {
    $rss->startElement('item');
    foreach ($row as $field => $value) {
      if ($field == 'pubDate') {
        $value = $this->getTimezoneOffset($value);
      } elseif ($field == 'link' && $this->_useURL) {
        $value = $this->_itemLink . $value;
      } elseif ($field == 'description') {
        $extract = Pos_Utils::getFirst($value, $this->_numSentences);
        $value = $extract[0];
      }
      $rss->writeElement($field, $value);
    }
    $rss->endElement();
  }
  $rss->endElement();
  $rss->endElement();
  $rss->endDocument();
  return $rss->flush();
}
```

Test the completed Pos_RssFeed class by uncommenting the following line highlighted in bold in generate_rss.php (or use generate_rss_05.php):

```
$result = $xml->generateXML();
if ($result) {
  // echo 'XML file created';
}
else {
  echo 'Error';
}
```

Load generate_rss.php or generate_rss_05.php into a browser. You should see XML file created displayed onscreen. When you open the XML file (mine is called oop_news.xml), you should see a full RSS feed similar to the one shown in Figure 9-8.

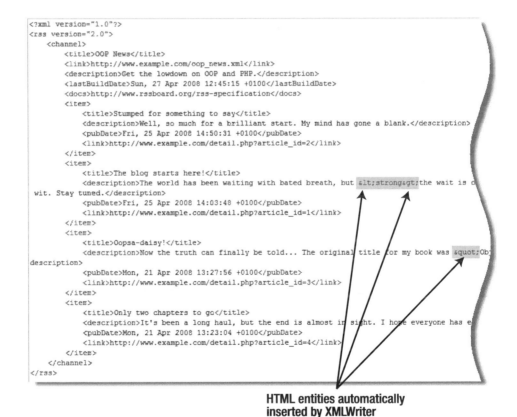

```
<?xml version="1.0"?>
<rss version="2.0">
    <channel>
        <title>OOP News</title>
        <link>http://www.example.com/oop_news.xml</link>
        <description>Get the lowdown on OOP and PHP.</description>
        <lastBuildDate>Sun, 27 Apr 2008 12:45:15 +0100</lastBuildDate>
        <docs>http://www.rssboard.org/rss-specification</docs>
        <item>
            <title>Stumped for something to say</title>
            <description>Well, so much for a brilliant start. My mind has gone a blank.</description>
            <pubDate>Fri, 25 Apr 2008 14:50:31 +0100</pubDate>
            <link>http://www.example.com/detail.php?article_id=2</link>
        </item>
        <item>
            <title>The blog starts here!</title>
            <description>The world has been waiting with bated breath, but &lt;strong&gt;the wait is o
wit. Stay tuned.</description>
            <pubDate>Fri, 25 Apr 2008 14:03:48 +0100</pubDate>
            <link>http://www.example.com/detail.php?article_id=1</link>
        </item>
        <item>
            <title>Oopsa-daisy!</title>
            <description>Now the truth can finally be told... The original title for my book was &quot;Ob
description>
            <pubDate>Mon, 21 Apr 2008 13:27:56 +0100</pubDate>
            <link>http://www.example.com/detail.php?article_id=3</link>
        </item>
        <item>
            <title>Only two chapters to go</title>
            <description>It's been a long haul, but the end is almost in sight. I hope everyone has e
            <pubDate>Mon, 21 Apr 2008 13:23:04 +0100</pubDate>
            <link>http://www.example.com/detail.php?article_id=4</link>
        </item>
    </channel>
</rss>
```

**HTML entities automatically
inserted by XMLWriter**

Figure 9-8. The Pos_RssFeed class generates an XML document fully compliant with the RSS 2.0 specification.

If your <description> elements contain HTML tags or quotation marks, you'll see that XMLWriter converts them automatically to HTML entities, as shown in Figure 9-8. Changing the angle brackets of HTML tags into < and > might seem odd, but don't worry; it won't make the HTML break. This is exactly the way that HTML should be rendered inside an XML document (unless you use a CDATA section). You can confirm that this is OK by testing the class to output the RSS feed directly to the browser. Locate the following line in generate_rss.php:

```
$xml->setFilePath('oop_news.xml');
```

Disable it by commenting it out, and then change the conditional statement at the end of the script like this:

```
if ($result) {
  header('Content-Type: text/xml');
  echo $result;
}
else {
  echo 'Error';
}
```

Save generate_rss.php, and load it into a browser (or use generate_rss_06.php). In a modern browser, you should see the RSS feed displayed as shown in Figure 9-9. As you can see, the <strong> tags in the second item have been rendered correctly.

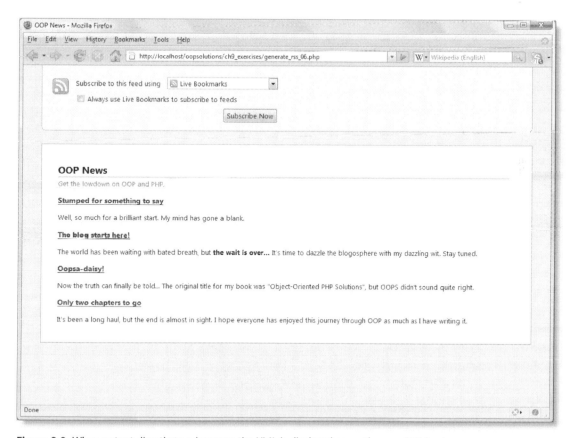

Figure 9-9. When output directly to a browser, the XML is displayed correctly as an RSS feed.

> *Eagle-eyed readers will notice that the* <description> *element of the second item contains three sentences, whereas the others contain the two specified by the default value of* Pos_Utils::getFirst(). *The reason for this discrepancy is that the end of the first sentence is wrapped in* <strong> *tags, so it fails to match the regular expression that finds the end of each sentence. This is such a minor issue, I have decided to ignore it.*

You can continue testing the class by setting various options, such as setLastBuildDate(), and changing the number of sentences or items displayed, but that completes this case study. It also brings us to the end of this book. As with all classes in this book, you might not agree with all of my design decisions, but you should now be equipped with the knowledge to customize the code to fit your own ideas and requirements.

Where to go from here

This case study brings to an end our journey through object-oriented PHP, but I hope you'll regard it as a jumping-off point, rather than an end in itself. As I said at the outset, OOP often requires much more code than a procedural script. Even though Pos_RssFeed inherits from Pos_XmlExporter, the definition of the child class is considerably longer than its parent. However, the advantage of both classes is that the code in your main script becomes much shorter and easier to read. Like all the classes in this book, they have been designed to answer generic problems, rather than specific ones. Pos_RssFeed can be deployed on any site, and generates a valid RSS 2.0 feed with just a few lines of code.

Building your own code like this can be immensely satisfying, but it's also time-consuming. However, the wonderful thing about open source software like PHP is that you don't always need to do everything yourself. A number of PHP OOP frameworks have been developed, putting ready-made class libraries at your disposal. Now that you have a thorough understanding of OOP and how it fits into PHP, you should be ready to take advantage of such a framework. The downside of frameworks is that they entail a learning curve, so it's difficult to choose the right one. You also need to be aware that at the time of this writing two of the most popular, CakePHP (http://cakephp.org/) and CodeIgniter (www.codeigniter.com), still use the obsolete PHP 4 object model. They're designed to be compatible with PHP 5 but don't take advantage of its greatly improved features.

When choosing a framework, it's important not only to make sure that it's based on the object model introduced in PHP 5 but also that it is actively supported. You don't want to base your projects on the latest hot framework only to discover that it fizzles out a few months down the line. Two frameworks that seem particularly worthy of investigation are the Zend Framework (http://framework.zend.com/) and symfony (www.symfony-project.org). Not only are they stable and rich in features but both have the backing of commercial ventures. The Zend Framework is backed by Zend, the company founded by the lead developers of PHP, and symfony is sponsored by Sensio Labs, a French web development company. This doesn't affect their cost; they're free and released under open source licenses.

With solid backing and the support of large development communities, these frameworks have good prospects of surviving and thriving. Both have extensive online documentation, and if you prefer a solid book in your hands, check out *The Definitive Guide to symfony* by Fabien Potencier and François Zaninotto (Apress, ISBN-13: 978-1-59059-786-6) and *The Definitive Guide to Zend Framework* (Apress, ISBN-13: 978-1-4302-1035-1). For a project-based approach to the Zend Framework, take a look at *Practical Web 2.0 Applications with PHP* by Quentin Zervaas (Apress, ISBN-13: 978-1-59059-906-8), which shows you how to build a sophisticated blogging system with the Zend Framework, the Ajax libraries, Prototype and script.aculo.us, and Google Maps.

Whichever route you choose, I hope this book has helped raise your PHP skills to a new level and inspired you to go further.

9

INDEX

Y

Z

Made in the USA
Lexington, KY
02 October 2013